D0993119

"The strength of the [Berlitz Travellers Guides] lies in remarks and recommendations by writers with a depth of knowledge about their subject."
—*Washington Times*

"The most readable of the current paperback lot."
—*New York Post*

"Highly recommended."
—*Library Journal*

"Very strong on atmosphere and insights into local culture for curious travellers."
—*Boston Herald*

"The [Berlitz Travellers Guides] eliminate cumbersome lists and provide reliable information about what is truly exciting and significant about a destination.... [They] also emphasize the spirit and underlying 'vibrations' of a region—historical, cultural, and social—that enhance a trip."
—*Retirement Life*

"Information without boredom.... Good clear maps and index."
—*The Sunday Sun* (Toronto)

CONTRIBUTORS

BARBARA COEYMAN HULTS, the author of a travel guide-book to Italy, has studied Italian civilization in Rome and has contributed articles to *Art & Antiques, Italy Italy,* and other magazines and newspapers. She has also written *Balloon,* a newsletter for travel fanatics, as well as a series of walking-tour tapes on several Italian cities. She travels in Italy five months a year and is the editorial consultant for this guide-book.

STEPHEN BREWER travels in Italy frequently. He is an editor and writer for several other volumes in this series, as well as for other publications.

JOANNE HAHN has lived and studied in Italy and returns there regularly. A contributor to several magazines, she is coauthor of a travel guidebook to Italy.

LOUIS INTURRISI is a writer, journalist, and longtime resident of Rome. His articles on Italy appear regularly in the *New York Times,* the *International Herald Tribune,* and *Architectural Digest.*

NUCCIO ORDINE teaches at the University of Calabria. His book on the 16th-century philosopher Giordano Bruno, *La cabala dell'asino,* has been published in Italian and French.

JEFFREY ROWLAND lives in Rome, where he is the assistant editor of *Italy Italy* magazine and writes for the *Washington Post.*

THE BERLITZ
TRAVELLERS GUIDES

THE BERLITZ TRAVELLERS GUIDE TO SOUTHERN ITALY
AND ROME
1993

ALAN TUCKER

General Editor

BERLITZ PUBLISHING COMPANY, INC.
New York, New York

BERLITZ PUBLISHING COMPANY LTD.
Oxford, England

THE BERLITZ TRAVELLERS GUIDE
TO SOUTHERN ITALY 1993

Berlitz Trademark Reg U.S. Patent and Trademark Office
and other countries—Marca Registrada

Published by Berlitz Publishing Company, Inc.
257 Park Avenue South, New York, New York 10010, U.S.A.

Distributed in the United States by
the Macmillan Publishing Group

Distributed elsewhere by Berlitz Publishing Company Ltd.
London Road, Wheatley, Oxford OX9 1YR, England

ISBN 2-8315-1780-X
ISSN 1057-4662

Designed by Beth Tondreau Design
Cover design by Dan Miller Design
Cover photograph © Angelo Tondini/Focus Team
Maps by Nina Wallace
Illustrations by Bill Russell
Fact-checked in Italy by Iris Jones
Copyedited by Norma Frankel
Edited by Katherine Ness

Printed in the United States of America
1   3   5   7   9   10   8   6   4   2

THIS GUIDEBOOK

The Berlitz Travellers Guides are designed for experienced travellers in search of exceptional information that will enhance the enjoyment of the trips they take.

Where, for example, are the interesting, out-of-the-way, fun, charming, or romantic places to stay? The hotels described by our expert writers are some of the special places, in all price ranges except for the very lowest—not just the run-of-the-mill, heavily marketed places in advertised airline and travel-wholesaler packages.

We indicate the approximate price level of each accommodation in our description of it (no indication means it is moderate in local, relative terms), and at the end of every chapter we supply more detailed hotel rates as well as contact information so that you can get precise, up-to-the-minute rates and make reservations.

The Berlitz Travellers Guide to Southern Italy 1993 highlights the more rewarding parts of Rome and the South so that you can quickly and efficiently home in on a good itinerary.

Of course, this guidebook does far more than just help you choose a hotel and plan your trip. *The Berlitz Travellers Guide to Southern Italy 1993* is designed for use *in* southern Italy. Our writers, each of whom is an experienced travel journalist who either lives in or regularly tours the region he or she covers, tell you what you really need to know, what you can't find out so easily on your own. They identify and describe the truly out-of-the-ordinary restaurants, shops, activities, and sights, and tell you the best way to "do" your destination.

Our writers are highly selective. They bring out the significance of the places they *do* cover, capturing the personality and the underlying cultural and historical resonances of a city or region—making clear its special appeal.

The Berlitz Travellers Guide to Southern Italy is full of reliable and timely information, revised and updated each year. We would like to know if you think we've left out some very special place. Although we make every effort to provide the most current information available about every destination described in this book, it is possible too that changes have occurred before you arrive. If you do have an experience that is contrary to what you were led to expect by our description, we would like to hear from you about it.

A guidebook is no substitute for common sense when you are travelling. Always pack the clothing, footwear, and other items appropriate for the destination, and make the necessary accommodation for such variables as altitude, weather, and local rules and customs. Of course, once on the scene you should avoid situations that are in your own judgment potentially hazardous, even if they have to do with something mentioned in a guidebook. Half the fun of travelling is exploring, but explore with care.

ALAN TUCKER
General Editor
Berlitz Travellers Guides

Root Publishing Company
330 West 58th Street
Suite 504
New York, New York 10019

CONTENTS

MAPS

THE
BERLITZ
TRAVELLERS
GUIDE TO
SOUTHERN
ITALY
1993

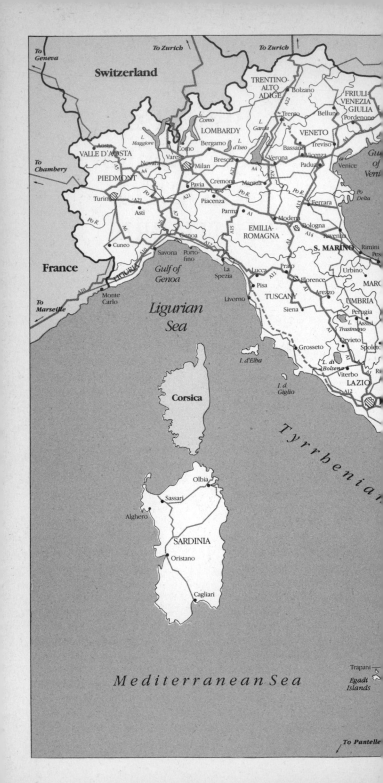

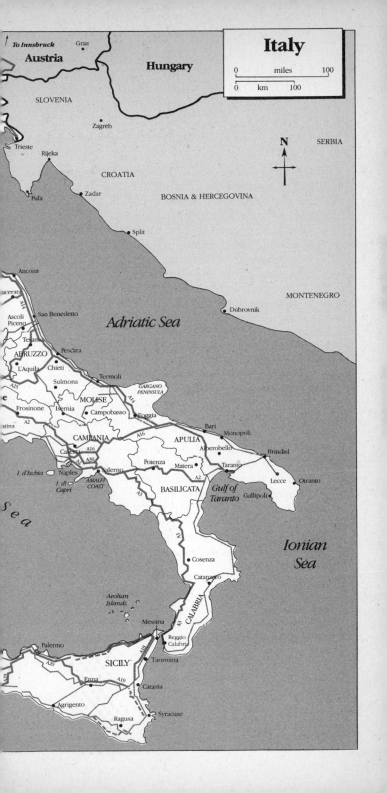

TRAVELLING IN SOUTHERN ITALY IN 1993

Reports of Italy's outrageously high prices are, unfortunately, not much exaggerated. An average hotel room in a major city would be considered a bargain at US$125. A full-course meal in an average restaurant costs about $50.

Avoiding these prices is not easy, but neither is it impossible. Off-season travel costs less, of course. Remember that Italy's low season in major cities includes August, when regular business clients and European tourists are at the seaside. Tour operators list reduced rates at very good hotels in their off-season, "independent" packages. We have mentioned many lower-cost but charming hotels in each city section.

Staying outside the cities costs far less, and many towns are within a day-trip's distance from Rome or Palermo. Towns provide a more personal view of the country, and better hospitality, and are usually less noisy. Family-run pensiones and hotels still abound, as do trattorias where Mama cooks while the beloved son smiles and dispenses menus.

The threat of terrorism seems negligible at present, despite last year's Mafia bombings of two much-respected judges in Sicily. Organized crime reaches tourists mostly through street criminals stealing for narcotics money, but rarely with violence. Preventive measures usually work, as we've outlined in the "Safety" section of "Useful Facts" at the front of the book. Some attention to safety is necessary, but it should not ruin your enjoyment. Italy is still the country of the Renaissance. Thieves were abundant then, too.

—*Barbara Coeyman Hults*

OVERVIEW

By Barbara Coeyman Hults

Barbara Coeyman Hults has lived, studied, and worked in Italy. Formerly the editor of Balloon, *a travel newsletter, she is the author of a travel guidebook on Italy and has written a series of walking-tour tapes on several Italian cities.*

There are three southern Italys.

One of them stretches luxuriously along the rocky coast from Sorrento to Amalfi, rushes up the cliffs to lofty Ravello, and jumps across the sea to the still-seductive Capri. This South is seen in other places: in Sicily's Taormina and along Puglia's eastern coast near Monopoli. This is the South of the sun worshiper, the sleek sailboat, the rich and famous, the boutique shopper. It's well groomed, glamorous, familiar.

The second is the South of antiquity: Roman Pompeii and Herculaneum; the ancient Greek cities of Agrigento, Siracusa, and Metapontum, and earlier shrines to Demeter and Diana; and Apulia's cone-shaped *trulli*. The more recent Baroque South—Sicily's Noto and Apulia's Lecce—would be included here as well.

The third South is in some ways more familiar because it has been transported to the Americas, Britain, and Australia in immigrant groups—the South of pizza and saint's day festivals, of Neapolitan exuberance and Sicilian restraint. It's also the South of Carlo Levi's autobiographical work *Christ Stopped at Eboli.* For many who live in this South, life has changed little since that postwar book. Parts of the Abruzzo, Campania, Apulia, Calabria, and Sicily belong to this Other South, both in memory and in reality.

For travellers, this Other South offers fewer comforts in hotels and transportation and far less street-cleaning. In return it allows the possibility of discovering a new world, one rarely explored by foreign (or Italian) tourists.

We've included the region called Lazio or Latium, which is often overshadowed by its unequaled and unruly capital, Rome, because it can be visited en route to the Mezzogiorno—the Midday—as the South is known.

Sardinia belongs more to itself than to North or South, with a history unlike that of any other region. Its Emerald Coast shelters yachts and year-round tans, and its stone structures, the *nuraghi,* stand as they did in prehistoric Italy.

Probably the best way to enjoy all aspects of the South is to choose comfortable bases in the first, the sleek South, from which to explore the others, mixing the familiar and the rare, the extravagant and the austere, the boutique and the souk.

The Geography of the South

Italy, we all know, is shaped like a delicate boot, with Sicily just off the toe. France, Switzerland, Austria, and Slovenia provide the northern political boundaries. The Alps turn into the Apennines, which follow the western part of the peninsula down its length. The eastern flatland ends in the marshy lagoons of Venice to the north, and beaches run down both coasts—with the best following Sardinia's island shoreline. Lakes dot the north above Milan, and the far northwest coast ends at the French border in an arc of Ligurian coast called the Italian Riviera.

Along their southwest boundaries, the north-central plains of Emilia-Romagna give over abruptly to the mountains of Tuscany, with Florence near its center. Umbria, between Tuscany and Rome's region of Lazio, follows ancient hills and valleys. The Abruzzo and Molise stretch from east of Rome to the Adriatic, rising at the center point to the Gran Sasso range, home to the highest peak of the Apennines. In the center of Lazio, on the west coast near the Tyrrhenian Sea, stands Rome, the Eternal City, to which all roads have led for 2,000 years—and where our journey begins.

Campania, south of Lazio, follows the beautiful rocky coast of Amalfi on the west side of Italy down to the toe of the boot, to Calabria's territory of mountains and lovely sea views. Eastward, the boot's instep is Basilicata, often neglected by travellers, partly because tourist facilities in its mountains and coastal villages are few. Its vineyards and olive groves, however, are beloved by those who take the time to know them. The high heel and spur of the boot are Apulia, the most industrially developed of the southern regions. Dramatic mountains cover its mystical northern Gargano peninsula; in the south, the stunning rocky eastern coast continues around the tip to the lovely white-sand beaches and gentle harbors along the inner heel south of Taranto.

The island off the toe, Sicily, has a mountainous center yielding to plains, encircled with small cove beaches along the coast. The other major island, Sardinia, west of the mainland, is ruggedly mountainous at the center, while its coasts are rimmed with white-sand beaches.

The History of the South

Italy's geographical variety is only part of its interest, however. Add to that the different historical destinies of its regions and you have the beginning of the myriad permutations in the country. Italy's history is exceedingly complicated, for rare is the conqueror who did not see something of value here, whether in natural resources or in enticing plunder.

"Ancient Italy" traditionally begins about 20,000 B.C., although areas throughout the peninsula and Sicily were inhabited long before then. Among many central Italian tribes, the Etruscans—whose origins have not been determined—emerged victorious during the sixth century B.C., only to be defeated by Rome in 351 B.C.

Tradition says that Rome was founded in 753 B.C. by Romulus and Remus, and this date, or at least that century, seems accurate, according to recent excavations. Rome ventured south to crush Pyrrhus—king of Greek Epirus and source of the term "Pyrrhic victory"—in Campania and Apulia during the third century B.C. Conflicts with Carthage (in present-day Tunisia) ensued, because the Phoenicians in Carthage had laid claim to part of the South. Under Hannibal's command, Carthage was victorious during the Second Punic War. Soon Rome demanded *Cartago delenda est,* and Carthage was indeed destroyed. Rome took its revenge on towns that had allied with Carthage by enslaving them, as Agrigento in Sicily would discover.

From the eighth to the sixth century B.C. Greek and Phoenician traders were establishing trading ports in southern Italy, and soon they set up colonies as well. Among the earliest Greek colonies were those at Cuma and on Ischia, both near Naples. The areas around Reggio Calabria, Sybaris, and Croton were soon to follow. The Aeolian Islands, off Sicily, had been established as trading ports by the Phoenicians because of the local obsidian, which made extremely durable knives and weapons. Greeks followed the Phoenicians to Sicily, creating colonies there that would rival their mother country.

The slave revolt, during which Spartacus fled to Mount Vesuvius to rally his fellow slaves, created problems for the republic and for the South (his followers were more intent on plunder than on independence), but Rome, whose sights were spreading in all directions, put down and crucified his men.

Southern Italy now became critical to Rome. Pompeii and Herculaneum were developed, and Sicily became a granary for the Roman legions. Finally in 27 B.C., under Augustus, Rome became a full-fledged empire that ultimately stretched as far west as England, through North Africa, and east to Syria.

Invasions of barbarians from the north began about the time of Marcus Aurelius, and by then the empire was on the wane. When Constantine (whose Edict of Milan ended the persecution of the Christians) moved the capital to Constantinople, the handwriting on the wall was etched in stone.

During the Middle Ages the Germanic Ostrogoths ruled from Ravenna while the papacy grew in influence, laying the groundwork for the Papal States that would follow. This was largely the work of Pope Gregory the Great (590–604), whose strength of purpose helped the papacy emerge as a major power from the muddle of the Middle Ages. In the year 800 the pope crowned Charlemagne Holy Roman Emperor, after which papal power increased as its troubles multiplied.

During the ninth century, Arabs from Arabia (usually called Saracens) established colonies in North Africa. In 827 they began incursions in Sicily, and soon afterward into coastal cities throughout the South.

A period of shifting allegiances followed, with the Byzantines and the Lombards being played off against each other while the Arabs were kept at bay on the mainland.

In Sicily an advanced Arab civilization was halted by the Normans, on their way to the Crusades during the 11th and 12th centuries. The Normans soon became rulers of the South, ousting the Muslim rulers and making Palermo their capital. The Norman king Roger was much influenced by Arab culture and ruled over a multicultural Sicily with great success.

In Northern Italy, Guelf and Ghibelline supported and opposed, respectively, papal power, while in the South, Frederic II Hohenstaufen, later called *Stupor Mundi,* eventually instilled order and early Renaissance values (although the Renaissance penetrated the South only slightly, mainly at Naples).

Charles of Anjou gave Naples supremacy over a neglected Palermo, the city that rewarded the Angevins with the Sicilian Vespers, in which the French were massacred. Robert the Wise of Anjou created a kingdom in Naples that saw the arts flourish, but wars continued among rival Angevin factions.

During the 15th century Naples and Sicily were united in name under the Spanish Aragons, who called the region the Kingdom of the Two Sicilies. A series of revolts and wars led to Spanish Bourbon rule under the childish Charles III (1734), whose value to the arts was immense: he rescued Pompeii from its lava grave, built the San Carlo Opera House in Naples, and created immense palaces—one of which was one of the first charity hospitals. His accomplishments were blurred by the disgrace of the later, reactionary Bourbons, who executed Joachim Murat, king of Naples, in 1815. Under two Ferdinands and Francis I, Sicilian rebellions were put down viciously, with opponents condemned to prison and servitude, while Spanish viceroy rule created an ever-more-exploitive nobility.

Italy was ready for a hero, and Garibaldi filled the bill when he landed in Sicily, on his way to help bring about the Risorgimento and Italian unity. The revolution began in 1860, and by 1870 Italy was an independent republic with a king. After the wars of the 20th century the king's popularity diminished, and the last king, Umberto II, died in exile in Portugal. Today the South remains in many ways separate from the North, ruled, most Southerners lament, by the regional Mafias.

Italy, once Europe's whiz kid with an economy bulging with Made in Italy labels, recently has been seeing hard times. The prestigious label sells at an ever-increasing price, for residents as well as tourists. Public debt and labor costs have made Italy one of the most expensive countries in the world. Entering the Monetary System would mean that the old method of coping with debt—devaluing the lira—would no longer be possible. Revelations of countrywide embezzlement and protection rackets created a nervous backdrop for a weakening economy. The lira was devalued and Italy withdrew (at least temporarily) from dreams of entering the European Monetary System. National elections in 1992 brought a new coalition government, this time without the Communist Party, once Europe's largest. No party, however, has been given a strong majority. Italians, like many Americans today, have little confidence in their government. The brutal car-bomb murder of the illustrious anti-Mafia judge Giuseppe Falcone, his wife, and their bodyguards in May 1992 plunged the country into despair.

Recent surprises from current data include a low birth rate (the lowest in Europe) and a growing population over age 70, the result, many think, of the very healthy diet and active life Italians enjoy. TV and fast food have not overtaken their vitality—a permanent condition, one hopes.

Northern and southern Italy are in many ways different countries. The South is Mediterranean; the North is European. The forces that fueled today's northern industries were largely French and Austrian, while in the South a history of exploitation and neglect, characteristics of Spanish viceroy rule, has contributed to the growth of the Mafia, which today discourages industry from expanding southward (with the exception of Apulia, whose prosperity is evident). A still-operative patronage system and public passivity are today's legacy, although demonstrations against organized crime have become frequent occurrences. The Renaissance, with its growth of the middle class, was by and large a northern phenomenon; even today, entrepreneurial exuberance in the South is possible only in certain areas, mainly where tourism is the industry.

At the time of Italy's unification in 1870, the North, many believe, took measures to encourage northern industry while keeping the South a source of cheap agricultural labor. The pattern has outlasted agriculture, which has shrunk in importance.

Organized crime—the Mafia in Sicily, the 'Ndrangheta in Calabria, the Camorra in Campania, and the Sacra Corona Unità in Apulia—is today recognized as a serious problem not just in the South but also in Italy as a whole. The war against organized crime is now being waged as never before. Although 1993 should find Italy's economic system merged to a great degree with that of the rest of the European Community, preliminary plans have proved to be overly optimistic. Centuries of a "second" economy make public disclosure of resources unlikely, and the current economic state is chaotic.

Yet to everyone's amazement, including the Italians', the country goes on—the pasta is *al dente* and the sun shines in the piazza. Despite the current fiscal disaster, Italy still belongs to the G-7, a group of the seven most industrialized nations. What does the future hold? *Che sarà, sarà.*

The Traveller's Southern Italy

Rome, the seductive, infuriating colossus, smugly aware that everyone will go there sooner or later, makes few adjustments to visitors. The traffic is ghastly, its unmufflered noise and gassy fumes at horror-show proportions. But should you then avoid Rome? Of course not. (Just be careful crossing the street when you get there.) Here you participate in Roman life; you do as the Romans do and you find it exhilarating. Rome provides visitors with layer upon layer of history—turning a corner may call up a new age altogether. You'll find the ghosts of Roman emperors and Renaissance popes, lavish Baroque churches and palaces, piazzas unchanged from the Middle Ages, arbors to dine under, and the Tiber winding calmly past it all. Each age makes its presence known in Rome, bizarrely juxtaposed as in a Fellini circus. An unexpected bonus in recent years is the unveiling of the many handsomely restored monuments, the magnificent column of Trajan among them.

Lazio, the region surrounding Rome, is a place where Etruscan tombs, ancient Roman apartment houses, and Renaissance castles are silhouetted against the sea and the sky, and where shepherds still lead their flocks along the airport road. (The urban sprawl around Rome is best sped past—unless you're a Roman who finds the modern comforts in these often unattractive areas more livable than the dark and unheated palazzi so romantic to the tourist.)

The **Abruzzo**, a land of wolves and witches and the highest mountains of the Apennines, is an eagle's nest a few hours east of Rome, and almost unknown to North Americans. The Abruzzo towns of L'Aquila and Sulmona are reached on roads that glide through a world of lush valleys, rushing streams, and medieval towns perched on terraced hills. The ski trails here are superb, and a national park protects chamois, fox, and bear.

Southeast of Lazio, **Campania**, balm to body and soul, is known mainly for its splendid, rocky Amalfi coast and Capri's isle, for the ancient cities of Pompeii, Herculaneum, and Paestum, and, of course, for **Naples**. Neapolitan cooking comes as a succulent surprise to those who think southern Italy is a poor cousin gastronomically.

In **Calabria**, down the Tyrrhenian coast from Campania, stark towns overlook mountain peaks and the sea, with its dramatic beaches and marinas. Cosenza's medieval quarter encloses a bright cultural life of music, literature, and a brand-new university. A trip from town to town in this rural, mountainous region is an introduction to yet another Italy, fast disappearing as tape decks and television bring the remotest areas in contact with the world beyond.

Apulia, on the opposite side of the boot from Campania, is a newcomer to travellers' itineraries, although it became better known in 1991 when its ports were trying to cope with thousands of Albanian refugees who sailed across the Adriatic seeking, and sometimes demanding, asylum from their oppressive regime. Yet the region's prime attractions remain undisturbed: white beaches; whimsical *trulli,* conical stone dwellings that have enlivened the landscape for millennia on southern hills amid almond blossoms in spring; the easy sophistication of the southwestern coast; the new hostelries created from old farmhouses that were once fortified for enemy onslaughts; and Lecce's Baroque elaborations. Consider also the windswept cliffs of the Gargano peninsula, mystical with its saints, dramatic with its views of caves and crashing surf.

Between Apulia and Calabria lies **Basilicata**, to which we have devoted little time because its accommodations are so few. But it has its rewards: mountains and streams, white beaches, and especially the city of Matera, which seems like a camouflaged, almost abandoned village molded into the mountains. Metapontum, on the coast, is filled with the excavated ruins of a once-thriving Greek colony.

Sicily reveals the brilliance of Arab-Norman cathedrals, the glory of Greek temples, elegant, restrained Baroque palaces, and the incomparably beautiful resort of Taormina, high on a terraced hill that looks out to beaches and sea and up to Mount Etna. Sicily's sophisticated cooking—more Arab in origin toward the island's west, more Greek to the east— takes advantage of the endless varieties of fish that fill the tropically blue seas around the island, and its desserts would please the sweetest tooth in Araby.

Sardinia is known for splendid white coves of beaches, but its dramatically varied interior is at once mountainous, carved with deep gorges, hollowed with grottoes, and flat with lagoons. Around the island are scattered some 7,000 *nuraghi,* ancient hollow stone structures as mystical as Stonehenge, some in the form of medieval cities.

In smaller southern cities, and often in larger ones, travellers find themselves the object of rapt attention. Southern Italians, who find people fascinating, *stare*. Where you are from, what you are doing there, what you think of where you are, and whether you know a cousin in Toronto are vitally important questions. Life is more communal, more piazza-oriented, in the South—although using piazzas for parking lots, and the spread of TV antennas, seem likely to draw people indoors into the alienation of which the rest of the industrialized world complains. But for the moment, people-watching wins over any TV rating.

The late Sicilian writer Leonardo Sciascia described a man on a train looking at a woman. After an hour he was wondering what to name the baby, having progressed gradually in his thoughts from the first word through courtship and marriage. This may be the Other South's most important gift to the traveller: the feeling of vitality that comes from living in the moment, observed and observing.

USEFUL FACTS

When to Go

Spring and fall (especially May, June, and October) are the ideal months—for climate, for flowers, and for lighter tourism and better prices. Summer is a cavalcade of tourists and winter is often drizzly. That said, both summer and winter have much to offer as well. Summer has the obvious advantages of beaches and water sports, and the unexpected discovery of cities—Rome in particular—when all the cars have gone. Anna Magnani said she felt the old Rome only in August, when she could walk through the medievally dark streets that surround the Pantheon and hear the echo of her own footsteps. Trattorias are unrushed then, and life is slow. The downside of summer is the same as the upside: Everyone *has* left the cities, leaving many restaurants and shops closed, and those that remain open are filled with non-Italian faces for the most part. Museums, however, have recently realized that summer days are among their best attended, and they often stay open through August.

However, summer can mean blistering heat, and you may find your touring is limited to the length of the hotel pool.

Winter, too, has advantages, especially cultural: the opera, the theater, concert halls, and uncrowded museums. Because there are fewer tourists, there are fewer lines to wait in, restaurants are on their best behavior (in summer they sometimes think no one will know the difference if they take short cuts with the sauce), and the weather is often lovely—although showers and fog are common even in Sicily.

Entry Documents

Just a passport is necessary for travellers to Italy, or an identity card for citizens of the EC. Motorists need a driver's license and a civil-liability insurance policy if they rent a car (usually provided when the car is picked up; see "Renting a Car and Driving," below).

Arrival at Major Gateways by Air

Alitalia offers direct daily flights from New York to Rome and frequent flights from Los Angeles, Chicago, Montreal, Toronto, Boston, and Miami. If you will be going from North America on to other destinations in Italy or elsewhere, Alitalia is the airline of choice at present, because of its excellent add-on plans. For example, with the "Visit Italy" program, those purchasing an Alitalia ticket from North America to Rome or Milan pay only $100 for a round-trip ticket to any additional Italian airport. (The cost would normally be double this or more.) The "Europlus" plan offers a round-trip ticket to any city serviced by Alitalia in Europe or North Africa for $119 each way. Another package provides a railroad ticket to Naples for passengers arriving in Rome: nonstop service between the Alitalia terminal at Rome's Leonardo da Vinci airport and Mergellina Station in Naples. Two trains daily in each direction are timed to meet Alitalia flights; travel time is about two and a half hours. The service is included in Alitalia's ticket price, which is comparable to or lower than other fares to Rome only. Passengers on other airlines can also use the airport train; the round-trip Rome-Naples fare is approximately $112.

All these special Alitalia tickets must be purchased in the United States or Canada when the transatlantic flight is booked.

As for the North American carriers, new routes are added almost monthly, and only travel agents can stay up to the minute. At present TWA, Delta, American, Canadian Airlines, and United have direct flights to Italy. Most flights from North America arrive in Italy during the morning, usually about 8:00 or 9:00. A good travel agent will work out the most convenient routing, by plane or train.

From London, Alitalia and some British carriers provide service to Rome and Naples. Qantas and Alitalia fly from Sydney and Melbourne to Rome.

Rome's principal airport, Leonardo da Vinci at Fiumicino, has undergone a transformation so glamorous that Clinique cosmetics has opened a boutique there, for a flying re-do. (Only a cosmetic surgeon in the wings is lacking.)

Added to this glamor is a shiny new train, ready to whiz you to the Eternal City. (The clumsy old airport bus to Stazione Termini has of course been banished. No style.)

Sounds celestial? Not quite.

Unfortunately you can't get from the airport luggage carousel to the train (or vice versa) if you need a luggage cart, as many international, and certainly intercontinental, passengers do. An escalator between airport and train prohibits carts, and lines can be long at the single elevator.

Next, there are the two new station stops in Rome: The first incoming stop, Trastevere, is convenient only for those with room reservations at the Vatican; the second, Stazione Ostienze, was apparently chosen for those who wish to see Keats's grave immediately upon arrival. There is public transportation at these stops, but you must know which city bus to take, where it stops, and where to buy bus tickets before getting on. The Piramide Metro stop is within walking distance of Ostiense, for those without luggage. Taxis may be waiting at the station if it isn't raining.

Bureaucratic irascibility worthy of Tiberius is behind this state of transit—or is it the taxi union? In any case, at present the only way to enter the Eternal City with luggage is by taxi: about 60,000 lire ($50).

Many independent air and hotel packages offer transfers from airport to hotel. This is a decided advantage.

When you are making your plans, also consider charter flights. Many charter-flight organizations at present use regularly scheduled airlines, and reserved seats can be arranged in advance. You'll probably be the one in the center if the plane is crowded, however, because the higher-paying passengers will of course get the more desirable aisle or window seats. The Sunday editions of major city newspapers, such as the *Los Angeles Times, New York Times,* and *Toronto Sun,* run ads regularly for special fares. In London, *Time Out* and the *Times* run similar ads.

Specialized travel agencies, such as Italy for Less (Tel: 800-794-8259 or 212-599-0577; Fax: 212-599-3288), will find the most economical fares. Summer and holiday fares are usually not discounted by the airlines. Other discounters are Access International (Tel: 212-465-0707) and TFI Tours International in New York (Tel: 212-736-1140), and Council Charter in New York (Tel: 212-254-2525) and Los Angeles (Tel: 213-208-3551).

Porters

A lack of porters is a chronic problem in Italy. Do not take more than you can carry unless you'll be renting a car at the airport or intend to rely on taxis. Most railway stations are cleverly designed with long stairways to the tracks, rendering even portable luggage carts useless.

Travelling Around by Air

Italy's domestic airlines are often attractively priced for weekend packages under the Nastro Verde (Green Ribbon) plan: You must leave and return on specific days and hours, which are different for each city but generally cover the weekend period. These can be purchased only in Italy, however, at any travel agent or Alitalia office. (All domestic airlines are owned by Alitalia.) In Rome, call Skyreps for discounted European and worldwide fares: via Calabria 17, Tel: (06) 488-4208. Many travel agents sell these tickets as well.

Airports in the South are located in Naples, Reggio Calabria, Catania, Palermo, Pantelleria, Trapani, Bari, Brindisi, Alghero, and Cagliari. These are serviced by Alitalia's domestic fleet, connecting with northern cities.

If you are making plans for railroad or air travel, make sure no strike (*sciopero*) is planned for your day of departure. Strikes are announced in the newspaper, and your hotel *portiere* should be able to forewarn you if you explain your plans.

Travelling Around by Train

Italy's rail service is excellent, and improving. The Rome–Naples express flashes from point to point in 2 hours. The glamorous new first-class-only ETR 450 travels between Rome, Naples, and Bari. Rome to Naples takes 1 hour 40 minutes; Rome to Bari, 4½ hours. Reservations are required. A regular Rome–Palermo express requires 13 hours; sleepers are available. (See also Alitalia's plane/train ticket, under "Arrival at Major Gateways," above.)

Before leaving on the trip, check with your travel agent for the numerous train passes available, each with different advantages. For example, the Kilometric Ticket costs about $238 first class and $140 second class. Valid for two months, it permits 20 trips or a total of 1,875 miles. As many as five people, even unrelated, may travel together on it. If you are travelling elsewhere in Europe, the Eurailpass is also available. Apart from these passes, which should be purchased before departure if possible (some *must* be bought in North

America), youth, senior, and family passes are also sold at special rates.

If you are travelling any distance, ask about the InterCity trains, which are nonstop, at least between important cities on a given route. They run from Sicily to Venice or Genoa. Always reserve a seat if possible, especially on InterCity trains. They are heavily used by Italians as well as foreigners, midweek and midday as well as peak seasons. It's worth the extra charge (no charge if you buy the special passes discussed above). Sleeping cars are available on long-distance trains and require supplements and reservations. For information, ask your travel agent.

Note: Italy's previously casual railroad officialdom has tightened up on its rules. Don't sit in first class without a first-class ticket; make sure the return portion of your round-trip ticket is stamped before you board; and don't assume you can buy a ticket on the train. All of these once-common practices (generally methods of avoiding lines and over-crowding) can incur a costly fine.

However you go, you can still expect experiences like D. H. Lawrence's, 70 years ago:

> Sicilian railways are all single line. Hence, the *coincidenza*. A *coincidenza* is where two trains meet in a loop. You sit in a world of rain and waiting until some silly engine with four trucks puffs alongside. Ecco la coincidenza! Then after a brief conversazione between the two trains, *diretto* and *merce,* express and goods, the tin horn sounds and away we go, happily, towards the next coincidence. Clerks away ahead joyfully chalk up our hours of lateness on the announcement slate. All adds to the adventurous flavour of the journey, dear heart. We come to a station where we find the other diretto, the express from the other direction, awaiting our coincidental arrival. The two trains run alongside one another, like two dogs meeting in the street and snuffing one another. Every official rushes to greet every other official, as if they were all David and Jonathan meeting after a crisis. They rush into each other's arms and exchange cigarettes. And the trains can't bear to part. And the station can't bear to part with us. The officials tease themselves and us with the word *pronto,* meaning *ready!* Pronto! And again Pronto! And shrill whistles. Anywhere else a train would go off its tormented head. But no! Here only that angel's trump of an official little

horn will do the business. And get them to blow that
horn if you can. They can't bear to part. *(Sea and
Sardinia)*

Travelling Around by Bus
Bus travel can best be arranged through travel agents. American Express, Italiatours, Central Holiday, and TWA offer good
programs, catering to independent travellers as well as
groups.

Regional bus companies vary from very comfortable, and
frequently faster than local trains, to the sardine-can variety.
From Rome to L'Aquila (in the Abruzzo), for example, bus
travel is faster, as it sometimes is from Palermo to Taormina.
Travel agents and tourist offices in Italy are your best sources
of information.

Long-distance buses connect Rome with Naples, Palermo,
and smaller cities; travel agents book these intercity buses.

By Boat
The islands of Sicily and Sardinia and smaller islands along
the coasts are connected to the mainland by car ferry and
sometimes by hydrofoil, especially in summer. The Tirrenia
line is the largest of the long-distance lines (Naples–Palermo,
Rome/Civitavecchia–Cagliari, etc.), and can be contacted in
North America through Extra Value Travel, Fountain Building,
683 South Collier Boulevard, Marco Island, Florida 33937
(Tel: 813-394-3384; Fax: 813-394-4848), or through a travel
agent. Always reserve and go first-class on the overnight runs.
(In summer the deck may be hidden under backpacks, and an
important soccer match will sell out the boat in a flash at any
time during the season.)

Smaller islands, such as Capri and the Aeolians, are
booked at the departure cities, as discussed in the "Getting
Around" sections of the regions in which they are located.

By Taxi
Metered yellow cabs (the only ones you want) usually line
up at cab stands, to be picked up there or telephoned. In
most cities they don't pick up en route. If you call a taxi, the
meter starts when and where the driver does. If you can't
find a cab, go into a hotel or bar and ask whether they will
call one for you. It's worth a tip.

Renting a Car and Driving
Although you'll want a car in the countryside to follow your
inclinations to sea resorts and Greek temples, driving in any

of the major cities is far more pain than pleasure. Congestion, speedway-style driving (Rome), hard-to-find parking, and auto theft in some cities are a few of the reasons you will be happier parking at the hotel or a good lot and walking or taking taxis or public transport.

All you will need to drive in Italy is a valid license from your own country. Major car-rental companies in Italy are Maiellano, Hertz, Avis, Budget, National (called Europcar in Europe), and Dollar Rent a Car (affiliated with InterRent). The smallest compact will probably be too small, so opt for at least the next larger. You may request an automatic (usually more than double the price of a standard, as is air-conditioning), but learn a bit about shifting gears just in case. Car rentals are subject to an 18 percent tax, higher for luxury cars.

In southern Italy, pick up your rental car in a smaller town, such as Salerno, rather than in Naples. Rental cars leaving the Naples area have been a frequent target for robbery.

Before leaving on the trip, investigate with your travel agent the cost of fly-drive programs, which are often less expensive (don't ask for the smallest car unless you're under four feet tall), and also about special promotional offers and independent packages, such as those that TWA, Alitalia's Italiatours, and CIT offer, which include a choice of hotels without the disadvantages of group travel.

Insurance for all vehicles is compulsory in Italy. A Green Card (*Carta Verde*) or Frontier Insurance, valid for 15, 30, or 45 days, should be issued to cover your car at the Italian border or by the rental company. Access America provides a health and theft policy that includes collision damage. Many automobile and health insurance policies cover the same emergencies.

Telephoning

The international telephone country code for Italy is 39. When telephoning from outside Italy, omit the zero from the local area codes. (For example, to call Rome from the United States, dial 011-39-6 and then the number.)

Plastic is the answer if you'll be using the telephone frequently, for calls within the country or abroad. For overseas calls, use your telephone card number. You can now reach an American operator to call collect or to use your telephone credit card: For AT&T dial 172-1011, for MCI 172-1022, and for Sprint 172-1877. You need a coin (200 lire) to activate the number. For other international operator assistance, dial 170 for non-European countries and 15 for Europe and Mediterranean countries. To dial directly (hotels charge a huge tax for this): dial 00-1 for the United States and Canada, 44 for the U.K., 61 for Australia, and 64 for New Zealand, and then the number. (New information is issued regularly from U.S. telephone companies; check with yours before you leave for the best way to phone home.)

To call within Italy, a SIP (Italian telephone company) card (*scheda*) is a great help, as Italian coins are heavy and phone calls require a lot of them. Buy SIP cards in denominations of 5,000 or 10,000 lire at SIP offices, airports, railroad stations, newspaper stands, or tobacconists. (Buy them when you are in a major urban area; smaller towns, especially in the South, are unlikely to have them.) The card is inserted in the phone box, and its remaining value is shown on a screen. An alternative is to use the telephone with a meter (*telefono a scatto*), which each town has in a bar (café) if you ask around; you pay the proprietor when you're through.

Regular calls within the same city cost 200 lire; tokens (*gettone*) are required less frequently, but it helps to keep a few with you.

In Rome, the main telephone center is located in piazza San Silvestro.

The Post

Mail service in Italy is rotten. Use the telephone or fax whenever feasible. Urgent letters should be sent by Federal Express, DHL, UPS, or another guaranteed service. When in Rome, try to do most of your mailing from the Vatican, which has its own—excellent—mail service (Italian stamps are not valid at the Vatican).

Local Time

Italy is six hours ahead of Eastern Standard Time, one hour ahead of Greenwich Mean Time, and nine hours behind Sydney. During the changeover to and from daylight saving time there are a few days when Italy is an extra hour ahead or behind, so double-check relevant hours near that period.

Electric Current

Italian current is 220 volts, 50 cycles; a converter/adapter is necessary for North American appliances. Most hardware stores, electronics outlets, and computer dealers in this country have them.

Currency

The monetary unit is the Italian *lira*, plural *lire*, written Ł. Notes are issued in denominations of 1,000; 2,000; 5,000; 10,000; 20,000; 50,000; and 100,000 lire. Coins are 10 (rare); 20 (rare); 50, 100; 200; and 500 lire. At this writing, the lira is valued at about 1,200 to the U.S. dollar, 1,004 to the Canadian dollar, 600 to the British pound, and 1,276 to the Australian dollar. However, the exchange rate is subject to daily variation; check with banks and daily newspapers for the current rates. On arrival at Rome's Fiumicino airport, you can change money just after clearing passport control, before claiming your luggage.

Traveller's checks are changed in banks at (usually) better rates than elsewhere. The American Express office in Rome cashes personal checks for members carrying their cards. Few hotels will accept a personal check, and some do not accept credit cards.

Cambio (exchange) offices vary in rates. Check the posted sign and ask about the commission charged.

Many banks throughout Italy give Visa and MasterCard cardholders cash advances. MasterCard advances are made in banks with Eurocard (EC) stickers on the door. (Eurocard is equivalent to MasterCard for other purposes as well.) Try to obtain such an advance in larger cities, as not all small towns are prepared for this service and you may have to travel to ten banks, waving your card, to find out whether any do. (An advance is an *anticipo*.)

Take your cash machine ID number with you, and ask your credit card company for a list of their automated teller machines in Italy.

Business Hours

Learning Italian business hours would require a university course. They vary from region to region, with the North adhering in general to more European hours and the South keeping the siesta tradition of closing for most of the afternoon and reopening in the evening; "normal" business hours in the South would be from 9:00 A.M. to 1:00 P.M. and 4:00 P.M. to 8:00 P.M. Many shops are closed Monday mornings. Banks are open usually from 8:30 A.M. to 1:30 P.M. and sometimes from 3:00 or 3:30 P.M. to 4:00 or 4:30 P.M., but individual differences require that you double-check. Exchanges (*cambio*) keep store hours. Local post offices are open from 8:00 A.M. to 2:00 P.M., and the central office is usually open late in the evening in large cities. Barbers open from 8:00 A.M. to 1:00 P.M. and 4:00 P.M. to 8:00 P.M. and are closed Sunday afternoons and Mondays. Women's hairdressers are open 8:00 A.M. to 8:00 P.M., but most close all day Sundays and Mondays.

Museum and Church Hours. State museums are open mornings all week but close on Mondays. Double-check the specific museum you want to visit before setting out. Churches that are open to the public at specific hours are usually open mornings only, although some open afternoons as well. The dress code for churches is: no bare shoulders or bare legs, for men or women. Many churches require a 100 or 200 lire coin in the light box to illuminate certain dark chapels or paintings. Keep a supply, preferably in a tube such as those used for camera film; Italian coins are large and heavy.

Holidays

Offices and shops in Italy are closed on the following dates: January 1 (New Year's Day); January 6 (Epiphany); Easter Monday; April 25 (Liberation Day); May 1 (Labor Day); August 15 (Assumption of the Virgin); November 1 (All Saints Day); December 8 (Day of Immaculate Conception); December 25 (Christmas Day); December 26 (Saint Stephen).

Banks, offices, and shops may also be closed for local feast days, such as June 29 in Rome (Saints Peter and Paul), July 15 in Palermo (Santa Rosalia), September 19 in Naples (San Gennaro), October 30 in Cagliari (Saint Saturnino), and December 6 in Bari (Saint Nicholas). While you might not be able to do any banking that day, these holidays are often colorful and festive, and the celebrations are worth seeking out (see "The Local Festa," below).

Note: Beware of *ponte* (bridge) weekends—the three-day weekends that include a holiday, when banking and other services will be closed. Remember that on Labor Day, May 1, absolutely *everything* in Rome and many other cities closes. This means the bus and subway lines as well, and taxis are far from plentiful. Few restaurants are open, but hotel restaurants and a few others will keep you from starving.

When banks are closed, you can change money in an emergency at the airport or railroad station or, with a higher service charge, at your hotel.

The Local Festa

Every region has its own feast days to honor favorite saints. Parades and local food specialties are the rule, and each celebration is individualized by ancient traditions. Here are but a few:

January 6: Epiphany, or La Befana (the good witch who brings toys to children). Piazza Navona in Rome turns into a Christmas fair, and Romans visit the *Bambino* (Baby Jesus) displayed in elaborate *presepi* (mangers) in dozens of churches and in St. Peter's Square.

Celebrations occur throughout Italy.

February 3: Catania, Sicily, honors its patron saint, Agatha, with processions and pastries.

Holy Week and Easter (Pasqua): Easter is naturally celebrated with pomp at the Vatican and elsewhere in Italy, where flowers, music, and spring specialties, lamb and asparagus among them, greet the day. The day after Easter (*Pasquetta*) is also a holiday.

Good Friday is solemnized with special fervor in the South, with processions bearing the Cross in most cities and towns. In Sicily the city of Trapani is famous for its procession of the Mysteries—large figures that are paraded through the town. Sweets include sculpted lambs in marzipan. On Easter Sunday in the nearby town of Prizzi, the triumph of Good over Evil is enacted with devils escorting Death, who will be vanquished by the risen Christ and the Madonna. The favored pastry is *cannateddi,* braided dough surrounding a colored egg.

In Calabria, Catanzaro relives the Good Friday scene of Christ's flagellation with a procession of flagellants, whipping themselves as they accompany the Cross to Calvary.

May 8: In Puglia, Monte Sant'Angelo celebrates Saint Michael's appearance there (also on September 29).

May 7–8: In Bari, Christmas's Saint Nicholas is the patron; his statue is taken out in the harbor for a ride, while on shore the Barese have a seaside party.

Last Sunday in May: The Cavalcata Sarda takes place in Sassari, Sardinia. In one of Italy's most beautiful celebrations, lavish folk costumes from all Sardinia are paraded, accompanied by amazing displays of horsemanship.

May 31: Cavalcade of the Turks. In Potenza, Basilicata, galleons are paraded through the streets with costumed figures representing the downfall of the Turks.

July 3: In Matera, Basilicata, the Black Madonna is carried by cart through the town, and the cart is demolished by a sometimes frenzied crowd.

July 11: In Palermo, Sicily, their patron, Santa Rosalia, is fêted with fireworks and feasting.

August 15: The Feast of the Assumption, a national holiday, is especially festive in Reggio di Calabria—puppets and sweets.

August 16: In San Rocco, there is a medieval-style religious procession of the lacerated *spinati,* who have pierced their flesh with thorns; votive offerings are sold along the streets.

September 1: Neapolitans celebrate the Feast of Piedigrotta, honoring the sanctuary with music, parades, and fireworks.

September 19: Naples' San Gennaro liquifies his centuries-dried blood in the cathedral, a sign of good fortune.

October 30: In Cagliari, Sardinia, the Feast of Saint Saturnino is celebrated with parades.

October 31: The Day of the Dead, or *I Morti.* Graves are visited and decorated with flowers throughout Italy. Artistic marzipan creations, from a delicate *pietà* to a cavalier to an octopus, are on sale at a fair in Palermo and at local bakeries.

Safety

A great many problems are easily solved by purchasing or making a money belt or a small undercover silk or cotton pouch. Carry a credit card and enough cash for the day. Small towns are far safer (from thieves) than cities; thievery is a major problem in Rome, Naples, and Palermo at present. Be sure your homeowner's or renter's policy covers your valuables when travelling. Many do.

Keep a list of all important document, credit card, and traveller's check numbers separate from those items. Or leave the numbers with someone at home whom you can call in case of theft.

If you *must* transport valuables, do so in a plain plastic shopping bag, or one from Upim or Standa, Italy's five-and-dimes. Cameras are easily cut off if you wear them around your neck. Pickpockets thrive in buses (in Rome the No. 64, which goes to and from the Vatican, is notorious) and other crowded areas. Gypsy children (with parental supervision) are among the most obvious; don't read any cardboard signs they put in front of you or your wallet will disappear. They normally work the railroad station areas, among others. Vespa-riding thieves, boys or girls, grab shoulder bags. The final word: Don't leave your valuables unguarded, even in St. Peter's.

The Emergency phone number throughout Italy is 115. For an ambulance, call 118. (Foreigners are not charged for emergency care.)

Restaurants

Eating out in Italy, even in out-of-the-way places, can be an expensive proposition. To avoid unpleasant surprises—and to alert you to unusually inexpensive options—we have tried to indicate the general, relative cost of a meal (first course, second course, dessert, and house wine) at the restaurants we describe. Any meal that comes in under 35,000 lire is inexpensive; from 35,000 to 50,000 lire we consider moderate. Most restaurants are in this category, and whenever we don't mention the price range, you can assume it's moderate. When the prices move from 50,000 to 100,000 lire, it's definitely expensive; and over 100,000 lire is devil-may-care territory. All restaurants charge a minimal cover charge, from 1,000 to 4,000 lire at inexpensive restaurants, and up according to the menu prices.

All restaurants are required by Italian tax law to issue a *ricevuta fiscale,* a computerized cash-register receipt that you must carry with you upon leaving. You can be fined if you don't have it.

Day Hotels

Many services are offered by day hotels (*alberghi diurnali*), which are generally located near the main railroad stations. They are handy for day-trippers, providing baths, showers, barbers, hairdressers, shoeshines, dry cleaning, telephone, baggage checking, writing rooms, and private rooms for brief rest periods (overnight stays are not permitted). Information desks in railroad stations or airports can tell you where day hotels are located. Usually signs indicating "diurnali" are clearly posted.

Hotels

Hotels are awarded stars by the government on the basis of amenities. If you don't need a television or a swimming pool, a deluxe hotel may not be required. (Deluxe hotels charge 19 percent IVA [value added] tax; others charge 9 percent.)

Ask your travel agent about independent packages, which often reduce hotel charges considerably.

The *pensione,* officially, is no more. They are categorized as hotels now. Some "hotels," therefore, will be located on a separate floor of a building. (The name "pensione" has been retained by some hotels.)

Motels

If you don't require traditional charm, Italian motels are excellent, and some have very good restaurants. AGIP and ACI are the organizations that operate motels, which are found near the main highways. (See the Tourist Office information booklet, below, for a listing.)

Youth Hostels

For a listing, see the Tourist Office information booklet, below, or contact the Associazione Italiana Alberghi per la Gioventù, via Cavour 44, 00184 Rome; Tel: (06) 46-23-42; Fax: (06) 47-41-26.

Country Living

A delightful way to see Italy is through the Agriturist organization, which arranges for stays in country houses that range from beautifully groomed villas and ancient castles to rough-and-ready farms. At present some Agriturist offices are not set up for English-speaking people, but if you can communicate in Italian, do write or call. The main office in Rome is located at corso Vittorio Emanuele 101, 00186 Rome; Tel: (06) 651-23-42. There are many individual provincial offices also; their addresses can be obtained from the Italian Tourist Office (see the booklet listed below) or the main Agriturist office. Consult the 1993 Agriturist book *Guida dell'Ospitalità Rurale,* which can be found throughout Italy; it lists relatively inexpensive accommodations (August sells out early). (Facilities in the South are well developed in Sardinia only.)

Campgrounds and Mountain Cabins

More than 1,700 official campgrounds are in operation in Italy, varying from the simple to the well equipped, some with cottages. Write or call the Tourist Office (see below) for a current directory.

Longer Visits

If you are staying in one city for a week or longer, your best bet may be a *residence,* a hotel apartment that enables you to have your own living room and kitchen, usually for less than the price of a hotel room for that period. Many hotels have suites that are rented on a weekly or monthly basis as well. Contact the Italian State Tourist Office or local tourist authorities for a list of residences; in Rome, the Tourist Office booklet *Here Is Rome* lists residences there.

Apartments and houses can be rented in Italy through

offices called Immobiliari, listed in the Yellow Pages. In Rome the newsletter *Wanted in Rome,* available at the Lion Bookstore (via Condotti 181), and at major newsstands, runs classified ads for those seeking and offering rentals in the city and throughout the country.

Many U.S. and British agencies handle villa and apartment rentals. The Italian Tourist Office lists a number of these (see below). This can be a great lira saver and a nice way to feel part of a community.

Cooking Classes

The ever-growing interest in Italian *cucina* has spawned a number of excellent cooking schools. These classes offer a long-lasting souvenir of your trip.

Country Cooking with Diana Folonari. Week-long courses in food and wine, conducted in a private home in Positano. Contact E & M Associates, 211 East 43rd Street, New York, NY 10017; Tel: (800) 223-9832 or (212) 599-8280.

Mario lo Menzo. Countess Franca and Count Giuseppe Tasca offer the opportunity to stay at Regaleali, their family estate and vineyard in Sicily (producing one of the island's finest wines), and learn the artistry of Mario lo Menzo, considered the last *monzù*—a term given to French master chefs during the 19th century. A rare and expensive week. Contact Ann Yonkers, 3802 Jocelyn Street NW, Washington, DC 20015; Tel: (202) 362-8228; or Anna Tasca Lanza, viale Principessa Giovanna 9, 90139 Palermo; Tel: (091) 45-07-27; Fax: (0921) 54-27-83.

Tourist Offices

Don't leave home without the booklet "General Information for Travelers in Italy," published annually by the Italian State Tourist Office. Major offices are located at:

630 Fifth Avenue, New York, NY 10111; Tel: (212) 245-4822; Fax: (212) 586-9249.

500 North Michigan Avenue, Chicago, IL 60611; Tel: (312) 644-0990; Fax: (312) 644-3019.

12400 Wilshire Boulevard, Suite 550, Los Angeles, CA 90025; Tel: (310) 820-0098.

1 Place Ville Marie, Suite 1914, Montreal, Quebec H3B 3M9, Canada; Tel: (514) 866-7667; Fax: (514) 392-1429.

1 Princes Street, London WIR 8AY, England; Tel: (0441) 408-1254; Fax: (0441) 493-6695.

BIBLIOGRAPHY

SIR HAROLD ACTON, *The Bourbons of Naples*. A witty evocation of an extraordinary time.

CORRADO ALVARO, *Revolt in Aspromonte*. One of the few books available in English by this prolific writer; discusses problems in the Italian South during the mid-20th century.

BURTON ANDERSON, *Vino: The Wines and Winemakers of Italy*. Even though it was published in 1980, it is still the best book on its subject—and with interesting asides on food, too—covering all 20 regions of the country.

VERNON BARTLETT, *Introduction to Italy*. An amusing and unusually comprehensive overview of the country's history from ancient times to the present day.

LUIGI BARZINI, *The Italians*. Dr. Barzini explains his countrymen, with wit and knowledge based on deep affection.

JAMES BECK, *Italian Renaissance Painting*. A comprehensive and readable survey of one of the most important aspects of Western civilization.

BERNARD BERENSON, *Italian Pictures of the Renaissance*. One of the essential guides to Renaissance art.

———, *The Passionate Sightseer*. Illustrated diaries of this essential art historian.

EDWARD BULWER-LYTTON, *The Last Days of Pompeii*. A graphic yet historically respectable version of those days.

JACOB BURCKHARDT, *Civilization of the Renaissance in Italy*. Remains a classic work on that period, though it represents a somewhat old-fashioned type of history.

———, *At the Court of the Borgia*. The days of Pope Alexander VI (father of Cesare and Lucrezia).

CHARLES BURNEY, *Music, Men, and Manners in France and Italy 1770*. Burney's account of his travels is one of the classics of the history of music.

JOHN HORNE BURNS, *The Gallery*. The Galleria Umberto in Naples as a metaphor for wartime Italy, with bartenders, prostitutes, gays, and WACs considered with a compassionate eye.

BALDASSARE CASTIGLIONE, *The Book of the Courtier*. An eyewitness account of one of the smaller ducal courts of the

Renaissance and a penetrating excursion into Renaissance thought.

BENVENUTO CELLINI, *The Life of Benvenuto Cellini*. One of the most fascinating autobiographies; Renaissance truth is as interesting as Renaissance fiction.

ELEANOR CLARK, *Rome and a Villa*. A novelist's portrait of the capital.

F. MARION CRAWFORD, *The Rulers of the South*. A two-volume history of southern Italy and Sicily.

VINCENT CRONIN, *The Golden Honeycomb*. A tour of Sicily that uncovers ancient myths and present pleasures.

DANTE ALIGHIERI, *Divine Comedy*. Heaven, Purgatory, and Hell, peopled with the author's candidates for each.

CHARLES DICKENS, *Pictures from Italy*. Evocative portraits of scenes encountered.

DANILO DOLCI, *Sicilian Lives*. Sicily experienced through individual life stories.

NORMAN DOUGLAS, *Old Calabria*. Historical and personal accounts of life in the South; many still hit home three-quarters of a century after publication.

———, *Siren Land*. The ancient Siren myth is related as it touches the Campanian coast.

———, *South Wind*. Once a cult book, it offers readers an escape to Capri, disguised as Nepenthe.

CAROL FIELD, *Celebrating Italy*. More than a cookbook, this sensitive and highly readable volume is an exciting adventure into the heart of Italy through its many legends, feasts, food, and mysteries.

M. I. FINLEY, DENIS MACK SMITH, and CHRISTOPHER DUGGAN, *A History of Sicily*. A brilliant three-volume history compacted into one volume.

SIDNEY J. FREEDBERG, *Painting of the High Renaissance in Rome and Florence*. The two volumes of this history by the former Harvard University professor are as personal as they are scholarly, the prose rising at times to near-poetic vividness.

EDWARD GIBBON, *The Decline and Fall of the Roman Empire* (1776–1788). It is not commonly known that this classic work—hard to find in an unabridged edition—ends with the 15th century, not the 5th, and so has much discussion of the Visigoths, Byzantines, Arabs, Carolingians, Lombards, and other peoples who figured in the transition from Augustus to the early Renaissance. Gibbon—still—should be read by anyone interested in Italy (or in graceful prose).

JOHANN WOLFGANG VON GOETHE, *Italian Journey*. One of the most important Italian journals of its time.

ROBERT GRAVES, *I, Claudius*. An imagined autobiography by the classical poet and translator.

PETER GUNN, *A Concise History of Italy*. True to its title.

AUGUSTUS HARE, *Augustus Hare in Italy*. A compilation of the author's travel writings in turn-of-the-century Italy.

BARBARA GRIZZUTI HARRISON, *The Islands of Italy*. A lavishly illustrated tour through Sicily, Sardinia, and the Aeolian islands with a lively and opinionated guide.

———, *Italian Days*. Her personal journey through the country of her ancestors rewards us with an affectionate but razor-sharp view of everything from history and politics to food and local lore.

HOWARD HIBBARD, *Bernini; Michelangelo;* and *Caravaggio*. Biographies of the artists by one of the most respected art historians.

PAUL HILLS, *The Light of Early Italian Painting*. This recent book is that rarity, art history capable of an immediate and powerful impact on the reader's visual perceptions.

PAUL HOFMANN, *O Vatican! A Slightly Wicked View of the Holy See*. An insider's appreciation.

———, *Rome: The Sweet Tempestuous Life*. Sketches of all aspects of life in the Eternal City.

———, *That Fine Italian Hand*. A revealing, shrewd, and amusing study of the Italian character: at work (or avoiding it), within the family (including the Mafia), always enjoying life.

HOMER, *The Iliad*. Read the Sicilian and southern coast sections, especially regarding the Cyclops, the Sirens, and other myths.

HENRY JAMES, *Italian Hours*. His love affair with Italy. "At last—for the first time—I live!" he wrote.

WERNER KERNER, *The Etruscans*. A scholarly look, with illustrations.

GIUSEPPE TOMASI DI LAMPEDUSA, *The Leopard*. The sensuous and evocative story of a Sicilian prince facing the next generation of rulers: "We were the leopards... those who take our place will be little jackals."

D. H. LAWRENCE, *Sea and Sardinia; Etruscan Places; Twilight in Italy*. All travel journals written with the Lawrencian passion.

CARLO LEVI, *Christ Stopped at Eboli*. Life in southern Italy during the Second World War.

GEORGINA MASSON, *The Companion Guide to Rome*. One of the best guides to Rome, divided by neighborhoods.

————, *Frederick II of Hohenstaufen*. A fine biography worth searching for.

————, *Italian Villas and Palaces*. A picture book full of good information.

AUBREY MENEN, *Speaking the Language Like a Native*. Lightness of touch and modesty of scale by no means preclude serious insight in this witty volume of social sketches by the Anglo-Indian-Irish writer, a long-term resident of Rome.

MICHEL DE MONTAIGNE, *Travel Journal*. The 16th-century essayist's Renaissance insights into church, state, tepid baths, and tough crayfish.

CHARLES DE SECONDAT, BARON DE MONTESQUIEU, *Considerations on the Grandeur and Decadence of the Romans* (1734). Published 42 years before Gibbon's *Decline and Fall,* Montesquieu's commentary focuses on the ancient Roman republican virtues and the institutions behind them—and of course on how and why they weakened, with the well-known result.

ALBERTO MORAVIA, *The Woman of Rome*. A novel of a prostitute under Fascism. Moravia's later works usually show Rome's bourgeoisie at calculated play.

H. V. MORTON, *A Traveler in Italy; A Traveler in Southern Italy; A Traveler in Rome*. All three are filled with the lore and musings of the beloved tale-teller.

PETER AND LINDA MURRAY, *The Architecture of the Italian Renaissance*. Not every fact here *is* a fact, but the writing is clear, the illustrations judiciously chosen, and the book probably the best short introduction to the subject for the general reader.

WILLIAM MURRAY, *The Last Italian: Portrait of a People.* An updated variation on Barzini's *The Italians,* written by a resident foreigner.

JOHN JULIUS NORWICH, *The Italians: History, Art and the Genius of a People.* A comprehensive cultural history.

————, *The Normans in the South* and *The Kingdom in the Sun.* Delightfully written accounts of Norman Italy.

AENEAS SYLVIUS PICCOLOMINI (Pope Pius II), *Memoirs of a Renaissance Pope.* Classical humanism and backstage real-politik blend in unexpected ways in this fascinating autobiography of the 15th-century Tuscan nobleman and pontiff.

GEORGE PILLEMENT, *Unknown Italy.* Up-to-date and off the beaten track, with a focus on architecture.

PINDAR, *The Odes.* Those on Sicily's Olympic heroes are especially interesting.

PLINY THE YOUNGER, *Letters.* Those that deal with his uncle's death at Vesuvius are riveting.

JOHN POPE-HENNESY, *Italian Gothic Sculptures; Italian Renaissance Sculpture; Italian High Renaissance and Baroque Sculpture.* These standard surveys distill the insights of one of the greatest connoisseurs in history. A straightforward main text is accompanied by informative appendices to each volume.

WAVERLEY ROOT, *The Food of Italy.* Anecdotes and a pleasurable introduction to the country's food and wine.

STEVEN RUNCIMAN, *The Sicilian Vespers.* The revolt as it relates to European history, written with immediacy and clarity.

LEONARDO SCIASCIA, *The Day of the Owl.* A mafiosi mystery with insight. Sciascia (pronounced approximately sha-sha), who died recently, is the best known of Sicily's writers.

MARY TAYLOR SIMETI, *On Persephone's Island.* A Sicilian book of the seasons, the journal of a critical and compassionate American resident.

————, *Pomp and Sustenance.* The definitive book on Sicilian cooking (a disguise for a textured work on Sicilian history), beautifully illustrated with rare engravings.

KATE SIMON, *Italy: The Places in Between* and *Rome: Places and Pleasures*. Both are full of insightful observations.

D. MACK SMITH, *Cavour and Garibaldi 1860*. The definitive English-language study of the Risorgimento.

WILLIAM JAY SMITH and DANA GIOIA, EDS., *Poems from Italy*. Almost 800 years of Italian poetry in parallel text form.

SUSAN SONTAG, *The Volcano Lover*. A brilliant, sensuous novel that evokes 1772 Naples, inspired by the lives of Vesuvius aficionado Sir William Hamilton, his wife, Emma, and her lover, Lord Nelson.

LAURENCE STERNE, *A Sentimental Journey Through France and Italy*. Musings on the Continent by the 18th century's top wit.

ALEXANDER STILLE, *Benevolence and Betrayal: Five Italian Jewish Families Under Fascism*. An illuminating and deeply moving account of the ordeal of five Italian Jewish families during the Fascist period.

ADRIAN STOKES, *The Stones of Rimini* and *The Quattro Cento*. Elaborately wrought, powerfully evocative travel writing-cum-criticism (of art and of life). The scholarship on which the English writer pinned his theories is dated beyond repair, but the unique sensibility and tone of voice remain fresh and stimulating.

SUETONIUS, *The Twelve Caesars*. He told what he knew and didn't know with great candor.

RACHEL ANNAND TAYLOR, *Invitation to Renaissance Italy* (1930). A vivid and highly entertaining account of the Renaissance and its major players and themes, forcing us to reconsider some strongly held notions of these fluid times.

TIME-LIFE BOOKS, *Pompeii: The Vanished City*. A very readable text that treats the excavation process as well. Beautifully illustrated.

LIONETTO TINTORI and MILLARD MEISS, *The Painting of the Life of Saint Francis in Assisi*. A unique study of the physical, day-by-day process by which a great fresco cycle came into being.

GIORGIO VASARI, *The Lives of the Artists*. The life and times of the Renaissance masters; gives a sense of how they were judged by their peers.

HORACE WALPOLE, *The Castle of Otranto.* This forerunner of the Gothic novel gives an amusing idea of how exotic Apulia was viewed in the late 18th century.

JOHN WHITE, *Architectural Principles in the Age of Humanism.* Not easy going, but possibly the single most influential modern interpretation of the theoretical basis of Renaissance architecture.

————, *Art and Architecture in Italy: 1250–1400.* A thorough study of the period that immediately preceded the Renaissance.

RUDOLPH WITTKOWER, *Art and Architecture in Italy, 1600–1750.* The noted Baroque historian's scholarly examination of the period.

A. G. WOODHEAD, *The Greeks in the West.* A concise, highly readable introduction to Greek expansion in Magna Graecia.

If the book you want is out of print or hard to find, stop when in Rome at **Books on Italy**, via Giubbonari 30, 00186 Rome, near campo dei Fiori. Call first for an appointment (Tel: 06-654-5285), or write to Louise McDermott at that address for her mail-order catalog.

In the United States, an excellent source is the Traveller's Bookstore, 75 Rockefeller Plaza, New York, NY 10019; Tel: (212) 664-0995. Ask for their catalog of travel books and related literature ($2). Another good source is the Complete Traveller, 199 Madison Avenue, New York, NY 10016; Tel: (212) 679-4339; their catalog costs $1.

VIDEOGRAPHY

Some of Italy's artworks are films, many of which are now available on videotape, dubbed or with subtitles.

Of the early classics, *Bicycle Thief* (De Sica, 1949) and *Umberto D* (De Sica, 1952) are among the most shattering, painful, and powerful films ever made, great works of art and of human compassion. Another fine wartime film, *Open City* (Rossellini, 1946), gives neo-realistic views of postwar Rome. A later (1971) De Sica film, *The Garden of the Finzi Continis,* photographs in exquisite color the elegant prewar world of a Jewish family as an unthinkable future descends.

Other directors who have brilliantly dominated the scene are:

Luchino Visconti (*Rocco and His Brothers*),

Federico Fellini (*Nights of Cabiria, La Strada, 8½, La Dolce Vita, Amarcord, Juliet of the Spirits*),

Michelangelo Antonioni (*Red Desert, L'Avventura*),

Paolo and Vittorio Taviani (*Night of the Shooting Stars, Padre Padrone*),

Giuseppe Tornature, the young Sicilian director whose *Cinema Paradiso* won an Oscar as Best Foreign Film.

Lina Wertmuller (*Seven Beauties, Swept Away,* and, in an unusual collaboration with Franco Zeffirelli, *Brother Sun and Sister Moon,* a life of Saint Francis, well played against a lyrical Umbrian landscape).

I, Claudius, is a fascinating, brilliantly acted series made for BBC-TV. Based on Robert Graves's novel, this look at Imperial Rome and its intrigue won many awards. A PBS video release.

ROME

By Louis Inturrisi and Barbara Coeyman Hults

Louis Inturrisi, the contributor to the Accommodations, Dining, Nightlife, and Shopping sections, is a writer, journalist, and longtime resident of Rome. His articles on Italy appear regularly in the New York Times, *the* International Herald Tribune, *and* Architectural Digest. *Barbara Coeyman Hults, who contributes to the Rome narrative and Getting Around sections, is the editorial consultant for this guidebook.*

Fountains whirling their watery arcs; Romans shouting and gesturing wildly; cars, buses, and motor scooters hurtling like chariots on a life-and-death course—Rome rushes at you. It can be overwhelming, overblown, exaggerated. Colossal as the Colosseum, pompous as the Baroque popes, melodramatic as a street vendor. But just when you've had enough and given up on it, something unexpected happens. You see the Tiber sparkling sapphire in the night light, a waiter brings you a fresh taste from the oven as a gift, you're charmed by a cat admiring a column once reserved for the Caesars, the apricot glow of a building warms you, and you decide to reconcile.

Federico Fellini once praised the city's expansive aspect: "Rome allows you all sorts of speculation, vertically. Rome is a horizontal city, made of water and earth, spread out, and is therefore the ideal platform for flights of fancy. Intellectuals, artists, who always live in a state of friction between two different dimensions—reality and fantasy—here find an appropriate and liberating stimulus for their mental activity, with the comfort of an umbilical cord that keeps them solidly attached to the concrete. Because Rome is a mother—the ideal mother because she's indifferent. She's a mother who has too many children and who, not being able to take care of any one of them, doesn't ask anything of you,

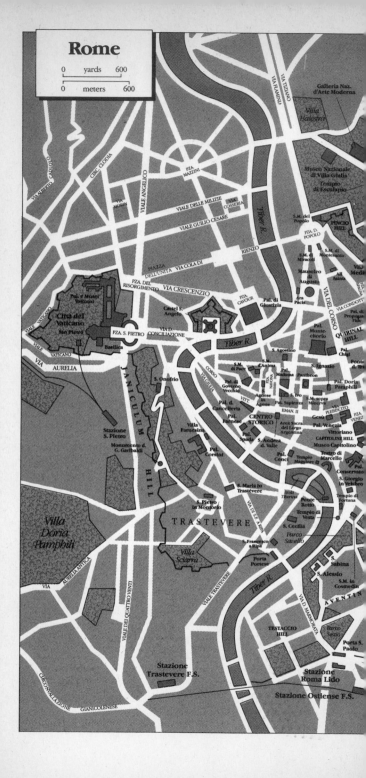

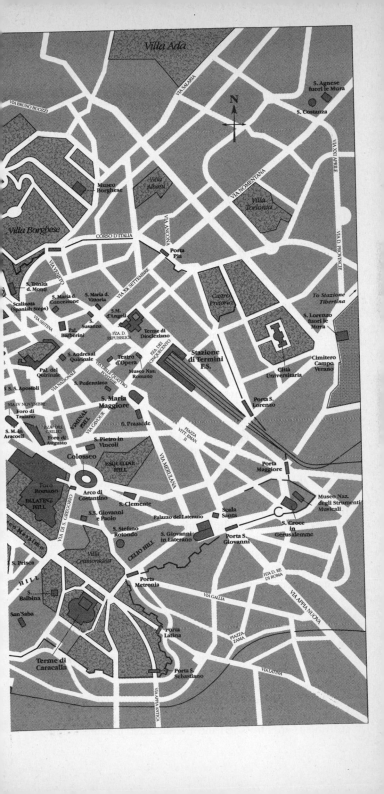

doesn't expect anything of you. She welcomes you when you come, lets you go when you leave."

Though quoted when he made his film *Roma* in the early 1970s, Fellini's words have an ageless quality about them—as befits the Eternal City. They recall the flights of fancy that created the legend about the foundation of Rome by Romulus and Remus, nursed by the she-wolf, the original mother of Rome.

Throughout the city the ancient and the modern are juxtaposed: A classical column protrudes from a building erected centuries later. A sleek, modern train station abuts a Roman bath that was redesigned by Michelangelo as a church.

Between the deep red of the ancient brick and the stark white of modern marble and concrete are the mellower tones, now fixed by law, that dominate Rome and might have come out of a fruit basket in a Caravaggio painting. Peach, apricot, pomegranate, and honey hues decorate its palazzos and villas, the colors made even more striking in combination with the stately Renaissance style imported from Florence, or the exuberant Baroque born in Rome and favored by the popes. Rome's present look is a blend of all such styles, with a touch (but just a touch) of order added when the government of a newly united Italy lined the Tiber with travertine embankments when the city became its capital.

Rome's principal attractions are highlighted in the narrative below, but don't expect—or even attempt—to see everything the first time around. The jumble of the centuries is simply too confusing, even to longtime residents, who are used to the distractions of the unexpected church closures, the signs announcing *chiuso per restauro* (closed for restoration) and *chiuso per mancanza di personale* (closed for lack of personnel), the delightful tangent of discovering a hidden courtyard, witnessing a dramatic bit of street theater (though it's just the Romans going about their daily business), or lingering a little at table over a meal enlivened with good wine and better conversation.

Today's residents often pronounce the city *invivibile* (unlivable), with its endless traffic jams and pollution. But like New Yorkers and Londoners, they seem never to leave. However, apartment rents have soared, sending residents out into the peripheral parts of the city, and thus making transportation still more difficult. In the Centro Storico (the historic center, which in Rome refers to that part of the city across the Tiber from the Vatican), rents of $3,000 a month and more for an ordinary apartment are not unusual. These apartments are furnished and are offered to foreigners only, because foreigners will pay the rents and they can be evicted. (Italians, once in, can rarely be gotten out.)

Begin your visit on a leisurely note and let Rome's charms wash over you slowly. Include a Sunday or public holiday in your plans in order to see the city free of the traffic that normally engulfs its streets and monuments despite legislation attempting to restrict it. If it's a nice day (and it usually is, for the South begins in Rome, as evidenced by the palm trees and the slower pace), rent a bicycle (see details below), or sit in one of the cafés or restaurants in piazza Navona and watch the drama unfold in front of you against the piazza's Baroque backdrop. As a visitor, you'll be as much a part of the street scene as the "real" Romans, whose heroine Anna Magnani personified their fierce vitality on film. For despite laments among many residents that the real Romans have been overrun by other Italians drawn to the capital to take patronage jobs, they are still here—at least in campo dei Fiori and Trastevere, the only areas where you are likely to see Romans whose grandparents were born in Rome.

And the city, which together with the Vatican is capital of church and state, is just as intensely bureaucratic and chaotic as any Fellini fantasy. But don't let it overwhelm you. Above all, take your time. Toss a coin into the Trevi Fountain to ensure you'll be back, for that oft-quoted expression about Rome, *non basta una vita* (one life is not enough), is true.

MAJOR INTEREST

The Roman Forum
The Palatine Hill
Trajan's Column
The Colosseum
The Pantheon
Piazza Navona's Baroque splendor
Walking through the Centro Storico (Old Rome, the historic center) for its large and small architectural pleasures
Piazza del Popolo's churches and cafés
The Spanish Steps
Shopping in the via Condotti area
The especially Roman areas of campo dei Fiori and Trastevere
Rome's restaurants, cafés, and bars
The museums at Villa Borghese, Palazzo Barberini, the Capitoline Hill, the ancient Roman Terme di

> Diocleziano, the Vatican (including the Sistine
> Chapel), and elsewhere
> St. Peter's basilica and piazza

The visitor is constantly confronted with visual reminders of more than two thousand years of history: from the outline left by the Circus Maximus, built in the second century B.C., to the Stadio Olimpico, refurbished for recent World Cup soccer finals. The Sabine and Etruscan kings ruled for more than two centuries (traces of the fortifications known as the Mura Serviane—traditionally attributed to the Etruscan king Servius Tullius, who ruled from 578 to 534 B.C.—may still be seen near the Mercato di Traiano [Trajan's Market]), until the Republic was founded around 500 B.C. The defeat of Carthage in 146 B.C. coincided with the conquest of Greek colonies in southern Italy, thus beginning the Greek influence on monumental Roman architecture, which expanded greatly during the Empire (27 B.C.–A.D. 395). It was during this era that most of what we see of ancient Rome was built, as well as when the engineering feats of the Aurelian Wall in the city (270–282) and the roads and aqueducts throughout the Empire were constructed.

Despite a series of sacks of Rome (by the Goths in 410, the Vandals in 455, the Saracens in 845, the Normans in 1084, and the German troops of Charles V in 1527), the papacy steadily established itself in the city, raising religious monuments and palazzi. The popes' effective political power began under Gregory I (590–604), but the development of the Holy Roman Empire—established when Leo III, in Rome, crowned Charlemagne emperor in 800—led to a series of conflicts between popes and emperors and eventually to the transfer of the papacy to Avignon (1309–1378). Rome's political and cultural importance was greatly diminished during this period.

With the end of the pope/antipope schism, and beginning with Martin V in 1417, Rome entered the Renaissance, and the popes began to commission great works from such artists as Michelangelo and Raphael. Sixtus V (1585–1590) began the first serious planning and development in the city in centuries, with straight roads, and under Urban VIII (1623–1644) and Innocent X (1644–1655) the Baroque we so associate with Rome today reached its zenith. During the relatively quiet political period that followed, such 18th-century works as the Spanish Steps and the Fontana di Trevi were built. Napoléon's troops occupied the city in 1798, and the French taste for Neoclassicism, typified by the works of

Antonio Canova, Napoléon's favorite sculptor, also invaded the city's arts.

Following the defeat of Napoléon in 1814, the Italian revolution (Risorgimento) began, and Rome became the capital of the united Kingdom of Italy in 1870. The overblown monument to King Vittorio Emanuele, completed in 1911, set the stage for Mussolini's march on Rome in 1922, and the Fascist government he established imposed its order on the city by destroying entire neighborhoods to create triumphant boulevards like via dei Fori Imperiali and via della Conciliazione.

The liberation of Rome by the Allies in 1943–1944 brought about the Italian Republic we know today, and except for such scattered modern buildings as the New Audience Hall and a few hotels, the most important contribution to postwar building in Rome seems to be the Grande Raccordo Anulare (the 44-mile-long highway that rings the city)—an impressive feat of engineering, given Roman bureaucracy, almost in the tradition of the ancient Romans.

The discussion of the city that follows begins at the beginning, with *ancient Rome*. It continues chronologically with the monuments of the *Pantheon* and *piazza Navona* (formerly Diocletian's stadium), in the area where the mixture of ancient, Baroque, and Renaissance is most apparent: the *Centro Storico*. You'll then go south of the Centro Storico and see how the real Romans of today live, in the lively neighborhoods of *campo dei Fiori* and—across the Tiber—*Trastevere*. Then we return to ancient history in the *Capitoline* and *Aventine* hills back across the river west of the Roman Forum.

After a breather in Rome's largest park, *Villa Borghese,* you can trace the presence of foreigners in Rome (among them Napoléon's sister Pauline, who lived in the Villa Borghese); then, from the *piazza del Popolo,* stroll to that high point of the Grand Tour, the *Spanish Steps,* and from there go on to the haunt of the Hollywood stars in the 1950s and 1960s, the *via Veneto*. That area becomes a springboard to the city's Christian past, in the general neighborhood of the *Quirinal* and *Esquiline* hills, beginning with the Palazzo Barberini, built for Pope Urban VIII, and then heading generally south (into the area east of the Roman Forum) and back in time to Michelangelo's conversion of a portion of the Terme di Diocleziano into a church, to early Christian churches, and to two of Rome's major basilicas, Santa Maria Maggiore and San Giovanni in Laterano. Finally, you'll traverse the Tiber once again to the separate state surrounded by the city of Rome—*the Vatican*.

ANCIENT ROME

Traces of old Rome—an arch, a column, a fragment of sculpture, or even the colossal marble foot that gave via di Piè di Marmo its name—are strewn about the modern city. The ancient city itself, however, inhabits its very own zone. Behind the Vittorio Emanuele monument radiate the forums and the Palatine Hill, the Colosseum, the Circus Maximus, and the Terme di Caracalla. It is a world of venerable ruins intersected by avenues of rushing Roman traffic.

Before entering, pick up a copy of the red loose-leaf book titled *Rome: Past and Present,* with plastic overleafs that show the Forum now and then; it is essential to re-creating the whole from the assembly of stray columns and fragments you'll see before you. (Buy the book in a store as opposed to a stand near the monuments, where it will be double the price.)

The Palatine Hill evokes the Rome of Classical fantasy, umbrella pines shading fragments of ancient palaces. It's reached from the Roman Forum, whose main entrance is around to the left of the Vittoriano, as Romans call the modern-day monument, and is the best place to get an overview of the otherwise complicated Forum before you explore it on ground level. When you reach the Forum grounds from the main entrance on via dei Fori Imperiali, you will see the Palatine ahead of you, rising above the ruins, an irregular mass of pine, oleander, and cypress interspersed with yawning arches. These arches are the ruins of the grand palaces that lined the hill (which gave us the very word "palace"): residences of Augustus, Nero, Caracalla, Tiberius, and Domitian. To reach the belvedere of the Palatine, from which you'll have a grand overview of the Forum, walk left through the Forum to its far side and then follow the path up the hill. Turn right and take the steps up to the terrace.

The Roman Forum

Few monuments so clearly represent the history and life of an entire civilization as does the great complex usually called the Roman Forum (Foro Romano). There are many forums, and the Roman is only a small part of the entire archaeological site, but for clarity the Roman Forum is

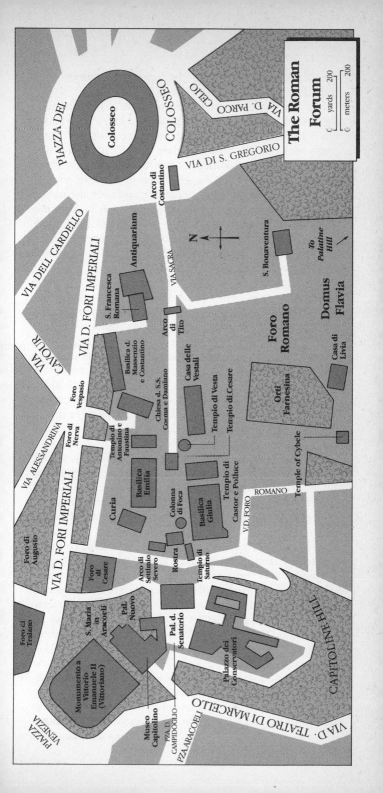

considered to be that section entered from via dei Fori Imperiali through the admission gate.

Built in the valley between the Capitoline and Palatine hills, the Roman Forum reached the peak of its importance under Julius and Augustus Caesar. Both these emperors—and later ones—enlarged the area with their own forums, but it was here at the original Roman Forum that the framework of Western civilization was forged. Much of our own government system derives from this forum, and even the names here are standard in Western thought: "capitol" from the Capitoline Hill next to the Forum; the word "forum" itself; "rostrum" from the Rostra, where Mark Antony delivered Caesar's eulogy; "money" from the mint at the Tempio di Giunone Moneta on the Capitoline.

The original Forum predates most of the buildings you'll see, which were built during the time of Augustus, the beginning of the Roman Empire. At the right, just past the entry ramp, stand the ruins of the **Basilica Emilia**. It was built in 179 B.C. and was later nearly destroyed by fire and the Vandals. The original basilicas had no religious purpose; they were commercial buildings with halls for conducting business. The building style was primarily functional, allowing light and air to circulate inside. The shape was rectangular and monumental, with two aisles and frequently a row of clerestory windows on top—the form adopted by many early Christian churches.

At the Emilia there were shops occupied by money changers—still an important profession for the tourist in Rome. When you walk up closer, in the nave you can see round green stains in the marble pavement, caused by copper coins dropped when the Goths set Rome ablaze in 410.

In front of the Basilica Emilia stands the original Forum as devised by Tarquin, the Etruscan king of Rome, in the eighth century B.C. He and other kings brought the tribes that inhabited these marshy hills together to complete a communal project—draining the malarial marsh of the Forum area. This done, the stage was set for the first forum—really an early piazza. The **Tempio di Vesta** on the east side was there at that time, as was the original Curia—next to the basilica— which was the meeting place of the senate. The black stone called *Lapis Niger,* in a sacred enclosure, covers the legendary site of the tomb of Romulus, founder of the city.

The look of the place at that time was of modest buildings made of tufa with a stucco coat and terra-cotta decorations.

Since wars laid claim to much of Rome's vitality for centuries, little was done to beautify the Forum until Augustus, who then boasted that he'd found a city of brick and transformed it into a city of marble.

City life was concentrated in the Forum, and all roads led there. Political candidates addressed the crowds from the once grand **Rostra**, now just a stone platform behind the Column of Phocas. The Rostra was named for the prows (*rostra*) of ships captured as war booty and lined up here as war trophies. A later trophy would be Cicero's head and hands (43 B.C.), when he got on the bad side of Mark Antony. It was also at this spot that Caesar was cremated and Mark Antony delivered the funeral oration. Elections were held nearby, and victorious generals paraded along the **Via Sacra** (the oldest street in Rome, currently being excavated by an international team of archaeologists) to the Capitoline Hill, where the **Tempio di Giove** (Temple of Jupiter) stood.

Plautus, in his comedy *Curculio,* described the crowds: "In case you want to meet a perjurer, go to the Comitium; for a liar and a braggart, try the temple of Venus Cloacina; for wealthy married spendthrifts, the Basilica. There will be harlots, well-ripened ones . . . while at the fish market are the members of the eating clubs." But Roman society of that time—well before the wild days of Tiberius—was relatively reserved in dress and manners. Women were forbidden to wear jewelry or expensive clothes, partly because of the war efforts. Later, when Carthage was subdued in the Punic wars and Gaul was pacified—both events that filled the treasury—Rome changed, and its first capitalist class was born, for whom wealth was not in land but in money. After that, temples and basilicas sprang up in all the forums, including the adjacent Foro di Cesare and the Foro di Traiano—Trajan's Forum—across the present-day via dei Fori Imperiali (built by Mussolini and covering further riches known at this moment only to the gods).

Beyond the basilica stands the **Curia**, a brick building begun by Sulla in 80 B.C. that replaced the original Curia thought to have been built by King Tullius. Before the days of the Empire senators had considerable power. Judgments were sometimes helped along by augurs, who revealed the workings of fate by reading patterns in flights of birds or in the feeding movements of chickens. The Curia was a consecrated building, with an altar and statue to a pagan god of victory. Christians hundreds of years later objected to the statue, and Saint Ambrose, archbishop of Milan, finally had it removed by appealing to reason: "Where was Jupiter [when the Gauls attacked]?" he asked. "Was he speaking to the goose?"

In A.D. 203 the **Arco di Settimio Severo** (for Septimius Severus, born in Africa, who led Rome to victory in Syria and later in the British Isles) was erected and on top of the arch was placed a sculpture of Septimius and his two sons in a chariot. One of his sons, however, was Caracalla, who murdered his brother, Geta, to ensure that he himself would become emperor—and erased Geta's name from this and other monuments throughout Rome, though the original inscription can still be made out under the obliterated fourth line across the top of the arch. Romans often used columns decoratively rather than structurally, which can be seen in the freestanding examples of the arch's portico.

To the side and slightly behind the Arch of Septimius Severus is the **Tempio di Saturno**, whose eight columns can still be seen. Dedicated to the god Saturn, it was the site of the Saturnalia, celebrated in December of each year, a time of wild public festivities and gift giving, with the quality and amount of the gifts no less carefully observed than they are today.

In front of the Rostra is the **Colonna di Foca**, dedicated to the tyrannical Eastern emperor who gave the Pantheon to Pope Boniface IV in 608. Next to the Temple of Saturn is the **Basilica Giulia**, named for Julius Caesar, who was murdered (not in the Forum but in Pompey's Theater, then near Largo Argentina) before its completion. Some of the stones in the pavement were used as ancient gaming boards, traces of which can still be seen.

The most beautiful fragment in the Forum comes from the **Tempio di Castor e Polluce**: the three elegant columns east of the basilica, often photographed as a symbol of Classical grace. The temple was created during the fifth century B.C. after Roman troops saw the divine twins Castor and Pollux (the Dioscuri) fighting at their side in battle far from Rome. Then the heavenly twins appeared at this site, proclaiming the Roman victory.

The round **Tempio di Vesta** nearby, where the goddess's flame was kept burning by the Vestal virgins, is a favorite site, and was modeled on the circular hut used by the area's earliest known inhabitants. The Vestal virgins, women of noble birth pledged for 30 years to this cult, were charged with never letting the flame die. If it went out, they were severely thrashed; if they lost their virginity, they were buried alive after being driven in a covered hearse through the streets and forced to descend to their own tomb on a ladder. Because they enjoyed great privileges in Rome, it is sometimes assumed that Vestal virginity was a sought-after honor, but Suetonius tells of noble families doing everything to keep their daughters' names from getting on the list when a virgin died.

The house of the Vestal virgins was like a luxurious convent, a self-contained unit surrounding a central garden court with pools and statues of the virgins. The name Claudia has been erased below the figure of one who converted to Christianity, an eternal reminder of her ignominy.

The **Tempio di Antonino e Faustina** (at the right of the entrance to the Forum area) is named for the emperor and his wife who adopted Marcus Aurelius and ruled after Hadrian in A.D. 138. Impressively set atop a long staircase, Etruscan style, it has nicely carved columns and a fragment of a statue on the porch. Alongside it is the church of **Santi Cosma e Damiano**, once part of the Vespasian Forum. If the Forum-side entrance is open, you can see a delightful Neapolitan *presepio* (an exuberant, expansive Nativity scene). The church also merits a visit to see its sixth-century mosaics, among the earliest in Rome. Christ as the Lamb Enthroned is on the triumphal arch.

The name of the large **Basilica di Massenzio e Costantino** makes it sound as if the building were a collaborative effort, but it wasn't. It was begun under Maxentius, but after Constantine defeated him at the battle of the Milvian bridge in 312 it was given his name as well. Its original form is easy to imagine, and part of the coffered ceiling can still be seen. In the Museo Capitolino lie some disembodied fragments of the 40-foot statue of the emperor Constantine that once stood inside the basilica. Encountering the enormous head and hand is an unforgettable Roman experience.

Three massive cross vaults of the nave rose 114 feet above the floor, their lateral thrust strengthened by concrete piers 14 feet in diameter. A Barberini pope appropriated the bronze tiles for St. Peter's, giving rise to the saying, "What the barbarians didn't take, the Barberini did." One of its gigantic marble columns ended up in front of Santa Maria Maggiore on via Cavour. This sort of papal modularism makes it seem probable that everything is really still here in Rome, if only massive rearranging could be done. But of course the jumble of the centuries is part of Rome's charm.

The **Arco di Tito** (Arch of Titus) at the end of the expanse of the Forum was built in A.D. 81 to celebrate the sack of Jerusalem by the emperor; the friezes show the spoils, including the altar from Solomon's temple and the seven-branch candlestick (menorah), being transported back to Rome in A.D. 70.

Next to the church (Santa Francesca Romana) between the basilica of Maxentius and Constantine and the Arch of Titus is the **Antiquarium**, a museum that has some interesting objects excavated from the Palatine and models of the huts in sarcophagus form. (A complete model of ancient Rome is on display at the Museo della Civiltà Romana in the suburban district of E.U.R.—but it is often closed; Tel: 592-61-35. E.U.R. is accessible by Metro.)

The Palatine Hill

But now look at the Palatine Hill behind you.

> Come and see
> The cypress, hear the owl, and plod your way
> O'er the steps of broken thrones and temples.
> Ye whose agonies are evils of a day
> A world is at our feet as fragile as our clay.

This atmosphere of antiquity that enchanted Byron when he wrote *Childe Harold* is readily evoked on the Palatine. Here you can wander amid the umbrella pines of Rome that must have inspired Respighi, and for the moment the world is perfect in classical beauty. The Farnese spread gardens along the hill, fragrant with roses and orange blossoms in the spring.

Although the Palatine Hill inspires dreaming under a tall pine or an ilex, it is the site of some of Rome's most interesting traces of civilization and merits exploration. In back of the splendid Farnese Gardens, down the steps, lie the remains of the **temple of Cybele** (also called Magna Mater, the Great Mother). This temple to the Mediterranean earth goddess was dedicated in 204 B.C. when the Romans learned from the Sibyl that they must build it in order to win a critical battle in the Second Punic War. In it they were to place an idol to be brought from Asia Minor, a black stone said to have fallen from the sky. (Phallic stones represented the goddess's fertility attribute.) You can see parts of a podium and a stairway from the original temple; the temple itself was rebuilt several times.

The huts being excavated in this area date from the eighth century B.C., at the time Romulus and Remus founded the city, according to tradition. They were circular huts of the Iron Age, similar to that reproduced in the Palatine Museum.

The legend of Rome's founding precedes Romulus and Remus, however. When Troy was sacked, Aeneas, son of Aphrodite, carried his crippled father out to safety and on to Italy. A female descendant, a priestess sworn to virginity, met the war god Mars, and the twins Romulus and Remus were the result. She was put to death when the births were discovered, and the twins were set afloat on the Tiber. They came aground at the Palatine Hill, where a compassionate she-wolf found them and nursed them (as you've no doubt seen on thousands of souveniers of Rome). The wolf lived in a cave, the Lupercal, a facsimile of which was venerated during the time of Augustus at the Feast of the Lupercal.

Near the temple you'll find a partly subterranean corridor called the **Crytoporticus**, the main branch of which is about 400 feet (130 meters) long. These passages linked the palaces of the hill, and if they could talk, even today's gossip gluttons might be shocked. (Read or watch Robert Graves's *I, Claudius* for a taste of those times.) On a corridor wall near the house of the evil Livia, fine white stuccoes contain figures of Cupid and floral motifs. The upper floor of **Livia's House** is fascinating, decorated with Egyptian frescoes (things Egyptian were coveted then). In another part of the house, three painted rooms show an interesting mix of fantasy and reality. The nymph Galatea flees Polyphemus upon a seahorse, while Polyphemus looks at her with unveiled thoughts. Elsewhere the architectonic aspects of the frescoes, although often unreal, give a good idea of the decorative scheme used. In the right wing a low frieze glows with a variety of scenes, one of the largest and best examples of landscape painting in Roman art: men and women practicing religious rites; fishermen; a man with a camel; and other scenes.

Nearby, the **Domus Flavia**, the reception area for the emperor Domitian's palace (A.D. 1), stretches in front of the modern building at the edge of the hill (the former Monastery of the Visitation). The large open area, with a fountain surrounded by a columned portico, is well preserved.

To the east, at the hill's edge, the **Paedogogium** was a slave quarters. Ancient graffiti on the wall can still be seen, but the most famous, a donkey crucified, thought to mock the early Christians, is now in the Antiquarium (Palatine Museum) nearby. An inscription reads "Alexamenos worships his God."

The Circus Maximus

Although an oblong field, with wildflowers here and there, is all that's left of the Circo Massimo's great chariot track, it is enjoyable to walk where four chariots raced together for seven laps around the two and a half miles. Originally, as many as 385,000 spectators sat here amid marble columns—nothing Rome did was less than colossal. Caligula loved the chariots, and during his reign the number of races doubled to 24 per day. In the stands, touts and wine-sellers worked the crowds. The last race was held in A.D. 549.

The Arch of Constantine

On a nice day you'll notice lots of people on the Palatine buried in books (or in one another's arms) under the trees, and you may want to follow suit. Otherwise walk back down the hill past the Arch of Titus and out on the via Sacra to via di San Gregorio and the Arch of Constantine (Arco di Costantino), the largest and best preserved of the ancient arches. It was erected to the emperor after his successful encounter with Maxentius. That battle is famous partly because of the vision that Constantine had before it began: He saw a flaming cross formed in the sky and heard the words, "*In hoc signo vinces*" ("In this sign thou shalt conquer").

The arch's unusual collection of reliefs was partly assembled from various other Roman monuments. On the inside of the central archway are reliefs from the frieze of a monument that commemorated Trajan's Dacian victories, but Constantine's head has been substituted for Trajan's. The frontality of the figures, a Byzantine convention, here foreshadows Constantine's transfer of the imperial capital from Rome to Byzantium (rebuilt as Constantinople) in 330, and the end of the glory days.

Beyond the arch looms the great oval mass that is the Colosseum, which may be contemplated alfresco at the **Hostaria Il Gladiatore** on the piazza in front of the Colosseum entrance.

The Colosseum

It was its colossal size that gave the Colosseum its name, but it was its games of bizarre cruelty that made this the most famous building in Rome. Tourist buses rattle its old stones hundreds of times each day, leading Romans to predict that it will soon "crumble like breadsticks," echoing an eighth-century prediction quoted by the Venerable Bede: While the Colosseum stands, Rome will stand. When the Colosseum falls, Rome will fall. The Empire had many coliseums, and some exist today in better condition than Rome's, but this will always be *the* Colosseum. During the years when Christians were literally thrown to the lions, along with other "criminals," Claudius used to arrive at dawn to see the spectacle.

The building was begun in A.D. 72, during the reign of the emperor Vespasian, on the site where Nero had excavated a lake for the gardens of his Golden House (now in ruins across the street and rarely open). Outside stood a colossal 96-foot statue of Nero. Vespasian's spectacles of persecution were so sadistic that Romans turned from them in disgust.

The niches that now seem to be open arches on the sides of the Colosseum were actually created to house Greek sculpture—including athletic motifs from Greece's unbloody games. The Greek athletic contests were introduced to the Romans but were apparently too tame in an age when combat to the death was the daily diet. Roman architects used niches not only for statuary but also to glorify the massiveness of the walls by emphasizing their depth—something Greek architects with their airy colonnades would never have dreamt of.

The Colosseum was built of blocks of travertine excavated from quarries near Tivoli and brought to Rome along a road created just for that purpose. It was apparently modeled after the Teatro di Marcello (see below), built during Julius Caesar's time. It rises in three levels, each decorated with columns, from the plain Doric at the bottom to Ionic and Corinthian; the fourth level held the cables that supported the huge awnings that could be billowed out across the spectators to protect them from rain or excessive sun. Scents were also sprayed on the crowd to keep the smell of blood away from their delicate nostrils.

At the first row of seats we can still see the names of important boxholders. In the second circle sat the plebians, with women and then slaves at the back. Galleries constructed between the seats and the outer walls provided a place to mill during intermissions. The Roman use of the crossed vault made such galleries possible.

Almost 50,000 could be seated with enviable efficiency. There were 80 entrances (four for the select boxholders), and each had a number that corresponded with the game-goer's ticket. Leaving was also facilitated by the vomitoria that "disgorged" the crowds down numerous ramps. Every detail was ingeniously worked out by the architects, who were sensitive to public comfort even as they watched gladiators and animals die agonizing deaths.

The games, too, were organized carefully. Gladiators were recruited from the ranks of those condemned to death and war prisoners—both groups with little to lose but the possibility of a dazzling future. They were housed nearby in the recently excavated *ludus magnus*. The floor could be flooded to create *naumachiae* (sea battles), and sometimes the gladiators fought in the water. (Not every program was just filled with gladiatorial strife, of course. There were circus acts with panthers pulling chariots and elephants that wrote Latin inscriptions with their trunks.)

During gladiatorial combat, participants sauntered around the arena, nonchalant, with their valets bearing their arms. They wore purple embroidered with gold, and when they came to the emperor's box they saluted by raising their right arm and saying, "*Ave Imperator, morituri te salutant*" ("Hail, Emperor. We who are about to die salute you"). The crowd screamed and cheered at each blow: *Verbera!* (Strike!) and *Ingula!* (Kill!). To ensure that a fallen warrior was dead, he was struck on the head with a mallet. A gladiator unable to continue could lie on his back and raise his left arm in appeal. Then the crowd could wave their handkerchiefs and show their raised thumbs to the emperor, who might take their advice and raise his, granting life. Or they might consider him cowardly and turn thumbs down. The emperor's down-turned thumb could not be contested.

Winners were given gold and the adoration of young girls. Cicero thought it a good way to learn contempt for pain and death, and Pliny the Younger thought the trials fostered courage. (Cicero and Pliny, however, did not have to fight.) What was fostered among the spectators was something basic to the Empire: Rome was about conquering.

Of all the forms created by Greek and Roman architects, the amphitheater, a huge bowl structure such as the Colosseum, has, in today's sports stadiums, been the most imitated. Maybe that's because it dovetails so neatly with our own modern sensibilities—in its utilitarianism as well as in its striving for and achievement of grandiose and overwhelming effects. In general, Rome's greatest contributions to architecture were practical: aqueducts and waterworks, roads and city plans.

Trajan's Column and
the Imperial Forums

Successive emperors laid out their own forums, and most are found across the via dei Fori Imperiali, Mussolini's idea of a triumphal highway, which split the forums into two parts.

The **Foro di Cesare** (Caesar's Forum) is mostly on the Roman Forum side of the avenue. On the far side, close to the Vittoriano, is the **Colonna Traiana** (Trajan's Column), a depiction of the emperor's battle (triumphant, of course), long classified as one of the wonders of the world. Its spiral frieze rises 100 feet, and it would, if marble could be unrolled, extend some 215 yards. This masterpiece of intricate composition contains 2,500 figures and was once more easily seen by a spiral staircase. Now binoculars would be handy.

Although you can see the column and much of the several forums by walking along the sidewalk, go inside the **Foro di Traiano** (Trajan's Forum; entrance at via Quattro Novembre 94), because then you can see the **Mercato Traiano** as well; besides, there is often an exhibition going on. Trajan's Market has the intimate fascination of ordinary places. It was a mall of 250 small shops on three levels where oil and wines, perfumes and shoes could be bought, and much of the original structure is well preserved. The forum itself is newly restored and will be the site of modern sculpture exhibitions.

Beyond the Foro Traiano is the **Foro di Augusto** and then the **Foro di Nerva**—where two fine Corinthian capitals have been restored above a relief of Minerva; the friezes tell the story of Minerva's jealousy of Arachne when she heard the peasant girl could spin more beautiful garments. She slit the web Arachne had created, and Arachne hanged herself in shame. Repentant Minerva changed her into a spider, restoring her skill in spinning.

Returning to the Mercato Traiano to leave, you'll see the **Torre delle Milizie** rising above it, part of what was the fortress of Gregory IX (pope from 1227 to 1241). The hilly streets that radiate from here and around nearby piazza del Grillo (off via di Sant'Eufemia) are so medieval in aspect they could be part of an Umbrian town, especially on Sunday when traffic is slow. The glimpses they afford of the forums through windows and arches and from parapets dramatize the ancient by contrasting the eras. From piazza del Grillo you can enter the **Casa dei Cavalieri di Rodi**, ancient seat of the crusading Order of St. John of Jerusalem. Go inside if it is open for the excellent view of ancient Rome from the loggia.

In December *presepi* (Nativity scenes) are displayed in churches throughout Italy, with lights, music, and even water effects. Now, a museum located near Trajan's Forum, open from October through May, displays more than 3,000 presepi from 29 countries, including Brazil, Palestine, and Madagascar. Lessons on constructing them are given during the month of November (in Italian). Open Wednesdays and Saturdays from 6:00 to 8:00 P.M., longer hours at Christmas. Call or write for an appointment: Museo Internazionale del Presepio, 31/AA via Tor de' Conti; Tel: 679-61-46.

The Baths of Caracalla

For more of ancient Rome, take a bus or taxi to the Terme di Caracalla south of the Colosseum. They were luxurious even for imperial Rome, their massive space shining with multi-colored marble, the pools filled by jets of water spouting from marble lions' mouths, the nymphaeum of gardens and pools and statues, gyms, theaters, and libraries. Everyone— rich and poor—went to the baths to socialize and gossip. Caracalla began this project in 212, and his successors added to the glamorous surroundings. The ruins today, the evocative site of Rome's summer opera season (see below), provide important insights into the social organization of ancient Rome.

THE CENTRO STORICO

The Centro Storico, Rome's historic center, is the name traditionally given to the part of the city that occupies the bend of the Tiber across from the Vatican, where the Pantheon, piazza Navona, and a world of Renaissance palaces and piazzas, Baroque drama, and spacious courtyards unfold—sometimes gradually but often abruptly, seducing the senses.

Begin at Palazzo Venezia, on the right corner of the via del Corso facing the Vittoriano, where the traffic is so frenetic that crossing brings on what Italians call *lo stress*. A traffic light eases some of the trauma, and once across you can weave a splendid path for yourself through streets that hold surprises even for those who tread their cobblestones daily. Most palaces along the way were created for noble families that numbered cardinals and one or even more popes among their members.

Peek into courtyards and look up at building decorations and tiny shrines. The traffic in this area is dreadful, so you might consider walking through it on a Sunday. Shops will be closed then, but almost everything else on this walk will be open, including the churches, though you will have to stop just before or just after mass to find them open to nonworshipers. If you can rent a bicycle to sail the virtually car-free streets, so much the better. Saturday morning strollers, on the other hand, can have a glimpse of noble Roman life at the **Palazzo Colonna**, via della Pilotta 17. It's closed all other days and in the month of August. The gallery maintains a fine collection, including 17th-century landscapes by Dughet and portraits by Titian and Veronese. But the Renaissance palace itself is the most fascinating part. The great hall's ceiling is decorated with stories of Marcantonio Colonna and family. A private chapel keeps a canopy and throne ready in case the pope should drop by. (One often has, particularly since Pope Martin V was a Colonna. His portrait hangs in the chapel.) The family church today is the church of the Santi Apostoli, on the adjoining piazza of the same name. An irreverent cool beer can be found at a beer hall of that name a few doors away.

Palazzo Venezia's crenellated, fortresslike mass was once the home of the Venetian Pope Paul II, but now it's better known for its balcony, at the center of the façade, from which Il Duce told Rome the Empire would rise again. Inside you sometimes can see his war room (Mappamondo). The museum in the palazzo has a good medieval collection and hosts frequent shows and exhibitions. In 1564 the pope gave the palazzo to Rome as the Venetian Embassy, but now it belongs to the Italian Republic.

Tucked almost out of sight behind the palace is one of Rome's Byzantine jewels, the basilica of **San Marco**. On its porch the popes once blessed the crowds as they do now from St. Peter's, but this small church usually escapes notice in a city where everything is grandiose.

The interior glows with mosaics and a coffered ceiling of blue and gold, with the heraldic crest and the crossed keys that always signify a pope. In the apse is a ninth-century mosaic of Pope Gregory IV offering Christ this church.

Across via del Plebiscito is the **Palazzo Doria Pamphilj** (Pamphili), still partly inhabited by the noble Doria family, whose anti-Fascist resistance during World War II is remembered by Italians. The Genoese admiral Andrea Doria is a

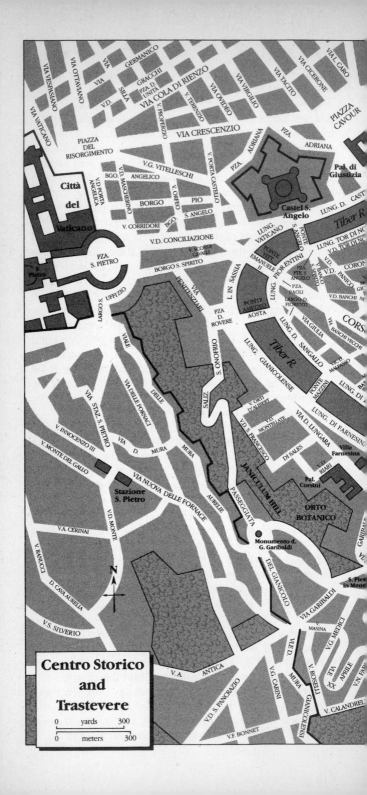

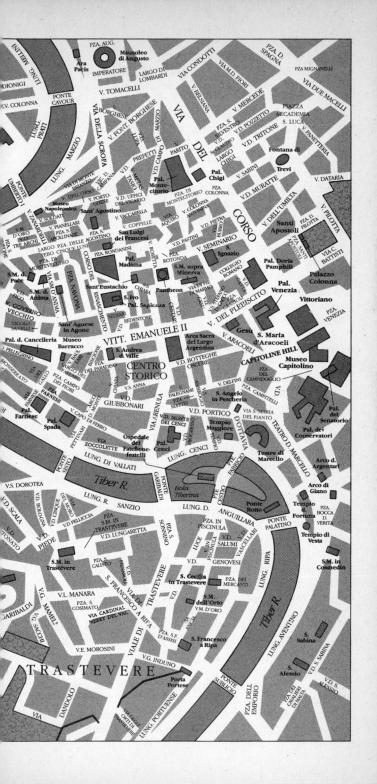

prominent ancestor. Cross via del Plebiscito and follow the little street behind the palace around to its inner courtyard and the museum, which is well worth seeing not only for the paintings but also for the apartment tour, a rare opportunity to see the interior of a Roman palace. (You must wait for a small group to be assembled, but you can see the paintings in the meantime.) The paintings have numbers only, so you may want to buy a catalogue.

Among the highlights of the collection are *Salome* by Titian, and Caravaggio's *Penitent Magdalen* and *Rest on the Flight to Egypt* (the angel is superb but the gallery lighting isn't—it takes angling to see the painting without glare). Farther along is Parmigianino's *Adoration of the Shepherds;* then the bizarre *Olimpia Maidalchini,* whose less-than-sweet face, in a bust by Algardi, is found at the corner. The brother-in-law she bedeviled is around the corner: Innocent X, as seen in one of the greatest portraits ever painted, by Velásquez, and also in a portrait by one who knew him better, Gianlorenzo Bernini. We owe much of the neighborhood to Innocent's forcefulness—that is, until Olimpia cheated him out of all worldly goods, taking his last coin when he was on his deathbed, according to some reports. Notice also, in Room IV, the lunettes by the Carracci family and the *Flight into Egypt* by Annibale Carracci.

For a leap into 20th-century luxury, when you leave, follow the street in front, via di Piè di Marmo, past the large marble foot planted nonchalantly at the side of the street. A clothing designer known to *tutta Roma* has a small shop in the piazza in back of the famous foot. **Teresa Trushnach** creates dresses, slacks, and blouses in sensuously beautiful fabrics and colors. Some ready-made clothes are also on display at her shop (via Santo Stefano del Cacco 27, Tel: 67-97-450). Take your Italian dictionary.

If fabric shopping is on your itinerary, turn left at via del Gesù to **Bises** at number 93, the 17th-century palace where Roman matrons have purchased fine yard goods for many years. The frescoed ceilings serve as a remembrance of times past.

At the Gesù intersection, you'll see **piazza della Minerva** rearing its lovely obelisk, placed atop Bernini's small elephant. The elephant seems quite undisturbed by the size of the obelisk on his back; his trunk curls out cheerfully, like a horizontal bazaar snake. The obelisk was found near here and presumably came from the Temple of Isis that stood close by this spot. In fact, the marble foot (above) may be the only remaining part of the figure of Isis. The beautiful

Holiday Inn Crowne Plaza Minerva, on the piazza, has reopened—perhaps too dazzlingly restored to luxury status.

The church of **Santa Maria sopra Minerva** has a plain façade that hides its considerable riches. It's one of the few ancient Gothic churches in Rome, and it stands on the site of a temple to Minerva (as the name indicates), Isis, and Serapis—Egyptian religions having been brought to Rome when the Empire spread to Egypt. The first Christian church on the site was built during the eighth century, and much of the existing one dates from the 13th century—the work of Dominican brothers Fra Sisto and Fra Ristoro. As you advance along the impressive but dark aisle on the right, the first large chapel is the Aldobrandini crypt, where the parents of Clement VIII were laid to rest with a memorial by Giacomo Della Porta and Girolamo Rainaldi. At the transept is the delightful Carafa chapel, merrily frescoed with the life of Saint Thomas Aquinas by Filippino Lippi between 1488 and 1492.

To the right of the high altar is the Capranica chapel, with a *Virgin and Child* attributed to Fra Angelico. Beneath the altar is the crypt of Saint Catherine of Siena, the main patron saint of Italy and a Doctor of the Church. She lived near here and was instrumental in persuading the popes to return from their "Babylonian captivity" in Avignon. At the left is the tomb of the mystical Fra Angelico. Beyond is *Christ with the Cross* (1514–1521) by Michelangelo, apparently finished by another when the master found a flaw in the marble. Cardinal Bembo is buried at the altar (there's a plaque in the floor), as are popes Leo X and Clement VII, in tombs sculpted by Sangallo the Younger. Works of art are clearly not lacking in this church; an inexpensive booklet is for sale here, detailing each of them, or take a look at the diagram near the entrance. Behind the altar you can see a small museum and some rooms once occupied by Saint Catherine.

The Pantheon

As you walk toward the right, the mass of the Pantheon seems to sit in wait for you, as it has for millions of admirers over the centuries. Its massiveness is what seizes you first, followed by the grace of its columns and the piazza (piazza della Rotonda) that opens in front. The obelisk-topped fountain of wonderfully absurd faces spraying water, the young people sitting at the base, the open windows—always someone leaning out—make this one of the loveliest piazzas in Rome for people-watching. Have a drink or coffee at one of the cafés while you pay your respects to the Pantheon, the best preserved of all Rome's ancient buildings.

Across the top of the Pantheon's façade you'll see the name Agrippa in the inscription, signifying the son-in-law of Augustus, who built the original temple (27 B.C.), which later burned down. The existing structure is the work of the always-building Hadrian, and was begun in A.D. 118. In 609 it was consecrated as a Christian church, having originally been a temple to all the gods.

The outside gives little hint of what's to come—there is nothing like it in the world. The circular opening, way on top—with clouds passing some days, or even raindrops or an occasional snowflake—comes as a shock. The immensity of the round space so high above and the coffered ceiling around it are awe-inspiring. The tomb of Raphael, especially, and of the Italian kings Vittorio Emanuele II and Umberto I are impressive, of course, but it is the space that hushes chattering visitors when they come through the door. In fact, it was the first building ever conceived as an interior space, aided by the use of concrete and cross vaults that allowed Roman architecture to soar.

Walk around the Pantheon to the left as you leave, until you see the stag's head and antlers of the church of **Sant'Eustachio**, the saint being the nobleman who converted to Christianity when hunting. His bow and arrow were aimed at a stag when suddenly Christ's face appeared in the antlers, according to the legend. Have coffee or cappuccino at the **Caffè Sant'Eustachio**, long considered by many the best in Rome. Take a few steps into the piazza and you'll see one of Rome's most exquisite sights, the white swirling tower of Sant'Ivo (see below).

Continue to the right into via della Scrofa for two streets to the church of **San Luigi dei Francesi** (Saint Louis). You'll want to run inside to see the Caravaggio paintings, but stop outside for a moment to see a bit of drollery. At the bottom right of the façade is a salamander that bears the head of François I of France. The salamander was his insignia, but in his version did not bear his face.

Inside, the Caravaggio canvases are in the last chapel on the left. *The Vocation of Saint Matthew* glows with unreal light that hits each figure in a different way, some to follow Christ, some to remain in shadow. *Saint Matthew's Martyrdom* is one of the most dramatic of his works in terms of lighting effects. (The plumed figure at the top left is thought to be the artist himself.) *Saint Matthew and the Angel,* painted in 1602, shows Matthew writing what the angel dictates.

Turn left from the church of San Luigi for two blocks, then left again to the church of **Sant'Agostino** for Caravaggio's *Madonna di Loreto*. This painting was not at all what was expected, because he used the poor and humble as her supplicants instead of the usual rich patrons. The model for the Madonna was a local woman who had rejected a lawyer who sought her hand. The lawyer called Caravaggio a "cursed ex-communicant" for painting her; the artist, in turn, wounded him with a sword and had to escape to Genoa until things cooled down. Raphael painted the *Prophet Isaiah* in fresco here after he had seen the Sistine ceiling; the high altar is the work of Bernini.

From San Luigi it's a short walk south on via della Scrofa to Sant'Ivo. Turn right into corso del Rinascimento. Ahead, the well-guarded **Palazzo Madama** was named for Madama Margaret of Austria, illegitimate daughter of Charles V, who married a Medici and then a Farnese. The palace is now the Palazzo del Senato, named for the government body whose traditions go back to the Curia of the Forum.

Just beyond, at number 101, is the **Palazzo della Sapienza**, whose Renaissance façade is the work of Giacomo Della Porta. Inside are the Vatican archives, but the reason to enter is to see Borromini's newly restored tower and church of **Sant'Ivo** and the courtyard there that Borromini also designed. The Barberini bees that have been worked into the design indicate that a Barberini pope, Urban VIII, was the instigator. The courtyard is elegantly planned to lead the viewer to the campanile's upward movement. The church, constructed from 1642 to 1660, is an intricate play of convex and concave shapes inside, with a hint of the Rococo. Borromini's search for geometric perfection as a spiritual state comes close to fulfillment here.

Piazza Navona

Just across the street, behind a row of palaces, is piazza Navona. The façades that grace the piazza make the owners of these buildings among Rome's most envied residents. The piazza is beautiful in all lights and moods: in early morning when the street-sweepers swoosh through, and by the golden light of sunset when shadows make casual encounters seem dramatic. On Sundays it is still the village piazza, with the entire family here to watch the youngest balance his first two-wheeler while papa hovers above him. Artists set out their paintings, Africans sell belts, pigeons swoop, and rendezvous are agreed on with the eyes.

Festivity has always characterized piazza Navona. In ancient Rome it often took the form of *naumachiae,* when the piazza was flooded to create a sea for real ships to play war in—but it was not play, and deaths were part of the "excitement." During that era the piazza was the stadium of Domitian, which accounts for its elongated shape. Athletic contests (*agone*) were frequent, and gave the name to the church facing the center, **Sant'Agnese in Agone**.

Pope Innocent X, wanting a symbol of his family to be indelibly imprinted on Rome, as well as to beautify the city, called in Bernini to create a monument, stipulating that an obelisk be fetched from the Circus Maximus to be part of the design. Bernini's **Fontana dei Quattro Fiumi** shows four rivers and their continents, each represented by a person. The head of the figure representing the Nile was covered to indicate that the source was then unknown, but Romans said it was because Bernini's statue couldn't bear to look at his rival Borromini's dreadful façade on the church of Sant'Agnese. The Danube's outstretched arm, meant to connect the fountain visually with the façade, was said to be raised to ward off the church's imminent collapse. The Plate and the Ganges complete the quartet. Bernini himself, it's thought, finished the horse, rock, lion, and palm while working here in situ. His poetic use of realistic objects in an exuberant style has made the Fountain of the Four Rivers symbolic of Rome itself.

The other two fountains in the piazza were finished by Bernini and his studio: Fontana del Moro con Tritone (the Moor) and Fontana del Nettuno (Neptune); the latter was largely rebuilt during the 19th century.

Inside the church of Sant'Agnese is a bas-relief of Saint Agnes by Algardi, showing the miracle in which she was stripped naked in preparation for martyrdom, only to be covered immediately by her long, luxuriant hair, which suddenly grew to conceal her body from her persecutors.

Piazza Navona is the place to eat a delicious chocolate ice cream called *tartufo* at **Tre Scalini**—so what if it's crowded with tourists; the *tartufo* and Bernini together are not to be scorned. **Mastrostefano**, the terrace restaurant on the piazza, is another good place to sit and observe the piazza life, and the food can be surprisingly good for such a heavily visited location. Prints are found at **Nardecchia**, a 30-year-old institution at number 25.

The streets off the western side of the piazza are popular

with the young and trend-conscious. Wine bars and shops have sprung up, enlivening the area at night. Walk down to the north end of piazza Navona (on your right when facing Sant'Agnese), turn left to the church of Santa Maria dell-'Anima, designed by Giuliano da Sangallo, past the charming vine-covered Hotel Raphael—protected by *carabinieri* because of its government guests—to the lovely church of **Santa Maria della Pace**. Be there just after 10:30 mass on Sunday morning to see the Raphael frescoes of the sibyls. If it's closed, the façade and the polygonal piazza are delightful anyway. Its cloisters, Bramante's earliest Roman creation, are open every day.

So popular it's often overflowing, the **Bar della Pace** on nearby via Santa Maria dell'Anima is a trendy, pleasant place to have an expensive drink.

One block north of Santa Maria della Pace is the merry **via dei Coronari**, an antiques-sellers' street that holds regular antiques fairs, when it is carpeted as if for royalty and festooned with flowers, banners, and candles. Paralleling the street to the north is the medieval via dei Tre Archi, and all around for strolling are delightful streets near the banks of the Tiber.

Nearby, **Jeff Blynn's** New York–style bar at via Zanardelli 12 may inspire you to order a cool martini in its posh surroundings.

Along the river at piazza di Ponte Umberto I is the **Museo Napoleonico**, with Bonaparte family portraits and the chaise on which Pauline reclined for her famous statue by Cavona (now in the Museo Borghese; see below).

From here you can follow the via dell'Orso (the Street of the Bear) as it makes its romantic meanderings. The **Hosteria dell'Orso** is as atmospheric a place as Rome has to offer—a medieval hostelry where you can stop for a drink at the beautiful bar on the ground floor or dine upstairs (though the food does not match the decor in quality). At night the lights from the river make the window views softly romantic.

Continuing back to the via del Corso, you may want to get an ice cream at Rome's venerable *gelato* institution, **Giolitti**. If so, make a detour when you reach via degli Uffici del Vicario. The *semi-freddo* (partly frozen) varieties and fresh fruit flavors are sought after; for pastry-lovers, the *bigne allo zabaglione* (a cream puff bursting with Marsala-laced custard) is one of its rich specialties. Farther along the same street, the **Gelateria della Palma** is a relative upstart favored by younger *gelato* aficionados.

Via degli Uffici del Vicario leads to piazza di Montecitorio, where, in the **Palazzo Montecitorio**, the lower house of parliament meets—thus the heavy security and milling journalists when congress is in session. The palace itself was completed by Fontana in 1634, as requested by the ubiquitous Pope Innocent X Pamphili. The back of the palace has one of the few Art Nouveau touches in Rome—the stairway and portal designed by Ernesto Basile, the Sicilian master of Liberty style, as Art Nouveau is called in Italy.

The obelisk at the center of the piazza was brought to Rome by Augustus, according to Pliny in his *Natural History;* it is one of the 13 that remain out of the nearly 50 that once graced the cityscape.

At the far end of the piazza a short street leads to **piazza Colonna**, dominated by the **Palazzo Chigi**, where the cabinet offices of the government are located. The Chigi Palace was designed by Giacomo Della Porta in 1562 for the Aldobrandini family, but the famous Chigi family of banking interests bought it. During the 18th and 19th centuries this piazza was sufficiently off the beaten track for coffee to be roasted here in the open air; the scent was then considered disagreeable. The column (recently restored) for which the piazza is named commemorates the campaigns of Marcus Aurelius and his victory over the Germanic tribes. The emperor's statue at the top was replaced by one of Saint Paul in 1588.

At some point along the way you'll doubtless notice people carrying portable phones (*telefonini*). Italians, for whom discourse on anything is as essential as pasta, took to these phones in record numbers. An informal survey revealed that 80 percent, despite their professional-looking briefcases, were talking of love and its modalities and most of the rest were registering their opinions on food. When the new president tried to call the parliamentary delegates to order in 1992, he was drowned out by ringing phones; phones are now prohibited during sessions.

For a grand finale to your walk, cross the via del Corso to the right of the arcaded Galleria and continue straight ahead until the rush of water tumbling over boulders tells you that the **Fontana di Trevi** is near. This Baroque version of a nymphaeum, bursting with gods and steeds, was just another fountain until Hollywood, with *Three Coins in the Fountain,* and Fellini, who splashed Anita Ekberg in it in *La Dolce Vita,* made it part of the standard itinerary. Recently restored to an almost too pristine whiteness, it's most magical at night when fewer tourist cameras are clicking. Tradition dictates that you toss a coin into it from over your shoulder to ensure a return to Rome.

Near the fountain, the **Academy of San Luca**, in a small square of that name, exhibits works by Titian, Rubens, van Dyke, Guido Reni, and others. The *Madonna di San Luca* is attributed to Raphael.

THE REAL ROMANS: CAMPO DEI FIORI TO TRASTEVERE

The Counter-Reformation, when the Roman Catholic church was attempting to draw back the parishioners who had strayed northward, was a time when popes commissioned artists, notably Bernini and Borromini, to seduce the viewer into the church's mysterious excitement. Façades waved convex and concave, statues gestured, putti cavorted over ceilings and dangled chubby legs from balustrade perches. What realism didn't accomplish, trompe l'oeil did.

No art form better expressed Italy's own vitality, and especially the famed exuberance of the people from Rome southward. To see the Baroque at its most opulent, start at the church of Sant'Ignazio (Saint Ignatius, founder of the Jesuit movement) and continue to the Gesù, where the saint is buried. The contrast between today's Jesuits—sometimes condemned by the Vatican for their leftist policies—and the priests who accumulated the Gesù's gold and precious stones is as dramatic as the art itself.

The church of **Sant'Ignazio** is near the Palazzo Doria, on a piazza best appreciated on a car-free Sunday. Sit on the church steps and you will discover yourself on a stage, the center of attention for the palaces that curve around the piazza, palaces whose waving convex and concave lines caused critics to call them "the bureaux"; the name spilled over into the tiny adjoining street, via del Burrò.

The church's visual impact starts with its façade, designed by the Jesuit Father Orazio Grassi, Algardi, and others, and financed by Cardinal Ludovisi, whose collection of antiquities is exhibited at the Museo Nazionale. Inside, a blaze of marble, stucco, and rich altar decorations sets the tone. Algardi created several large statues for this church, but the pièce de résistance is the nave's vault, entirely frescoed by the Jesuit Andrea Pozzo and showing Saint Ignatius's ascent into Paradise. Stand at the marble disc on the floor for the trompe l'oeil effect. (Baroque churches relied on viewer participation.)

The expensive trattoria **Cave di Sant'Ignazio**, with an outdoor terrace on the piazza, is still a favorite with Romans at night, when the setting is even more scenic.

Several blocks south of the church is the via del Plebiscito. Turn right into it and soon you will see the church of the **Gesù** (now behind scaffolding), whose opulence makes Sant'Ignazio seem stark. The façade was designed by della Porta in collaboration with the Jesuit Father Valeriani. The church is the prototype for Counter-Reformation churches, with room for the congregation to hear the priest's address comfortably and wide aisles for seating. The church was designed by Vignola for Cardinal Alessandro Farnese, and the idea was to lead the spectator into contact with the mystical by artistic means.

Father Pozzo again created a great ceiling in the chapel. The master of the quadrature painters, who treated entire ceilings as canvases, he organized the groups of heavenly participants by dark and light areas. Bernini's influence is seen here in the rays of light at the center, to which your eyes gravitate. There also appears the monogram IHS, signifying the Name of Jesus, a subject for contemplation in Ignatian meditation. But not everyone saw it as mystical: The grand duke of Tuscany said it meant "*Iesuiti Habent Satis*"— "the Jesuits have enough."

Another story attached to the church is that of the devil and the wind. The two were out walking in Rome when they came upon this church. "Wait for me," said the devil, entering the Gesù. Since he never came out, the wind is still waiting, which explains why that corner is one of the windiest in Rome.

- Continue along corso Vittorio Emanuele II to the **Area Sacra del Largo Argentina**, where some of Rome's oldest buildings, temples from the period of the Republic (fourth century B.C.), can be seen—in the traditional home of Rome's largest stray cat colony, whose benefactors are numerous. Near the via di Torre Argentina stood the Curia Pompeii, where Julius Caesar was murdered. To visit the grounds at Largo Argentina (most of it can be seen from the street), apply to Ripartizione X, via del Portico d'Ottavia 29; Tel: 671-038-19.

Continuing on the same street, on the left is where *Tosca* begins: the church of **Sant'Andrea della Valle**, designed by

Carlo Maderno but publicized by Giacomo Puccini and, later, Franco Zeffirelli. Domenichino's contribution was considerable: the frescoes of the *Life of Saint Andrew*. The dome is the second highest and largest (after St. Peter's) in the city. A recently canonized saint of the family of Tommaso di Lampedusa (author of *The Leopard*) is buried here to the right of the high altar. Along corso Vittorio Emanuele II and off to the left on via Baullari (the trunkmakers' street) are the busy streets that surround piazza Campo dei Fiori.

The **Museo Barracco**, farther along on the Corso, occupies an elegant Renaissance palace and houses excellent collections of Egyptian artifacts and classical sculpture.

The Campo dei Fiori Area

On sunny mornings there is no merrier market scene than the one in this piazza—a medieval Covent Garden of cheeses and meats, fruits and flowers, greens and vegetables like none you've ever seen before, and all fresh from the fields, with the bakery **Il Forno** to provide fragrant bread and the **Enoteca campo dei Fiori** for wine. Prices at the luggage stands and flower stalls are usually lower than in stores. On gray or stormy days the campo is more fascinating and moody. Then the atmosphere of the Middle Ages at their most intense permeates the area around the statue of Giordano Bruno, who was burned here as a heretic in 1600. **Da Francesco** on the piazza is a good trattoria for lunch; the crowded **Carbonara** rests on its shaky old laurels. The **Grotte del Teatro di Pompeo** on via Biscione is a favorite in the evening for its fiery *penne all'arrabbiata* (flat tubes of pasta with a red-peppery sauce), *liguine al radicchio* (narrow ribbon pasta with a spicy chicory sauce), and the pizza from its wood-fired oven.

To the north of the campo is the lovely **Palazzo della Cancelleria**, whose court with a double loggia is a Renaissance masterpiece and is thought to be partly the work of Bramante. (A glimpse through the gate may be all you'll get, though its hallowed halls ring with chamber music during the Christmas season.) To the southwest of the campo, the next square is the **piazza Farnese**, reached from the via del Gallo. There stands one of the most influential of Renaissance palaces—it was reproduced all over Europe. The **Palazzo Farnese** was begun by Sangallo the Younger for Cardinal Alessandro Farnese, who would become Pope Paul III. Exactly what part Michelangelo played is disputed, but it appears that the central balcony, the cornice, and the third floor were his contribution. The palace is today the French Embassy; for admission, which may or may not be granted, apply to the French cultural attaché. While on the piazza, have a look at the tiles in the **Galleria Farnese** boutique. If you are antiques hunting, stroll along the via Giulia, which runs parallel to the Tiber.

Continue along via di Monserrato southeast to the **Palazzo Spada**, in piazza Capo di Ferro. The piazza was designed by Francesco Borromini, who built a wall to screen the palace's resident, Cardinal Spada, from prying eyes. Windows later broke the wall, however, and the fountain was replaced by a more modest one.

The palazzo's busy façade blends whimsy and artistry, and depicts heroes of ancient Rome fêted with garlands of stucco. The palace was built about 1550, but Borromini wasn't called in until 1632. Because the Italian Council of State is the present occupant, access is not easily obtained, but the gallery and the garden are open. When you enter the courtyard—a fantasy of tritons, centaurs, and delicate garlands—stop at the custodian's corner office and ask him to show you the gardens (*giardini*) and the palace (*palazzo*). He often waits to assemble a small group—so you will know whether to stay there or head into the gallery, which has regular hours. (The custodian expects a tip.)

The garden has a charming secret—a colonnade that leads to a life-size figure . . . but no, it's an illusion created by diminishing columns; the figure is only about a foot tall in reality. We owe this fancy to the Augustinian priest Giovanni Maria da Bitonto (1653), not, as was thought until recently, to Borromini.

If you can enter the sumptuously decorated palace, you'll see the statue of Pompey under which Caesar was murdered (or a reasonable facsimile thereof). It's the "dread statue" to which Byron addressed this question: "Have ye been victors of countless kings, or puppets of a scene?" Borromini's stairway, the Corridor of Bas-Reliefs, and the state rooms are appropriately impressive.

The gallery is interesting partly because it is housed in its original setting, four rooms of the cardinal's palace. Of the artworks note especially Titian's *Musician,* the *Visitation* by Andrea del Sarto, a portrait of Cardinal Spada by Guido Reni, and works by Brueghel and Lorenzo Lotto. (A piece of paper enclosed in plastic, found in each room, lists the surrounding works.)

The Ghetto and Isola Tiberina

From piazza Mattei, south of the Area Sacra, via Sant' Ambrogio leads south to **via del Portico d'Ottavia**, named after the monument at the end of the block to the left (currently being restored). Augustus rebuilt the second-century B.C. portico of Cecilius Metellus, which surrounded the temples to Jupiter and Juno, and created two libraries—one Greek and one Latin—dedicating the portico to his sister, Octavia. It became a fish market (*pescheria*) during the Middle Ages, and now houses the fishmongers' church, Sant'Angelo in Pescheria, named in the fishmongers' honor.

Today, via del Portico d'Ottavia is the main street of what was Rome's Jewish **Ghetto**, one of the least touristed and most evocative sections of Rome. Formerly residents of Trastevere, the Jews of Rome moved to the Isola Tiberina following the pillage of Rome in 1084. Then, crossing over the ponte Fabricio (which was once known as the pons Iudeorum, or the Bridge of the Jews), they moved into the area next to the Portico d'Ottavia, ironically the very site where Vespasian and Titus had convened the senate the day Rome conquered Jerusalem. Paul IV officially confined the Jews to the Ghetto in 1555, and although much of it was razed in 1885 to destroy what had become a crowded and insalubrious district over the centuries, many of Rome's Jews chose to remain here. People still come to the area for its characteristic cuisine, which may be sampled at **Da Luciano** or **Da Giggeto** on the via del Portico d'Ottavia, or more expensively at **Piperno** on via del Monte dei Cenci. There is also an excellent pastry shop, **Il Forno del Ghetto**, at number 119. Try the ricotta cheesecake.

Another unfortunate site nearby is the **Palazzo Cenci**, in piazza Cenci. Never a part of the Ghetto, the palazzo was the home of the bloody Cenci family. In a 16th-century scandal, the brutal and perverted Francesco Cenci was murdered by a killer hired by his wife and three of his twelve children. Although public opinion held that this was legitimate self-defense, his wife and daughter Beatrice were beheaded near the ponte Sant'Angelo, his son Giacomo was drawn and quartered, the other son was sentenced to life imprisonment, and the pope confiscated all the family property. The Cenci exploits inspired many literati, including Shelley and Antonin Artaud, and every year on the anniversary of their deaths a mass is celebrated for the repose of Beatrice's soul in the church of San Tommaso, next to the palazzo.

One block away is lungotevere Cenci, where, to your left, is the **Tempio Maggiore**, Rome's synagogue. Built in 1904, it also houses a museum of Roman Jewish memorabilia (Tel: 656-46-48; closed Saturdays). Across from it is the boat-shaped island called the **Isola Tiberina**, reached by ponte Fabricio, Rome's oldest standing bridge, which dates from 62 B.C. (Farther downstream may be seen the remains of the older ponte Rotto, or Broken Bridge, which collapsed in 1598, the year Francesco Cenci was murdered.) The Isola Tiberina was sacred to Aesculapius, the god of medicine, and had hospitals on it long before the present-day Ospedale dei Fatebene-fratelli (literally, the do-good brothers).

Trastevere

After walking through the ever-rushing crowds in the center of the city, crossing the Tiber to Trastevere (tras-TAY-var-ay) can be like entering a country town (first the speedway along the Tiber must be bested; push buttons for lights are found about every 50 feet). Go to Trastevere late in the afternoon, when the light on the buildings glows rose and gold, and at night (money belt–only zone). You can stroll through lanes where green tufts of grass sprout from little cracks in thick-walled buildings; tiny shrines are lit to the Madonna; the smell of fresh bread entices; artisans repair statues, sand tables, solder tin pots; children play in long smocks and dark stockings; fountain steps harbor meetings; and on enviable roof gardens the long arm of gentrification is seen. The people of Trastevere consider themselves the true Romans and have made little accommodation to the "foreigners" who have adopted their quarter, although they themselves are warm and friendly by nature.

Start in the southern part of Trastevere at the church of **Santa Cecilia in Trastevere**, whose large, tranquil courtyard is frequented by local mothers watching their *bambini* taking their first steps. Life was far from tranquil for Santa Cecilia, however, who lived in a patrician villa on the site (excavations have been made of her rooms below ground; entrance from inside the church). Her husband, Saint Valerian, was beheaded because, as a Christian, he refused to worship the Roman gods. Cecilia was locked in the steam room of her house, which was then heated by a roaring fire; instead of dying, she was found singing in a heaven-sent shower. Three days of heat did not kill her, and even the blows of an ax failed. By the time she died, hundreds had converted, inspired by her courage. Thus armed with the legend, enter the church to see her statue by Stefano Maderno at the high altar, a figure lying down with her head turned away, as she was when her sarcophagus in the catacombs was opened. On November 22 concerts are held in her honor, and the Academy of Santa Cecilia in Rome, among the most prestigious of music academies, was named for her. During the late afternoon, you may hear the nuns singing mass from behind the grate.

In the nearby **piazza in Piscinula** (named for an ancient Roman bath) stands the 12th-century Palazzo Mattei (now private), once the home of the family that reigned over this neighborhood in medieval days by force of intrigue and murder. Though both acts were common in the Middle Ages, apparently the Mattei went too far and were thrown out of Trastevere. They landed on their feet, however, amassing a great fortune and a cluster of palazzi at piazza Mattei across the river near the Fontana delle Tartarughe.

The spiritual side of the Middle Ages is also well represented at the piazza, with the church at the opposite side built above the house where Saint Benedict spent his childhood, and which he left to create one of the most widespread monastic organizations in the world. The tiny campanile (the smallest in Rome, with the oldest bell) can be seen to best advantage along via in Piscinula, leading from the piazza. Ceramics from all over Italy are beautifully displayed at the **Galleria Sambuca** on via della Pelliccia, several blocks to the west and just north of piazza Santa Maria in Trastevere, a good place for gift buying.

Stop at nearby via dei Genovesi 12 and ring for the *custode* to see the *chiostro,* one of the loveliest small cloisters in the city. Follow via Anicia south from via dei Genovesi, past the church of Santa Maria dell'Orto, with the odd little obelisks on its façade, to piazza San Francesco d'Assisi. Here the church of **San Francesco a Ripa** shelters Bernini's statue of *Blessed Ludovica Albertoni,* strikingly similar to his more famous Saint Teresa. Bernini was in his seventies when he made this statue but was still in command of his formidable powers. The chapel is a domed space, strangely illuminated over the body of the saint lying in her final agony. Howard Hibbard, in his book *Bernini,* describes it in terms that recall a host of Baroque scenes in Rome: "The waves of draperies in front echo her position, their heaving billows reflect her agony, their colors accentuate her pallor . . . the chiaroscuro of this drapery and the diagonal of Ludovica's arms, broken by [the position of] her hands, create an almost symphonic treatment of physical suffering and death . . . the frieze of bursting pomegranates below the painting signifies the immortality to which her soul is passing."

A living Baroque scene takes place daily (except Sundays) at the produce market in **piazza San Cosimato**, across the viale di Trastevere (a major bus artery) from the church of San Francesco. If the market doesn't have something to entice you, the streets that surround it are likely to. On **via di San Francesco a Ripa**, which runs from piazza Santa Maria to San Francesco, you'll find freshly made mozzarella and ricotta, banks of new cheeses to try, fresh bread, pizza squares, and pastries—the *bignè* (cream puffs) *con zabaglione* are rich with Marsala. On Sunday mornings the bakeries are open and filled with people seeking the traditional *cornetti, sfogliatelle* (a Neapolitan transplant), and their more sugary associates.

Come early (8:00 or 9:00 A.M.) on Sunday morning for the Porta Portese **flea market**, which extends for blocks and is filled with sometimes interesting antiques, old books and prints, stacks of jeans and shoes, fresh coconut and raw fava beans (*fave*) to munch on, and a liberal assortment of pickpockets. Roman authorities would close the market, but the *populus Romanus* yells a resounding no. Stop first at the bakeries on via di Francesco a Ripa (above) for fresh *cornetti* and coffee to fortify you. After 11:00 A.M. only the crowd-loving need apply—it's the thing to do on Sundays for many Romans. The entrance where the "antiques" dealers ply their trade, off via degli Orti di Trastevere, is the easiest. The section around Porta Portese, on the Tiber, is often mobbed by 11:00. (Remember that state museums are open Sunday mornings, however.)

From here to the famous **piazza Santa Maria in Trastevere** is only a short walk. Its dominant feature, the church of **Santa Maria**, is enchanting, especially at night, when the façade mosaics glisten. By day it's a mini–piazza Navona, with crowds of local residents and visitors, soccer games, and entangled lovers on the fountain steps.

The church's portico, embedded with ancient relics, was built by Carlo Fontana in 1702. Its campanile (restored) has surveyed the piazza since the 12th century. Although the church we see dates from then, it was erected over what is traditionally thought to be the oldest church (first century) in Rome dedicated to the Virgin Mary. Inside is a gilded ceiling designed by Domenichino; the wonderful polychrome marbles and mosaics sparkle above the Cosmatesque pavement. In the mosaic of the *Madonna with Christ,* a very real woman sits with her son's arm about her in touching tenderness.

A few streets north, on via della Lungara, you'll arrive at the **Palazzo Corsini**, which houses an impressive collection of Renaissance and later masterworks from Fra Angelico to Poussin (open every morning). Across the street, the **Villa Farncsina** contains several rooms frescoed by Raphael with voluptuous and dramatic tales of the gods. The villa was built (1508–1511) for the Sienese banker Agostino Chigi, whose bedroom on the upper floor is frescoed with scenes from the marriage of Alexander the Great and Roxanna. No mere banker's fantasies for him. Given to drama, he once had the servants throw all the gold and silver utensils into the Tiber, outside the dining room, when dinner was finished. The startled guests didn't know that wily Chigi had laid nets in the river to catch his finery.

Stop also at the fine print collection on the second floor, called the **Gabinetto Nazionale delle Stampe**. The Farnesina is closed Sundays but open Mondays.

Near the Farnesina and perfect for a hot day's escape is the **Orto Botanico**, at largo Cristina di Svezia 24, an enchanting garden with greenhouses of orchids and cactus. On its higher level some of the ancient oaks and beeches that once covered the Janiculum have miraculously survived the onslaught of centuries. Open daily except holidays from 9:00 A.M. to sunset; Saturdays and Sundays until noon.

For a Trastevere evening, **Sabatini's** on the piazza is a popular place to dine, especially for the view, or stop at **Noiantri**, another landmark nearby. The English-speaking (or -learning) crowd in Rome turns out in force at the Pasquino, a second-run movie house on vicolo del Piede. **Vicolo delle Cinque** to the north is an attractive old street of stylish boutiques and trattorias. On via della Scala the **Birreria della Scala** is the spot for jazz and beer. Trastevere has several jazz clubs (Billie Holiday, Folkstudio, Big Mama) with American musicians in regular attendance. For a more elegant note, sit in the garden at the **Selarium** (just off via dei Fienaroli) and listen to live music. When it's late, **Yes Brazil** at via Francesco a Ripa 103 will follow up with Brazilian music; the crowd is young and Roman.

Janiculum Hill

High above Trastevere to the northwest, and overlooking the Centro Storico on the other side of the river, the Gianicolo (Janiculum Hill) is frequently climbed (or driven) not only for the superb views of Rome it affords but also for the church of **San Pietro in Montorio**, built over the spot west of

Santa Maria in Trastevere where Saint Peter was once believed to have been crucified. In the courtyard is Bramante's lovely Tempietto, smug with Renaissance harmony. Beatrice Cenci is buried in the church, within sight of her place of execution on the ponte degli Angeli.

If you walk farther west up via Garibaldi and then to the passeggiata del Gianicolo, you'll see the monument to Garibaldi, hero of a united Italy. The passeggiata continues past the statue of his wife, Anita, who fought and died at his side.

CAPITOLINE HILL TO AVENTINE HILL

An exhilarating walk (mostly downhill) leads with very few street crossings from the piazza Venezia to the Tiber (stopping off at the Capitoline museums, Santa Maria d'Aracoeli, and piazza Bocca della Verità) and then turns up the Aventine Hill, where during the warmer months the simple charms of early Christian basilicas are entwined with the scent of rose gardens and the orangery, exquisite in spring.

The monument to Vittorio Emanuele II, or the **Vittoriano**, as it is frequently called, has few redeeming architectural features, and its never-darkening white marble in a city of apricot and honey tones is a shock. But to the Italian tourists who come to Rome to see their capital of only a little more than a century, it is a powerful image of unity and durability. The Tomba del Milite Ignoto (Tomb of the Unknown Soldier), midway up the steps and guarded 24 hours a day by the military, adds to its nationalistic appeal. An oddity just in front on the left is a fragment of ancient wall—left there because, when the area was being razed for the monument, it proved to be the tomb of one Caius Publicius Bibulus, who died about 2,000 years ago. Since graves had to be outside the city limits, this provided a historical clue to the configuration of the first century B.C. city walls.

Around to the right as you face the monument are the steep steps that lead to the Aracoeli church. These are suitable for penitents on their knees, but if you feel guilt-free you might opt for Michelangelo's Cordonata, the sloped staircase on the right that leads to the Capitoline Hill's summit and piazza del Campidoglio.

The church of **Santa Maria d'Aracoeli** (pronounced ara-CHAY-lee, or -SHAY-lee in Roman dialect) was built on the site of an ancient temple to Juno Moneta and to Jupiter—a holy place above the Forum where every Roman offered sacrifices. The earliest church on the site dates from the sixth century. In the ninth century a Byzantine monastery occupied the hill, and the present basilica was built around that time. Saint Bernard of Siena lived here, and his life is celebrated inside in a series of frescoes by Pinturicchio. The flight of 124 steps was built by the architect Simone Andreozzi, in gratitude for being spared from the plague in 1346; the parishioners contributed the funds. The church's name, which translates as Saint Mary of Heaven's Altar, is derived from the 12th-century *Mirabilia,* which tells of the time when the emperor Augustus consulted the sibyl about a problem: The senate wanted to deify him, but the idea didn't appeal to him as it had to his predecessor Julius Caesar. The sibyl prophesied that "from the sun will descend the king of future centuries." At that moment the Virgin Mary with the Christ Child in her arms descended from heaven and voices said to him: "This is the Virgin who will receive in her womb the Savior of the World—this is the altar of the Son of God." On that spot Augustus created the altar that was called the Ara Coeli. Later chroniclers mention the altar, which is now lost. A column in the church came from Augustus's bedroom in his palace on the Palatine Hill. It's marked *a cubiculo Augustoranum* and stands third on the left in the nave.

The sumptuous ceiling of gilt-coffered panels was built to honor the victory at Lepanto, which ended the Turkish fleet's rule of the Mediterranean (the papal fleet had taken part in the rout).

Pinturicchio's frescoes of Saint Bernard, painted in 1486, are among the best examples of the artist's work. In the right transept is a Roman sarcophagus festooned with fruit and flowers. Across from it at left is the octagonal tomb of Saint Helen, mother of Constantine. The altar beneath her burial urn is what was thought to be the Ara Coeli but is instead a fine 13th-century work that depicts the miracle. Also in this transept is the tomb of the 13th-century Cardinal Matteo d'Acquasparta, an exceptional work by Arnolfo di Cambio.

In the sacristy, or in the left aisle at Christmas, is the little gold- and gem-encrusted figure of the *Santissimo Bambino* (the Most Holy Child), whose intercession is still sought. Among the many legends surrounding the Bambino is one of a very wealthy woman who was so ill she wanted desperately to keep the Bambino with her through the night. In the morning she felt better but decided she couldn't part with him and had a replica made to return to the church. One medieval night, stormy to be sure, the monks at the church were aroused by a loud knocking at the outer door. It was the Bambino come to his rightful home. At Christmas every year, children come to the church and recite poetry to him; and Christmas Eve mass here is among the most festive celebrations in Rome.

Piazza del Campidoglio

The adjoining piazza del Campidoglio is one of the most pleasant places in Rome to sit, and especially so in the evening. The museums here are open certain weeknights and Saturday evenings. Though you may have to make do with a bit of curbing to sit on, the beauty of the piazza and the lack of cars make it exceptionally conducive to a respite. Since Michelangelo was the planner, this is not entirely surprising. Even the approach along the Cordonata alerts the senses to something out of the ordinary at the top.

The Campidoglio (Capitoline Hill) is the smallest of Rome's famous seven hills, but it is the most imposing because it was the spiritual and political center of the Roman world—the Forum was built on its slope—and it remains the seat of city government to this day. It is especially brilliant each April 21, when the city celebrates its birthday by illuminating the façades of the buildings with hundreds of dish candles.

The equestrian statue of Marcus Aurelius that once graced the center of the piazza (the only equestrian statue that has survived from Imperial Rome) has been relocated to a side courtyard after restoration, and the dramatic if less brilliant statues of Castor and Pollux stand at the top of the steps. At the right is the **Palazzo dei Conservatori**, in which the Conservators' Palace Museum is found. Its courtyard is unmistakably Roman; the enormous head and hand of Constantine, and odds and ends of limbs from the statue that was in his basilica in the Forum, line the warm apricot walls of the court.

On the stairs is the figure of Charles of Anjou, whose ambitions were ended by the Sicilian Vespers revolt; it is the only medieval portrait statue in Rome. In this extensive Classical collection—the statues are mainly copies of Greek originals—the *Thorn Extractor* is notable, but the portrait busts from Augustus to Nero and Tiberius are the prizes. Here Roman art did not follow the Greek patterns but showed the rulers in unidealized portraits. The Etruscan bronze statue of the she-wolf with the nursing twins, Romulus and Remus, that Pollaiuolo added, is also here; its imprint is on everything in Rome, from state seals to sewer covers. The Museo Nuovo wing is devoted to the Renaissance: paintings by Bellini, the Carracci, Caravaggio, Lotto, Reni, and others.

Directly across the piazza, in the Palazzo Nuovo, is the **Museo Capitolino**, where the ancient god Marforio lies in seductive indolence in the courtyard. His name is assumed— he's one of the "talking statues" to which verses were attached, usually satiric poems directed at the celebrities of the time.

Hadrian's villa at Tivoli was awash with splendid mosaics, and some of them are now here, in the Room of the Dove. The theme is Love: Eros and his Roman counterpart, Cupid, with Psyche and the Capitoline Venus. Among the fine statuary are the poignant *Dying Gaul;* the *Marble Faun* (a satyr figure attributed to Praxiteles, and the marble faun of Hawthorne's last novel); and the *Wounded Amazon* (a copy), which was sculpted for a competition at Ephesus, where the cult of Diana thrived.

The remaining building on the piazza is the Palazzo del Senatorio, where the local government meets. In back of it splendid views of the Forum unfold (by day and night).

Toward the Aventine Hill

To the west a couple of blocks on the via del Teatro di Marcello, in front of piazza del Campidoglio, is the **Teatro di Marcello**, Julius Caesar's first contribution to the dramatic world. Its impressive if fragmentary current state is enhanced by the oddity of its having apartments above. Known as the Palazzo Orsini, it is still inhabited by the Orsini family, who have perhaps the best view in Rome. (The stylish **Vecchia Roma** restaurant is close by, and is recommended for lunch.)

Down via del Teatro di Marcello toward the Tiber, before piazza Bocca della Verità, stands the sturdy, newly restored **Arco di Giano** (Arch of Janus) in a valley (now behind a parking lot) where cattle dealers gathered in the days of the Empire, sheltering themselves inside the arch. On the far side of the arch is the delightful church of **San Giorgio in Velabro**, named for the marsh in which Romulus and Remus were found. (The Palatine Hill is just beyond.) The church often bears the red carpet that awaits a wedding party, presided over by 13th-century frescoes.

The beautifully sculpted arch adjoining the church, erected in A.D. 204 in honor of Septimius Severus and his sons, is called the **Arco degli Argentari** (Arch of the Money Lenders). And again, after Caracalla murdered his brother, Geta, he removed Geta's name from the arch, as on the Arch of Septimius Severus in the Forum. On the pilasters contemporary views of the Forum provide the background.

As you turn back toward the Tiber, across the broad boulevard is the exquisite round marble **Tempio di Vesta**, really a temple to Hercules, some think, and the so-called **Tempio della Fortuna Virile** (both second century B.C.).

At the end of the street is the medieval church of **Santa Maria in Cosmedin**, famous for the open mouth of truth, the *Bocca della Verità,* on the porch. Hordes of tourists wait in line to see if it will snap off their hand if they tell a lie. The face was a medieval drain cover, but its appeal is not diminished by that knowledge. The sixth-century church was later enlarged and given to the colony of Greek refugees. The floor is a rare example of mosaics produced by the Cosmati themselves, most floors being only Cosmatesque; geometrical designs signal their work.

The Aventine Hill

Turn left at the corner by Santa Maria and walk to the next wide street, via del Circo Massimo. Across it, a winding road from the piazzale Romolo e Remo ascends the Aventine Hill; by following it you'll see the loveliest rose gardens in Rome (in May) and the orange trees of the church of **Santa Sabina**—and the view of Rome from the balustrade in the little Savello park by the church. The church is an elegant example of a fifth-century basilica, wonderfully lit by clerestory windows and impressive-looking with its Corinthian columns, but the drama is in its simplicity. In 1222 it was given to Saint Dominic, who was founding a new religious order, and the Dominicans still preside here. On the porch is a carved cypress door (under glass); the crucifix at the top left is apparently the oldest known representation of Christ on the Cross.

Continue southwest after Santa Sabina to **piazza dei Cavalieri di Malta**, a Piranesi-designed space most famous for the keyhole at number 3 that frames St. Peter's dome so beautifully. The Aventine is an obviously wealthy residential neighborhood (money belts advised), and it is a joy to stroll up and down its slopes, away from the hubbub of the city. If you have time, stop also at the ancient churches of Santa Prisca, built over a Mithraic temple (being excavated), and San'

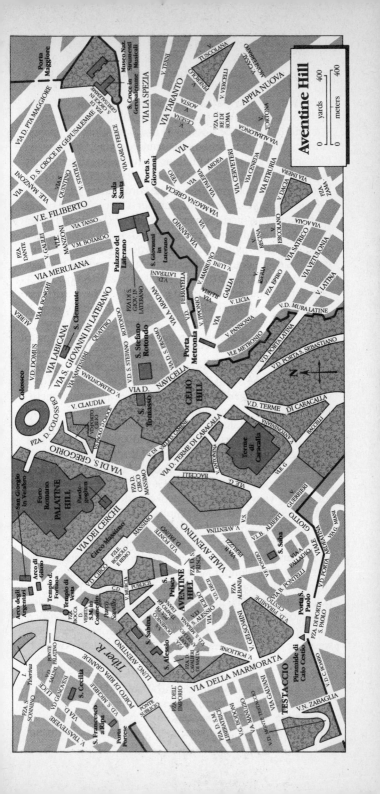

Saba, on the other side of piazza Albania to the southeast of the hill.

For lunch, go across via della Marmorata from the Aventine to the outskirts of **Testaccio**, an old neighborhood where the slaughterhouses once stood, and that is still famous for restaurants that specialize in cooking innards. Wonderful vegetables are also a specialty of the inexpensive trattorias that dot the area. **Perilli** is a favorite on via della Marmorata, which leads from the ponte Sublicio to the Porta San Paolo, but stop first up the street at **Volpetti** (number 47) to see one of the most marvelous (and expensive) shops for cheese and other delicacies, including a mortadella like no other. Try the very strong Pugliese *ricotta forte* and varieties of fresh mozzarella; tasting is encouraged. Rome's housing shortage has brought the young and chic to this once-funky neighborhood. See it before the wine bars move in.

ROME'S LEGACY OF FOREIGNERS

Begin one of your days in Rome early, at the **Museo Borghese** in the small palace of the **Villa Borghese** (not a villa but a large park built for Cardinal Scipione Borghese, the pleasure-loving nephew of Pope Paul V, on the Pincio Hill). Today the Villa Borghese, just north of the Spanish Steps/via Veneto area, is one of the greenest and most relaxing public places in Rome, a favorite spot for a picnic, a trip with the children to the zoo, or a promenade to its piazzale Napoleone I on the west side of the **Pincio** for a traditional view of Rome over piazza del Popolo. Bicycles can be rented on via di Villa Giulia, but you must leave your passport.

For the purpose of this one early morning visit, however, go primarily for the museum, where the cardinal amassed, by patronage and plunder, an extensive collection of paintings (temporarily closed to the public) and sculpture. The display begins dramatically, if not scandalously, with the statue of Napoléon's sister Pauline, who, when she married Prince Camillo Borghese, commissioned it from Antonio Canova as a wedding present for her husband. She insisted on posing as Venus, almost entirely in the nude. When asked how she could have done so, she replied, "Oh, there was a stove in the studio," anticipating Marilyn Monroe's remark about having a radio on in similar circumstances.

Scipione Borghese was an early patron of Bernini, a number of whose most outstanding sculptures are on display here, including *David, Apollo and Daphne,* and *Pluto and Persephone.*

From the museum it is a pleasant walk (or, perhaps better for scheduling your time, taxi ride) to Villa Giulia at the northwest corner of the park, which actually *is* a 16th-century suburban villa, built after a design by Michelangelo and Vignola for Pope Julius II. It houses the **Museo Nazionale di Villa Giulia**, an outstanding collection of the art of the mysterious Etruscans who once inhabited central Italy. Highlights include the *Apollo of Veii,* found in the excavations here, and the *Bride and Groom,* a sarcophagus depicting a smiling, dreamy-eyed couple reclining as if at a banquet with an equality that shocked other ancient societies. Upstairs are attenuated bronze statues and other objects covered with drawings that, to our eyes, look strikingly modern. The Castellani collection of antique jewelry also is superb.

If modern art is what interests you, head next to the **Galleria Nazionale d'Arte Moderna**, which you passed on your way from the Museo Borghese. It contains works of modern painters such as De Chirico, Boccioni, Modigliani, and Pistoletto, as well as some foreign works.

Piazza del Popolo Area

From Villa Giulia, ride or walk west to the ancient via Flaminia; turn south on it and you'll be entering Rome as travellers have traditionally for centuries, through the grand gate called the **Porta del Popolo**, at piazza del Popolo. One such arrival was that of Queen Christina of Sweden, who converted to Catholicism and came to Rome in 1655, an occasion for which Bernini decorated the inside of the great arch and Pope Alexander VII composed the arch's inscription: *Felici faustoque ingressui MDCLV.* Across the piazza are the twin churches of **Santa Maria di Montesanto** (on the left) and **Santa Maria dei Miracoli** (on the right), playful exercises in the art of illusionary design begun by Carlo Rainaldi. The church on the left is narrower than that on the right, so Rainaldi topped the left church with an oval dome and the right with a round one in order to make them look symmetrical—and they do. Good news is that the glamorous piazza is being cleaned and polished, and that the central Egyptian obelisk will be floodlit. Even better news is that it is closed to traffic.

Immediately to the left of the gate is the church of **Santa Maria del Popolo**, which was constructed with funds from the *popolo* (people) and gives the piazza its name. It was built originally in the Middle Ages over what was thought to be Nero's grave, in order to exorcise his malign spirit. Best known for its two paintings by Caravaggio, *The Conversion of Saint Paul* and *The Martyrdom of Saint Peter,* it also contains the Cappella Chigi by Raphael and works by Pinturicchio, Annibale Carracci, Sebastiano del Piombo, and Bernini (who was responsible for the restoration of the church).

Between the twin churches runs the renowned **via del Corso**, named after the horse races that were run during Carnival along its entire length between piazza del Popolo to the north and piazza Venezia and the Vittoriano to the south. One new addition to the otherwise static street is the **Fondazione Memmo**, a private foundation that hosts art exhibitions in the Palazzo Ruspoli (via del Corso 418, Tel: 683-21-77). Between shows, continue your tour by looking left (south) at via del Babuino (which leads to piazza di Spagna) and to the right at via di Ripetta. Either of the cafés at the beginning of these streets is a nice place to pause for some morning refreshment. Most evocative of the *dolce vita* era is **Canova**, on the left, since it is modern in style and popular with employees of the nearby Italian television office, RAI, across the river. **Rosati**, on the right, with its original Art Nouveau decor, comes alive at night, when it is frequented by slick young lotharios on the prowl in noisy sports cars and motorcycles.

Follow the narrow **via di Ripetta**. For a look at the building where Antonio Canova once created his masterpieces, turn onto via Antonio Canova, the third street on the left. You'll find his former studio on the right, a low building with bits of classical sculpture set into its apricot-colored façade, which also has a bronze copy of a self-portrait bust of the artist.

Two streets ahead on via di Ripetta is the **Ara Pacis Augustae**, an altar finished in 9 B.C. to celebrate the Augustan peace, which not only brought peace to the Empire but also ushered in the Augustan Age lauded by Virgil in the *Aeneid* and by other writers such as Livy, Ovid, and Horace. Much of the altar was rediscovered in Rome in the 1930s and transported to its present site, now covered with a protective piece of Fascist-era architecture. Missing segments were reclaimed from museums throughout the world or replicated.

On one side of the altar, Augustus walks first but remains, modestly, almost unseen in the procession. Sir Mortimer Wheeler wrote of the marble, "If we would understand the

Augustan period—its quiet good manners and its undemonstrable confidence—in a single document, that document is the Ara Pacis Augustae." As a work of art it is brilliant, and as a portrait gallery it gives us an image of the Augustan *dramatis personae*. His daughter Julia (banished to the Tremiti Islands for her sexual exploits) and her husband, Agrippa, who built the temple that Hadrian later transformed into the Pantheon, are at the center. The scenes of everyday life here are superb: A child pulls at his mother's robe and a woman silences a chattering couple with a finger to her lips. The child who wears the laurel crown would eventually be grandfather to Nero. The intertwined floral motifs on the far side are some of the finest examples of decorative art created in Roman times.

Across the street is the odd mound that is the **mausoleum of Augustus**. Now stripped of its original travertine covering and obelisks, it was once counted among the most sacred places in Rome. Like Hadrian's tomb (Castel Sant'Angelo), it took the cylindrical Etruscan form, and Augustus's ashes and those of his family were buried within. At his funeral pyre, which was nearby, an eagle was released when the emperor's body was committed to the fire, symbolizing his immortal soul soaring to divine heights.

Hold this thought and cross the Tiber at Ponte Cavour, where Rome's most curious museum awaits. Under glass are the face of a soul in purgatory that was printed on a wall; handprints of the dead priest Panzini that appeared on various objects, among which (without comment) was the chemise of Isabella Fornari, abbess of a convent; and other supernatural manifestations. Ask the sacristan if you may visit this **Museo delle Anime del Purgatorio** (Museum of the Souls in Purgatory) in the church of Sacro Cuore, lungotevere Prati 18.

Continuing along via di Ripetta, the first piazza you will encounter is **piazza Borghese**. Here, in the morning, stalls are filled with antique books and prints, often of high quality and reasonably priced. Nearby on via della Lupa is **La Grapperia**, a bar dedicated to the consumption of hundreds of varieties of the Italian aquavit, grappa. Back at the beginning of the street, via del Clementino and via Fontanella Borghese lead to the Corso, across which begins via Condotti. Lined with designer shops, **via Condotti** is Rome's most famous shopping street, though the two streets parallel to it on the south—via Borgognona and via Frattina—are lined with equally luxurious shops. If you're interested in serious shopping (see "Shops and Shopping," below), avoid

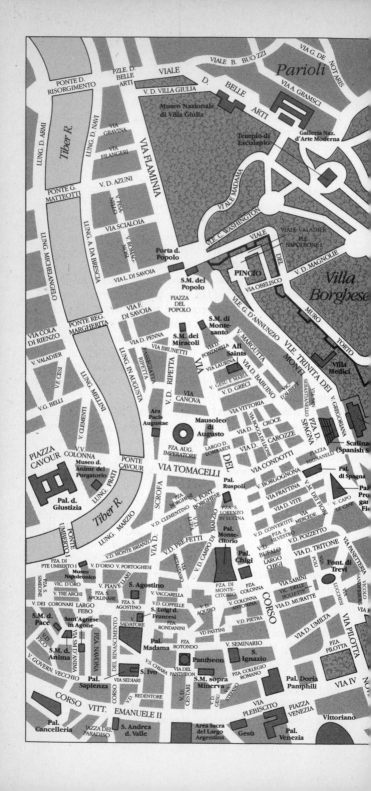

**Piazza
del Popolo —
Via Veneto**

0   yards   300

0   meters   300

the area on a Saturday, when the nearby metro stop of piazza di Spagna disgorges hordes of young people from the suburbs who look but don't buy, much to the consternation of the owners of Gucci, Ferragamo, Fendi, and other shops in the area.

Via Condotti goes straight to the Spanish Steps. Along the way, peek into number 68, the palazzo where the Sovereign Military Order of the Knights of Malta has its headquarters. Granted extraterritorial rights by the Italian state, it issues a limited number of passports and license plates with its S.M.O.M. insignia. If the Vatican is the world's smallest inhabited state, this is the only one entirely enclosed in a palazzo.

The Spanish Steps

Piazza di Spagna is laid out in the shape of a butterfly—without doubt a mellow subtropical species. The tall palms that greet you immediately and the languid crowds on the steps are beautiful reminders of how balmy Rome really can be. The piazza takes its name from the Palazzo di Spagna at number 57, the Spanish Embassy to the Holy See. Many other foreigners, however, have been active in the area. The Spanish Steps (Scalinata della Trinità dei Monti), which rise in the middle of the piazza, actually were paid for by the French to create an easier access to the church of Trinità dei Monti, built by their kings at the top of the hill, and the piazza once was known locally as piazza di Francia. The whole area, in fact, was called *er ghetto del'Inglesi* by the Romans, assuming that all foreigners were English, just as the Greeks before them had referred to all outsiders as barbarians. Keats lived and died in the house at number 26 piazza di Spagna, and is commemorated with a death mask and cases full of memorabilia (as are Shelley and Byron) in the Keats-Shelley Memorial there, where you can purchase tiny volumes of the poets' works.

Goethe and Dickens also knew the Spanish Steps. In his *Pictures from Italy,* Dickens described the characters of the day who went to the steps to hire themselves out as artists' models. "There is one old gentleman, with long hair and an immense beard," he writes, "who, to my knowledge, has gone through half the catalogue of the Royal Academy. This is the venerable, or patriarchical model." He then goes on to describe other colorful types who posed as "the *dolce far niente* model," "the assassin model," "the haughty or scornful model," and writes that "as to Domestic Happiness, and Holy Families, they should come very cheap, for there are lumps of them, all up the steps; and the cream of the thing, is, that they are all the falsest vagabonds in the world, especially made up for the purpose, and having no other counterparts in Rome or in any other part of the habitable globe." The theatricality of the Italian street scene is nothing new. These days, though, you're likely to encounter all sorts of vendors as you climb the steps, for amid the pots of azaleas in the spring, the Nativity scene at Christmas, and all over the steps throughout the year are the people selling crafts and offering modern-day Daisy Millers a coffee that turns out to be drugged, as the tale of their robbery will reveal in Rome's daily *Il Messaggero* the next morning. Like large metropolises everywhere, Rome is not immune to crime, and the Spanish Steps have been getting their share lately, particularly at night.

Yet the steps are still a welcome resting place for tourists. Romans know that spring has come when large pots of azaleas are brought from the Villa Celimontana, where they've wintered and budded, and are hoisted into place on the steps and in the surrounding streets.

You'll need some sustenance to scale the 137 steps, however. Fortunately, the historical presence of travellers and the piazza's contemporary guise as a center for luxury shops (increasingly affordable, it seems, only to Italians) have ensured a number of cafés and restaurants in the area. If you're feeling fancy, try **Ranieri's** on via Mario dei Fiori, a remnant from the Grand Tour days. Otherwise, the pleasant outdoor courtyard of **Otello alla Concordia** on via della Croce is a fine spot for lunch. For a postprandial pickup, the antique **Caffè Greco** on via Condotti has been offering coffee and other refreshment since the early 18th century. **Babington's**, to the left of the steps in the piazza, serves high-priced tea, and the bar at the Hotel D'Inghilterra, as well as **Baretto** at via Condotti 55, serve as watering holes for the elegant locals.

Or you may simply want a sip of water from the fountain called the Fontana della Barcaccia, at the base of the steps. Designed by Pietro Bernini, or possibly his son Gianlorenzo, it takes its shape from the boats that once came to the papal port of Ripetta, formerly nearby on the Tiber.

Before making your ascent up the steps, follow via del Babuino off the piazza to the left. Turn right on vicolo d'Alibert to the charming **via Margutta**, which is lined with an open-air art show every spring and fall (and art galleries year-round), and double back at via della Fontanella to via del Babuino, where amid the elegant antiques shops you'll notice the statue of Silenus, dubbed by residents "the baboon" and giving the street its name. The Anglican church of **All Saints** is at number 153, the English-language **Lion Bookstore** is at number 181, and, if you're in need of some refreshment, try the ultramodern **Café Notegen** at number 159. Cross piazza di Spagna to its southern triangle, where you'll see the column dedicated to the Immaculate Conception. Here each December 8 the pope crowns the statue of the Virgin with a garland of flowers; its height requires that the deed be performed by a member of Rome's trusty fire brigade from the ladder of a truck. The building behind the column is the **Palazzo di Propaganda Fide** (Palace of the Propagation of the Faith), the missionary center of the Catholic world. Bernini and Borromini both worked on its façades, but not at the same time. The side facing the piazza is the work of Bernini, and his rival's concave façade is to the right.

Perhaps braced with another sip of water from the Fontana della Barcaccia, you're now ready to climb the delightfully curving travertine steps to Trinità dei Monti, with its views of the shoppers below. In honor of the Trinity, the staircase is divided into three landings; each in turn is divided into three. The French occupy not only the church but the adjacent **Villa Medici**, just to the left as you face the church, on viale della Trinità dei Monti. It was here that Louis XIV established the Académie de France and the Prix de Rome in 1666. French artists still come to study at the academy within, which also hosts important art exhibitions. The street eventually leads to the view from the Pincio, but come back at sunset to enjoy that at its best, preferably from the **Casina Valadier** café-restaurant. Now is the time to turn around and head down via Sistina to piazza Barberini and the beginning of via Veneto. The centerpiece of the piazza is the Fontana del Tritone (Fountain of the Triton) by Bernini, and at the corner of via Veneto is the Fontana delle Api (Fountain of the Bees), named after its numerous symbols of the Barberini family, who commissioned the work from Bernini. (The Palazzo Barberini here is the starting point of our "Centuries of Christianity" section below.)

Via Vittorio Veneto

The shady curves of via Vittorio Veneto recall the days when it was a cow path only a century ago but mask the more frenetic activity that has taken place there in recent years, most infamously in the 1960s, when it was the stage for the extravagances of international film stars working at Rome's film studio, Cinecittà. The way of life was dubbed *la dolce vita* (the sweet life) and fictionalized by Fellini in a movie of the same name. Before musing on that time, however, stop into the church of **Santa Maria della Concezione** for a memento mori about where the sweet life eventually leads. Its five chapels were decorated in bizarre Rococo patterns formed by the bones of some 4,000 Capuchin monks.

These days the street scene is quieter, interrupted occasionally by the clicking heels of the (usually transvestite) prostitutes who walk the street at night and the cars that screech to a halt to meet them. But the overall atmosphere is peaceful, and the street activity can be taken in over leisurely refreshment at **Café de la Paix**, the best-known café from the days of the sweet life.

The Veneto ends in glory, however, with piazza Barberini's restored statue of **Il Tritone**—a masterwork by Bernini, who understood the exuberant sensuality of his city.

CENTURIES OF CHRISTIANITY

Ever mindful of museum hours, begin one day's tour on via delle Quattro Fontane at the entrance to the **Palazzo Barberini** (number 13). Begun in 1625 for Pope Urban VIII (Maffeo Barberini) by Carlo Maderno, construction of the palazzo was taken over by Borromini, who was responsible for the oval stairs on the right, and then by Bernini, who designed the central façade and the rectangular staircase on the left. The palazzo remained in the hands of the Barberini family for years. Among its tenants was the American sculptor William Story, who entertained the Brownings, Henry James, and Hans Christian Andersen in his apartments here. In 1949 it was sold to the Italian government and now houses the **Galleria Nazionale d'Arte Antica**, which is not a gallery of antique art at all. The gallery contains paintings by such artists as Fra Angelico, Filippo Lippi, Bronzino, Caravaggio, Tintoretto, and El Greco, as well as Raphael's portrait of *La Fornarina*, the baker's daughter who was his mistress. The sumptuous Baroque and Rococo decoration of the rooms, especially Pietro da Cortona's ceiling fresco *Allegory of Divine Providence* (note the ever-buzzing Barberini bees in the center) in the salon, gives some idea of the splendor in which the popes lived.

Southeast up via delle Quattro Fontane, where it intersects via del Quirinale, are the four facing Baroque fountains for which the street is named. This is also the crossroads of the wide streets laid out under Sixtus V (1585–1590), with sweeping views leading to Porta Pia to the northeast and to the obelisks of the Quirinal Hill to the southwest, the Esquiline Hill to the southeast, and Trinità dei Monti to the northwest.

On the far corner of via del Quirinale is Borromini's church of **San Carlo alle Quattro Fontane**, known affectionately as San Carlino, with a lovely adjacent cloister. The geometric complexity of the church's interior provides an obvious contrast (and convenient comparison) to the interior of Bernini's church of **Sant'Andrea al Quirinale** just down the street, which is relatively simple in spite of its rich marble and gilt decor.

Farther down the street is the **Palazzo del Quirinale**. Designed by Maderno, Bernini, and many others, it was formerly a summer residence of the popes and was later used by the kings of Italy. It is now occupied by the president of the republic. Its rich decoration by such artists as Melozzo da Forlì and Pietro da Cortona can be seen only by permission (write the Ufficio Intendenza della Presidenza della Repubblica, via della Dataria 96, 00187 Rome). No appointment is necessary, however, to see the *corazzieri,* the presidential guard, all over six feet tall and dashing in their crimson and blue uniforms, gleaming boots, and shining helmets with tossing plumes. The changing of the guard takes place every day at 4:00 P.M.

Take via della Consulta south off piazza del Quirinale and turn left on bustling via Nazionale, where you'll pass the recently reopened **Palazzo delle Esposizioni** at number 194, where interesting art exhibitions are held, and the Neo-Gothic American church of St. Paul on the corner of via Napoli. The street leads to piazza della Repubblica, with its tall spray of water shooting out of the Fontana delle Naiadi, an 1885 bronze fountain by Alessandro Guerrieri of naiads cavorting with sea monsters. The piazza is commonly called piazza Esedra because the arcades of the two curving palaces around it are built where the *exedrae,* or semicircular benches, of the Terme di Diocleziano (Baths of Diocletian) once existed. (Coincidentally, the ring around the fountain is still a popular trysting place.)

Baths of Diocletian Area

Begun by Maximilian and completed by Diocletian, the baths (*terme*) were the largest of all such Roman facilities, able to accommodate 3,000 people and covering an area of

32 acres. Today the church of **Santa Maria degli Angeli** is housed within the original Tepidarium. It was begun as a Carthusian church by Michelangelo, who converted the baths' vast central hall into the nave, but when Vanvitelli took over the design he changed the nave into a transept. What has not changed is the sense of space, a uniquely Roman contribution to the course of architectural history. The church and its adjacent convent have just been restored to house the **Museo delle Terme di Diocleziano**, displaying art from the late Roman Republic.

Coin collectors will want to stop at the **Museo Numismatico della Zecca**, at via XX Settembre 97. Because it's in the Italian Treasury Building, your passport will be required; closed Sundays.

Before leaving the area, stop into the church of **Santa Maria della Vittoria** on via XX Settembre. (The American Catholic church of **Santa Susanna**, with a magnificent façade by Maderno, presently under restoration, is in the next block.) The interior of Santa Maria della Vittoria also was designed by Maderno in the Counter-Reformation style of the Gesù, and Bernini's theatrical Cappella Cornaro is Baroque at its most flamboyant. Here, members of the Cornaro family are portrayed in marble as spectators in theater boxes to the statue of Saint Teresa of Avila, whose ecstasy seems decidedly secular. If her sensuality gets the best of you, cool off in front of the horned statue of Moses in the Fontana del Mose around the corner. The fountain was designed by Domenico Fontana, who allegedly died after seeing how badly his work compared to Michelangelo's statue of Moses in the church of San Pietro in Vincoli (see below), though the story is held to be apocryphal.

Better to sublimate your desires into lunch and take the five-minute taxi ride from piazza della Repubblica in front of the Terme di Diocleziano a few long blocks south to the simple setting of the restaurant **Cicilardone** at via Merulana 77. There you'll be able to sample the endless varieties of homemade pasta by ordering *assaggini* (little tastes), which go a long way. (A less expensive alternative would be to buy provisions at the boisterous food market in nearby piazza Vittorio.)

If you haven't already done so on your travels, give a passing glance to **Stazione di Termini**, the railroad station often overlooked in the context of the city's more venerable architecture. Begun under the Fascists, as the neo-Roman side sections show, the construction of the station unearthed part of a wall built after the invasion of the Gauls in A.D. 390,

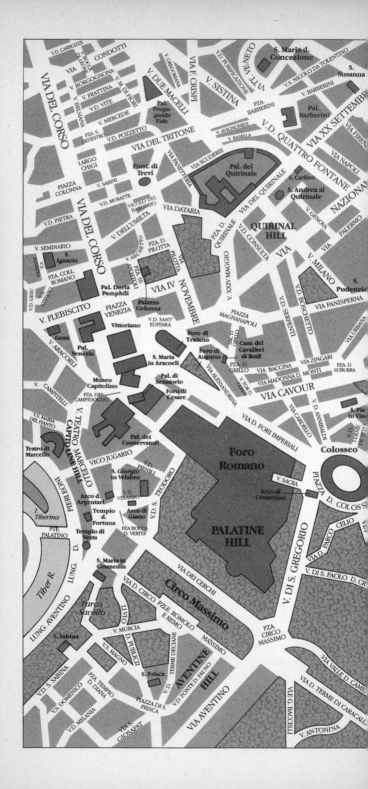

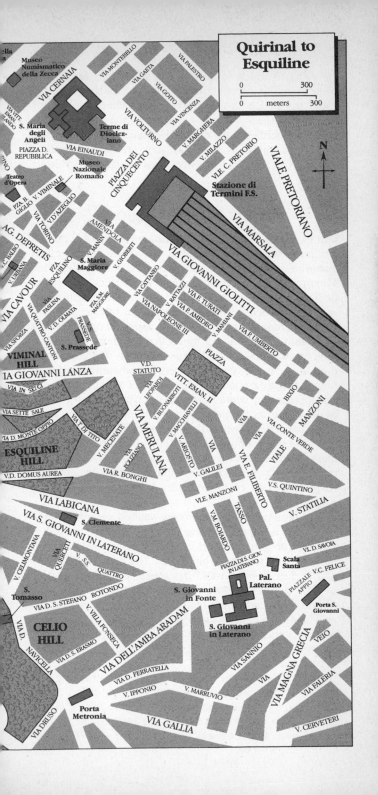

the ruins of which in front of the station provide a stark contrast to the sweeping travertine curve of the entrance. Today the piazza in front serves as a gathering place for immigrants from Asia and Africa, a phenomenon reminiscent of the farthest-flung days of the Roman Empire. Gypsies will no doubt be interested in your *lire* here. Beware— especially of children carrying signs designed to distract you.

Santa Maria Maggiore

From Cicilardone take via Merulana to the double-domed basilica of Santa Maria Maggiore, one of the four so-called major basilicas of Rome, this one built on the Esquiline Hill. Many myths and legends surround the basilica, which was dedicated to the Virgin Mary after the Council of Ephesus in A.D. 431 affirmed that she was the mother of Christ. One of the most charming is that the Virgin appeared on this site on the night of August 4, 352, saying that her church should be built on an area she would cover—and did—with a snowfall the following morning. The event is commemorated each August 5 with a pontifical mass in the Cappella Borghese, accompanied by white flower-petal flurries from the dome of the chapel as a simulated snowfall in the piazza at right. (The chapel is also where the tiny coffin of Pauline Borghese lies.) The basilica preserves the relic (displayed each Christmas) of the Holy Crib in which the infant Jesus was laid, mentioned by Petrarch in a letter to Pope Clement VI in Avignon as one of Rome's sacred treasures to lure the papacy back.

The basilica has a magnificent vaulted ceiling covered with what is supposedly the first gold to have arrived in Europe from the New World, but even more precious are its mosaics, best seen with binoculars. The nave mosaics contain scenes from the Old Testament; the triumphal-arch mosaics depict the infancy of Christ; and the apse mosaics illustrate the Coronation of the Virgin. In the afternoon it is also likely you'll find a sacristan to admit you to the oratory of the manger beneath the Cappella Sistina, which houses the remains of Arnolfo di Cambio's original 13th-century decoration.

Outside, notice the campanile, which is the tallest in Rome. Its bells are said to speak in Roman dialect. When they ring, try to make out the words *Avemo fatto li facioli, avemo fatto li facioli* (We made the beans). The bells of San Giovanni in Laterano then ask, *Con che? Con che?*

(With what?), and Santa Croce in Gerusalemme responds, *Co' le codichelle, co' le codichelle* (With *cotechino* sausage).

Nearby are **Santa Prassede** and **Santa Pudenziana**, two early Christian churches dedicated to sister saints, the daughters of a Roman senator named Pudens, who was a Christian and a friend of Saint Peter. Off the piazza di Santa Maria Maggiore is the side entrance to the brick church of Santa Prassede, on via Santa Prassede. The church was once a *titulus,* a private residence where Christians were sheltered and rituals took place during the time of persecution. In the apse mosaics the sisters are being presented by Saints Peter and Paul to the Redeemer, but the most spectacular Byzantine mosaics entirely cover the Cappella di San Zenone, which contains a column, brought from Jerusalem, on which the flagellation of Christ is believed to have taken place. Many relics are found in the church, among them a circular porphyry stone under which Santa Prassede is said to have placed the blood and bones of thousands of Christian martyrs.

On the other side of Santa Maria Maggiore, off piazza del Esquilino (with its obelisk that originally stood in front of the Mausoleo di Augusto), you'll find via Urbana, where the church of Santa Pudenziana stands. Its apse contains one of the oldest mosaics in Rome, dating from the fourth century.

San Pietro in Vincoli Area

Follow via Urbana down the hill to piazza degli Zingari, which means Gypsies in Italian, a reminder that bands of Gypsy pickpockets roam the area (and much of Rome)—so be alert. The street then leads to piazza della Suburra, named after the most notorious district of ancient Rome—which today seems quite peaceful, even trendy, with restaurants and rents both rapidly on the rise. Taking the steps up to via Cavour (where you could slip into **Enoteca** at number 313 for an afternoon refresher), cross the busy street, and on your right locate the steep staircase to the church of **San Pietro in Vincoli**. The church preserves a relic said to be the chains (*vincoli*) that shackled Saint Peter during his imprisonment in Jerusalem as well as in Rome, but most people come here to see Michelangelo's statue of Moses. (The horns are an artistic convention meant to indicate the subject's status as a prophet.) The figure is part of Julius II's ill-fated tomb, originally intended for St. Peter's and supposed to contain some 40 statues but never finished; some of its statuary was dispersed to the Louvre and to Florence's

Galleria dell'Accademia. The *Moses* was completed, however, and Vasari writes about how the Jews of Rome went there "like flocks of starlings, to visit and adore the statue." Many legends surround the statue: The mark on the knee supposedly comes from Michelangelo throwing his hammer at it, commanding it to speak.

Descend the Esquiline Hill on via degli Annibaldi and take the stairway that leads to piazza del Colosseo; around to your left, via San Giovanni in Laterano will bring you east to piazza di San Clemente. On the left is the fascinating **Basilica di San Clemente**, a three-level house of worship run by Irish Dominican brothers since the 17th century. Its upper level has a lovely 12th-century marble pavement by the Cosmati family, 12th-century mosaics, and 15th-century frescoes by Masolino da Panicale. Underneath, and reached by the right aisle, is the lower church, which has frescoes dating from the ninth century. Beneath it, and accessible at the end of the left aisle, are the remains of a first-century *domus* and third-century Mithraic temple, which has a bas-relief representing the sun god Mithras slaying a bull. And even farther below is another evocative phenomenon: If you listen carefully, you'll hear the Charonic sounds of an underground river, which leads to Rome's ancient Cloaca Maxima sewer.

San Giovanni in Laterano

Continuing along via San Giovanni in Laterano, lined with nondescript residential apartment buildings, you will soon come across another of the major basilicas of Rome, San Giovanni in Laterano (Saint John Lateran). It is the cathedral church of Rome and the titular see of the pope as bishop of Rome; he usually celebrates Maundy Thursday services here. The basilica takes its name from the patrician family of Plautius Lateranus, whose huge estate on the site was confiscated by Nero but later was returned to the family and became the dowry of Fausta, wife of Constantine, who built the original basilica here. (Constantine later had her drowned in her bath.) It subsequently underwent a series of disasters: a fifth-century sacking, a ninth-century earthquake, and a 14th-century fire; as a result, the present church has more historical than aesthetic appeal. The original Palazzo del Laterano next to the church was the residence of the popes until they moved to Avignon, and many important events in the history of the church took place here, including the 1123 Diet of Worms. (The current palazzo dates from the 16th century and is the seat of the Rome vicariate.)

Today you see an 18th-century façade on the church, crowned with gigantic statues of the saints surrounding Christ. Borromini designed the nave and aisles of the interior, which has a magnificent ceiling and statues of the apostles by followers of Bernini. Among the other sights of the church are a heavily restored fresco by Giotto in the Cappella Corsini; reliquaries containing (legend has it) the heads of Saints Peter and Paul and a piece of the table on which the Last Supper took place; and cloisters dating from the 13th century. Next door, **San Giovanni in Fonte** (the Baptistery of St. John) was the first of its kind, built by Constantine (the one who drowned his wife) in about 320. Its octagonal form became the prototype for baptisteries throughout Italy.

The Scala Santa, on the opposite side of the Palazzo del Laterano from the baptistery, contains the **Sancta Sanctorum**, the old private chapel of the popes, and, leading up to it, what are believed to be the steps Christ climbed in Pilate's house, brought to Rome by Saint Helena, Constantine's mother. Today the faithful still climb them on their knees.

Farther on, at the other end of via Carlo Felice, is the church of **Santa Croce in Gerusalemme**, one of Rome's seven pilgrimage churches. It contains two 15th-century works of art worth stopping for—an apse fresco, *The Invention of the True Cross* (the church was built to house the relics of the True Cross brought back from Jerusalem: three pieces of wood, a nail, and two thorns from Christ's crown), and a mosaic in the Cappella di Santa Elena—as well as another lovely marble floor by the Cosmati. The **Museo Nazionale degli Strumenti Musicali** next to the church, at piazza di Santa Croce in Gerusalemme 9A, houses an impressive collection of musical instruments from ancient times to the 17th century (closed Sundays).

Cannavota, Rome's oldest fish restaurant, is found in piazza San Giovanni in Laterano, near the obelisk. The restaurant itself is worth a dinner reservation (Tel: 06-77-50-07; closed Wednesdays). If you need to cast about beforehand, have a look at the colorful street market outside Porta San Giovanni in via Sannio, or check out the local branch of Italy's Coin department-store chain.

THE VATICAN

If all roads lead to Rome, they soon after lead across the Tiber to the Vatican. Since 1929, when Benito Mussolini and Cardinal Pietro Gasparri signed the Lateran Treaty between Italy and the Holy See, Vatican City—the seat of the Roman Catholic church and the cradle of all Christendom—has been an independent state ruled by the pope, the only absolute sovereign in Europe. The Vatican, as it is most commonly known, has its own flag and national anthem, mints its own coinage, prints its own postage stamps (many Romans have more faith in its postal system than in Italy's, and go to the Vatican just to mail their letters and packages), has its own polyglot daily newspaper (*L'Osservatore Romano*), Latin-language quarterly (*Acta Apostolicae Sedis*), multilingual radio station, and plans for a television station. (The pope, it's said, gets his news from an all-Latin news show broadcast by Finnish shortwave.) All these activities take place in an area of just over 100 acres, a considerable part of which is taken up by St. Peter's, the world's greatest basilica in the world's smallest state. In addition to establishing the sovereign territory contained within the high walls of the Vatican, the Lateran Treaty granted special extraterritorial privileges to the churches of San Giovanni in Laterano, Santa Maria Maggiore, and San Paolo Fuori le Mura. Together with St. Peter's they constitute the four major basilicas of Rome.

Because of the limited visiting hours of many of the Vatican's attractions, you'll need careful planning to see the sights in the span of a day. *Begin early,* on Italian territory in piazza ponte Sant'Angelo across the Tiber from the Castel Sant'Angelo. You will be facing Rome's most beautiful bridge, the glorious ponte Sant'Angelo, which Gianlorenzo Bernini intended as the initial part of the approach to St. Peter's. Statues of Saints Peter and Paul greet you as you walk over the Tiber, virtually escorted by ten statues of angels, each carrying a symbol of Christ's crucifixion, to herald your visit.

The massive round object across the Tiber, topped with a statue of the Archangel Michael, is **Castel Sant'Angelo.** The ancient mausoleum of Hadrian, it was once landscaped, clad in travertine, covered with sculpture, and topped by a bronze statue of the emperor himself. In the Middle Ages it became part of the Aurelian Wall, and through a gate on the castle grounds called Porta San Pietro became the main point of entry to the Vatican for religious pilgrims. It also has

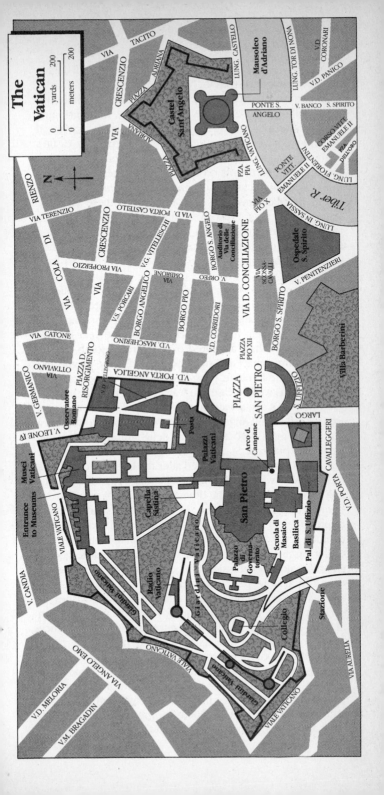

served as a refuge for the popes, who entered it through a private passageway from the Vatican, and as a prison. One of its illustrious captives was the Renaissance goldsmith Benvenuto Cellini, whose escape is one of the most gripping moments of the dashing life he recounted with bravura, if not braggadocio, in his *Autobiography*. Bypass the castle's grim displays of weapons and prisons and opt for the sumptuous papal apartments on the top floor instead. The painting collection includes Lorenzo Lotto's *Saint Jerome* and works by Mantegna and Signorelli. From there take the staircase that, after a display of military paraphernalia, leads to the terrace familiar from the last act of *Tosca,* the one from which the heroine jumps to her death in the Tiber. (The river today is too far from the castle for her to have made it.)

The terrace has one of the best views of Rome and offers a close-up of Peter Anton Verschaffelt's 18th-century bronze statue of the Archangel Saint Michael, commemorating Pope Gregory the Great's vision during the plague year of 590, when Saint Michael appeared over Hadrian's tomb sheathing his sword, an act that signified the end of the plague and gave the castle its name. (Castel Sant'Angelo is open Monday afternoons as well, in case you want to see it later in the day.)

In Bernini's day, a walk down the narrow medieval streets from Castel Sant'Angelo directly west through the area known as the Borgo led to the delightful surprise of his expansive piazza at St. Peter's. Now, however, the grandiose **via della Conciliazione**, named after the Lateran accord, has ludicrously overextended the welcoming arms of Bernini's colonnade and ruined the dramatic element of turning suddenly into piazza San Pietro. In all fairness, a monumental boulevard had been planned since the middle of the 15th century; it was unfortunate that *domani* finally came in 1936 under Fascism. The wide swath, with double obelisks goosestepping along either side, was completed in 1950, just in time for a Holy Year (they officially occur every quarter century but can be declared as often as the pope wishes, as seen in recent years). Walk quickly and fix your gaze on St. Peter's, heading straight for the tourist information office in the colonnade on your left as you face the basilica.

The **Vatican Gardens** are now open to guided tour groups only, so make the most of your time if not your money (the price of admission to most things at the Vatican is lofty) and get to the office no later than 10:00 A.M. to sign up for the daily tour. The cost is £15,000 on Tuesdays, Fridays, and Saturdays. On Mondays and Thursdays the tour includes the

Sistine Chapel and costs ₤27,000. (Between November and February, tours take place only on Saturdays.) The tour begins at the Arco delle Campane (Arch of the Bells), watched over by the Swiss Guards, whose red-yellow-and-blue striped uniforms—supposedly designed by Michelangelo—add a playful air to the increasingly serious job of protecting the pope. From there, guides escort visitors to a number of sights on the extensive grounds, given an occasional assist by a minibus. Included in the tour are sights most visitors to the Vatican have not seen—**Circo di Nerone**, where the first Christian martyrs (including Saint Peter) met their deaths; the 18th-century mosaic studio, which still sells stones as souvenirs; the train station (used primarily for the delivery of duty-free merchandise to fortunate employees and friends of the Vatican); the Palazzo del Governatorato, where the governor has his office; the radio station; and the prison. The most pleasant part of the tour is the gardens themselves, meticulously groomed and presided over by cypresses, umbrella pines, and—most magnificently—the only good views of the largest brick dome in creation, part of Michelangelo's original plan for St. Peter's.

The garden tour ends back at the tourist information office, and whether or not you've gone on it, this is where you should take the bus to a side entrance of the Vatican Museums. This bus also goes back through the gardens and is a pleasant alternative to the long walk from St. Peter's Square around the walls to the main museum entrance on the viale Vaticano to the north.

The Vatican Museums

The Vatican Museums have become so crowded that the authorities have had to resort to four color-coded tours to impose order. The only one that covers all the important sights is the yellow tour, which supposedly lasts five hours, but by following the yellow route and stopping only at the highlights listed below you can cut that time in half. (Ticket sales stop at 1:30 P.M. except at Easter and from July to September, when they stop at 3:30. The museums are closed on Sundays, except for the last Sunday of the month, when they're free. Wear comfortable shoes; take binoculars and a fan.)

The Egyptian Museum. Head straight for Room V, where the most impressive relics are the colossal granite statue of Queen Tuia, mother of Ramses II, and the sandstone head of Pharaoh Menuhotep across from it. Before leaving the room, peek through the door into the outdoor niche, which contains the giant bronze fir cone found near the Thermae of Agrippa, and to which Dante compared the giant's face ("just as wide as St. Peter's cone in Rome") in the *Inferno*.

Braccio Nuovo. Here stands the famous statue of Augustus, found in 1863 on the grounds of the dread Livia's estate at Prima Porta.

Chiaramonti Museum. Rather than dwelling on any single work of art here, take a look at the display, which was laid out in the early 19th century by Neoclassical sculptor Antonio Canova. The realistically human portrait busts of ancient Romans are the prized objects here.

Pio-Clementino Museum. Two of the most celebrated antique sculptures in the world are exhibited in Room VIII. The undisputed star is the *Laocoön*, described by Pliny the Elder as "a work to be preferred to all that the arts of painting and sculpture have produced." The first original Greek work of art to be discovered in Rome (it was unearthed in 1506 on the Esquiline Hill), it depicts a passage from the *Aeneid* in which Virgil describes the wrath the gods released on the priest Laocoön for warning the Trojans about the horse, sending two serpents to destroy him and his two sons. In the same room is another famous work, the *Apollo Belvedere* (a Roman copy of a fourth-century B.C. Greek statue once displayed in the Agora in Athens), which influenced Canova's nearby Perseus. Apollo's face came to symbolize beauty incarnate.

Father Nile is a favorite, resting on a cornucopia and a sphinx, dotted with babies. Other highlights of this museum are the *Apollo Sauroktonos* (Room V), the *Cnidian Venus* (Room VII), the *Belvedere Torso* (much preferred by the Romantics and Pre-Raphaelites to the Apollo Belvedere; Room III), the *Jupiter of Otricoli* (Room II), and the sarcophagi of Helen and Constantia, mother and daughter, respectively, of Constantine (Room I).

Gregorian-Etruscan Museum. Highlights in this newly reopened section are the Etruscan Regolini-Galassi Tomb (Room II) and *Mars of Todi* (Room III), the Greek *Head of Athena* and funerary stele (Room of Greek Originals), and the Greek amphora of *Achilles and Ajax Playing Morra* (Room XII).

Stop in the Sala della Biga (Chariot Room) for a sweeping view of St. Peter's from the window.

Raphael Rooms. These four rooms were the official apartments of Julius II, who commissioned frescoes from Raphael, the masterpiece of which is *The School of Athens*.

According to tradition it contains portraits of Leonardo as Plato, Michelangelo as Heraclitus, and Raphael himself as the figure in the dark cap second from the extreme right. Truth, beauty, and justice were his themes throughout.

The Borgia Apartments. Here, Alexander VI had Pinturicchio paint frescoes, of which the richly decorated Room of the Saints is considered the major work.

Sistine Chapel. The chapel has been undergoing cleaning for a decade. Its most famous feature—the ceiling, which depicts scenes from the Book of Genesis—has been uncovered to reveal the brilliant colors of Michelangelo's original palette. The scaffolding at the end wall partly covers his *Last Judgment,* the success of whose restoration will not be up for our judgment until completion in 1994.

The Apostolic Library. Two paintings predominate here, the Greek Odyssey landscape series and the Roman *Aldobrandini Wedding*. In addition, temporary exhibits display the wonders of the library's rare book and manuscript collection.

Pinacoteca. Paintings by Giotto, Melozzo da Forlì, Raphael, Bellini, Reni, and Domenichino will delight the retina still capable of retaining anything after having seen the rest of the museums. Leonardo's unfinished *Saint Jerome,* although poorly restored, conveys the saint's pathos. Caravaggio's *Deposition* and Poussin's *Martyrdom of Saint Erasmus* present an interesting comparison—the former's immediacy contrasting with the latter's academic distance.

Before leaving, have a look at the museum gift shop, which, among its many reproductions and religious articles, sells men's ties patterned with papal coats of arms.

The sin of gluttony is not exactly catered to around the Vatican. However, take via del Pellegrino from the museum exit to **Borgo Pio**, the east–west street running parallel to via Corridori/via Borgo Pio to the south, where you'll find a number of prim little restaurants, such as **Marcello**, with tables in a vine-covered courtyard during the warmer months and, like its neighbors, serving a standard Italian menu. Fancier and more imaginative is **Papalino** at Borgo Pio 170 (Tel: 686-55-39; closed Mondays).

St. Peter's Square

After lunch, return to the immense oval of piazza San Pietro, which can now be enjoyed at a leisurely pace without having to worry about the pearly gates of the morning's attractions slamming shut. At noon on Sundays Pope John Paul II gives a blessing from his window in the Apostolic Palace, the second from the right on the top floor. At variable times on Wednesday mornings he holds an audience. In the summer, until the pope moves to his summer residence at Castel Gandolfo (see the Lazio chapter), it takes place in the piazza. In the winter the audience is held in the new audience hall designed by Pier Luigi Nervi in 1971, for which permission must be received by writing to the Prefect of the Pontifical Household, Città del Vaticano, 00120 Rome, or applied for in advance and in person at the bronze door to the right of the piazza.

On audience days the square is filled with religious pilgrims, often grouped together and carrying banners announcing their places of origin. Even at other times the square is bustling with large-scale activity, as befits a monumental space. Tight phalanxes of black-clad nuns and priests scuttle back and forth on official Vatican business. Schoolteachers lead groups of their uniformed charges and try to distract them from the surrounding grandeur with lectures. Fatigued tourists squint at the immensity of the piazza and the façade of St. Peter's. And the occasional self-contained honeymoon couple from the provinces wanders dazedly toward the basilica. Keeping watch upon it all are the 140 stone saints above Bernini's colonnade and the 13 giant statues over the façade of St. Peter's. For aerial variation, flocks of pigeons swoop freely to and fro, and if you're especially fortunate, it's all topped off by the colossal clusters of cumulus clouds that God seems to have designed especially for Baroque Rome.

The focal point of Bernini's oval piazza is the obelisk at the center, originally from Alexandria, where it had been erected by Augustus, and brought to Rome by Caligula. Not until much later was it erected on its present site; in 1586, chroniclers tell us, 900 men, 140 horses, and 44 winches accomplished the feat. Another account tells of a Ligurian sailor who, defying the papal order to remain silent during the dangerous enterprise, saw that the ropes were about to give out and cried, *"Aigua ae corde!"* an admonition to wet the ropes. He thus saved the day and Pope Sixtus V not only spared his life but rewarded him by starting the tradition of supplying the palms for Palm Sunday from his native port of Bordighera. Apocryphal as the tale may be, it is a charming example of the innumerable secular legends that surround the Vatican.

On either side of the obelisk spout the jets of two Baroque fountains, and between the two fountains and the colonnades is a circle of black marble in the pavement. If the squealing schoolchildren will allow you to stand on it, look toward the colonnade and you'll see the four rows of columns blend into one.

St. Peter's Basilica

Built under Constantine on the site of the tomb of Saint Peter, the original St. Peter's basilica, constructed in 326, was a sumptuous early Christian edifice almost as large as the present one. When the basilica began showing signs of age, the popes decided to build a new one and appointed a succession of architects to supervise the project. Bramante, Raphael, Sangallo, Michelangelo, and others were involved at one point or another, and their designs alternately called for Greek- and Latin-cross plans. Michelangelo's design for a Greek cross and dome was being carried out at the time of his death in 1564, but under Paul V it was decided to extend the front portion to conform to the outlines of Constantine's original basilica. This unfortunately makes Michelangelo's dome appear to sink as you approach the entrance, although it is the glory of the Roman skyline from elsewhere in the city. Carlo Maderno designed the façade and portico (where Giotto's *Navicella* ceiling mosaic from the old basilica was installed) in an early Baroque style.

As you step inside (you will not be admitted wearing shorts, skirts above the knees, or sleeveless dresses—St. Peter's dress code is stricter than Lutèce's or Claridge's, but the ambience is worth it), the effect is as dazzling as was intended. Perfect proportions mask the vastness of St. Peter's, but spotting the minuscule forms of other visitors beneath the gigantic statues, or a look at the comparative lengths of other European churches—traced in metal on the floor of the nave—confirms its enormous size. The immensity of history is also immediately present at the round porphyry slab set into the pavement in front of the central door: On this stone, on Christmas in the year 800, Leo III crowned the kneeling Charlemagne the first emperor of the Holy Roman Empire.

In the first chapel on the right, Michelangelo's **Pietà** stands behind the glass erected after the sculpture was assaulted in 1972. At the right end of the nave is Arnolfo di Cambio's bronze statue of *St. Peter Enthroned,* its foot worn by the touches and kisses of the faithful over the centuries. Over the high altar soars Bernini's gilded bronze **baldacchino**, its four fluted columns spiraling up to support a canopy crowned by an orb and cross a hundred feet above the floor. Be sure to note the more down-to-earth, human dimension of the carvings of a woman's features in the marble pedestals that support the columns; the facial expressions become progressively more contorted, culminating in the smiling visage of a newborn infant. Legend has it that Pope Urban VII asked Bernini to add the sequence in gratitude for his favorite niece surviving a difficult childbirth.

Bernini was entrusted with the decoration of the interior of St. Peter's, and his works abound throughout. In the apse behind the *baldacchino* is his reliquary of the throne of Saint Peter, topped by a stained-glass representation of the Holy Spirit. His tomb of Alexander VII in the passage leading to the left transept is but one highlight among many magnificent monuments in the church by other artists. The Treasury, reached from the left aisle near the transept, houses a valuable collection of sacred relics. Room III contains Pollaiuolo's tomb of Sixtus IV.

Back near Arnolfo's statue of Saint Peter is the entrance to the **Vatican Grottoes**, a dimly lit church containing a number of chapels and tombs. Beneath them are the famous excavations of what is held to be the original tomb of Saint Peter, where in the 1940s an ancient crypt containing bones and the remains of a garment fitting the description of Saint Peter's were discovered by archaeologists. Permission to enter must be obtained from the Ufficio Scavi, at the left of the Arch of the Bells, in piazza San Pietro (Tel: 698-53-18; open from 9:00 A.M. to 5:00 P.M.). They will call to confirm your visit, so make sure you have your phone number with you.

For a final survey of your visit to the Vatican, take the elevator at the front of the left aisle for a walk on the roof. Inspired souls may then continue up the 537 steps to the lantern for a last inspirational view of the Vatican, Rome, the Alban Hills, and the surrounding blessed countryside.

GETTING AROUND

International flights generally land at Leonardo da Vinci Airport in Fiumicino, about 30 km (18 miles) southwest of Rome. A train leaves the airport for the center of Rome every 20 minutes and takes about 25 minutes, with a stop in Trastevere, to reach its destination, Ostiense, near the Pyramid of Cestius. From there you can take the B line metro to the main train station (four short stops) or catch a taxi.

Tickets for the train from the airport cost 5,000 lire and must be purchased before boarding from a booth in the arrivals area or from machines at the turnstiles (requiring exact change). Tickets must be retained for on-board control. The train operates from 6:30 A.M. to 12:45 A.M., after which there are night buses into the center of Rome every hour on the hour until 5:00 A.M.

Rome's other airport, Ciampino, is about 16 km (10 miles) southeast of the city and is used mainly by charter flights. ACOTRAL buses provide service to the Cinecittà metro stop, which will take you into the center of Rome. But unless you are familiar with the metro, taxis are your best bet. Take only authorized "yellow" cabs, make sure the meter is turned on, and be forewarned that cabdrivers are entitled to charge a 10 percent surcharge when travelling to or from either airport. In addition, there are late-night rates, Sunday and holiday surcharges, and a small fee for each piece of luggage you put in the trunk.

International (and most national) trains arrive at Rome's central station, Stazione Termini, where you can catch a bus, a taxi, or the subway. Some trains arrive at Stazione Tibertina or Stazione Trastevere; these are less central but are served by taxis and buses.

Driving in Rome is best left to those who can trace their ancestry back to a charioteer or two. Crossing the street should satisfy anyone's taste for the heroic, but if you must have a car and want to rent it, make all the arrangements before coming to Europe to avoid paying the hefty value-added tax.

Rome's two subway lines, A and B, are inadequate and inconveniently located. Expansion is always in the air, but screeches to a halt every time the digging unearths another major artifact. Nevertheless, the *Metropolitana* (marked by a large M at the entrances) connects many of Rome's main tourist sights and runs from 5:30 A.M. to 11:30 P.M. (line B stops at 9:00 P.M.). Tickets can be purchased in major subway stations from machines, which require the exact change in coins, or from tobacconist shops, newsstands, and bars.

Rome's public bus system is extensive and relatively cheap. Various types of tickets—as well as a routes map—are available at the ATAC information booth in the parking area in front of Stazione Termini, the main train station. (Telephone information is available by dialing 469-51.) Tickets are good for unlimited use on any bus line for a 90-minute period. There are also daily, weekly, and monthly passes that permit unlimited travel on any bus line (but not the metro). In addition, passes allow the passenger to enter from the front of the bus, which is convenient during rush hours. Otherwise, buses are boarded from the rear and exited from the middle doors. (Passes for the metro are available at the ticket office next to the metro entrance on the lower level of Stazione Termini.)

Once you board the bus, place your ticket in the validating machine, which will stamp it with the time, date, and bus number. Failure to display a correctly stamped ticket or a pass to the controllers, who can board buses at any time and any place, could result in a hefty 50,000-lire fine—payable in any currency.

The same rules apply to the more limited tram service. A ride on tram 30 is an excellent way to get to know the city. The tram passes most of the major monuments and takes about an hour. If you have a 90-minute ticket, you can get on and off as many times as you want, so long as you stamp in your last ride before the time limit is up.

Each bus or tram stop, called a *fermata,* has a yellow sign that lists all the stops on the route and shows you where you are—provided you can read the small type. Most buses run from 5:00 A.M. until midnight, although some stop at 9:00; the hours are indicated at the bottom of each route listing. Popular routes have a night service listed under the *servizio notturno* column. Night routes often differ from day routes, so check carefully. Night buses have conductors who sell tickets.

A special tourist bus gives tours of the city every day at 2:30 P.M. The tour is a real bargain (about $5.00) because it lasts three hours and includes all of the major sights. Tickets are available at the ATAC information booth in front of the Stazione Termini (Tel: 469-51), which is also the departure point for the bus.

Rome is not a good taxi city; cabs are few and far between, expensive, and not air-conditioned, and they cannot be flagged down. The meter starts at 6,000 lire. The average fare in the city is 10,000 lire. On the plus side, tipping is optional. Taxis are found at stands throughout the city or may be called by dialing 35-70, or 49-94.

Whatever means of public transport you use, do not underestimate pickpockets. They are extremely enterprising with their hands, razor blades, and other means of getting into your pocket or purse. Make photocopies of your documents for easy replacement and leave the originals and any other valuables you don't really need in your hotel safe.

Violence is rare in Rome, but petty crime is not, so keep your money in a money belt or neck pouch and don't carry a bag or a conspicuous camera case. If your bag is snatched by a passing motorcyclist, do not hold on to it or you may incur more injury than the bag is worth. Report the loss to the police and the embassy, as very often the bag, minus the money, turns up in a post box or somebody's back yard.

Rome's hills, heavy traffic, and cobblestones make the city less than ideal for bicycles, but in some cases a bike can be the best way to explore the city. Bicycles can be rented for 3,000 lire an hour, 10,000 lire a half-day, or 15,000 lire a day at piazza San Lorenzo in Lucina off via del Corso, at piazza Sonnino in Trastevere, and at St. Peter Moto at 43 via Porta Castello near the Vatican (Tel: 687-57-14). Other locations are just outside the metro at piazza di Spagna and in the Borghese Gardens. A nine-mile bike path traces the Tiber, on the Trastevere–Vatican City side, beginning north of Ponte Cavour.

Rome city tourist offices are located in the customs area of both airports, in the track area of Stazione Termini (Tel: 487-12-70), and at via Parigi 5, behind the Grand Hotel between the train station and via Veneto (Tel: 488-37-48).

ACCOMMODATIONS

The rates given below are projections for 1993; always check for up-to-date information before making reservations. Wide ranges may reflect the differences between low- and high-season rates. Unless otherwise noted, the figures indicate the cost of a double room (per room, not per person) with bath. Air-conditioning is included in the price except when a surcharge is specified, as is breakfast. The service charge is included in the rate; inquire about the tax.

The telephone and fax area code for Rome is 06. When telephoning from outside the country, omit the zero in the city code.

"We were well accommodated with three handsome bedrooms, a dining room, larder, stable and kitchen," wrote Montaigne's secretary of their lodgings in Rome. It's possible to get an idea of the value of the 20 crowns a month they paid in the 16th century when Monsieur le secretaire goes on to estimate that the beds in their rooms must have cost between four and five hundred crowns apiece. In that light, the room was a real bargain, especially when you consider that nowadays, the price—in dollars—of a room in one of Rome's top hotels is closer to what the beds cost—and without the larder, stable, or kitchen.

The Eternal City, in case you haven't heard, is no longer the *dolce vita* dreamland of cheap lodgings and gargantuan meals for a song. You have to hunt around and choose carefully now, but it is still possible to find reasonably priced accommodations, especially if you are willing to compromise on location or forego the stable and larder and some of the other conveniences of home.

The hotels in the following list are arranged according to neighborhoods. The Centro Storico (Old Rome) area offers proximity to the major monuments; the Villa Borghese area skirts the park; piazza di Spagna is close to Rome's elegant shopping district; via Veneto has the highest concentration of luxury hotels and an active nightlife; and the area near Stazione Termini, the central train station, is convenient for those who need to come and go in a hurry.

Centro Storico

A windy medieval street off the via della Scrofa opens into a tiny piazza where two enormous stone angels blow Judgment Day trumpets atop the Portuguese national church. Tucked into a corner of the church is the 150-year-old **Albergo Portoghesi**, a small, relatively inexpensive hotel that at first glance looks like a Paris bistro decked out in wrought-iron fencing and bunches of white globe lamps. Inside, the Portoghesi has kept its somewhat eclectic charm in spite of a recent effort to update. There are 24 rooms on three floors, all with antique furnishings, private bath, and air-conditioning. An elevator rises to the rooftop terrace, where breakfast is served in good weather and from which you can almost touch those trumpeting angels next door. Via del Portoghesi 1, 00186; Tel: 686-42-31; Fax: 687-69-76. L130,000; L10,000 extra for breakfast and L20,000 for air conditioning.

Discretion is the rule at the vine-covered **Raphael**, a favorite of journalists and Italian politicians. The somewhat gloomy lobby unsuccessfully blends antiques with modern furniture, and although most of the 85 rooms are small and far from luxurious, the views of piazza Navona from the upper floors are quite expansive—and expensive. The service is professional—down to the pink terry-cloth robes. Largo Febo 2, 00186; Tel: 65-08-81 or 683-88-81; Fax: 687-89-93; L385,000. L22,000 extra for breakfast.

Sole al Pantheon claims to be the oldest hotel in Rome (1493). Plaques attest to stays here of the poet Ariosto and the composer Pietro Mascagni, who wrote *Cavalleria Rusticana*. The Sole was also a favorite of Jean-Paul Sartre and Simone de Beauvoir, and one can see why just by opening the shutters onto the Pantheon—one of western architecture's most venerated monuments. The neighborhood teems with cafés, restaurants, and crowds of late-night revelers, so you'll appreciate the double glass in the windows and the central air-conditioning because you won't be able to open your windows—at least on the piazza side—and sleep in summer. Nor will you lament the Jacuzzi in the bath after a long day of sightseeing and shopping. Via del Pantheon 63, 00186; Tel: 678-04-41; Fax: 684-06-89. ₤250,000–₤380,000.

Even closer to the Pantheon and more moderately priced is **Hotel del Senato**. Its jazzy postmodern lobby leads to less jazzy but serviceable rooms. The tiny elevator is an appropriate prelude to the size of the rooms, but when you open your window and look down over the Pantheon, you'll probably stop counting square feet. Piazza del Pantheon 73, 00186; Tel: 679-32-31; Fax: 684-02-97. ₤110,000–₤146,000; ₤18,000 extra for breakfast; ₤22,000 a day for air-conditioning.

Toward the back of the Pantheon, the **Holiday Inn Crowne Plaza Minerva** recently reopened after the property, once a hotel where George Sand and Marie-Henri Beyle (Stendhal) slept on separate occasions, was renovated and modernized. You'll pay handsomely for business-traveller-style amenities, such as nonsmoking rooms and satellite TV, but the convenient location, panoramic rooftop terrace, and barbecue lunches may make it worthwhile. Piazza della Minerva 69, 00186; Tel: 684-18-88; Fax: 679-41-65. ₤438,000–₤492,000; ₤30,000 extra for breakfast.

For much less, the 97-room **Hotel Santa Chiara**, just across the street from the Minerva, has rooms furnished with antiques, recently completely renovated to include air-conditioning, color TVs, refrigerator, and lavish marble bathrooms. Via di Santa Chiara 21, 00186; Tel: 654-01-42; Fax 687-31-44. ₤76,000–₤150,000; ₤25,000 extra for breakfast; ₤20,000 for air-conditioning.

Teatro di Pompeo is located in a tiny piazza near Campo dei Fiori and is built on top of the ruins of the Theater of Pompey, where Julius Caesar was assassinated on the Ides of March in 44 B.C. (and not in the Forum, as many think, because the Curia, like many public buildings in Italy today, was closed that day for renovation). Breakfast is served either in your room or in the cavernous cellars of the notorious theater. The 12 rooms are tastefully understated with their white walls, dark-beamed ceilings, and terra-cotta floors accented by hand-painted tiles and colorful geometric rugs. The rooms on the top floor look out onto the dome of the adjoining church, which seems to be coming right into the room. Central air-conditioning, refrigerator, and color

TV are included. Largo del Pallaro 8, 00186; Tel: 687-28-12; Fax: 654-55-31. Ł175,000; Ł21,000 extra for breakfast.

The **Hotel Forum** has a stunning view over the imperial forums, particularly from its rooftop terrace and bar. The hotel is a converted convent, and part of its ancient bell tower forms part of the lobby, along with various capitals and other fragments from the surrounding archaeological zone. The air-conditioned rooms are done up in polished woodwork and brocade and are small but comfortable. Via Tor de' Conti 25, 00184; Tel: 679-24-46; Fax: 678-64-79. Ł300,000–Ł400,000; Ł25,000 extra for breakfast.

Near the antiques stores on via Giulia and the outdoor market in Campo dei Fiori is **Ponte Sisto**. The best rooms look out onto a large, palm-shaded courtyard where breakfast is served in good weather and where a bar crowd holds court at night in summer. Some of the 129 rooms (room 601 in particular) have views of St. Peter's and the Janiculum hill; most do not, but if you value large luminous rooms more than sweeping vistas, Ponte Sisto is where you'll get the most for your money. There is no air-conditioning, but parking is available. Room 107 has a large terrace. Via dei Pettinari 64, 00186; Tel: 686-88-43; Fax: 654-88-22. Ł146,000; Ł13,000 extra for breakfast.

Hotel delle Nazioni is just a coin's throw from the newly restored Trevi Fountain. It has small but comfortable rooms with air-conditioning and its own restaurant-pizzeria. If you come off-season, you get a 20 percent discount. Ask for one of the top rooms with a terrace—far from the 24-hour crowd at the fountain below. Via Poli 7, 00187; Tel: 679-24-41; Fax: 678-24-00. Ł225,000–Ł330,000.

Budget choice: Around the block from piazza Venezia and just off the Corso is the ideally located **Pensione Coronet**, a leftover from the era of cheap pensioni that still provides clean, functionally ugly rooms in a glorious setting overlooking the garden of the Palazzo Doria Pamphili. Piazza Grazioli 5, 00186; Tel: 679-23-41. Ł86,000; Ł10,000 extra for breakfast. No credit cards.

Villa Borghese

Perhaps due to its past as a house of ill-repute, the sumptuous **Valadier** has some of the largest bathrooms in Rome. Situated just below the Pincio hill, near the trendy piazza del Popolo, the hotel also has spacious air-conditioned rooms and lounges tastefully accented with gleaming marble, polished brass, mahogany, and fresh flowers. Ask for one of the three rooms that have terraces. There is a 20 percent weekend discount if you book in advance. Via della Fontanella 15, 00187; Tel: 361-19-98; Fax: 320-15-58. Ł270,000–Ł405,000.

Villa Borghese looks—outside and inside—like a country house set in the middle of the park, but there is no air-conditioning, and it gets noisy in summer when the windows are open. In the fall and winter, however, it's one of the coziest spots in Rome and far from the noisy crowds. Via Pinciana 31, 00198; Tel: 844-01-05 or 854-96-48; Fax: 844-26-36. Ł160,000; Ł28,000 extra for breakfast.

On a side street facing the venerable brick walls that the emperor Aurelius built in the third century A.D. to protect Rome is the **Hotel Victoria**, a small hotel with a solid reputation for comfort and good service. The air-conditioned rooms on the top floors have splendid views of the Villa Borghese park, which is convenient for joggers and strollers—but only during the daytime. Via Campania 41, 00187; Tel: 473-931; Fax: 487-18-90. Ł240,000–Ł280,000.

Piazza di Spagna

The **Carriage** is named after the street in which the touring carriages of yesteryear used to stop for repairs. The Old World atmosphere is still evident in the gilded furnishings of this small bur comfortable hotel. All rooms are air-conditioned, but the best are clustered around a terrace on the top floor; number 32 has an enormous bathroom. Via delle Carrozze 36, 00187; Tel: 699-24-01 or 679-33-12; Fax: 678-82-79. Ł185,000; Ł25,000 extra for breakfast.

Rooms with views of the tile rooftops and domes of Rome are part of the offering at the newly renovated **Condotti**, just off Rome's super-chic shopping street of the same name. The 21 small rooms also are drop-dead chic, in cheerful peach and gray or light blue moiré silk. Some rooms on the top floor have terraces, while those on the second and third have small balconies. Via Mario de' Fiori 37, 00187; Tel: 679-46-61; Fax: 679-04-57. Ł133,500; Ł25,000 extra for breakfast; Ł20,000 a day for air-conditioning.

With its Oriental rugs, crystal chandeliers, and marble tables, the **De la Ville Intercontinental** at the top of the Spanish Steps is for many the quintessence of Old World charm. Its upper floors and roof-garden terrace (which offers a Sunday brunch) have spectacular views, while the rooms on the lower floors overlook a central courtyard. If you book in advance, there are special weekend and August rates. Via Sistina 69, 00187; Tel: 673-31; Fax 678-42-13. Ł415,000–Ł484,00.

The **D'Inghilterra** used to be a refuge for writers in Rome

(Henry James, Mark Twain, and Ernest Hemingway all stayed here), but its prices nowadays have placed it beyond most writers' means. It can be noisy and the rooms are small, but it has one of the best bars and by all accounts the best bartender in Rome. Via Bocca di Leone 14, 00187; Tel: 672-161; Fax: 684-08-28. Ł335,000–Ł446,000; Ł22,000 extra for breakfast.

The **Hassler–Villa Medici** is the preferred hotel of many distinguished visitors, from American presidents to movie stars, but if you do not fall into a similar category, the service can be cold and unfriendly. Right at the top of the Spanish Steps, the Hassler is crowned with one of the city's most elegant restaurants. At these prices, ask for a room with a view of the Steps or the gardens behind. Piazza Trinità dei Monti 6, 00187; Tel: 678-26-51; Fax: 678-99-91. In U.S., Tel: (212) 838-3110 or (800) 223-6800; Fax: (212) 758-7367. In U.K., Tel: (0800) 18-11-23; Fax: (071) 353-19-04. Ł400,000–Ł600,000; Ł25,000 extra for breakfast.

Opposite the Hassler and sharing the same views for a lot less money is the **Scalinata di Spagna**. Reservations are strictly required in this small family-run hotel. The two rooms on the top floor share the rooftop terrace and are usually filled by honeymooners. Breakfast is served in your air-conditioned room or on the flower-filled rooftop terrace, where you can bask in all the Roman standards: red-tiled rooftops, cascading geraniums, and a landscape of domes, large and small, in the distance. Piazza Trinità dei Monti 17, 00187; Tel: 679-30-06; Fax: 684-05-98. Ł130,000–Ł260,000. No credit cards.

Down Via Sistina, the **King** is a dependable, reasonably priced hotel in the Spanish Steps area. Its sparsely decorated rooms are nonetheless comfortable, and the rooftop terrace has more of those wonderful views. Via Sistina 131, 00187; Tel: 488-08-78; Fax: 487-18-13. Ł145,000; Ł25,000 extra for breakfast; Ł25,000 a day for air-conditioning.

Located at the top of the Spanish Steps in a former convent on the street that houses many of Italy's high-fashion ateliers, the small, stylish **Gregoriana** was decorated by Erté, and the doors of each room bear his anthropomorphic letters rather than numbers. Rooms F, M, and R have small balconies overlooking an inner courtyard, and room C preserves elements of what was a chapel in the days when the Gregoriana was a convent. (The leopard-skin wallpaper in the halls was added later.) There are only 19 rooms, which are often booked solid by models or rag-trade buyers, and the service is legendary. Via Gregoriana 18, 00187; Tel:

679-42-69; Fax: 678-42-58. Ł85,000–Ł142,000; Ł25,000 extra for breakfast; Ł20,000 a day for air-conditioning. No credit cards.

The newest of the small elegant hotels in the Spanish Steps area is the **Hotel dei Borgognoni**, on a narrow street where the inhabitants of Burgundy settled in Rome in the 17th century. The 50 rooms are small but richly decorated; some overlook a glass-enclosed, flower-filled inner courtyard. Number 109, 110, and 112 have small terraces. There are the usual amenities—air-conditioning, color TV, refrigerator, room safes, and a private garage—and the Borgognoni also offers a free baby-sitter service. Via del Bufalo 126, 00187; Tel: 678-00-41; Fax: 684-15-01. Ł330,000–Ł390,000.

Nestled in among the deluxe hotels at the top of the Spanish Steps is the unassuming **Albergo Internazionale**, which has long been considered one of the city's best-run hotels in the moderate price category. Parts of the building date from the 16th century, which accounts for the ornately carved wood furnishings and frescoed ceilings in some of its 40 rooms. Rooms on the fourth floor have terraces, and a few on the ground floor have whirlpool baths. All of the rooms have satellite TVs, and free parking is available. Via Sistina 79, 00187; Tel: 679-30-47; Fax: 678-47-64. Ł160,000–Ł220,000; Ł25,000 extra for breakfast; Ł20,000 a day for air-conditioning.

On a tiny, quiet side street off Via del Babuino and a few yards from the foot of the Spanish Steps is the **Margutta**, a small, inexpensive hotel, decorated in bold colors that reflect the artistic spirit of the nearby street from which it takes its name. Two of its 26 rooms are on the roof and come with fireplaces and private terraces that overlook palaces, bell towers, and the Pincio gardens. Via Laurina 34, 00187; Tel: 679-84-40 or 322-36-74. Ł94,000; Ł10,000 extra for breakfast.

Budget choice: Reflecting its name, the **Suisse** (Swiss) is an efficiently run, moderately priced hotel with large rooms furnished in both antique and modern styles. A charming terrace, a loyal clientele, and low rates make reservations well in advance a must. Via Gregoriana 56, 00187; Tel: 678-36-49. Ł80,000–Ł88,000; Ł12,000 extra for breakfast.

Via Veneto

Opposite the American Embassy, the **Ambasciatori Palace** offers 150 large, luxurious rooms in a modern setting and impeccable service. It has a lively bar, popular with embassy people. Via Vittorio Veneto 70, 00187; Tel: 474-93; Fax: 474-36-01. Ł400,000; Ł30,000 extra for breakfast.

The **Excelsior** was the preferred residence of Elizabeth Taylor and other Hollywood luminaries during the *dolce vita* era. Most of its roomy, luxurious suites and well-appointed rooms decorated in French Empire style still live up to its glamorous past. Via Vittorio Veneto 125, 00187; Tel: 47-08; Fax: 482-62-05. In U.S., Tel: (212) 935-9540 or (800) 221-2340; Fax (212) 421-5929. In U.K., Tel: (071) 930-41-47 or (0800) 289-234; Fax: (071) 839-15-66. £392,000–£619,000; £30,000 extra for breakfast. Pets accepted.

Offering the most discreet service of the Via Veneto luxury hotels, the **Flora** is a favorite of many for its Old World charm, spacious rooms, and traditional service. It is just inside the Aurelian walls and across the street from the Villa Borghese park, which is convenient for joggers. Via Vittorio Veneto 191, 00187; Tel: 48-99-29 or 482-03-51; Fax: 482-03-59. £330,000–£500,000; £35,000 extra for breakfast.

The **Hotel Alexandra** is a charming 19th-century mansion at the bottom of Via Veneto that has been managed by the same family for four generations. All 45 rooms have recently been renovated and sound-proofed against the traffic on Via Veneto. Breakfast is served in an antiques-filled salon of faded gentility decorated with black-and-white photos of turn-of-the-century Rome. Air-conditioning, refrigerator, color TV, free parking restaurant, bar, and room service. Via Vittorio Veneto 18, 00187; Tel: 488-19-43; Fax: 487-18-04. £140,000–£200,000; £20,000 extra for breakfast; £20,000 a day for air-conditioning.

La Residenza, on a quiet street one block from Via Veneto, was a private villa and then a convent before it became a hotel. Seven of the 27 rooms have terraces; others have only small balconies but are larger. The public rooms have Louis XVI furniture, fireplaces, and Baroque mirrors. Many claim that the breakfast buffet here is the best in Rome. Via Emilia 22, 00187; Tel: 488-07-89; Fax: 485-721. £210,000; £25,000 extra for breakfast; £30,000 a day for air-conditioning. No credit cards.

Near the Station
The Neoclassical grandness of **Le Grand Hotel** is not diminished by its location near the train station, which used to be one of the most fashionable areas of the city. The Grand boasts majestic rooms and suites whose elegance is matched by the appointments in the public areas, where an elaborate tea is served each afternoon, and Roman matrons lunch to harp music and eat finger sandwiches and petits fours. Via Vittorio Emanuele Orlando 3, 00185; Tel: 47-09; Fax: 474-73-

07. In U.S., Tel: (800) 223-6800 or (212) 838-3110; Fax: (212) 758-7367. In U.K., Tel: (0800) 18-11-23; Fax: (071) 353-19-04. Ł390,000–Ł624,000; Ł30,000 extra for breakfast.

The **Mediterraneo** is one of five hotels in the Bettoja hotel group that offer accommodations from luxury to reasonably priced. Situated on the Esquiline Hill, the highest of Rome's seven hills, the hotel has a roof-garden terrace, where breakfast is served in summer, that provides sweeping views of the city. The rooms are traditionally furnished but have modern conveniences like direct-dial telephones and satellite TVs. The concierges at the Mediterraneo have a long-standing reputation for service and knowledge. Via Cavour 15, 00184; Tel: 488-40-51; Fax: 474-41-05. In U.S., Tel: (800) 223-9832 or (212) 599-8280; Fax: (212) 599-1755. Ł180,000–Ł360,000; Ł20,000 extra for breakfast.

The recently refurbished **Hotel Nord** is another Bettoja hotel in a more economical price range. It faces the new Roman Archaeological Museum and is within walking distance of the train station and the opera house. Free parking is available. Weekend and off-season discounts are available when you book through a travel agency. Via G. Amendola 3, 00185; Tel: 488-54-41; Fax: 481-71-63. In U.S., Tel: (800) 223-9832 or (212) 599-8280; Fax: (212) 599-1755. Ł210,000; Ł30,000 extra for breakfast.

The Vatican

The most creature comforts–oriented hotel in the area is the modern **Atlante Star**, which also has a lush roof-garden restaurant with close-up views of St. Peter's and a unique policy (which it shares with its less expensive sister hotel, **Atlante Garden**) of picking up its guests at the airport free of charge. Via Vitelleschi 34, 00193; Tel: 687-32-33; Fax: 687-23-00. Ł240,000–Ł420,000; Ł27,000 extra for breakfast. Atlante Garden: Via Crescenzio 78, 00193; Tel: 687-23-61; Fax: 687-23-15. Ł180,000–Ł295,000; Ł27,000 extra for breakfast.

Formerly the Renaissance palazzo of Pope Julius II's family, the **Columbus**—even though due for renovation—abounds in red velvet drapes, antique tapestries, and frescoed ceilings in some of the rooms (number 221), although the management has opted for efficient simplicity in most of the others. That combination and the fact that the Columbus is on the main avenue leading into Vatican City make reservations in advance a must. Free parking. Via della Conciliazione 33, 00193; Tel: 686-54-35; Fax: 686-48-74. Ł140,000–Ł220,000; Ł30,000 extra for breakfast; Ł20,000 a day for air-conditioning.

Hotel Sant'Anna is a small hotel located 50 yards from St.

Peter's Square on a busy street crowded with restaurants, food stores, and souvenirs shops. The 20 rooms are very small but attractive. Breakfast is served in a frescoed dining room or around the courtyard fountain. There's no elevator to take you there, but ask for one of the spacious blue-and-white attic rooms, each with its own tiny terrace. Borgo Pio 143, 00193; Tel: 654-16-02; Fax: 68-30-87-17. Ł150,000; Ł30,000 extra for breakfast; Ł20,000 for air-conditioning.

Budget choice: The **Alimandi** is a clean, well-run pensione with a charming breakfast terrace, and it's only a short walk back—for tired feet—from the Vatican Museums. Via Tunisi 8, 00192; Tel: 38-45-48; Fax: 31-44-57. Ł80,000–Ł110,000; Ł13,000 extra for breakfast. No air-conditioning.

Elsewhere in Rome

With a pool, tennis courts, and a famous restaurant, the **Cavalieri Hilton** is such a self-contained unit that many of its guests never leave it for very long. Moreover, its privileged position atop Monte Mario (north of the Vatican) gives it some of the best views of Rome at night. A bus regularly shuttles guests (and their dogs and cats) to the Spanish Steps and back. Via Cadlolo 101, 00136; Tel: 315-11; Fax: 315-122-41. Ł395,000–Ł540,000; Ł30,000 extra for breakfast.

On a quiet side street between piazza del Popolo and the Tiber, the very low-key **Locarno** is many people's favorite small hotel in Rome. Although it has lost some of its finer fin-de-siècle features to modernization, the Locarno is still a good example of a Roman hotel that has managed to retain some of its original charm while yielding to the demand for color TVs, refrigerator, and air-conditioning. There are Belle Epoque touches in the lobby, such as Tiffany-style lamps and sinuous beveled glass doors, and in winter the open fire, dark woodwork, and brass ornaments give a warm glow to the parlor. In good weather breakfast is served in the garden under the ubiquitous Roman *umbrelloni*. A unique feature: The Locarno provides free bicycles. Via della Penna 22, 00186; Tel: 361-08-41; Fax: 321-52-49. Ł160,000; Ł25,000 extra for breakfast; Ł20,000 a day for air-conditioning.

In the exclusive residential neighborhood of Parioli behind the Villa Borghese, the luxurious **Lord Byron**, decorated in subtle tones and bursts of fresh flowers, attracts a well-heeled clientele. Moreover, it boasts a restaurant that many say is Rome's best. Via Giuseppe de Notaris 5, 00197; Tel: 322-04-04; Fax: 322-04-05. In U.S., Tel: (800) 223-6800 or (212) 838-3110; Fax: (212) 758-7367. In U.K., Tel: (0800) 18-

11-23; Fax: (071) 353-19-04. £510,000; £25,000 extra for breakfast.

Somebody at the **Viminale** went to hotel school, because here you get all the extras—valet parking, remote-control color TVs, credit card keys, room safes, adjustable air-conditioning, and a newspaper slipped under your door in the morning. The 46-room hotel is in a converted Art Nouveau villa near the basilica of Santa Maria Maggiore. Most of the rooms have been fully restored, but there are still a vintage 1920s cage elevator on the inside and graceful Art Nouveau—or "Liberty," as Italians call the style—touches on the outside. Via Cesare Balbo 31, 00184; Tel: 488-19-10; Fax: 474-47-28. £155,000; £27,000 extra for breakfast; £20,000 a day for air-conditioning.

The **Plaza** is halfway between piazza del Popolo and piazza Venezia and has been catering to a sophisticated clientele since 1860. Its Old-World grandeur has not diminished since the queen of Mexico inaugurated it. The Belle Epoque reception room, with its potted palms and stained-glass ceiling, has recently been restored to its former Art Nouveau glory. The best rooms (number 257, for example) are set around a cool, quiet inner courtyard. Via del Corso 126, 00186; Tel: 67-21-01; Fax: 684-15-75. £255,000–£310,000; £18,000 extra for breakfast; £15,000 a day for air-conditioning.

Many people claim that the residential area on the Aventine hill above the Circus Maximus is the quietest in Rome, and for that reason the **Sant'Anselmo**, although a bit out of the way, has become popular. The garden breakfast terrace and afternoon bar reflect the lush, hushed surroundings of the area, where sleeping peacefully at night is never a problem. No air-conditioning. Piazza Sant'Anselmo 2, 00153; Tel: 574-35-47; Fax: 578-36-04. £90,000–£147,000; £18,000 extra for breakfast.

Also outside the center (but a quick bus or taxi ride away) are several hotels along via Nomentana, a wide tree-lined boulevard bordered by parks and private villas. Two hotels are the best in the area:

Villa delle Rose is a venerable old villa set back from the avenue with a tranquil, leafy garden and a gurgling goldfish pool. Once the residence of a series of wealthy Roman families who built their villas on what was then the outskirts of the city, Villa delle Rose has kept some of that atmosphere in its rooms and parlors. Via Vicenza 5, 00185; Tel: 445-17-88. £136,000; £17,000 extra for breakfast; £11,000 a day for air-conditioning.

Hotel Villa del Parco is a converted 19th-century villa set back from the street by a tree-lined drive, which gives it the air of a Mediterranean country house. The cozily furnished rooms have high ceilings and large double-door windows. In addition, it offers air-conditioning, refrigerator, color TVs, free parking, and a garden where breakfast is served. For joggers there is the ample Villa Torlonia park next door. Via Nomentana 110, 00161; Tel: 855-56-11; Fax: 854-04-10. ₤136,000–₤202,000; ₤23,000 extra for breakfast; ₤20,000 a day for air-conditioning.

Budget choices: The 22-room **Pensione Parlamento**, off the central via del Corso, has the kind of relaxed, run-down atmosphere that some people find charming, and that (along with its rooftop terrace) has made it a favorite among expatriates. Via delle Convertite 5, 00187; Tel: 678-78-80. ₤62,000–₤95,000; ₤12,000 extra for breakfast.

Located in the quiet Prati quarter north of the Vatican, the comfortably furnished **Forti's Guest House** is a block from the Tiber and convenient to all forms of public transportation. The Italian-American management is friendly and helpful and sometimes even prepares family-style meals for guests. Via Fornovo 7, 00192; Tel: 320-07-38; Fax: 321-22-22. ₤85,000–₤95,000; ₤14,500 extra for breakfast.

Residences

If you are planning to spend at least a week in Rome, you should look into staying in a *residence* instead of a hotel or pensione. Residences are mini-apartments that include an outfitted kitchen, a bedroom and bath, and a parlor. The advantages are that you can have breakfast whenever you want, cook your own simple meals, and entertain guests in a living room instead of a bedroom. During the off-season, many residences let you stay for less than a week.

The best in this category is the **Palazzo al Velabro**, a vine-covered palazzo at the bottom of the Palatine Hill on a quiet street between the Tiber and the Circus Maximus (where you can go jogging). The 35 mini-apartments have a modern, functional decor, and some of them have terraces that overlook a lush inner courtyard that has the Palatine Hill as a backdrop. The ₤1,600,000-a-week price includes linens, kitchen utensils, color TV, air-conditioning, and maid service. Via del Velabro 16, 00186; Tel: 679-34-50; Fax: 679-37-90.

Ripa Residence in Trastevere is next door to Rome's renowned Sunday morning flea market. It offers monthly as well as weekly rates and boasts all the comforts of a hotel plus the privacy of your own home. The comforts do not include an iota of aesthetic charm and the (sometimes noisy) dog pound is nearby, but the convenience, location, and price may entice you to ignore the downside. Via degli Orti di Trastevere 1, 00153; Tel: 586-11; Fax: 581-45-50. £1,000,000 a week; £2,700,000 a month.

Monasteries and Convents

Another alternative to commercial hotels is a monastery or convent. These are not former houses of worship that have been converted into trendy hotels, but religious communities that take in guests for a nominal fee (no credit cards) that sometimes includes meals. Accommodations are spartan but immaculate. Some monasteries have an 11:00 P.M. curfew, but the ones listed here give guests their own keys, so they are free to come and go as they wish. The following accept families as well as single men and women of any or no faith.

The **Franciscan Sisters of Atonement** is an American order of nuns whose motherhouse is in Garrison, New York. All rooms have private baths; there is a dining room; and parking is available. There is also a spacious pine-shaded garden to stroll about in. (This convent is recommended by the Vatican City Tourist Information Office.) Via Monte del Gallo 105, 00165; Tel: 53-07-82. £60,000 per person for room with full board; £45,000 for half board.

The **Convent of Santa Brigida** is in one of Rome's most beautiful Renaissance piazzas—piazza Farnese. The rooms are more expensive than at the other religious establishments that lodge guests but cheaper than in a hotel. Guests must eat at least one meal here. The rooms—all with private baths—are modest and spotlessly clean. The guest house is operated by an order of Swedish sisters who also have guest houses in Farfa and Assisi. Piazza Farnese 96, 00186; Tel: 698-52-63. £90,000 per person for room with full board; £70,000 for half board.

The **Casa di Santa Francesca Romana** is in the heart of Rome's bohemian quarter—Trastevere—a short distance from the Tiber Island. The pensione is housed in what was once a noble Roman family's vast palazzo, and it offers hospitality to groups, families, or individuals in single, double, or triple rooms with private baths. There is central heating (but no air-conditioning), an elevator, and a cool inner courtyard. Rooms 23 and 35 have picturesque views of Trastevere. Via dei Vascellari 61, 00153; Tel: 581-21-25. £87,000 for a double with bath.

The **Casa Kolbe** at the foot of the Palatine is a religious

guest house that caters mainly to groups of pilgrims, but it
sometimes has vacancies. The rooms are very basic, but the
location is perfect and the public rooms and garden are
quiet and relaxing. Via San Teodoro 44, 00186; Tel: 679-49-
74; Fax: 684-15-50. £70,000–£82,000 for a double with bath;
£7,000 extra for breakfast.

—*Louis Inturrisi*

DINING

Despite the abundance of roads leading to Rome, remarkably few culinary influences have flowed into or out of the
Eternal City in its more than 2,000 years of existence. The
sprinkling of non-Italian restaurants in the capital today
(mostly Chinese) are looked upon with suspicion (and
rightly so), while the others offer more or less the same
Roman standards, none of which—with the possible exception of spaghetti *alla carbonara*—has ever achieved international recognition. The result is that although it is rare to eat
badly in Rome, it is also true that the food is not very
exciting—unless you count knuckles, shanks, and tails
among the world's epicurean delights.

Roman cooking, like the people who created it, is simple,
straightforward, and unpretentious: In a word, it is emi-
nently practical—as befits a people better at road construction and plumbing than at painting or sculpture. It doesn't
bother with subtle cream sauces or expensive ingredients
like truffles because it didn't come out of the kitchens of the
emperors or the popes, but out of the *cucina povera*—the
good, solid home cooking of the common people. This
characteristic still survives in the plain and hearty Roman
dishes made from whatever was left over, whatever they
could get their hands on, or whatever pieces of meat or fish
nobody else wanted. It also accounts for the preponderance
of tripe, brains, innards, and intestines in Roman cooking, as
well as the ubiquitous presence of preservatives like hot
peppers and garlic.

A complete meal in a Roman restaurant, osteria, or
trattoria (there is not much difference nowadays) includes a
first course (*primo*) of pasta, rice, or soup; a *secondo* of
meat, poultry, or fish; and a dessert of fresh fruit, cheese, or,
less often, sweets. The meal often begins with an antipasto of
appetizers selected from a table near the entrance of the
restaurant where a variety of grilled vegetables, cold cuts,
and shellfish are displayed. Another favorite Roman appetizer is *bruschetta* (slices of toasted garlic bread topped with
chopped tomatoes and sprinkled with olive oil).

The most common Roman *primi* are spaghetti *alla carbonara* (bacon, egg yolk, Parmesan, and black pepper), said to have been invented by coal (*carbone*) miners to satisfy their need for a simple sauce that could be prepared without cooking; *bucatini all'amatriciana* (long, narrow pasta tubes in a sauce of salt pork, onions, tomatoes, and grated sheep's-milk cheese); *penne all'arrabbiata* (short pasta with a peppy tomato and garlic sauce, topped with fresh parsley); spaghetti *alla puttanesca* (the sauce made from tomatoes, capers, and black olives), which tradition says was popular with whores (*puttane*) because of its lack of garlic; and *gnocchi* (potato dumplings), which are traditionally served every Thursday topped with one of the two standard Roman sauces: *sugo* (tomato and basil) or *ragù* (tomato and ground beef). If you can't decide which pasta to order, ask for *un assaggino* (a taste) of two or three. If it all sounds like too much, ask for *una mezza porzione* (a half portion).

The most common *secondi* are *saltimbocca alla romana* (literally, "jump-in-your-mouth" veal filets topped with prosciutto and a few sage leaves and then sautéed in butter); *coda alla vaccinara* (oxtail stewed in wine, onions, tomatoes, and celery); *peperonata* (chicken stewed in roasted peppers); *osso buco* (braised veal shank in tomato sauce); and *abbacchio al forno* (roast baby lamb served with roasted potatoes and rosemary). There are also *secondi* of grilled steaks and chops, the veal in Rome being especially good and reasonably priced. Try *lombata di vitello,* a veal chop that is best grilled over charcoal and doused with fresh lemon.

Fish is also available in most restaurants, but it is not a Roman specialty and the distance from the sea makes most claims to freshness suspect. Remember also that fish served on Mondays anywhere in Italy can't be fresh, as the fishermen do not take in a catch on Sunday.

To accompany the *secondi* there are a wide variety of *contorni* (raw or cooked vegetables) and salads. Some traditional Roman vegetables you should try if they are in season are: *puntarelle,* the crunchy stalks of the chicory plant, which are unknown outside the Rome area and are served in a dressing of anchovies, crushed garlic, olive oil, and vinegar; *rughetta,* a wilder variety of what is called rucola or arugula in other parts of Italy (and rocket in England) for the peppery nutlike flavor it adds to salads; and the tender, sweet, chopstick-thin wild *asparagi* (asparagus), which appear in early spring and are served with lemon or butter and Parmesan or *alla Bismarck*—with a fried egg on top.

To accompany the meal, try one of the wines from the Castelli Romani, the hills southeast of Rome, with names like Colli Albani, Frascati, and Marino. Most of the house wines served in trattorias come from the Castelli. The whites are very raw, but cheap; the reds are better—among the best are Torre Ercolana and Colle Picchioni.

Many Romans, like other Italians, like to end the meal with a *digestivo,* an alcoholic herbal brew that settles the stomach after the onslaught of three courses. The most common *digestivo* is an *amaro,* which means bitter, and you'd better believe it. *Amari* range from the mildly musty herbal flavor of a Montenegro or an Averna to the cough-medicine-gone-bad taste of the bracing elixir known as Fernet Branca. Nevertheless, they do seem to work at relieving the heaviness.

Other after-dinner drinks include the sweet anise-flavored Sambucca, which is served *alla mosca*—with three *mosce* ("flies") floating in it. These are really coffee beans to crunch on. There are also a wide variety of *grappas* (fruit brandies) that are kept near-frozen in summer and come in bottles full of pieces of fruit.

Romans eat lunch between 1:00 and 3:00 P.M.; dinners don't begin until 8:00. In summer, it is not at all bizarre to start a meal just before midnight.

In between, Romans snack on *pannini* (sandwiches in buns), *tramezzini* (half-sandwiches on slices of bread), or rice croquettes stuffed with mozzarella (*arancini*) or tomato sauce and ground meat (*supplí*) and deep-fried. Take-out pizza is available throughout the day; it's sold by weight in rectangular rather than triangular slices. In addition to the well-known red-sauce pizzas, there is also pizza *bianca* (white pizza), covered only with olive oil and salt or rosemary. Another favorite snack is sandwiches made with slices of *porchetia* (roast suckling pig), sliced before your eyes from the propped-up animal (with his or her head but minus the trotters).

As a rule of thumb, when choosing a restaurant always look for a handwritten daily menu, a fresh display of antipasti on the table inside, and an appreciative local crowd. Avoid places that display menus in five languages or with pages of dishes too numerous to prepare well. Another sure sign of low quality is a place that offers concoctions like pasta *allo champagne* (white wine) or risotto with kiwi.

The tap water in Rome is drinkable everywhere, but most people prefer to drink bottled mineral water (*aqua minerale*) with bubbles (*gassata*) or without (*non gassata*).

Since only the owner of a restaurant or trattoria is entrusted with writing the bill, it often takes more time than you would expect for it to arrive, depending on who and where the owner is. If you are in a hurry, ask for the bill when you order dessert or coffee and remind the waiter when he brings it. Even so, it could take up to 20 minutes or more to get the bill. Heading for the door, as a last-ditch effort, causes a commotion but produces results.

On the bill, in addition to what you ordered, you will find a small cover charge (*pane e coperto*) and a service charge of 10 to 15 percent. If the bill does not include the service charge, add it to what you pay; if it does, one usually leaves an additional Ł1,000 per person on the table for the waiter.

A note on Roman waiters: Roman waiters are a breed apart. They are not there to cajole the public. They are salaried and therefore do not perform for tips. Moreover, they are more or less assured of lifelong employment, so service with a smile is not one of their priorities. Threats to bring your business elsewhere go over their heads. On the plus side, they do not give lengthy biographies or wish you a nice day.

In the following list—arranged according to neighborhoods—a three-course dinner with a house wine in an inexpensive Roman restaurant or trattoria will cost about Ł25,000, in a moderately priced restaurant, Ł27,500–Ł47,500; and in an expensive restuarant, between Ł50,000 and Ł97,500. The very expensive category, such as hotel dining rooms and three-star restaurants, starts at about Ł100,000 and keeps on going.

The Pantheon

On a side street leading from piazza del Gesù toward the Pantheon is **Chianti Corsi**, one of the few inexpensive trattorias in the area that serves good Roman food. Corsi is filled to capacity at lunchtime with politicians, shop assistants, and workmen, so go early. A typical Corsi lunch begins with pasta in an artichoke cream sauce, goes on to roast veal or meat loaf with gravy and roast potatoes flavored with rosemary, and ends with dessert. But you don't have to order all of it. One of the best items on the Corsi menu is the *insalata completa*—an Italian version of Niçoise. Via del Gesù 88. Closed Saturdays and Sundays; lunch only. Tel: 679-08-21.

Da Fortunato is an expensive restaurant just off piazza del Pantheon; it's popular with Italian politicians from the nearby parliament and American journalists eavesdropping on them. Veal from the milk-fed calves in the Campania grazing lands south of Rome is a must to sample. The *scaloppine* (flour-dusted veal filets sautéed in white wine or lemon) at Da Fortunato is always tender. If you order an orange for dessert, the waiter will peel it at your table and turn it into a work of art. Reservations are required in summer, especially if you want one of the outdoor tables with a slice of the Pantheon to look at during your meal. Via del Pantheon 55. Closed Sundays; no credit cards. Tel: 679-27-88.

If you must eat fish in Rome, **La Rosetta**, with a Michelin star to its credit, is a good place to have it. It claims a fresh catch arrives every day from Sicily, but you will pay dearly for that privilege. Forget about spaghetti with clam sauce—that you can get anywhere. Concentrate instead on *tonnarelli alle uova di spigola* (homemade spaghetti with sea-bass roe) or *risotto all'aragosta* (lobster risotto). Via della Rosetta 9. Reservations required; closed Sundays, Monday lunch, and August. Tel: 686-10-02.

Hostaria L'Angoletto is located on a little corner—which is what its name means—in the maze of side streets that leads out of the piazza where the Pantheon holds reign. In addition to serving a variety of seafood and wild mushrooms in season, it is one of the few moderately priced restaurants in the center that serves food after midnight—or as long as the customers keep coming. Piazza Rondanini 51. Closed Mondays. Tel: 686-80-19.

La Cave di Sant'Ignazio is tucked into a corner of the miniature piazza in front of Sant'Ignazio, which has so many entrances and exits that it looks like an opera set. Arrive early to get one of the outdoor candlelit tables to enjoy the show. The owners of this expensive restaurant claim that the fish arrives fresh from the port at Fiumicino every day. Try spaghetti with shrimp, garlic, tomato sauce, and fresh parsley, but leave room for the chocolate soufflé with vanilla sauce, which you should order at the beginning of the meal because it goes very quickly. Piazza Sant'Ignazio 169. Closed Sundays; reservations recommended. Tel: 679-78-21.

Piazza Navona

Many consider **El Toulà** the best all-around luxury-class restaurant in Rome. The decor of softly lit earth tones, comfortable armchairs, and glimmers of color in the antique paintings and Baroque flower arrangements is elegant but discreet. The cuisine is predominantly from the Veneto, so the rice dishes are especially well prepared. One of its

Veneto specialties is *radicchio alla griglia,* grilled radicchio—the long, feathery variety that is grown in Treviso in the Veneto. Via della Lupa 29. Reservations required; closed Saturday lunch, Sundays, and August. Tel: 687-37-50 or 687-34-98; Fax: 687-11-15.

If you join the Sunday morning cappuccino-sipping, newspaper-reading, crowd-watching group in piazza Navona, you'll be glad to know about **Fiammetta**, one of the very few inexpensive trattorias open for lunch on Sundays. Just five minutes from the southern curve of the piazza, Fiammetta makes one of the best eggplant parmigianas in Rome. Get there early (it opens at 12:30) for one of the outdoor tables under an arbor. Piazza Fiammetta 8. Closed Tuesdays. Tel: 687-57-77.

Once a famous inn for the privileged, **Hosteria dell'Orso** has hosted, among others, Dante, Leonardo Da Vinci, and Rabelais. The 13th-century palace still retains much of its medieval splendor, and there is no lack of faded tapestries, gilded mirrors, and red velvet. This is the place to go if you want to dress up and have a special night in a very expensive restaurant. Many diners go from the dinner table to the Cabala discotheque upstairs. Via del Soldati 25. Reservations required; dinner only; closed Sundays. Tel: 686-42-50.

La Maiella specializes in dishes from the Abruzzi region east of Rome, such as *maccheroni all chitarra* (pasta cut into strings by pressing it through a guitar-like cutter)—but its risottos (*verdi,* with spinach, or *fiori di zucca,* with zucchini blossoms) make a visit to this expensive restaurant worthwhile, especially at night when the outdoor tables are crowded with Roman glitterati. Piazza Sant'Apollinare 45. Closed Sundays. Tel: 686-41-47.

Of the restaurants in the piazza, the best—and it is a qualified best at that—is **Mastrostefano** on the east side of the piazza. The view of Bernini's Fountain of the Four Rivers and Borromini's undulating church façade behind it is what puts this place in the expensive category, but the food, especially the *abbacchio* (roast suckling lamb), at least resembles the Roman food you find in less tourist-trodden areas. Piazza Navona. Closed Mondays and the last two weeks in August. Tel: 654-28-55.

Tucked away in a tiny piazza off via dei Coronari, which is lined with elegant antiques stores, **Osteria L'Antiquario** serves refined and unusual dishes that you won't find elsewhere, like *lasagne con melanzane al sugo di anatra* (lasagna with eggplant in duck sauce) or *coscio di anatra alle erbe in casseruola* (herbed thigh of duck in casserole).

The price is high, but the candlelight and surrounding Renaissance palaces make it one of the most intimate outdoor dining experiences in Rome. Piazza San Simeone. Dinner only; reservations recommended; closed Sundays. Tel: 687-96-94.

Next door to the church of Sant'Agostino south of the piazza is the tiny eight-table, family-run **Da Pietro**, but this is not a cheap ma-and-pa operation. The food is expensive but prepared with exquisite care according to old family recipes. Among the best is *manzo al barolo* (very tender beef in a Barolo wine sauce). Via dei Pianellari 19. Closed Sundays. Tel: 686-85-65.

Campo dei Fiori

Besides being set in the ancient diamond-shaped brick ruins of the theater Pompey built to celebrate his triumph in 61 B.C., **Costanza** offers some of the most imaginative Roman cooking in town, two examples of which are *risotto con fiori di zucca* (risotto with zucchini blossoms) and *ravioli con carciofi* (artichoke-stuffed ravioli). The grilled meats are also good in this expensive restaurant—especially *abbacchio scottadito* (tiny grilled lamb ribs), which are best eaten with your fingers. But be careful not to "burn your fingertips," which is what *scottadito* means. Piazza del Paradiso 65. Closed Sundays and August. Tel: 686-17-17 or 654-10-02.

Filetti di Baccalà, in a tiny piazza off via de' Giubbonari, is always filled with young people, especially on Friday nights when they come to taste the Roman specialty for which the restaurant is named—baccalà—battered and deep-fried salt cod filets, which are served at paper-covered communal tables and accompanied by cheap raw Castelli wine. You may never want to eat one again, but the experience is pure Romano. Largo dei Librari 88. Closed Sundays and August. Tel: 686-40-18.

Il Pianeta Terra di Patrizia e Roberto is an elegant, very expensive restaurant run by a Tuscan rugby player and his Sicilian laywer wife. Its inventive, somewhat nouvelle menu has earned it a Michelin star and includes such rarities as *ravioli d'oca al barolo* (ravioli stuffed with goose in wine sauce) and *petto d'oca in salsa di prugne* (breast of goose in plum sauce). Via Arco del Monte 94. Dinners only; closed Mondays and August. Tel: 686-98-93.

Il Drappo means the drape and there are a lot of them, especially on the ceiling, in this expensive Sardinian restaurant. Sisters Angela and Valentina, together with their brother Paolo, have produced loving variations on the hearty cuisine of their native island. Try the *maialino arrosto* (roast piglet) accompanied by the flat, crunchy disk-shaped Sardinian bread called *carta da musica* (sheet music). For dessert try *sebada,* cheese-filled deep-fried dough balls. Vicolo del Malpasso 9. Reservations recommended; closed Sundays. Tel: 687-73-65.

If you're tired of pasta or want just a salad, try **L'Insalata Ricca,** which is next door to Sant'Andrea della Valle, the church in which the first act of Puccini's *Tosca* takes place. Salads come in both small and super sizes in this inexpensive restaurant. One super has olives, feta cheese, and artichoke hearts. There are also some pasta dishes in case you are still hungry afterward. Largo dei Chiavari 85. Closed Wednesdays; no credit cards; no smoking indoors. Tel: 654-36-56. There is also a **L'Insalata Ricca II** in piazza Pasquino, near piazza Navona; closed Mondays; Tel: 68-30-78-81.

If you get to **Hosteria Romanesca** early enough to get a table outdoors, you can get a moderately priced lunch and watch the vendors dismantle the outdoor food market in the campo, which closes shop every day (except Sundays) at about 1:30. As its name indicates, this trattoria serves heaping bowls of traditional Roman home cooking that has not been doctored to appear upscale or thinned down to accommodate tourists. Campo dei Fiori. Closed Sundays. Tel: 654-89-73.

Da Giovanni ar Galleto is on a street that connects campo dei Fiori with piazza Farnese and its magnificent Renaissance palace, which you can admire from an outdoor table. This moderately priced trattoria specializes in game and wild mushrooms (also truffles when they are in season), so be sure to try the *gallina faraona* (guinea hen) or the *galletto alla diavola,* a whole Cornish hen flattened and spiced and then baked to crispy perfection. Piazza Farnese 102. Closed Sundays; no credit cards. Tel: 686-17-14.

At **Pallaro** there is a fixed menu that includes three courses and wine for Ł26,000. The menu changes each day and the seating is family style, but the price is hard to beat in Rome these days. Largo del Pallaro 15. Closed Mondays. Tel: 654-14-88.

One of the liveliest places for outdoor dining is **Pierluigi,** on a side street near piazza Farnese. The *ravioli di pesce* (ravioli stuffed with seafood) and the *straccietti* (strips of sautéed beef) with raw *rughetta* on top are reason enough to reserve a table, but you may also be attracted by the fact that Pierluigi is one of the few expensive restaurants in Rome in which you can find homemade chocolate cake with whipped cream for dessert. Piazza dei Ricci 144. Closed Mondays; reservations recommended. Tel: 686-13-02 or 686-87-17.

In spite of what Shakespeare or Hollywood may have claimed, Julius Caesar was not killed in the Forum on the Ides of March in 44 B.C., but rather in the Teatro di Pompeo, because the Curia in the Forum where the Roman Senate usually met was closed for renovation (sound familiar?). The dining room of the **Da Pancrazio** restaurant is housed in the vaulted brickwork remains of the same Teatro di Pompeo, which once covered the whole area from the campo to largo Argentina. The ambience tends to be better than the food in this expensive restaurant, so it's best to stick to standards like *spaghetti alla carbonara.* Piazza del Biscione 92. Closed Wednesdays. Tel: 686-12-46.

Trevi Fountain

The pomposity of the owner of **Al Moro** was legendary even before he played to type in Fellini's *Satyricon,* but it has never stopped Fellini and a host of other luminaries from sampling what many people consider the best-prepared *funghi porcini* in Rome. The noise is unbearable, the waiters are schooled in the owner's protective disdain, and the smoke will kill you—but the wild mushrooms in this expensive trattoria are almost worth dying for. Vicolo delle Bollette 13. Closed Sundays and August; reservations recommended. Tel: 678-34-95.

Al Piccolo Arancio is on a *vicolo* (alleyway) off via del Lavatore, around the corner from the fountain. It has the most reliable menu of the eateries in this heavily trafficked area and offers fresh fish on Tuesdays and Fridays. Try *fusilli alla melanzana* (corkscrew pasta with an eggplant and tomato sauce) and the lemon mousse for dessert. Vicolo Scanderberg 112. Closed Mondays and August. Tel: 678-61-39. The same owners have two other moderately priced restaurants, **Da Settimo all'Arancio** (via dell'Arancio 50; Tel: 687-61-19) and **Arancio d'Oro** (via Monte d'Oro 17; Tel: 686-50-26), which also serves pizza. Both are closed on weekends.

The Colosseum

La Taverna dei Quaranta (The Tavern of the Forty) is a cooperative run by 40 would-be actors who take turns operating it. Located about a block away from the Colosseum, it has a rustic trattoria atmosphere and is popular with workmen and students. The offerings tend to be hearty Roman standards like *polenta* or *carbonara,* but there are always some interesting new ideas like risotto with radicchio. Via Claudia 24. Closed Sundays; no reservations; moderately priced. Tel: 73-62-96.

Osteria da Nerone is located on a hill just above the Colosseum and is one of the few moderately priced restaurants in the area that still serve good food. Try, for example, the homemade ravioli stuffed with ricotta cheese and spinach, garnished with melted butter and tiny sage leaves. The house specialty, *fettucine al Nerone* (ribbon pasta with peas, mushrooms, egg, and salami), seems well suited to an emperor (Nero) who is remembered for his excesses and whose house lies under the hill on which the restaurant sits. Via delle Terme di Tito 96. Closed Sundays. Tel: 474-52-07.

The Ghetto

Da Giggetto is the least fancy of the Ghetto restaurants and the most reasonably priced. It serves all the traditional Roman-Jewish specialties, mostly batter-dipped and deep-fried fish and vegetables, as well as *carciofi alla giudia* (a Jerusalem artichoke that is flattened so it looks like a chrysanthemum and then deep-fried until it is both crunchy and tender—a hard balance to achieve, and sometimes the artichokes are hard and greasy). The best of the offerings fried in this manner, however, is *mozzarella in carrozza,* tiny pieces of bread soaked in broth, dipped in egg, filled with mozzarella, and deep-fried to a golden crisp. Via del Portico d'Ottavia 22. Closed Mondays. Tel: 686-11-05.

The most celebrated restaurant in the Ghetto is **Piperno**, which is on a little hill in the corner of a tiny piazza next to the palazzo where Beatrice Cenci plotted her famous parricide. Piperno is pricey, but if you want exemplary (though non-kosher) versions of the Jewish classics such as *fritto misto* (a mixture of batter-fried delicacies) in a quiet, charming setting, this is the place. For dessert, ponder *le palle di nonno* (grandfather's balls), two hot cream puffs filled with sweetened ricotta cheese and chocolate bits. Monte de' Cenci 9. Closed Mondays, Sunday dinner, and August. Tel: 654-06-29.

Al Pompiere is the place to go if you want to sample one of the glories of Ghetto cuisine: *fiori di zucca ripieni* (batter-fried zucchini blossoms stuffed with tiny pieces of mozzarella cheese and anchovies). This moderately priced restaurant shares a part of the *piano nobile* of the Cenci Palace, which has several legends surrounding it and was a frequent goal of the English Romantic poets, who saw in Beatrice

Cenci one of their ideal tragic heroines. If that doesn't interest you, consider that this is the only place in Rome that serves a pasta dish as delicate and tasty as *pennette* with lemon sauce. Via Santa Maria dei Calderari 38. Closed Sundays. Tel: 868-83-77.

The Roman artichoke is bigger and tenderer than those found in other countries. Nowhere is it better prepared than at **Da Evangelista,** where they do not deep-fry it, as they do elsewhere in the Ghetto, but rather flatten it between two bricks and then bake it in the oven—a method the owner's grandfather invented. The result is light and greaseless and melts in your mouth. Via delle Zoccolette 11. Closed Sundays and August; expensive. Tel: 687-58-10.

The excellent food and charming outdoor setting recommend the expensive **Vecchia Roma** in spite of the waiters' rudeness, which is so extreme that it has become a joke among customers. It is less amusing when they tamper with the bill. Nevertheless, the candlelight, the looming chiaroscuro background of the surrounding palaces and churches, and especially the sorbets made from whole fresh fruit are so memorable that they often make people more forgiving than usual. Piazza Campitelli 18. Reservations recommended; closed Wednesdays. Tel: 656-46-04.

Trastevere

If you prefer fish restaurants with a refined setting and excellent quality, at **Alberto Ciarlà** you will find everything from Maine lobster to Scottish salmon and Normandy oysters. The olive oil and wine (Bianco di Velletri Vigna Ciarlà) come from the owner's own property, and the sea bass with almonds and raw sea bream with ginger are just two of his excellent creations. Piazza San Cosimato 40. Reservations recommended; dinner only; closed Sundays; very expensive. Tel: 581-86-68; Fax: 688-43-77.

When **Augusto** fills up, which is almost every day and night in summer, the customers are expected to take things into their own hands, which often means getting your own bread and wine or replacing the paper tablecloths. The food in this family-run trattoria near piazza Santa Maria in Trastevere is hearty, healthy, and heaping and the price low, but don't go if you are in a hurry. Piazza de Rienzi 15. Closed Sundays. Tel: 688-57-21.

Ciak gets its name from the owners' passion for the movies (*ciak* is the "clack" sound the "take" board makes). It also explains the old movie posters and photos on the walls. This moderately priced restaurant near piazza Trilussa specializes in Tuscan cuisine. Start with an appetizer of mixed *crostini* (circles of bread spread with pâté, olive paste, or mushrooms). Then move on to *ribollita*—a hearty Tuscan vegetable soup with pieces of bread on top. A Florentine steak (with olive oil, lemon, and black pepper) could come next, or *spiedini* (skewers of grilled meat, sausage, bay leaf, and peppers). Vicolo del Cinque 21. Dinner only; closed Mondays. Tel: 589-47-74.

Da Lucia is a moderately priced trattoria located in a part of Trastevere that has not yet become so gentrified that it has nothing left but fake charm. The surrounding apartments and street-level shops, often festooned with the colors of rival soccer teams, testify to the fact that it is still a vibrant neighborhood of working-class Romans, and the menu reflects their interests. One of the best items, *penne all'arrabbiata* (short pasta in a spicy hot tomato and garlic sauce, garnished with fresh parsley), is a common Roman dish—rarely prepared as well these days as it is at Da Lucia. Via del Mattonato 2; Closed Mondays. Tel: 580-36-01.

At the moderately priced **Osteria-Pizzeria da Anna** just off viale Trastevere, you can eat outdoors or inside the air-conditioned dining room. The menu features all the Roman standards, which are prepared by the owner and served by her two daughters. Papa makes the pizzas at a wood-burning oven. Try *fettucine alla burina* (ribbon pasta with peas, tomatoes, mushrooms, and ham) or pizza with gorgonzola and rughetta. Via San Francesco a Ripa 57. Closed Thursdays. Tel: 589-39-92.

Eating in Trastevere's beautiful neighborhood living room, piazza Santa Maria in Trastevere, is a very expensive affair nowadays, but just around the corner is the moderately priced **Hosteria-Pizzeria Der Belli**. The view from the outdoor tables is not as picturesque as it is in the piazza, but the food is always good and sometimes inventive—like *formaggio arrosto con miele*—grilled cheese steaks with coarse honey. Piazza Sant'Apollonia. Closed Mondays. Tel: 580-37-82.

Il Ponentino ia named after the cool evening breeze that blows into Rome from the Alban hills in late afternoon in summer, so alfresco dining is one of the benefits of this inexpensive restaurant, which serves both pasta dishes and pizzas (in the evening). Try its *spaghetti alla Trasteverina*, made with cream, mushrooms, and peas. Piazza del Drago 10. Closed Mondays. Tel: 588-06-88.

One of the best restaurants in Rome in the moderately priced category is not Roman, but Sicilian. You will be hard bent to find better pasta in the capital than **La Gensola**'s rigatoni with broccoli, or its penne with eggplant and tomatoes, or the exquisite Arab-Sicilian *pasta con le sarde* with sardines, pine nuts, and raisins. The *secondi* in this small trattoria off piazza in Piscinula are typical Sicilian dishes like grilled swordfish or *involtini* (braised veal rolls stuffed with bread crumbs, parsley, and cheese). It also makes the lightest greaseless *calamari fritti* anywhere. Via della Gensola 15. Closed Sundays; reservations recommended. Tel: 581-63-12.

For many tourists, dining in Trastevere still means **Sabatini**, right in the piazza facing the church and sparkling fountain. The main dining room has beamed ceilings and frescoed walls, but even better are the crowded and noisy outdoor tables where you can indulge in some people-watching between courses. The food at Sabatini and its twin around the corner, **Sabatini II** (closed Tuesdays), is not any better than at less expensive Roman restaurants, and nothing on the menu has ever won critical acclaim, but what you really pay for is the view. Piazza Santa Maria in Trastevere. Closed Wednesdays. Tel: 581-20-26.

The full name of **Tentativo** reads like the title of a Lina Wertmuller film: *Tentativo di Descrizione di un Banchetto a Roma* (Attempt at a Description of a Banquet in Rome). The creative and very expensive menu includes such un-Roman entrees as *ravioli d'anatra* (duck-filled ravioli) and *fileto di manzo affumicato con funghi porcini* (smoked beef filet with porcini mushrooms). The setting is intimate and free of the usual operating-room lighting that abounds in most Roman eateries. Via delle Luce 5. Dinner only; closed Sundays and August; reservations necessary. Tel: 589-52-34.

Piazza del Popolo

The late Roman restaurateur Alfredo, self-proclaimed king of fettucine and creator of *fettucine all'Alfredo,* was popular with American tourists from the day he served his pasta dish to Douglas Fairbanks and Mary Pickford with a golden spoon and fork. **Alfredo alla Scrofa** continues the tradition (for much more than the fettucine, butter, cheese, and cream could ever cost) with what they say are the original utensils, and with a lot more show than class. (The drama is enhanced by live music.) Via della Scrofa 104. Closed Tuesdays. Tel: 654-01-63.

The location of **Casina Valadier**, on the Pincio Hill in the Villa Borghese gardens and overlooking piazza del Popolo, makes its outdoor terrace the perfect place for Sunday brunch. The prices are high but the view of the domes and rooftops of Rome is perfect, as is the carefully prepared *caprese* (Capri-style) salad of mozzarella balls, cured ham, and fresh tomatoes dressed with basil and olive oil. Save room for the vanilla ice cream topped with bits of caramelized orange peel. Piazza Valadier. Closed Mondays; reservations recommended for Sunday lunch. Tel: 679-20-83.

Dal Bolognese, right in piazza del Popolo, specializes in the cuisine of Bologna, which many say is Italy's finest. The pasta is all homemade and you should order it *al ragù,* with the meat sauce typical of Bologna. Though *cotolette alla bolognese* (breaded veal cutlet covered with a slice of prosciutto and melted cheese) is a standard, also try the *bollito misto,* a sampling of boiled meats and poultry accompanied by a green sauce of parsley, capers, and chopped onion. Piazza del Popolo 1. Closed Sunday dinner and Mondays, reservations recommended. Tel: 361-14-26.

La Buca di Ripetta, a moderately priced family-run trattoria two blocks from piazza del Popolo, is one of the few in that category that is air-conditioned and open for Sunday lunch. Go early because there are no reservations and it is small. Ask about the daily specials, which do not appear on the menu. On any Thursday, try the traditional Roman Thursday standard, *gnocchi* (potato dumplings). Via di Ripetta 36. Closed Sunday evening, Mondays, and August. Tel: 321-93-91.

Al Ristorante 59, on a street leading out of the piazza, is a fine clublike restaurant popular with journalists and businessmen who often meet there for interviews or power lunches. The most popular item on the excellent Bolognese menu is *tortelli di zucca,* little pockets of pasta filled with pumpkin squash and garnished with butter and sage leaves—it's the only place in Rome where you can get them. Via Angelo Brunetti 59. Closed Sundays; no credit cards. Tel: 321-90-19.

Piazza di Spagna
Tucked away on a side street behind the American Express office is **Alla Rampa,** where lunch is an enormous smorgasbord that includes everything from stuffed olives to eggplant parmigiana. This moderately priced restaurant also has pasta dishes and outdoor tables under the typical Roman canvas *ombrelloni* (umbrellas). If you want to sit outdoors, go early, because La Rampa does not take reservations. Piazza Mignanelli 18. Closed Sundays and Monday lunch. Tel: 678-26-21.

Nino, on a street leading out of the piazza, is what many consider the finest Tuscan restaurant in Rome. Its white bean soup (*zuppa di fagioli*) steamed in bottles (*al fiasco*) is a perennial favorite of regulars, especially in winter. Nino also makes excellent *bistecca alla fiorentina* (a huge charcoal-grilled steak with a bit of olive oil, lemon, and black pepper)—to be eaten with the excellent house Chianti *a consumo,* meaning you pay only for what you drink from the carafe on the table. Via Borgognona 11. Closed Sundays and August; expensive. Tel: 679-56-76.

Via Margutta, off via del Babuino, which leads out of the piazza in the direction of piazza del Popolo, is lined with artists' ateliers and is the site of an annual art fair in May. The small vegetarian restaurant **Margutta** has a warm, inviting atmosphere. The entrées, like tagliatelle with avocado and mushrooms, are generally expensive, but at lunch there is an economically priced buffet that includes an interesting assortment of vegetables and cold pastas. Via Margutta 119. Closed Sundays and August. Tel: 678-60-33.

Otello alla Concordia, on another side street leading out of the piazza, is a moderately priced trattoria that provides both indoor seating and outdoor tables beneath a vine-covered pergola. It serves classic Roman dishes, with a few concessions from other parts of Italy, and is very popular with office workers and shop assistants in the area. The cannelloni—always a chancey dish because you never know when it was prepared—is excellent here, but save room for *melone e lampone*—fresh melon with raspberries for dessert. Via della Croce 81. Closed Sundays; no reservations. Tel. 679-11-78 or 678-14-54.

The Hotel d'Inghilterra has opened its own expensive restaurant, **Roman Garden**, which has quickly become a popular spot for business lunches. Among the refined Italian dishes it serves are *insalatina di sogliola e salmone con spinaci* (a sole and salmon spinach salad) and *tortelli di anatra al tartufo* (duck-filled dumplings with truffles). Via Bocca di Leone 14. Open seven days. Tel: 67-21-61.

Via Veneto

A creative menu, flawless service, and an intelligent wine list have earned **Andrea**, an expensive diplomats' and business-men's restaurant, a faithful clientele. Among its best dishes are lobster bisque and *straccetti di manzo con porcini e tartufi* (strips of sautéed beef with porcini mushrooms and truffles). One eats very well here. Via Sardegna 26. Closed Sundays and Monday lunch. Tel: 482-18-91.

The hearty specialties of Emilia-Romagna are served in a

quiet country trattoria-like setting at **Colline Emiliane** near piazza Barberini at the foot of via Veneto. Homemade pasta (rolled out before your eyes) is what to order here, or one of the boiled meat dinners that are a signature piece of the region. There is an excellent selection of Lambrusco and other Emilia wines. Via degli Avignonesi 22. Closed Fridays. Tel: 481-75-38.

The best thing to do at **Piccolo Abruzzo** is to let the owner, Eduardo, keep bringing the food until you can't eat anymore. That's what he'll do anyway. He usually passes around the tables with a bowl of whatever has just come out of the kitchen (shrimp risotto or spaghetti and eggplant) and insists that you try a little. You can stick to the standard menu, but the bill in this moderately priced trattoria featuring food from Abruzzo won't be that different. Via Sicilia 237. Closed Saturday lunch. Tel: 482-01-76.

For those looking for an "international" atmosphere, **Sans Souci** is the very expensive answer. A black-and-gold decor sets the scene for elaborate Italian-based dishes, often heavy-handed, such as the *ravioli di pesce* (fish-stuffed ravioli), which come swimming in a lake of heavy cream. But Michelin has given the filet of sole with strawberries a star. Via Sicilia 20. Dinner only; reservations recommended; closed Mondays and August. Tel: 482-18-14.

Others

The **Abruzzi**, located at the far end of piazza Santi Apostoli, a short walk from piazza Venezia, is an inexpensive restaurant that consistently serves well-prepared, dependable dishes from both Rome and the Abruzzo region east of Rome. You will always find here, for example, a delicious homemade *stracciatella* (chicken soup with ribbons of egg batter and Parmesan cheese floating in it). Via del Vaccaro 1, Closed Saturdays. Tel: 679-38-97.

In the warren of alleys that constitutes the area between corso Vittorio and the bridge to Castel Sant'Angelo is the tiny (seven-table) inexpensive trattoria called **Alfredo e Ada**, which remains one of the few trattorias in the old-fashioned "ugly, banal look" that has not been given a new glazed-over white-pine update. The quality of the good old-fashioned Roman food like *spezzatino* (veal stew) or *seppie con piselli* (baby squid with peas) hasn't changed either. There is no menu, and Ada does everything from cooking to serving to writing up the bill, so relax and enjoy it. Via Banchi Nuovi 14. Closed Sundays; no credit cards; no telephone.

Al Ceppo is located in Rome's elegant residential area,

Parioli, near piazza Ungheria. The atmosphere is rustic: wood-beamed ceilings, dark wood tables, and an open-grill fireplace stocked with tree stumps, which is what *ceppo* means. The food is geared toward pleasing Italian families out for a good (and expensive) meal who expect entrées that are a little more special than what they prepare at home—such as cannelloni stuffed with pumpkin or giant ravioli filled with eggplant purée. Via Panama 2. Closed Mondays. Tel: 841-96-96 or 855-13-79.

Keep **Ambasciata d'Abruzzo** in mind when you are ready for a big meal. For a blanket price of ₤30,000 including wine, you can eat all you want and the waiters will still keep bringing the food. After a while you don't taste anything, but the outlay is impressive and induces lots of camaraderie with fellow diners, who exchange friendly grimaces and groans. When you sit down, there is a basket of sausages and bread already waiting. Skip it and make some selections instead from the antipasti table—keeping in mind that you will have to sample at least three pastas, two meat dishes, and as many desserts as your heart can take before you finish. Via Pietro Tacchini (in Parioli). The best way to get there is by cab; closed Sundays. Tel: 807-82-56.

One of the best all-time, old-time restaurants in Rome is **Cannavota**, near San Giovanni in Lateran. Its specialty is seafood, but the dish that has kept generations of neighborhood families coming regularly to this moderately priced restaurant is *bucatini alla cannavota,* pasta with a secret tomato-and-cream seafood sauce that is mildly spicy and delicious. Piazza San Giovanni in Laterano. Closed Wednesdays; reservations recommended. Tel: 77-50-07.

For a special evening in Rome, have dinner on a barge in the Tiber at **Canto del Riso**, just below the Ponte Cavour bridge. There are both outdoor and indoor tables, but get one of the outdoor candlelit ones and watch the sun go down while you sip an aperitivo. The food will pale by comparison, but try the seafood risotto or the salad with mozzarella, fresh tomatoes, and basil. Lungotevere Mellini 7. Closed Mondays; reservations recommended in summer; expensive if you order fish; Tel: 361-04-30.

The chicest place these days to sample the various Roman innards is **Checchino dal 1887**, auspiciously located across the street from the former slaughterhouses in the newly gentrified section of Testaccio, near the Ostiense train station. The owners claim their ancestors invented the Roman specialty *coda alla vaccinara* (oxtail stew), which has more bone than tail to it, but the pasta garnished with the same sauce is another matter. Checchino has two sommeliers in charge of one of the best wine cellars in Rome, downstairs carved out of the mountain of pottery shards that gives the area its name. And for dessert? Gorgonzola and coarse honey with a glass of very good Marsala. Via di Monte Testaccio 30. Closed Sunday dinner, Mondays, and August; reservations recommended in summer; expensive. Tel: 574-63-18.

Coriolano, just off via Nomentana, is an expensive classic Roman restaurant near Porta Pia that has kept its fan club of gourmets because of its absolute adherence to quality and freshness. The very small dining room is decorated with antiques the owner's father collected from Switzerland and Germany. The daughter speaks English and will explain the menu, which includes perfectly prepared items like *tagliolini all'aragosta* (very thin fettucine with lobster sauce). Coriolano is especially proud of its secret way of preparing porcini mushrooms. It's a shame the restaurant ruins it by passing out cigars and allowing smoking everywhere. Via Ancona 14. Closed Sundays and August; reservations recommended. Tel: 855-11-22.

Severino a Piazza Zama is beyond the Baths of Caracalla, but many Romans and travellers alike go there to sample the Roman dish it is justly famous for—*saltimbocca alla romana* (literally, "jump-in-your-mouth" filets of veal covered with prosciutto and cheese and then braised). If you order this dish, you get to take the decorated plate home with you. Piazza Zama 5. Closed Sunday dinner, Mondays, and August; reservations advised; expensive. Tel: 700-08-72.

La Campana, on a side street of the same name off via della Scrofa, began as an inn 500 years ago and has been consistently serving high-quality Roman dishes for more than 100 years. That makes it one of the oldest continual in-service restaurants in Rome. The food is still good. Take, for example, *vignarola,* a thick vegetable stew that is a meal in itself. But its pasta with artichoke cream sauce and home-made ricotta cheesecake are what have won this restaurant a loyal clientele. Vicolo della Campana 18. Closed Mondays and August. Tel: 687-52-73.

An Alternative to Restaurant Dining

If you find the traditional Roman three-course meal overwhelming for both your stomach and your pocketbook, one solution is to eat in wine shops that serve food (*enoteche*). These are not wine *bars,* but wine *stores* that have converted part of their establishment into a lunchroom. Most have only a few tables with paper tablecloths, a limited menu, and no service, but others have taken the idea upmarket by adding creative menus, waiter service, and a sophisticated ambience.

Most enoteche are open only for lunch, but some serve food until late at night. Another benefit is that you can try different wines and buy a bottle of what you like on the way out. Enoteche are quick, cheap, and ideal for those times when you want more than a sandwich or a pizza and less than a three-course meal.

Da Benito (via dei Falegnami 14; lunch only; closed Sundays) is a tiny one-room shop in the Ghetto with a few tables and a counter. The food is hearty (*gnocchi*—potato dumplings—every Thursday) and cheap and the atmosphere is crowded and harried. At **313 Cavour** (via Cavour 313; closed Sundays), however, you can take your time and choose from a wide selection of salads, pâtés, and *torte rustiche*—vegetable pies made from organically grown vegetables. The same is true at **Cul de Sac** (piazza Pasquino 73; closed Mondays; Tel: 654-10-94), near piazza Navona, where the wine bottles lie in racks over the tables and the red lentil or white bean soup is especially good with the warm home-made bread.

The most recent incarnation of the eat-in wine shop is a model in which the food is as important as the sale of wine. These smart in-places cater to young professionals and are more expensive. Among the best are **Spiriti** (via di Sant'Eustachio 5; closed Sundays), which features combination platters of daily specials like Greek salad, Sardinian lasagna, or grilled eggplant; and **Semidivino** (via Alessandra 130; closed Sundays), which is very upscale and offers such rarities as smoked breast of goose, sturgeon carpaccio, and rabbit pâté with truffles. But the best of the new enoteche is **La Bottega del Vino** (via Santa Maria del Pianto 9; lunch only; closed Saturdays and Sundays), where the wine cellar has been converted into a smart dining area and the menu features items like smoked salmon rolls filled with crabmeat and ricotta cheesecake from a bakery in the nearby Ghetto.

Pizzerias

The outdoor pizzerias at the beginning of viale Trastevere are still as loud and blindingly lit as they were in Fellini's *Roma*, but they are the place to go if you want to sample the Roman version of Italy's most famous culinary invention. Roman pizza is flat, wafer-thin, and crunchy, because it is usually baked in a wood-burning oven so that the crust blisters and it acquires a slightly smoky flavor. In addition to the standards—*margarita* (tomato sauce, cheese, and basil), *napoletana* (cheese and anchovies), *funghi* (mushroom), and *salsicce* (sausage)—Romans have invented *la capricciosa,* a capricious blend of just about everything, including a hard-boiled egg. Most pizzerias do not open for lunch and do not take reservations.

Among the best—and therefore the most popular and most crowded—are **Baffetto** (via del Governo Vecchio 114; closed Sundays and August) near piazza Navona, where the lines are long but the turnover fast; **Da Ivo** in Trastevere (via San Francesco a Ripa 157; closed Tuesdays), which is well known for its meat-and-sausage–filled *calzone* (covered pizza); **Da Gildo** in Trastevere near Porta Settimiana (via della Scala 31; closed Sundays), which charges more but serves large pizzas with unusual toppings like shrimp or salmon; **La Capricciosa** at the end of via Condotti (largo dei Lombardi 8; closed Tuesdays), which claims to have invented the *pizza capricciosa* described above; **Le Volte,** located in a frescoed 16th-century palazzo (piazza Rondanini 47; closed Tuesdays) near the Pantheon; **Corallo** (via del Corallo 10; closed Mondays) off via Governo Vecchio, which also serves *foccacia;* **Osteria Picchioni** off via Nazionale (via del Boschetto 16; closed Wednesdays), which serves very expensive pizzas with truffles and sun-dried tomatoes; **Tulipano Nero,** a boisterous, busy outdoor pizzeria in Trastevere (piazza San Cosimato; closed Wednesdays) that serves large, inexpensive pizzas of all kinds; and **Taberna Piscinula** in piazza in Piscinula (number 50; closed Mondays), which is very upscale and expensive and offers far-out toppings like corn niblets or crabmeat at outside tables or in an air-conditioned inside room.

—Louis Inturrisi

NIGHTLIFE

Nightlife in the Eternal City is not as varied as it is in other, more cosmopolitan capitals. The symphony still lacks a permanent auditorium, there is no national ballet company, art galleries are few and unvaried, most cinemas are expensive and closed in summer, and the museum situation is legendary. However, recently the situation has shown positive signs of improvement. Wildcat strikes, inferior quality, and totally inconvenient ticketing, which often discouraged people in the past, occur less frequently; many theaters have adopted air-conditioning and computerized ticketing; the opera has a new inventive impresario; and there is even a museum (Palazzo delle Esposizione on Via Nazionale) that stays open until 11:00 P.M.

Rather than looking at after-hours as a time for partying, young Roman professionals put on their best clothes, take a walk or—less often these days—a ride into the center, have an aperitif at one stop, a meal at another, and a digestivo at a third, then go to a disco or to a piano bar to hear live music.

Activity in cafés and bars starts picking up after dinner at around 10:00 P.M. Piano bars and clubs begin to get lively at midnight, and nightclubs don't even open until after midnight in summer. Most of the clubs charge a cover, and some require a membership fee. In summer Roman nightlife can easily extend into the wee hours of the morning.

Information on what's happening in Rome can be found in Italian in the Rome daily *Il Messaggero* and in the Thursday supplement of *La Repubblica,* or in English in two biweekly English-language magazines, *Wanted in Rome* and *Metropolitana.* Both of the latter are available at kiosks and English-language bookstores.

Opera, Symphony, Theater
The **Rome Opera** season runs from December to May (box office: piazza Beniamino Gigli near via Viminale; Tel: 675-957-25 in English); in summer it mounts productions outdoors at the Terme di Caracalla, which always include a spectacular version of Verdi's *Aida.* The **Accademia di Santa Cecilia** symphony orchestra (via delle Conciliazione in front of the Vatican; Tel: 654-10-44) has regular concerts from October to June and moves outdoors to the Villa Giulia near the Modern Art Museum in summer. The **Teatro Argentina,** in largo Argentina (Tel: 654-46-01), mounts stage productions in Italian of classical and modern playwrights like Pirandello and Goldoni from October to June. Musicals in both Italian and English (by international touring companies) are performed at **Teatro Sistina** near the top of the Spanish Steps (via Sistina 129; Tel: 482-68-41) regularly throughout the year.

Cinema
All foreign films in Italy are dubbed. But the dubbers are carefully chosen (and sometimes become celebrities themselves), so that you would swear Woody Allen had grown up in Italy. Nevertheless, films are shown daily in English exclusively at the **Pasquino Cinema** (vicolo del Piede 19; Tel: 580-36-22) just off piazza Santa Maria in Trastevere, and on

Mondays at the **Alcazar Cinema** (via Cardinale Merry del Val 14; Tel: 588-00-99) near piazza Sonnino in Trastevere. Cinemas do not open until around 4:00 P.M. and close for lack of air-conditioning and customers in August.

Cafés and Bars

The mecca of serious people-watching has shifted recently from the bars on via Veneto like **Café de Paris** (number 90) or **Doney** (number 145) to **Rosati** and **Canova** on the curve of piazza del Popolo. The men here tend to be Roman, the women foreign. The opposite is generally true of the bars on via Veneto. In Trastevere, **Caffè-Bar di Marzio** in piazza Santa Maria is packed at night and on Sunday mornings, when you can't see the customers for the open newspapers. The best cappuccino in Rome is still at **Bar Sant'Eustachio** in the piazza of the same name near the Pantheon, but you have to tell the waiter *senza zucchero* if you don't like it sweet. Young professionals and students like **Vineria** in campo dei Fiori (number 15), whereas would-be actors and actresses prefer **Bar della Pace** in front of Cortona's fanciful Santa Maria della Pace or its new rival, **Bar Bramante**, across the street. Purists still go to **Caffè Greco** on via Condotti (number 86) near the Spanish Steps to revel in the atmosphere that once attracted the likes of Mark Twain, Dickens, and Buffalo Bill. At **Biancaneve** (Snow White) in piazza Paoli at the end of corso Vittorio, a young crowd sits at night on the side facing the illuminated Castel Sant'Angelo and munches on *mele stregate* (bewitched apples)—balls of *zabaione* ice cream coated in dark chocolate. Two cafés that have good panoramic views are **Cafe Ciampini**, across from the Villa Medici at the top of the Spanish Steps, and **Zodiaco**, on Monte Mario near the Hilton Hotel, which has a spectacular overview of Rome (viale di Parco Mellini 90).

Gelaterias

In Juvenal's time, Roman citizens used to collect snow from the foot of the outlying hills and mix it with honey and fruit to make libations they called *nix dulcis*—sweet snow. Modern Romans do not travel quite so far in their pursuit of *gelato,* but they are still very particular about how and where they enjoy their sweet snow. Rome, in fact, holds the title for ice cream consumption in Italy—more than five gallons per person. In summer it is part of the *passeggiata* (ritual evening stroll) to wind up at one of the following crowded gelaterias, currently considered among the best. (Remember, they are all closed on Monday.)

The mecca for serious gelato eaters is the via del Pantheon, a crooked street that leads out of piazza del Pantheon. Home of four of the best gelaterias in Rome, it has been nicknamed "ice cream alley." The first—and best—is **Fiocco di Neve** (number 51), which offers a limited number of fresh homemade flavors as well as a few in which rice has been added. Try *riso alle fragole,* which combines strawberry ice cream and rice. Farther down the opposite side of the street (which changes names) is **Gelateria della Palma** (via della Maddalena 20), a slick, high-tech gelateria that specializes in exotic fruit-flavored ices. Continuing to the end of via della Maddalena and turning right will bring you to **Giolitti** (via degli Uffici del Vicario 40), one of the oldest and most respected ice-cream parlors in Rome. Its *coppa olimpica* is an expensive combination of ice creams, sherbets, and whipped cream and a wafer chimney that weighs in at half a kilo.

Elsewhere in Rome, **Tre Scalini**, in piazza Navona, is justly famous for its *tartufo,* a ball of rich dark chocolate ice cream that includes chunks of even richer chocolate and a cherry in the middle, all smothered under dollops of whipped cream.

Other gelaterias in the center where you can find fresh homemade gelato are **Gelofestival** in Trastevere (viale Trastevere 27), which also has ice-cream sandwiches; **Pasticceria Cecere** (via San Francesco a Ripa 153) in Trastevere, which is famous for its *zabaione;* **Fassi** at via Nomentana 127; **Al Ristoro della Salute** (behind the Colosseum), which also makes fresh-fruit milkshakes; **Bar Europea** in piazza San Lorenzo, where you can get Sicilian specialties like *cassata* ice cream; and **Alberto Pica** (via della Seggiola), between largo Argentina and the Garibaldi bridge.

As an alternative to gelato, try a *granita* (crushed ice that has been made from fresh fruit juice) or a *grattachecca* (shaved ice over which a variety of syrups or fruit juices are poured). Most bars have *granite* in summer, and you will find *grattachecche* at the kiosks along the Tiber. A good way to lift flagging spirits is to order a *granita di caffè,* a coffee ice topped with whipped cream, or a *granita di limone,* with fresh lemon juice. **Tazza d'Oro**, at via degli Orfani 84, near the Pantheon, makes the best of both.

Piano Bars and Live-Music Clubs

For live music the choices are wide and scattered throughout the city. **Big Mama** (vicolo San Francesco a Ripa 18, in Trastevere), true to its name, is the leading jazz club in

Rome, but there are many others. The **Mississippi Jazz Club** (borgo Angelico 16, near the Vatican), **Music Inn** (largo dei Fiorentini 3, off via Giulia), and **Billie Holiday Jazz Club** (via degli Orti di Trastevere 43, in Trastevere) are all just as well established. **Saint Louis** (via del Cardello 13/a, near the Colosseum) is still enormously popular, but lately has been displaced by **Caffè Latino** (via di Monte Testaccio 96, in the trendy Testaccio neighborhood) as the current favorite.

For other kinds of music, there's **Four Green Fields** (via Morin 40, near the Vatican) for Irish music; **Yes Brazil** (via San Francesco a Ripa 103, Trastevere) for Brazilian; **Makumba** (via degli Olimpionici 19, near the ponte Flaminio) for African reggae and salsa (weekends only); and **Folkstudio** (via Sacchi 3, in Trastevere) for folk.

Birrerias

Romans are not about to forsake *vino,* but beer (*birra*) is becoming a popular drink, especially in summer. Imported beer is expensive; Italian brands like Nastro Azzurro and Peroni are less expensive but not as good. Nevertheless, an evening in a crowded Roman *birreria* can be a boisterous, rowdy, fun-loving affair. One of the most popular these days is **Birreria della Scala** in Trastevere (piazza della Scala 58; closed Wednesdays), which has live music and serves pasta as well. Other lively birrerie are **Birreria Bavarese** (via Vittoria 47; closed Mondays) and **Birreria Wiener** (via della Croce 21; closed Wednesdays) near piazza di Spagna; **Birreria Dreher** in piazza Santi Apostoli; and **Birreria Peroni** (via Brescia 24; closed Mondays), which dates from the turn of the century.

Nightclubs

Nothing is eternal about Rome's nightlife, which has become increasingly trendy. Jaded jet-set types still frequent **La Cabala** and the **Blue Bar** (via dei Soldati 25), both upstairs from the Hostaria dell'Orso restaurant near piazza Navona. More "in" at the moment, however, are **Gilda** (via Mario de' Fiori 97, near the Spanish Steps), and, especially, the recently opened **Alien** (via Velletri 13/19, near piazza Fiume), both frequented by beautiful people from the worlds of politics and entertainment. The poor rich kids of the Parioli residential district north of Villa Borghese—so much a cultural phenomenon that *pariolini* has become the Roman term for "gilded youth"—are dragging themselves to the new **Krypton** (via Luigi Luciana 52) with renewed lack of enthusiasm. And the latest gay hangouts for both sexes are **L'Angelo**

Azzurro (via Cardinal Merry del Val 13, in Trastevere) and **Hangar** (via in Selci 69/A, near Santa Maria Maggiore). But who knows when the new emperors of entertainment will turn their thumbs down on what Cicero called the *aura popularis* (popular breeze) of these "in" establishments. Before you go, you'd better have your hotel check to make sure they're still in business.

—*Louis Inturrisi*

SHOPS AND SHOPPING

Though T. S. Eliot's women may "come and go, talking of Michelangelo," when shoppers come and go in Rome today the talk is more likely to be of Valentino, Fendi, and other designers who keep their ateliers here. For despite Milan's prominence in the ready-to-wear fashion world, Rome still reigns supreme for *alta moda.*

Rome's sartorial splendor extends to men as well. The fabrics of made-to-measure shirts rival anything you'll see on Savile Row, and the tailoring is often superior. Quality, and the traditions of pomp and circumstance running from the ancients through the popes and now to the headquarters of Italy's major television networks and film industry, are what distinguish shopping in the capital.

Shops in Rome generally are open from 9:00 or 10:00 A.M. to 1:00 or 1:30 P.M., unless they're on *orario no-stop* (chic Italian for nonstop schedule); they reopen between 4:00 and 5:00 P.M. and stay open until between 7:00 and 8:30 P.M. All shops are closed Sundays and Monday mornings, except around Christmas. Food shops close Thursday afternoons in fall and winter and Saturday afternoons in spring and summer. In addition to national holidays, many shops close on Rome's birthday, April 21.

Most of the shops listed below accept credit cards, but if you find that you need cash outside of normal banking hours, try one of the new automatic machines in the center or Banca Nazionale del Lavoro (via Veneto 11; Tel: 482-44-21) or 482-76-60), which stays open *no-stop* until 6:00 P.M., including Saturdays.

The most elegant (and expensive) shopping in Rome centers around the streets leading out from piazza di Spagna. Less expensive—but by no means less crowded—are the shops on via del Tritone and via Nazionale. Other, less-trafficked shopping streets are via Cola di Rienzo (near the Vatican), via dei Giubbonoari (near campo dei Fiori), via Salaria, and the daily open-air market specializing in used clothes along via Sonnio next to San Govanni in Laterano.

Spanish Steps

Before leaving the piazza to shop in the side streets, you may want to stop at **American Express** (number 38). Having put your credit cards and money safely in a waist pouch, not in a shoulder bag or wallet, you are ready to do some serious shopping.

Begin by wandering up **via Babuino**, off the piazza to the north, where two designers have their less expensive boutiques: the **Armani Emporium** at number 140 (his more-expensive men's and women's lines are at via Condotti 76) and Valentino's **Oliver Boutique** at number 61 (his women's store is at via Bocca di Leone 15; his men's, on the corner of via Condotti and via Mario Fiori). On the same street, along with women's wear by **Missoni** (number 96/a; his men's shop is in the piazza at number 78), you will find some of Italy's leading antiques dealers. **Antonacci** (number 146) and **W. Appolloni** (number 133) are the most famous. If you're looking for a painting, double back down the parallel **via Margutta** and have a look into the art galleries that line that street.

Return to the piazza and go down fashion's most famous shopping street, **via Condotti**, where you will find internationally known stores like **Richard Ginori**, **Gucci**, **Cartier**, **Bulgari**, **Beltrami**, and **Hermes**. **Ferragamo** has a men's shop at number 66 and a women's shop at number 74. **Trussardi** is at number 49; **Barilla** (number 29), which makes classic hand-sewn shoes for men and women, and **Battistoni** (number 61), which makes made-to-measure menswear, are less well known but worth visiting. The hairstylist **Sergio Valente** has his salon at number 11.

Via Borgognona and **via Frattina** are two more streets leading out of the piazza where you will find more famous name showrooms. The **Fendis** have their shop at number 36; **Gianni Versace** has his men's shop at number 29 (his women's shop is at via Bocca di Leone 26); and **Gianfranco Ferrè** has a men's shop at number 6 and a women's shop at number 42/b. At number 4/d is the black-and-white shop of the publicist **Franco Maria Ricci**, where you can purchase elegant cards, art books, and copies of his very expensive art magazine *FMR*. Finally, if you love stationery stores that are full of bric-a-brac and cleverly designed office supplies, have a look in the two **Vertecchi** stores on via della Croce (numbers 38 and 70) before leaving the area.

Specialty Shops in the Center

Antiques and engravings. Besides the daily outdoor print market in piazza Fontanella di Borghese, some reputable shops that sell antique prints are **Roberto Boccalini** (via del Banco di Santo Spirito 61), **Casali** (piazza del Pantheon 82), **Cascianelli** (largo Febo 14), **Nardecchia** (piazza Navona 25), and **Giuliana Di Cave** (piazza di Pietra 24), near the Pantheon.

The largest concentration of antiques dealers is on via dei Coronari, and if you are there in May or October, you will see the street decked out in carpets and torches for the two annual antiques fairs. Some exceptions to the mostly 19th-century English furniture in the shops are **Mario Morisco** (number 136), which sells French Empire furniture; **La Mansarde** (number 202), which deals in Piedmontese period furniture; and **Metastasio** (number 33), which sells unusual nautical paintings. Other streets where antiques are sold are via Giulia near piazza Farnese and via del Babuino off piazza di Spagna.

Crafts and ceramics. Via dell'Orso, just off Ponte Umberto, is lined with crafts shops and holds an annual fair every October. Elsewhere, the antique craft of tile making is still practiced at **Galleria Farnese** (piazza Farnese 50); mosaic tiles may be made to order at **Opificio Romano** (via dei Gigli d'Oro 9), and **Canguro** (via di Campo Marzio 45) sells high-quality yarns.

Expensive handmade beeswax candles are available at **Pisoni** (corso Vittorio Emanuele 127); master bookbinding is the specialty of **Mario Rossini** (via dei Lucchesi 25); and **Papiro**, near the Spanish Steps (via Capo le Case 55), makes a wide line of products from handmade marbleized paper. If pottery from Deruta, Vietri, or Apulia, or country furniture from Umbria and Tuscany interests you, **Galleria Sambuca** near Santa Maria in Trastevere (via della Pelliccia 30) has the most representative line of both in Rome.

Housewares. **Croff Centro Case** has well-designed Italian housewares and furniture (via Cola di Rienzo 197); **Spazio Sette** (via Barbieri 7), near largo Argentina, has inventive hi-tech everything from soup spoons to floor lamps; and **De Sanctis**, at number 84 in piazza Navona, has all the latest Alessi home products as well as De Simone folk pottery. The housewares department in the basement of the piazza Fiume branch of **La Rinascente** department store has a good selection of espresso pots and pasta makers.

Men's made-to-order. **Caleffi** (via Colonna Antonina 53) has been making men's shirts, suits, and ties for three generations. **Caraceni** (via Marche 1 and via Campania 61/b) is another respectable family dynasty in custom tailoring; and **Camiceria Piero Albertelli** (via dei Prefetti 11) specializes in men's nightwear.

Bargain outlets. **Discount dell'Alta Moda** (via Gesù e Maria), between piazza di Spagna and piazza del Popolo, and **Discount System** (via del Viminale) near the Basilica of Santa Maria Maggiore sell designer clothes and accessories from the top names in Italian fashion at a 50 percent reduction.

Linen and embroidery. **Frette** (piazza di Spagna 10 and via del Corso 381) is an old, very respected vendor of quality linens; **Cir**, at largo Susanna 88, has fine handmade embroidery.

Leather goods. **Bottega Veneta** (via San Sebastianello 18) just off piazza di Spagna has very distinctive—and expensive—bags and wallets; jackets and other clothing can be found at moderate prices at **Gerard** (via San Silvestro 55); excellent hand-crafted belts, bags, and luggage can be custom ordered at **Polidori** (via Piè di Marmo 7) near the Pantheon, and gloves are available in all sizes at a tiny store without a name at via di San Claudio 70, near La Rinascente department store and piazza Colonna.

Children's toys and clothes. There is a children's toy store at either end of piazza Navona: **Al Sogno** (number 53) sells gigantic stuffed animals, and **Berte** (number 108) has hand-carved Pinocchios (with exchangeable noses) and a variety of children's games. **La Cicogna** (via Frattina 38) and **Cir** (piazza Barberini 11) are expensive children's clothes boutiques. For less expensive clothes, try **Chicco** (via della Penna 16) near piazza del Popolo. **Mondo Antico** (via dei Pianellari 17) sells miniature stage sets and puppets.

Books. **Rizzoli** is in the Galleria Colonna at largo Chigi; the **Economy Book & Video Center** (via Torino 136) near the opera house sells English books and rents English-language videos; the largest English-language bookstore is **Lion Bookstore** (via del Babuino 181). Also recommended for English and American books are the **Anglo-American Bookstore** (via della Vite 57) near the Spanish Steps and the **Corner Bookshop** at via del Moro 48 in Trastevere.

Department stores. Romans have never gotten the hang of department stores. They prefer their neighborhood boutiques, where they can count on personal service and a discount. As a result, the department stores in Rome are very low-key. **La Rinascente** has a branch in piazza Fiume and another in piazza Colonna; **Coin**, in piazzale Appio near San

Giovanni in Laterano, is more upscale; and **Upim** (via del Tritone 172) sells cheap clothes, household goods, and cosmetics.

Unusual shops. Via dei Cestari runs between largo Argentina and the Pantheon, and the shops on it specialize in religious articles, statues, and gilded angels. For more mundane purchases, **Art'è** (piazza Rondanini 32) sells witty replicas of urban architecture; Rome's only magic shop is **Curiosità e Magia** (via Aquiro 70); **La Gazza Ladra** (via del Bianchi Vecchi 29) has an extensive stock of 19th-century walking sticks; **Ai Monasteri** (piazza delle Cinque Lune 76), near piazza Navona, sells liqueurs, honeys, and herbal elixirs made by monks and nuns; **Olfottoteca** (piazza della Cancelleria 88) mixes perfumes to order; **Giovanni Borghi** (via della Scrofa 52) sells trilobites and other fossils; **Borsolino** (via del Corso 39) sells hats, straw or otherwise; **Postcards** (piazza del Pantheon 69) has postcards from every region and of every famous artwork in Italy; **Moriondo & Gariglio** (via della Pilotta 2) is Rome's oldest and best fancy chocolate store; **Trimani** (via Giotio 20) has the best selection of wines, olive oil, and balsamic vinegar at affordable prices; **Numismatica** (via Sistina 10) sells ancient Roman coins; **Pineider**, the elegant Florentine stationers at via Due Macelli 68, will help you design your own stationery; **Arte del Pane** (via Merulana 54) sells every kind of bread imaginable; **F.A.M.A.R.** (piazza dell'Unità 51) has blazer buttons with designer logos on them, and there's a taxidermist, **L'Imbalsamatore**, with a stuffed cobra, at via Sant'Agostino 5, near piazza Navona.

Finally, for a Sunday morning shopping event, there is the open-air flea market at Trastevere's Porta Portese, where you can browse among everything from vintage postcards to fake Etruscan pottery. The pickpockets make the most money, they say, and it has become a common dictum that if your wallet is stolen on the way in, you can buy it back on the way out.

—*Louis Inturrisi*

LAZIO
DAY TRIPS FROM ROME

By Barbara Coeyman Hults

Lazio (LA-dzio), a land of forests, castles, and ancient abbeys, is rarely experienced by tourists, except when they hurry along the crowded and rarely attractive major arteries to Rome. Besides Rome, the Villa d'Este is apt to be the only part of the region visited. (The Roman name for Lazio, Latium, is sometimes used in English.)

This isolation has been a great boon to Lazio, for it has been able to go its own way, for the most part without the click of cameras or the exclamations of the adoring to make the region self-conscious. Actually, Lazio is one of the most beautiful parts of Italy, with a rare mystical quality all its own, born of monasticism and pine forests, mountain grottoes worn deep in the porous tufa rock, lakes and spas, and quiet towns. As to its superlatives, Lazio has more lakes than any other region of Italy—still, shadowy volcanic lakes in the midst of thick forests.

Lazio's boundaries extend north to Viterbo and the borders of Umbria and Tuscany, south beyond Anzio and Gaeta to the border of Campania, and east to the mountainous Abruzzo.

Its castles and abbeys are often rugged and isolated on mountaintops covered with pine and *macchia,* the pervasive Mediterranean shrub. Its gastronomy has the same simple, fresh, and hearty character: rice or pasta with beans, pasta *all'amatriciana* (with *pancetta* and the local pecorino cheese) or *all'arrabbiatta* (in a tomato sauce made "angry" with hot peppers), lamb or pork roasted outdoors, chicken done in hundreds of ways, roasted artichokes, oxtail stew, tripe, and Rome's famous *saltimbocca* (slices of veal, cured ham, and sage leaves in a tangy sauce).

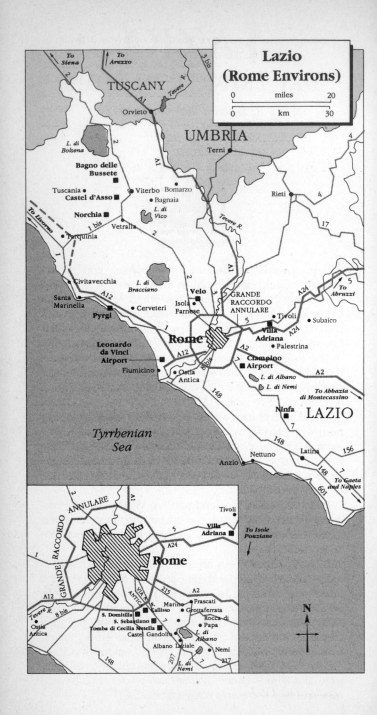

Autumn is Lazio's season, when a cool breeze picks up the scent of wood fires and the red wine is uncorked.

MAJOR INTEREST

The Catacombs
Archaeological excavations at Ostia Antica and Palestrina
Tivoli for Villa d'Este and Villa Adriana: frescoes, gardens, fountains
The Castelli Romani, castles and villas in the Alban Hills: Frascati, Castel Gondolfo, and others
Viterbo
Major Etruscan sites: Tarquinia, Cerveteri, and Tuscania
The ancient Benedictine Abbey of Montecassino
The gardens of Ninfa
The island of Ponza

THE CATACOMBS

Shaded with cypress trees, the graceful symbol of death, numerous elaborate tombs of wealthy ancient Romans border the Appian Way (*Via Appia*), the consular road built by the censor Appius Claudius and opened in 312 B.C. to link Rome with the south. In the early years of Christianity, the bodies of several saints were buried in the tombs, and soon others wanted to be interred alongside them. They became places of worship for Christians, but there is no evidence that they were also hiding places.

Catacombs are systems of underground galleries on several levels, extending often for miles. The openings to the tombs were closed with slabs of marble, and a name— originally in Greek, later in Latin—was carved into them. Over the centuries the tombs have been looted by invaders and local thieves, but much of interest remains. Saints' bones have been removed to churches in Rome.

Caveat: Many of the catacombs are dark, most of the steps are uneven, skulls and bones are quite visible, and retreat is often impossible once inside—and some people do want to retreat.

The **Catacomb of San Callisto** is one of the most important. Named after Saint Calixtus (the slave who became pope), who was appointed guardian of the site by Pope Zephyrinus (199–217), it constituted the first specifically designated cemetery of the early bishops of Rome and was the burial place of the early popes (but not of Calixtus, who was perhaps crowded out) as well as Saint Cecilia, who is commemorated by a copy of the Carlo Madreno statue in the crypt. It is also the most extensive of the catacombs, stretching some 15 miles underground, and has not yet been fully explored. Just behind the catacomb of San Callisto is the **Catacomb of Santa Domitilla**, which contains the fourth-century basilica of San Nereus and Sant'Achilleus, as well as some beautiful paintings, including the first known representation of Christ as the Good Shepherd, painted in the second century.

The **Catacomb of San Sebastiano**, a few minutes away, developed around the spot where Saint Sebastian was martyred and buried, and is also where the bodies of Saint Peter and Saint Paul were first buried. It is an enormous structure on four levels, much visited over the centuries, partly because during the Middle Ages Saint Sebastian was thought to have influence against the Black Plague. The tunnels are covered with graffiti. In the room honoring Peter and Paul words invoking the apostles can be seen. A beautifully decorated pagan tomb adds to the mix.

Along the Appian Way at number 119A is the entrance to the **Jewish Catacombs**, where names and symbols can still be seen on the tombs. For permission to visit, ask at the Synagogue in Rome, Lungotevere Cenci 9.

The best-known of the Roman burial monuments is the **Tomb of Cecilia Metella**, a vast circular shape created for the daughter-in-law of the triumvir Crassus, who shared office with Caesar and Brutus. The crenellated top was part of a fortified castle built around it during the 14th century. Unlike most monuments of the period it has been preserved with much of its marble facing intact, and is decorated with charming relief scenes. Nearby is the restaurant **Cecilia Metella** (via Appia Antica 125; Tel: 06-513-67-43; closed Mondays), which makes for a pleasant (moderately expensive) outdoor lunch or dinner during the warm weather.

The number 118 bus from the Colosseum stops at the Catacomb of San Callisto; the other sites are all within walking distance from San Callisto. Each catacomb closes on a different day, and they all close from 12:00 to 2:30 P.M. daily.

OSTIA ANTICA

If the Palatine Hill is one of your favorite places in Rome, Ostia Antica will be your favorite excursion. To the charm of umbrella pines and ancient ruins is added the complexity of a city, with apartments and storehouses, fish markets and shrines.

The extensive excavations of the ancient commercial and military seaport precinct of Ostia are most important to archaeologists for their examples of Roman residential architecture, ranging from the patrician villa, called the *domus* (much more common at the wealthy resort town of Pompeii), to the apartment block called the *insula*. Set in a park unbothered by the intrusions of the centuries and gracefully landscaped with cypresses and umbrella pines, the site gives a more vivid picture of everyday life in the Empire than anything in Rome does. From the entrance, follow the Decumanus Maximus, the town's main street, to the **Terme di Nettuno** (Baths of Neptune), where mosaic marine monsters cavort with cupids and naked deities. Continue on to the theater and the tree-shaded piazzale delle Corporazioni, the former business district, where the mosaic pavement in front of the various offices depicts the nature of the businesses inside. Several blocks later you'll reach the **Capitolium**, a large temple dedicated to Jupiter, Juno, and Minerva. Behind it is the **Museo Archeologico Ostiense**, housing well-displayed sculptures from the excavations, noteworthy among them *Cupid and Psyche, Family of Marcus Aurelius,* and *Lion Attacking a Bull.* Farther on are some remarkable mosaics in the ancient residences called the **Casa delle Muse** (House of the Muses) and the **Domus dei Dioscuri** (House of the Dioscuri). Nearby, at the Marine Gate, go up into the former tavern if sexually explicit material doesn't bother you. At the farthest end of the excavations are the remains of one of the oldest synagogues yet discovered, dating from the first century. Buy an illustrated guidebook at the gift shop to identify the buildings.

The most picturesque way of getting to Ostia is on the boat sponsored by the Amici del Tevere, which leaves from the ponte Marconi in Rome. Otherwise, take metro line B to the Magliana stop, where a connecting train goes to Ostia Antica. The crowded-in-season resort Lido di Ostia, which leaves much to be desired as a beach, can be reached by metro or on foot. Lido di Ostia has a number of seafood restaurants, of which **Da Negri** is among the nicest (via Claudia 50; Tel: 06-562-22-95; closed Thursdays; fairly expensive).

TIVOLI AND VILLA ADRIANA

Medieval in appearance, the town of Tivoli (30 km/19 miles east of Rome) is the bastion of the Renaissance **Villa d'Este**, built for Cardinal Ippolito II d'Este (son of Lucrezia Borgia) by Pirro Ligorio. The villa itself contains frescoes by 16th-century artists, but more noteworthy are its gardens, where hundreds of fountains freshen the air and add water music. Though the *giochi d'acqua,* the sprays of water that surprised unsuspecting visitors, are no longer in use, the fountains themselves are just as wondrous. The Organ Fountain, Terrace of the Hundred Fountains, Ovato Fountain, Little Rome (a tiny replica of Rome's Tiber Island), and Dragon Fountain are but a few. Dry for centuries, the fountains have been restored by the Italian government, which also illuminates them at night during the summer.

Tibur (Tivoli's ancient name) was founded, some say, by the Siculi, and later became an important resort for wealthy Romans. It was here that the Sybil Albunea, whose shrine was sacred to her cult, was consulted.

The most pleasant warm-weather dining option in the area is **Sibilla** (via della Sibilla 50; Tel: 0774-202-81), a regional restaurant whose outdoor garden overlooks the temples of Vesta and Sibilla. Seeing the fountains at Villa d'Este is perhaps best combined, however, with a surreptitious picnic dinner at **Villa Adriana** (Hadrian's Villa), 4.5 km (3 miles) south of Tivoli. Now in ruins, it was once the largest villa in ancient Rome (180 acres). The Emperor Hadrian built it for his retirement, reconstructing some of his favorite sights from around the world to keep him company. Among them were the entrance colonnade, called the Poikile, from Athens, and the Canal of Canopus from Egypt. The Maritime Theater is a round building inside which a moat surrounds a small island. On the island, a miniature villa contains a reception room and of course a bath. Hadrian could receive or shut out guests by merely raising or lowering the drawbridges. Finding the emperor at the Villa Adriana took connections of a high order.

The **Antica Trattoria del Falcone** (via del Trevio 34; Tel: 0774-223-58; closed Mondays), where Lazio's dishes—such as chick-pea soup, baccalà, and fresh fruit pies—as well as pizza are featured, is a refuge for the weary visitor.

ACOTRAL provides regular bus service from Rome (via Gaeta, near the piazza dei Cinquecento) to Tivoli, depositing passengers near the entrance to the Villa d'Este; buses stop about a mile from the entrance to the Villa Adriana.

The local CAT bus in Tivoli goes near the Villa Adriana stop as well. Taxis from the town of Tivoli go to the door.

PALESTRINA

Known to the ancient Romans as Praeneste, Palestrina was founded, according to legend, by the son of Ulysses and Circe. Then the site of the oracle at the **Temple of Fortuna Primigenia** (the first daughter of Jupiter)—one of the richest and most elaborate sanctuaries of antiquity and the largest Greek-style building in Italy, dating from 80 B.C.—today the town is visited for the archaeological excavations surrounding the temple, magnificently located on the slopes of Monte Ginestro, 37 km (23 miles) east of Rome. Its adjacent museum, the **Museo Archeologico Prenestino** (in the Palazzo Barberini), houses material from the excavation, the highlight of which is a second-century B.C. mosaic depicting the floodwaters of the Nile.

Music lovers might want to have a look at the monument to the town's most famous native son, 16th-century composer Giovanni Pierluigi da Palestrina, in the main piazza. Just outside town (via del Piscarello, Tel: 06-955-77-51) is the restaurant **Trattoria del Piscarello**, where you can enjoy a classic Roman menu—in an outdoor setting in fair weather.

ACOTRAL buses leave Rome regularly for Palestrina from piazza dei Cinquecento; there is also train service from Stazione Termini to the Palestrina station, from which a local bus takes you to the town center.

East of Palestrina, the abbeys of Santa Scolastica and San Benedetto at **Subiaco** merit a visit.

CASTELLI ROMANI

The Castelli Romani (Roman castles) are, collectively, the 13 towns about 21 km (13 miles) southeast of Rome where wealthy Romans built castles and villas in the Colli Albani, or Alban Hills, best known today for their crisp white wine.

Frascati is the most popular of the Castelli Romani, and though its lovely 16th-century **Villa Aldobrandini** has spectacular views of Rome, it is best known as a gathering place for *fagottari,* people who buy or bring bundles of *porchetta* (pork roasted with herbs) and other delicacies to enjoy on open-air terraces next to the wine shops while drinking healthy amounts of the Frascati wine. **Cacciani** (via Armando

Diaz 13; Tel: 942-03-78; closed Tuesdays) is an excellent restaurant here, with an expansive outdoor terrace from which to enjoy the scenery (expensive; reservations are recommended).

The woods and vineyards of **Grottaferrata** shelter the Abbazia, a Basilian abbey founded in 1004, where the Greek Orthodox rite was reinstituted with the pope's permission during the last century. The monks will show you around the grounds and the museum of religious artifacts, and also sell olive oil and a good local wine.

The elegant **Grand Hotel Villa Fiorio**, in its park of pine trees, is the place to stay and to dine, an ideal retreat unless it's to be a wedding party weekend—ask in advance (viale Dusinet 28; Tel: 06-945-92-76). In the town, the **Taverna dello Spuntino** is a charming spot to relax in over home-made pasta, veal with arugula, roast pig, and homemade desserts (via Cicerone 20; Tel: 06-945-93-66; closed Wednesdays). Both restaurants are fairly expensive.

The wine of **Marino** is considered the best of all the Colli Albani whites, and is especially celebrated during the Sagra dell'Uva (Festival of the Grape) on the first Sunday in October, when, after a procession and an offering to the Madonna, the Fontana dei Mori flows with wine, and so do the crowds.

Castel Gandolfo is believed to be the location of Alba Longa, the most powerful city in ancient Latium, founded by the son of Aeneas and destroyed by the Romans. The current town contains the church of **San Tommaso da Villanova** and a fountain, both by Bernini, in its main square. Its **Palazzo Pontificio** is part of the Vatican State and serves as the summer residence of the pope, who gives addresses here on Sundays and holds audiences on Wednesday mornings (apply for admission at the Vatican).

Albano Laziale is on a lake on the site of the Castra Albana, which was built by Septimius Severus for a Roman legion in the second century. Ruins of the ancient town and subsequent medieval additions may be seen.

The Nemus Dianae, or Grove of Diana, sacred to the primitive cult with which James Frazer opens *The Golden Bough,* gave its name to the town and lake of **Nemi**, today famous for its strawberries. Though very few of them are wild, they are all celebrated in the Sagra delle Fragole, or strawberry festival, in June. **Rocca di Papa**, named after the castle, or *rocca,* built by the popes, is the highest of all the Castelli Romani. The upper portion of the town is medieval, and if you ascend Monte Cavo above that (as did the Roman legions when the Temple of Jupiter Latialis was located here), you'll be treated to magnificent views of the Castelli, the lakes of Albano and Nemi, and the surrounding country-side as far as the coast.

The most convenient way to see the Castelli Romani in a day is undoubtedly by car, beginning on the Roman via Tuscolana (route S 215) and following signs for the individual towns; otherwise, select the one or two towns that appeal most to you and check train and bus schedules. Trains from Stazione di Termini serve Albano, Marino, and Frascati. ACOTRAL buses from Cinecittà (a stop on metro line A) serve all the towns.

The **gardens at Ninfa**, south of the Castelli, exude a melancholy magic from the 12th century, when the overgrown ruins were a prosperous town. The gardens, with plants brought from all over the world, are open the first Saturday and the first Sunday of every month from April to October. For admission, contact the Amministrazione Caetani, via delle Botteghe Oscuri 32, Rome (Tel: 06-686-61-01), or the Oasi di Ninfa (Tel: 0773-432-31).

VITERBO

Few medieval cities convey their era as dramatically as **Viterbo**. The priorities of the Middle Ages—defense, defense, and prayer—are met in Viterbo's massive walls and brooding introspection. This mood doesn't extend, however, to the young soldiers in today's town, putting in their year of compulsory military service at the Viterbo base. Their preoccupations are predictable, and not very militant.

On rainy days the city seems too dour for some travellers, like many cities of its time, but when the weather is fair it is superb, flourishing at the foot of the Cimini hills. The tufa, a soft, porous volcanic stone typical of central Italy, changes color with the weather, absorbing foggy grays and warm sun tones with equanimity.

The capital of its province, Viterbo is 104 km (50 miles) northwest of Rome. It has been a city to be reckoned with since the 13th century, when it was the papal seat during strife between the papacy and the empire, and the place where the first conclave in Catholic church history was held.

The heart of Viterbo is the **piazza del Plebiscito**, where yesterday and today vie for supremacy, overlooked by tufa lions. Here the **Palazzo dei Priori**, or Communale (town hall), begun in 1460, still maintains the city's records. Its fine

Renaissance courtyard and loggia are usually open to visitors, and you can glimpse the current powers of Viterbo as they pontificate within. The building with the clock tower is the 13th-century Palazzo del Podestà (Mayor), the secular authority of its time.

Across the square, near the door of the church of Sant'Angelo, a Roman sarcophagus has been set into the wall. It is called the tomb of the beautiful Galiana, who was killed with an arrow by a Roman officer whom she'd refused, thus sparing the city from siege, we're told.

Along the via San Lorenzo, a twisting street through the ancient city, stands the imposing Renaissance form of the Palazzo Chigi, enhanced with a lovely court and loggia. Beyond it is what is now the Jesuit church of the Gesù, a simple 11th-century structure, but restored. Inside, it seems, two brothers of the Monforte family beat up Prince Henry of Cornwall during Mass, avenging the death of their father, which had been ordered by King Richard.

At the triangular piazza della Morte, probably the site of executions yet today green and cheerful, the vicolo Pellegrini leads to the Ponte del Duomo, set on an Etruscan base that can be seen if you descend the stairs at the bridge's side. The bridge united the city with an ancient castle.

Nearby, the beautiful 14th-century Palazzo Farnese, birthplace of the Farnese pope Paul III, has a stylish courtyard.

The cathedral of San Lorenzo is a 12th-century Romanesque building with a splendid campanile in Gothic form. The interior was severely damaged during World War II. In the left apse the *Madonna della Carbonara,* and in the sacristy the painting of *Christ Blessing the Saint,* both by Girolamo da Cremona, are among the treasures. On the altar, *Saint Laurence in Glory* is the work of the Baroque artist Giovanni Romanelli, who also painted the *Holy Family* in the right aisle.

In the piazza, the Palazzo dei Papi, with its open loggia, is the true cornerstone of the city. It was built between 1257 and 1266, and soon after was used to house the first Conclave. Even the Second Vatican Council is unlikely to have had a stormier session, and it was not a longer one (1268–1271). To end the impasse over the election of Gregorio X as pope, the Viterbese removed the roof of the congress hall. The Princes of the Church, sequestered beneath, erected tents and continued, until their subjects resorted to stones; holes can still be seen where they hit the floor. Gregory was thus pelted in, and despite this electoral process four more popes were elected here.

Returning to the piazza della Morte: The little street in front of the fountain will take you through the beautifully preserved 12th-century **Medieval Quarter**, with its pinnacle, the **piazza San Pelligrino**, considered the most comprehensive medieval piazza in Italy. The **Palazzo degli Alessandri** here is a typical example of an austere private palace. This section is the place to wander, on the lookout especially for the superb fountains that are typical of Viterbo and for other signs of the Middle Ages—towers, covered passageways, gently arched bifurcated windows, and dark streets. The **Fontana Grande**, off the via Cavour (near where you began), is one of the city's finest.

The **Museo Civico** at piazza Crispi is housed in the convent of the church of Santa Maria della Verità. The Etruscan objects on the ground floor reflect Viterbo's other dominant influence. To the west of Viterbo lie some of Italy's most important Etruscan sites, notably at Tarquinia, Cerveteri, and Tuscania; they are described below. In the gallery, the star is Sebastiano del Piombo's *Pietà,* based on a lost drawing by Michelangelo. There is also a lovely cycle of frescoes on the life of the Virgin by Lorenzo da Viterbo (1469). Currently closed for restoration, the museum is scheduled to reopen sometime in 1993.

The **church of San Francesco**, near the northern city walls and close to the Public Gardens, houses the tombs of Pope Clement IV and Hadrian V, the latter attributed to Arnolfo da Cambio.

Viterbo has one notable restaurant, **Il Richiastro**, which is open only Thursday through Sunday. The Scappucci family restored a 12th-century building for the atmosphere they wanted, and in 1981 opened this delightful trattoria. Here traditional recipes have been carefully researched, and the best of Lazio emerges. Hearty soups of beans and grains, steaks, and the less popular (in North America) cuts of meat are done to perfection. Many of the products, including the olive oil, are home-grown or homemade. Call to reserve (via della Marrocca 16–18; Tel: 0761-22-36-09; no credit cards; closed in August).

As to hotels, the best-appointed are the **Mini Palace** and the **Balletti Palace**. The **Tuscia** is fine for an overnight and within most budgets.

The **Villa Lante** at Bagnaia, a suburb of Viterbo, is a Renaissance treat, and its gardens are among Italy's finest. Also near Viterbo, the amazing **Parco dei Mostri** at Bomarzo suited the bizarre fancy of Prince Vicino Orsini. Massive stone ogres, harpies, mermaids, and a leaning tower make up an early Disneyland-on-the-edge (about 16 km/10 miles east of Viterbo, connected with ACOTRAL bus several times a day). In Bomarzo you might want to stay in a 17th-century castle, part of the Agriturist project, called the **Azienda Pomigliozzo**; its dining room uses its own products.

Rome's transit authority, again in its infinite wisdom, has changed things around so that getting to Viterbo is a project. We can only hope that the situation will be changed by the time you want to go.

At present the way to get there is to go to Saxa Rubra, near Prima Porta, a stop on the Roma Nord line that starts near the Flaminia metro stop, just outside the gate of Rome's piazza del Popolo. (To save time and frustration, take a taxi to Saxa Rubra.) At Saxa Rubra a bus will take you on to Viterbo. The train will too, but the trip is long, although a nice way to see the countryside (unless you get one of the old wooden-seaters). In any case, leave as early as possible if you're making a day trip. In Viterbo, cars can be left outside the walls at piazza Martiri d'Ungheria.

On the way back you might want to dine in Saxa Rubra at the **Grotte di Livia**, a pleasant family-run restaurant on the grounds of a villa that Livia and Augustus shared during Rome's imperial golden age. Its homemade pasta is superb, and the steaks are excellent. On a hot evening in Rome, its outdoor dining is the right choice (piazza Saxa Rubra 9; Tel: 06-691-12-53; closed Mondays).

ETRUSCAN SITES

Most of the beautiful removable objects—sculpture, vases, and gold artifacts—unearthed from Etruscan necropolises over the last century are on display at museums such as the Museo Nazionale di Villa Giulia and the Musei Vaticani in Rome. The tombs themselves, however, which so fascinated D. H. Lawrence (he wrote about them in *Etruscan Places*) and others, are easy to visit from Rome, and a look at their faded frescoes and homelike arrangement makes the ancient civilization seem both closer and more distant.

The area west of Viterbo is one of the richest parts of Italy in Etruscan excavations. The principal sites, from northern Lazio to near Rome, can be seen in a day trip from Rome.

Begin at the site farthest from Rome, the medieval-looking town of **Tarquinia**, about 90 km (56 miles) up the coast, where the **Museo Nazionale Tarquiniese** has an extensive collection of Etruscan art from the nearby necropolises (about 3 km/ 2 miles west of town)—only a few of which are also open to the public (apply at the museum) on any given day because of their delicate condition and to protect them from grave robbers (*tombaroli*). The unrivaled collection of wall paintings gives a vivid impression of the partying afterlife that the Etruscans anticipated—perhaps the reason they are always smiling. (Open 9:00 A.M. to 2:00 P.M.; Tel: 0766-85-60-36.) Tarquinia today is home for hundreds of refugees from Eastern Europe, an unsettling experience for all concerned.

Toward Viterbo, more necropolises are to be seen surrounding the hill town of **Tuscania** as well as farther along the road at **Bagno delle Bussete**. **Castel d'Asso**, on a small road southwest of Viterbo, has a large cliffside necropolis, as does **Norchia**, to the west of Vetralla. From Tarquinia, the coastal road south is dotted with both Etruscan and Roman sites at Civitavecchia, Santa Marinella, and Pyrgi. **Cerveteri**, perched on a spur of tufa, enjoyed a comfortable Etruscan life during the seventh and sixth centuries B.C., if the paintings on the tombs don't lie. The **Museo Cerite**, located in the Orsini castle, exhibits objects from the surrounding tombs, including some fascinating sculpture and red-figured vases. But the **Necropolis**, on the hill called Banditaccia, about 2 km (1 mile) from the town's center, is the prize. Tombs are laid out in avenues here amid an attractive park of cypress trees and flowers. If you can arrange for a guide at the ticket office, do so, for many of the tombs with frescoes remain closed. The Tomba dei Rilievi (fourth century B.C.), for example, is decorated with scenes of everyday life, but can only be seen with a guide. (Closed Mondays.)

About 2 km (1 mile) south of Cerveteri is the oldest tomb, the huge tubular **Regolini-Galassi tomb**, dating from the seventh century B.C. Its conical top with tall grass growing on it was the typical tomb design, and influenced Hadrian's and Augustus's tombs in Rome.

You may want to picnic somewhere along the way, but good food can be had at the restaurant **Nazareno** (località San Paolo; Tel: 06-995-23-82).

Because many of the Etruscan sights are tombs in the open countryside, the best way to visit them is by car. Depending on how long you want to stay at the individual sites, this can take one lengthy day or two leisurely days, with the best accommodations for a stopover at Tarquinia's **Tarconte e Ristorante Solengo**, via Tuscia 19; Tel: (0766) 85-61-41; closed Wednesdays. Otherwise, buses leave from via Lepanto in Rome for Tarquinia and Cerveteri.

ANZIO AND NETTUNO

Anzio was the birthplace of both Caligula and Nero, a bloody legacy continued more recently by the landing in World War II of American and British troops. Today it and Nettuno are modern seaside resort towns with decent beaches and family-style accommodations, about 60 km (37 miles) south of Rome. In addition, Anzio boasts the excavations of the **Villa di Nerone** (Nero's Villa). Both towns are of particular interest for their cemeteries: The British Military Cemetery is located at Anzio, the American at Nettuno. Anzio also has a panoramic seafood restaurant, **All'Antica Darsena** (piazza Sant'Antonio 1; Tel: 06-984-51-46; closed Mondays); Nettuno's is **Il Gambero II** (via delle Liberazione 50; Tel: 06-985-40-71; closed Mondays and from September 15 to June 15).

ACOTRAL buses leave for Anzio from Rome at Cinecittà, at Osteria del Curato; trains from Stazione Termini.

ABBAZIA DI MONTECASSINO

The abbey at Montecassino as one of the most important outposts of Christian culture during the Middle Ages, when much of the world was dark. Begun in the sixth century by Saint Benedict, founder of the Benedictines, it has existed for more than 14 centuries, despite destruction by an earthquake in 1349 and the Allied bombardment of 1944, in which hundreds of tons of bombs were dropped to destroy a German stronghold. After the war an inspired work of reconstruction was begun, and today the monastery is almost restored to the original.

The abbey commands as dramatic a position as nature allows, atop a high peak that overlooks a breathtaking panorama of rolling hills and valleys. To reach it, hairpin curves must be executed along a 9-km (5-mile) road.

Saint Benedict, who had been living as a hermit in nearby Subiaco, was asked by a group of monks to be their abbot—but apparently things didn't work out, as they tried to poison him. When he returned to Subiaco he attracted a great number of disciples. An orderly man, he divided the monks among 12 monasteries, appointed a prior for each one, and made manual work a part of the program. Subiaco quickly developed as a center of spirituality and learning. Benedict left suddenly, apparently because of bad rapport with a prior, and settled at Montecassino, destroying the temple to

Apollo on the mountaintop and constructing an altar on the site. In about 530 he began to build the monastery, attracting many disciples, whom he organized into a monastic community. He then wrote the Rule of Saint Benedict, prescribing a life of moderation in asceticism and a program of prayer, chastity, study, and work, in community life with one superior. Obedience, stability, and zeal were the watchwords, and his Rule has affected monastic life throughout the centuries since.

At the abbey's entrance three cloisters lead to the Loggia del Paradiso, from which the view of the valley is superb. The original loggia, which has been reconstructed exactly, was designed by Sangallo (who designed Orvieto's famous well). The basilica's altar, originally the work of Fanzago, has also been duplicated, as has Sangallo's tomb of Pietro de'Medici, the son of Lorenzo. The original crypt remains, where Saint Benedict was buried. A museum is open but the library, with thousands of the original books and manuscripts, is available only to those with requests for serious study.

Among nearby restaurants are **Boschetto**, via Ausonia 54 (Tel: 0776-30-12-27), with good local cooking, and **Canguro**, via Appia Nuova 8500 (Tel: 0776-442-59; closed Mondays). Both are inexpensive.

PONZA

Lazio's dramatically beautiful island of Ponza, off the coast of Anzio south of Rome, had been kept in the family until recently; foreigners didn't flock there, except perhaps in August when every puddle in Italy speaks a different language. In recent years easier transit, including hydrofoils, has changed all that, facilitating weekend trips. Yet despite it all, Ponza maintains a striking individuality.

The Pontine Islands (Isole Ponziane), of which Ponza is the largest and most important, are volcanic islands whose past extends to the Paleolithic era. Their early history followed the course of their supply of obsidian, the hard stone best suited for knives. Used first as a trading post, Ponza became a convenient isle for receiving those who had fallen out of favor with emperor Tiberius. Monks lived on the island through the Middle Ages, and colonists arrived during a tax-incentive program of the Bourbons in Naples. During World War II the island was again used for exiles—and also for Mussolini during a short period after the war.

The island's charm is its 6 miles of amazing configurations: Jagged, pale tufa cliffs rise high above the sea, and beaches and grottoes soften the rocky shoreline. The principal town, also called **Ponza**, is pastel-colored and simple. The island's interior is usually reached through tunnels, like the one the Romans dug to the **Chiaia** (kee-AY-ya) **di Luna** (Moonlight Bay), where a 300-foot-high crescent of cliff shelters a beach below (at low tide). A boat trip around the island circles grottoes and beaches, but the real joy is the drama of the island itself against the sea. If you climb **Monte Guardia** to Punta della Guardia (1 hour) you will discover extraordinary, bizarre rock formations. At sea, scuba divers may find coral and sunken ships amid the sea creatures.

The **Grand Hotel Chiaia di Luna**, on a cliff that overlooks the bay, is an unusual complex of small buildings united by terraces and stairways. The beach is reached through a Roman tunnel, but the pool and bar, solarium, and restaurant are close at hand. The **Torre dei Borboni** takes a bit of walking to get to (they'll send a porter), but this hotel and its site in an old Bourbon fort are worth the effort, especially if your room is in the 18th-century castle that overlooks the port. Ponza's lobster (*aragosta*) is served in the sea-view dining room, and the hotel's private beach is down a stairway. The good budget-hotel choice on Ponza is **Gennarino a Mare**, with balconies overlooking the sea.

Ponza's festivals occur on the last Sunday in February and on June 20, both commemorating San Silverio, the pope who drew the wrath of the Byzantine empress Theodora, who backed another candidate. Legend has it that he was murdered on Ponza on June 20.

To arrive at Ponza from the port of Fiumicino (near Rome's airport), take the Medmar hydrofoil or ferry (about 40,000 lire); the trip takes about 6 hours. Reserve well in advance during the summer (piazza Barberini 5, 00187 Rome; Tel: 06-482-85-79; Fax: 06-481-45-01). Helios runs ferries from Anzio and Formia on the Lazio coast (Anzio: 06-984-50-85; Formia: 0771-70-07-10).

If you're held up at Fiumicino (the airport or the nearby harbor town), or if you need a respite between flights, stop at the **Ship Museum** near the airport on via Portuense at km 5, and at the **Isola Sacra** excavations of ancient Roman tombs, on the road to Ostia at km 3.5. For lunch at Fiumicino's port, stop at **Il Pescatore**, via Torre Clementina 154 (Tel: 06-650-51-89; closed Thursdays), or at the famous **Bastianelli al Centro**, on the same street at number 88 (closed Wednesdays; Tel: 06-650-50-95).

ACCOMMODATIONS REFERENCE

The rates given below are projections for 1993; always check for up-to-date information before making reservations. Wide ranges may reflect the differences between low- and high-season rates. Unless otherwise indicated, the figures indicate the cost of a double room (per room, not per person). However, half-board (mezza pensione) rates, which include breakfast and one other meal per day, are per person. The service charge is included in the rate; inquire about tax and breakfast.

▶ **Agriturismo Pomigliozzo.** 01020 **Bomarzo** (Viterbo). Tel: (0761) 92-44-66.

▶ **Balletti Palace.** Viale Trento 100, 01100 **Viterbo.** Tel: (0761) 34-47-77; Fax: same. Ł120,000–Ł143,000.

▶ **Gennarino a Mare.** Via Dante 64, 04027 **Ponza.** Tel: (0771) 800-71; Fax: (0771) 800-98. Ł70,000.

▶ **Grand Hotel Chiaia di Luna.** Via Chiaia di Luna, 04027 **Ponza.** Tel: (0771) 801-13; Fax: (0771) 80-98-21. Open at Easter and May 22–October 4. Ł150,000–Ł300,000; half board Ł100,000–Ł195,000.

▶ **Grand Hotel Villa Fiorio.** Viale Dusmet 28, 00046 **Grottaferrata.** Tel: (06) 945-92-76; Fax: (06) 941-34-82. Ł110,000–Ł160,000; half board Ł150,000.

▶ **Mini Palace.** Via Santa Maria della Grotticella 2, 01100 **Viterbo.** Tel: (0761) 30-97-42; Fax: (0761) 34-47-15. Ł120,000–Ł180,000.

▶ **Torre dei Borboni.** Via Madonna 1, 04027 **Ponza.** Tel: (0771) 801-35. Ł60,000.

▶ **Tuscia.** Via Cairoli 41, 01100 **Viterbo.** Tel: (0761) 22-33-77; Fax: (0761) 34-59-76. Ł64,000–Ł100,000.

THE ABRUZZO

By *Jeffrey Rowland and Joanne Hahn*

Jeffrey Rowland lives in Rome, where he is the assistant editor of Italy Italy *magazine and writes for the* Washington Post. *Joanne Hahn has lived and studied in Italy and returns there regularly. A contributor to several magazines, she is coauthor of a travel guidebook to Italy.*

When the tourist-crowded piazzas and car-filled streets of Italy's major cities begin to overwhelm, or museums packed with Renaissance and Baroque masterpieces become all but a blur, there is a region in which to seek refuge. Eastward across the Italian peninsula from Rome, where the Apennines meet the Adriatic Sea, lies the Abruzzo region. By taking the A 24 autostrada east out of Rome, you can find yourself, within the span of an hour, enjoying the solitude of a majestic mountain world once known for its witches and wolves, including *lupi mannari,* or werewolves. The emphasis is on nature in this sparsely populated region, which has been isolated historically and geographically from Italy's grander currents of political and artistic history. Although today it is easily accessible by the country's modern road system, you can still glimpse men and women in colorful peasant dress, see farmers making cheese in their gardens, and marvel at barns constructed of reeds, as they have been for centuries. Life still proceeds here at a sauntering pace, and yet from this same mountain-bound land came two of Italy's most sophisticated and passionate poets, Ovid and the flamboyant Gabriele D'Annunzio, as well as philosopher Benedetto Croce.

The breathtaking mountains—the highest of the Apennines—were largely responsible for cutting the Abruzzo off from the north and directing its traffic toward Apulia and the south as well as to the port of Pescara on the Adriatic. These peaks are high enough to be snow-covered year-round and can be seen from every side. The white crests of the Gran Sasso form a barrier 9,000 feet high. Natives claim that the weather here is the best in Italy, with 11 cool months and only one cold one.

The well-constructed roads from every direction to Abruzzo's capital, L'Aquila, glide through a landscape that never fails to delight: lush valleys, rushing streams, and medieval towns perched on terraced hills. Voyagers who arrived at these villages were once in for a rough night in whatever passed for lodgings; inedible food and beds crawling with "little strangers" were commonplace. Now there are modern hotels not only in the larger towns but in the mountains as well—the latter opened up as ski resorts in the winter and as havens for nature and wildlife lovers in the summer. For those who ski, there are outposts in every direction—Campo Imperatore, Campo Felice, Campo di Giove. If you're searching for interesting flora and fauna, head toward the south, where the hills below Sulmona and Scanno lead to the Parco Nazionale d'Abruzzo.

MAJOR INTEREST

Wild, mountainous landscape
Medieval villages
Strongly flavored food

L'Aquila
Churches of Santa Maria di Collemaggio and San
    Bernardino
Castello and its Museo Nazionale d'Abruzzo
Fontana delle 99 Cannelle
Tre Marie restaurant

Teramo (mountain town)
Gran Sasso d'Italia and its ski resorts
Scanno (jewelry in Roman style)
Sulmona (medieval hill town)
Parco Nazionale d'Abruzzo
Chieti (Roman ruins)
Saepinum (preserved ancient Roman town)

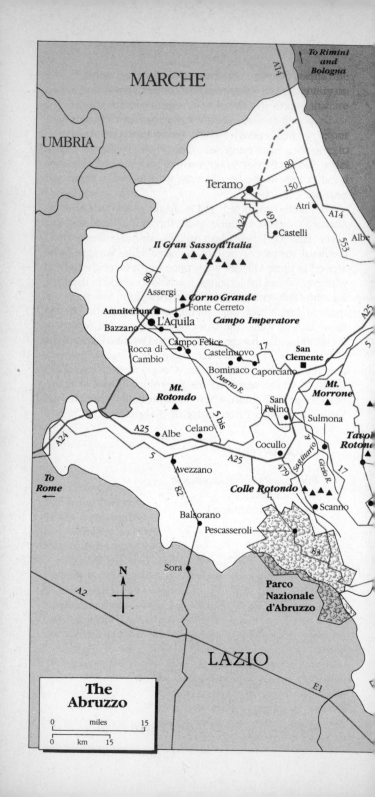

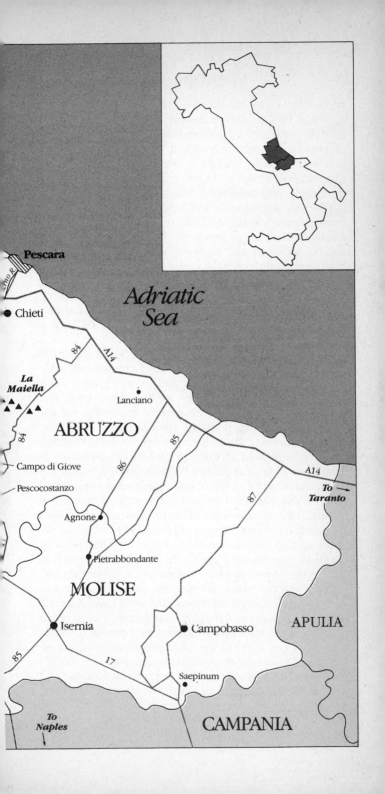

L'Aquila

Beautifully set on the steep slope of a mountain valley encircled by the massive heights of the Apennine range, L'Aquila is the region's principal city for historical and artistic interest. But unlike Chieti and Teramo, Abruzzo's other provincial capitals, L'Aquila is not an ancient city. It was founded only in the mid-13th century, along an important trade route that connected Naples with Florence.

From its Romanesque and Renaissance churches to its perfect Spanish castle, L'Aquila is a town of architectural treasures. The narrow streets that connect one piazza with another are lined with medieval homes and churches that have changed little over the centuries.

A northern outpost of the Kingdom of Naples during the 16th century, L'Aquila was controlled by Spanish viceroy Don Pedro of Toledo. Under his tutelage the great **Castello** was built, among other buildings, thus giving the town a feeling of a Spanish town, similar to Granada.

Situated in a park on the northern edge of town, the Castello, begun in 1534, is an extraordinary structure with formidable triangular bastions and an impressively deep moat. The entire cost of the Castello's construction was foisted on the people of L'Aquila, in retribution for the revolt they had waged against Spanish rule in 1528. The Castello was never put to the test, however, for no warring armies ever showed up. For centuries the fortress served as little more than an expensive barracks. Today it houses the **Museo Nazionale d'Abruzzo**, with collections of archaeological treasures, medieval art, and Renaissance sculpture. The ground floor contains some of the most interesting exhibits, including the overwhelming *elephas meriodinales,* the remains of a 1.5-million-year-old pachyderm, found by chance about 40 years ago on a site not far from L'Aquila, as well as numerous Roman portraits, statues, and a wonderful polychrome wooden statue by Silvestro d'Aquila. During July and August, concerts sponsored by the Societa Aquilana Concerti are held in the castle's auditorium. (An attractive modern hotel, appropriately named the **Castello**, is conveniently located opposite the castle in the piazza Battaglione Alpini and marks the entrance to the main street, via Vittorio Emanuele. It's a bit noisy here, so ask for a back room.)

The natural daughter of Charles V, Margaret of Parma, retired to L'Aquila after two not very happy marriages: one to a Medici (murdered), the other to a Farnese. She was, by all accounts, a kindred spirit to Christina of Sweden, often riding forth from her palace (now the Palazzo di Giustizia) dressed as a man. The heart of L'Aquila has changed little since then. Its narrow streets and old shops invite strollers to search for the rare *tombola* lace, one of Abruzzo's treasures; to enjoy a *passeggiata* down the corso Federico II at sunset or to stop at the **Magic** shop for a winning *tiramisù* and coffee, or its delicious *gelato* (via dell'Indipendenza 25); to see its small piazzas with their fountains in the evening under the stars; and then to witness the hubbub of the market in front of the Duomo the next morning. A perfect stand-up lunch can be had here, with stands offering chickens roasted on a spit and a wonderfully spicy *porchetta* sandwich.

At the end of corso Federico II at the juncture with via Rendina is the **Grand Hotel del Parco**, an excellent choice for lodging, with formal furnishings, a marble lobby, fine antiques, excellent rooms (the quietest are in the back), and a fine restaurant, **La Grotta di Aligi** (reservations needed; Tel: 0862-652-60; closed Mondays). On a grander scale, although the atrocious façade belies the comforts within, is the **Duca degli Abruzzi**, viale Giovanni XXIII 10, with a lovely roof garden and a splendid restaurant offering superlative mountain views. Ask for a room on the third floor, which is the quietest.

The cathedral, because of the earthquakes that plague the Abruzzo, has fared badly; but it never did compare with the two outstanding churches of L'Aquila. One, **Santa Maria di Collemaggio**, is on the edge of town and reached via a tree-lined avenue. It has a boldly designed façade of pink-and-white stone, and its patterned polychrome is interrupted by three Romanesque portals and three rose windows. Santa Maria was founded by an aged hermit named Pietro Angeleri at the end of the 13th century to honor a miraculous appearance of the Virgin. Later, when Pietro was living in Monte Morrone, the College of Cardinals, which had reached an impasse, almost dragged him from his mountain retreat to become pope. But that was the last thing that the naïve Pietro wanted to be, and once his ill-suitedness for the job was recognized he abdicated, only to be imprisoned by the succeeding pontiff, Pope Boniface VIII, who wasn't naïve at all. Pietro was kept in a castle at Fumone until he died at the age of 81, and only then was it considered safe to bring his remains back to his own church, to canonize him as Saint Celestine, and later to build him the fine Renaissance tomb that graces the church.

The other saint who ended up in L'Aquila was Saint Bernar-

dino of Siena, the great revivalist preacher who arrived at the
Franciscan convent in L'Aquila just in time to die—to the
everlasting fury of the Sienese, who never got his body back.
The people of L'Aquila gave him a superb Renaissance
church, however: The **Church of San Bernardino** has one of
the most elegant and balanced of façades, with an imposing
mausoleum sculpted by Silvestro dell'Aquila, the master
Abruzzese sculptor who created one almost equally fine for
Maria Pereira in the north chancel.

Very much the point of visiting L'Aquila are the smaller
churches and their respective piazzas, which are scattered all
over town: San Giusta and San Flaviano (Romanesque); Santa
Maria di Paganica, surrounded by Gothic palaces; San
Silvestro, with its frescoes; and San Giuseppe, with its Gothic
tombs. Near the Porta Rivera is San Vito, and below it is the
Fontana delle 99 Cannelle, built in 1272, where 99 sculpted
masks of humans, animals, and grotesques spout water. It is
currently being restored, and unfortunately little of its charm
can be appreciated while it is under wraps. According to
legend, L'Aquila rose from the earth, like Athena from the
brow of Zeus, with 99 of everything: quarters, fountains,
churches, and 99 villages around it to come to its rescue in
time of need. The truth is that the city was founded in 1240
by Emperor Frederick II as yet another bastion against Rome.
Near the fountain is the hotel **Le Cannelle**, on via Tancredi da
Pentina, with 115 modern rooms, a pool, tennis courts, and
other amenities.

L'Aquila is an excellent base from which to explore the
area's archaeological collections, medieval villages, and monastic sites. By taking scenic route 17 east, which cuts
through fields of lavender and saffron, past **Bazzano**—
where the 13th-century church of **Santa Giusta**, with its
vaulted campanile and frescoes, is worth a visit—you'll
come to the small hill town of **Castelnuovo**. Beyond it lie the
ruins of Peltuinum, an important city in Roman times. Amid
the remains of a theater and town walls rises the church of
San Paolo, erected in the eighth century. Threaded through
these grassy fields is the ancient *Tratturo Magno,* a ribbon
of white stones and part of a larger network of *tratturi,*
migration paths that was used by shepherds to herd their
flocks from summer pastures in the mountains to winter
ones along the Adriatic. In just a short distance you'll see the
turnoff for the little town of Caporciano, beyond which is the
tiny hamlet of **Bominaco**, perched on a hill and dominated
by the ruins of a castle above. Here are two of the most
celebrated monuments in Christendom, the churches of

Santa Maria Assunta and the small San Pellegrino, founded by Charlemagne. The primitive oratory of San Pellegrino has fascinating colorful naïf frescoes. The upper church, Santa Maria, has none of the delicate charm of the oratory, but it is a handsome Romanesque basilica richly endowed with carved doors, an outstanding pulpit, and a giant Paschal candelabrum. A spirited custodian who lives right across from the churches will admit you and fill you in on the details.

Retracing route 17 through L'Aquila and then travelling route 80 for a few miles, you will come to the ruins of Amniterium, the Sabine city that was the birthplace of the Roman historian Sallust.

THE FOOD OF L'AQUILA AND THE ABRUZZO

If the Abruzzesi don't have a monumental cathedral designed by the likes of Michelangelo or a museum packed with the works of a Leonardo or a Raphael, what they do have and are rightly proud of is their cuisine. Unencumbered by culinary invasions from other regions, the cuisine of the Abruzzo has a pure quality that reflects the simple and genuine nature of the region.

There are quite a few regional specialties, the most interesting perhaps being the traditional dish called *Le Virtu*. The key to this dish is the number seven—referring to the seven virtues. Hence it is composed of seven types of pasta, seven types of pulses, and seven different vegetables. Once all these ingredients are tossed into a pot, the concoction is simmered for seven hours. It is not only a highly flavorful and protein-packed meal, but it also empties the cupboard of every last bean and tube of rigatoni.

Pasta made in the Abruzzo is seasoned with the salty flavors of the sea or with lamb and pork, and is nearly always enriched with the perfumes of the mountain herbs—saffron, pepper, mint, parsley, sage, basil, and chile pepper. In fact, the region's red-hot pepper, *diavoletto,* is thrown around with almost Moroccan abandon, and little jars of fire and oil grace many tabletops.

The delicious soup called *mbusse* in local dialect is made with scraps of fresh pasta and sprinkled with Parmesan. Meats are almost always treated with rosemary, white wine, and olive oil, and saffron and capers turn up in many dishes. The various cuisines of the province—mountain, hill, and sea—were once more separate than they are now, and renowned cheeses appear in every area: *Pecorino* is often used in cooking, and the pear-shaped *scamorza,* made from the milk of cows that graze high in the mountains, is exported on a large scale.

The Abruzzo is also well known throughout the peninsula for a soft honey-and-almond sweet called *torrone.* Produced in L'Aquila from an age-old recipe, it is a favorite at Christmas time.

Of the various regional wines you may sample, the most renowned is the white Trebbiano d'Abruzzo. This delicate, naturally dry wine goes well with white meat dishes and is best served cool. Montepulciano d'Abruzzo is a noteworthy red to accompany all kinds of savory dishes with strong ingredients, and with roast meat, game, and hard piquant cheeses. Other fine labels are Zaccagnini from Bolognano and Monti of Controguerra.

Each region of Italy has its own home-brewed liqueur, usually drunk after dinner. In the Abruzzo, it is the powerfully peppery brew called *centerbe*—100 herbs. This green liqueur packs a real punch.

In L'Aquila you can sample some of the best regional cuisine at the venerable **Tre Marie** restaurant, tucked away at number 3 on via Tre Marie, off piazza del Duomo (closed Sunday evenings and Mondays; Tel: 0862-41-31-91). The story of how the restaurant first opened begins in the 19th century, when the great-grandfather of the present owner went off to the hills to buy cheese and lamb for his inn. He was killed by bandits, and his widow was left with three daughters to raise. The widow taught her daughters to cook, and a restaurant was started when they passed on her recipes to their children. The menu changes with the season, of course, but quite conveniently always includes the basic local dishes. Most diners will opt for the Abruzzo's favorite pasta: *maccheroni alla chitarra,* also called *tonnarelli.* Pressed into very thin strips through the strings of the wood-and-steel harp once found in every household here, the pasta is then served with a sauce either of tomato or of diced meat and *pecorino.* Polenta with chopped sausage is an alternative, and so are the short, flat *fusilli* served with a game sauce. All the local cheeses are on the menu of the Tre Marie, with the *scamorza* prepared *allo spiedo* (on a skewer). The best of the desserts are the *dolcetti paesani di mandorle,* a selection of every sort of almond sweet, from the rich soft marzipan made in the southern hills of Maiella to a crisp variation of Spanish *turron.* In the midst of this gustatory ecstasy, don't forget to look up at the pretty antique majolica plates on the wall.

The ham of L'Aquila was certainly a Spanish innovation—cured here but resembling that of Serrano. Fresh mountain river trout are served at the Tre Marie on a bed of potatoes and black olives; also from the mountains come the truffles, sliced and served with breast of chicken. The two favorite local meats are roast lamb and pork, both cooked with herbs. For the spring festivals, pork is served out on the piazzas, and roast suckling pig is sold at stands with accompanying slabs of bread.

More modest dining can be found at **Trattoria San Biagio**, at number 4 in the piazza of the same name. The simple furnishings here pair well with the honest cooking such as grilled meats, a delicious side dish of bitter greens called *agretti*, and fresh fruit for dessert. Closed Sundays. Tel: (0862) 221-39.

Teramo

The mountain town of Teramo, 75 km (45 miles) northeast of Aquila and reached by beautiful roads (route 80), is the capital of its own province within a province. A picturesque place, it is a Roman town in origin, though much of the city is medieval and Renaissance in appearance. Its heyday occurred during the Angevin reign, and there are many fine buildings dating from this period. Eventually the city was incorporated into the Kingdom of Naples. In the 12th-century red-brick **Duomo**, there is a silver altar consisting of 34 panels depicting scenes from the Bible, by Nicola da Guardiagrele (1448). Located in the old part of town, the Duomo also has a stunning Cosmati portal, good Romanesque statues of saints, and a swallowtail crenelated roofline indicating its Ghibelline allegiance. Roman ruins, including a first-century A.D. amphitheater, have been excavated near the center of town.

At the **Church of Madonna della Grazie**, in the east end of town, there is a 15th-century Virgin made of wood, by Silvestro dell'Aquila. The Villa Comunale houses a museum with artworks by local and Neapolitan artists. In Teramo, the restaurant **Duomo**, via Stazio 9 (Tel: 0861-24-17-74; closed Mondays and August), has been turned by its proprietor, Carlo Rossi, into a place for both traditional dishes and some of his own creations, such as rigatoni *alla Candida,* an aromatic dish with olives, herbs, and prosciutto. Lamb or roast kid can follow, and the wines here are particularly good. Also high on the list is **Antico Cantinone**, which has been serving authentic regional cooking for about 50 years at via Ciotti 5; Tel: 0861-24-88-63.

The best hotel in Teramo is the **Sporting**, via De Gasperi 41, which is situated on a gorge across from the old city. Offering not much in the way of architectural appeal, the hotel does have a host of modern conveniences, such as an indoor pool, air-conditioning, sauna gym, and a pretty good restaurant, **Il Carpaccio** (closed Mondays). One annoying detraction is noise: The walls are thin in this hotel, and every sound reverberates.

EXCURSIONS FROM TERAMO

The road south from Teramo, along route 80, which connects to route 491, requires some careful driving along twisting roads and culminates at the dramatically situated village of **Castelli**, set high on a hill of the Gran Sasso. The town is a haven for pottery lovers and, as one of the oldest ceramic capitals in Italy, contains an impressive collection, which you can see in the **Museo delle Ceramiche di Castelli**. Don't miss the small country church of **San Donato**, just outside of town. Its ceiling, covered with more than 1,000 beautifully painted tiles, is appropriately called the Sistine Chapel of Italian majolica. The church is kept locked, so ask at the Commune office in piazza Roma to have it opened before making the trip from Castelli.

Another worthwhile detour from Teramo is to the little town of **Atri**, reached by scenic route 150 east, and then 553 south. Along the way there are two Romanesque gems of churches to see, both near the juncture of route 553. The first, **San Clemente al Vomano** in Guardia Vomano, is a sweet stony quilt made up of bits of Roman ruins. Built in the ninth century and rebuilt in the twelfth, it contains a highly original ciborium and a statue of (who else?) Saint Clement. A few miles beyond is the Romanesque-Gothic church and abbey of **Santa Maria de Propezzano**, which has 12th-, 13th-, and 15th-century frescoes, and 17th-century frescoes by the Polish artist Sebastiano Majewski, in the spacious cloister. (Obtain keys from the nearby house.)

A good stop for lunch in Guardia Vomano is **Tre Archi**, a simple place serving good regional cuisine (closed Tuesdays and November; Tel: 085-89-81-40).

Atri, the legendary Hatria, which stands on the site of the ancient Sabine city, became a Roman colony in 282 B.C. Vain and somewhat of a big deal during its checkered past, it is credited by some for giving its name to the Adriatic—although another proud contender for this distinction is the

Veneto town of Adria, whose name does sound a bit closer to Adriatic. Ancient scholars such as Pliny and Livy hotly debated these claims. Atri even went so far as to engrave the claim on its coins, the heaviest minted coins in Western Europe (exceeding in weight the oldest Roman coins). Controlled intermittently during the Middle Ages and Renaissance by the Acquaviva dukes, whose **Palazzo Ducale** is now the city's municipal building and post office, the city has recently unearthed some Roman remains in the piazza and under its fine Duomo. The 13th-century Romanesque-Gothic **Duomo**, with its graceful campanile and elegant façade, contains beautiful 15th-century frescoes by Andrea Delitio on the life of the Virgin. It also contains the largest church organ in the Abruzzo (6,000 pipes). In the crypt you'll see the remains of a Roman *piscina* (pool), and mosaics under the altar.

The **Museo Capitolare** (open mid-June to mid-September; reserve in advance at other times) has an excellent collection of jewelry, ecclesiastical items, and wooden sculptures. There's a pretty good restaurant in town, too: the inexpensive **Campana d'Oro**, piazza Duomo 23 (Tel: 085-87-01-77).

The Gran Sasso

Not called "The Big Rock" for nothing, **Il Gran Sasso d'Italia** is truly a sight to see, especially after you arrive from the rolling hills of Lazio or Tuscany, which are indeed puny in comparison. This snow-capped ridge of limestone, 22 miles long, is one of the most compelling reasons to visit the Abruzzo. The highest peak, the Corno Grande (9,581 feet), is higher than any peak in southern Italy except Sicily's Etna. Consisting of two almost parallel chains, the Gran Sasso divides the Abruzzo from the Marches to the north and can be seen all the way from the coastal town of Pescara. In fact, in that seaside city the rock has been known as "the sleeping beauty" ever since the poet and patriot Gabriele D'Annunzio claimed that from that eastern angle, the mount looked like a girl sleeping.

Hikers equipped with good maps, which are available at newsstands, can walk to *rifugi* (inexpensive inns). The Club Alpino Italiano, via XX Settembre 8, L'Aquila, is the best source of information, but a knowledge of Italian is essential. To make the trek to the top of the massif from L'Aquila, take a city bus to Fonte Cerreto, near the village of Assergi (or travel route 17 *bis* north), and from there take the cable car to Campo Imperatore (about a 15-minute ride) at the foot of the

Corno Grande. The hike to the top will take you about seven hours. **Campo Imperatore**, at 7,029 feet and once the bed of a prehistoric lake, is also connected by bus with L'Aquila (about 25 km/15 miles away) and is a lively ski and hiking resort that brims with flowers in spring and sleek skiers in winter. There are three ski lifts at Campo Imperatore and nearby **Monte Cristo**, with runs rivaling the best the Alps have to offer and cross-country ski trails, too. **Campo Felice**, south of L'Aquila off route 5 *bis,* also has good skiing and bobsledding. From here you can visit the picturesque village of **Rocca di Cambio**, the highest in the Abruzzo.

The Gran Sasso is certainly more accessible to present-day travellers than it was to Otto Skorzeny, who was sent to these mountains by Hitler in 1943 to rescue Mussolini. After his arrest, Il Duce had been shifted from one isolated prison to another, and it took two months for the Germans to discover where he was. Once found, the hideaway—a hotel on the Gran Sasso—was surrounded by German commandos who had been landed by glider. The Italian guards put up no resistance, and Skorzeny rushed to the room where Mussolini was lodged, explained what was happening, and with the help of a crack aviator named Gerlach managed, in a damaged plane, to get the dictator to Vienna that very evening.

The Southern Ranges

Many travellers will want to head southeast to the range of La Maiella and Monte Morrone above Sulmona, or to the Colle Rotondo above Scanno, because this southern region culminates in the **Parco Nazionale d'Abruzzo**. Nearly 200 square miles of highland forest of pine, beech, and chestnut trees and sweeping green valleys, the Parco Nazionale d'Abruzzo is home to 40 species of mammals, including wolves, wild chamois, and nearly 100 Marsican bears. There are about 30 species of birds and dozens of snakes, including the deadly Abruzzo viper.

One of the most compelling reasons to visit the region, especially for nature lovers and hikers, is that in June and July its meadows are carpeted with red poppies and yellow gorse, and wild strawberries are there for the picking. The park is ideal for hiking and horseback riding. During the winter both cross-country and downhill skiing are popular, and when the crowds clear out after the Christmas holiday, skiers will find uncrowded slopes where the loudest noise is the crunching of snow under ski.

Most people begin their excursion at **Pescasseroli**, the

largest village in the park, where you'll find a museum, gardens, and a small zoo, as well as a reception center that can provide excellent hiking itineraries. The trails to the Camosciara, a superb mountain area embracing woods, waterfalls, and the Val Fondillo, which is thick with beech, pines, and crystalline waters, are the most favored. A lovely trail of moderate difficulty is the two-hour hike up to the Valico di Monte Tranquillo. The less ambitious may take the *funivia* to the summit of Monte Vitelle. The grandest hotel in the Pescasseroli area is the **Grand Hotel del Parco**, which is beautifully situated and has a garden and pool.

The roads south from Teramo and L'Aquila to the Parco Nazionale, however, also pass through or near places of interest: **San Pelino**, with its Romanesque church, and **Pescocostanzo**, off route 84 near route 17, a gabled medieval town of artisans and once famous for its delicate lace. The church of **Santa Maria del Colle** is noteworthy, with an exceptionally fine ceiling in the nave and a lovely painting of the Madonna and Child on the high altar.

SCANNO

Situated between routes 83 and 17 and reached by route 479, Scanno is a dreamy city perched on a hill and dusted with antiquity; on Sundays the town's matrons don traditional headdresses and long black Middle Eastern dresses that seem frightfully cumbersome. Any attempts to snap a shot of these ladies should be suppressed, for they take none too kindly to gawking tourists and "the sight of a camera is enough to send the old women in black scurrying into archways and vanishing from balconies," as H. V. Morton says in his superb book *A Traveller in Southern Italy.* It is believed that the unique customs and costumes of the Scannesi come from the ancient Macau Scammons tribe, who settled in the area. During the Renaissance, when the wool trade was the town's main business, Scanno was overwhelmingly populated by sheep: 130,000 of them compared to about 2,500 human inhabitants. Today the jewelry trade has replaced wool production, and the population of sheep just about equals that of people.

Of particular interest in the town is the 13th-century church of **Santa Maria della Valle**. Its foundations stand on those of a small ancient temple. From this position there is a beautiful view of a valley below. Scanno is also known for its statue of a Virgin that is said to bring rain. In the first week of May, the little statue, no more than a foot high, is removed from her shrine and draped in fancy Spanish vestments.

Dripping with gold and other gifts, she is carried the two-mile run into town and is then placed in the altar of the village church, where she remains for a month.

There are hotels aplenty, thanks to winter sports, both in town and on the nearby lake. The best hotel is the inexpensive **Mille Pini**, simple, neat, Alpine in style, and, as the name suggests, surrounded by pines. It is situated at the foot of the chair lift to the small winter resort of Monte Rotondo. If you don't mind staying a five-minute drive outside of town, you might try the rustic **Hotel del Lago**, which sits right on tiny Lago di Scanno and offers simple but comfortable lakeside rooms, as well as enclosed terrace dining and boating facilities. Or you can try the smaller **Garden** nearby, which is comfortable and homey. And across the lake is the little frescoed chapel of the Madonna del Lago, where the presiding Virgin of the rain stands. Scanno's top restaurant is **Gli Archetti**, a wonderful old-fashioned tavern in a 16th-century cellar tucked away on a quiet back street, serving excellent bean dishes and grilled trout seasoned with red pepper, at very reasonable prices (via Silla 8; Tel: 0864-746-45; closed Tuesdays).

SULMONA

The best known of the region's hill towns remains Sulmona, right off route 17, just south of the A 25, ideally situated in a rich green basin ringed by mountains. It doesn't take long to discover who the favorite native son of Sulmona is. "Sulmo Mihi Patria Est," declared the Roman poet Ovid, and the Sulmonese have taken his word for it. The principal thoroughfare is the corso Ovidio, the town's coat of arms bears the letters SMPE, a statue of him graces the largest piazza, and there are plenty of indications as to where "Ovid's Villa" can be found. Whether or not it even belonged to his distant kin, its size reminds us, as Ovid himself was wont to do, that he was a knight and born into a wealthy family, in a land "cool and rich in water." (The mountains around Sulmona frame a valley laced with streams.) The poet himself, hardly elegiac, was by no means addicted to country life; highly urbane, he preferred metropolitan Rome. His elegant, completely amoral verses described nature of another sort—without, miraculously, ever using an obscene word. Later, the natives of Sulmona became confused about his powers; it was said that Ovid was more literate than even Cicero because he could read with his feet (his statue in Sulmona has him standing on a book).

When Frederick II made Sulmona capital of its own province, it flourished as a center of learning and religion; today the town earns its prominence in a sweeter commerce—the production of *confetti* (colorful candy-coated almonds) and other nuts indispensable throughout Italy for conferring good wishes at weddings and christenings.

Along corso Ovidio you'll find the handsome church of **Santa Maria Annunziata** and its adjacent palazzo, a harmonious blend of three architectural styles—medieval, Renaissance, and Baroque. Begun in 1320, the church is considered one of the finest in the Abruzzo.

Sulmona was noted for its superior goldsmiths during the 14th and 15th centuries, and there is a magnificent collection of jewelry in the **Museo Civico**, which also houses medieval sculptures and archaeological remains.

Bounding the bustling **piazza Garibaldi**, from which the main street leads, are the fragments of a 13th-century aqueduct that supplied water to the town and its many mills. And across from this thriving marketplace, where stalls teem with everything from fruit to the latest duds, stands the remarkable Gothic portal of **Santa Francesca della Scarpa**, a medieval prop covering the presbytery of a newer church behind it, in the piazza del Carmine. Across from here is the **Fontana del Vecchio**, so named because of the sweet old man who tops it.

The cathedral of **San Panfilo**, at the north end of town, built on the remains of a Roman temple, has a fine Gothic portal, and inside is a crypt containing a lovely 12th-century Byzantine-style relief of the enthroned Madonna, as well as a bust of Saint Panfilo and a 12th-century bishop's chair.

The **Europa Park Hotel**, roughly 3 km (2 miles) north of town on strada Statale 17, offers perhaps the most comfortable lodging here, with tennis courts and a good restaurant on the premises. For dining, choose between **Da Nicola**, piazza XX Settembre 26 (closed Mondays and the first half of July; Tel: 0864-330-70), serving wonderful homemade pasta and grilled meats in a homey setting, and the inexpensive **Ristorante Cesidio**, via Sollimo 25 (closed Fridays; Tel: 0864 527-24), with simple furnishings that never detract from the dazzling antipasti and homemade soups and pasta with beans.

As you walk through the streets of Sulmona, you'll see shops festooned with the handicrafts of the region. Many are worth toting home—such as the gaily colored and handsome bedspreads and carpets that you are unlikely to find outside of the Abruzzo.

As for ski resorts in this region, the town of **Campo di Giove**, 85 km (53 miles) southeast of L'Aquila and just 18 km (11 miles) east of Sulmona, stands in the shadow of Tavola Rotonda (6,703 feet), which is one of the peaks of the Maiella mountains. In the old village there are still some houses dating from the 15th century. The **Abruzzo**, a modest hotel popular with skiers here, has 22 rooms and is very reasonably priced.

A mountain retreat on a grand scale at a very reasonable price is the **Castello di Balsorano**, a fine outpost on the western side of the national park (about 35 km/22 miles southeast of Avezzano) from which to make forays into the park or nearby Lazio. This 13th-century fortress, miraculously spared by the barbarians and the earthquakes, is medieval to the core. Inside, coats of armor, shields, and daggers abound. Some bedrooms, though a bit frayed, are done up in baronial style, with silk wall hangings and ornately carved beds. Proprietor Mary Ricci is English, a help in this region where little *inglese* is spoken. The hotel is very small, however (five doubles, one suite, all with bath and central heating), so reserve well in advance. Meals are good and moderately priced; even so, you will pay more for them than for the room.

Elsewhere in the Abruzzo

PESCARA

The Abruzzo produced another poet, one of our century, and his birthplace is one of the few sights that the Adriatic port of Pescara has to offer. Gabriele D'Annunzio was to be as famous in his time as Ovid was in imperial Rome—and with some similarities: Both, in their youth, shocked the world with their poems of unbridled sensuality; both became the darlings of the aristocracy; and both treated their subject matter as masters of style. But there the resemblance ends. D'Annunzio was born into a humble family, and he was finally a very serious man who loved his country (he lost an eye for it in World War I, and soon after secured the town of Fiume for Italy with his own army of companions). Ovid showed nothing but scorn for the rustic Abruzzesi, whereas D'Annunzio, though born on the coast, was fascinated by the people of the mountainous interior, and in particular by their ventures into sorcery and witchcraft. This dabbling in the occult was, indeed, quite widespread. Because for centuries the people of the region were isolated from other cultures, including the influence of the fledgling Christian church of the third and fourth centuries, the Abruzzesi continued practicing many ancient rites and worshiping ancient gods. In fact, pagan rituals have stubbornly resisted Christianity here; medieval abbeys took the place of pagan temples only in the eighth and ninth centuries. Caves in which ritual ceremonies had been carried out by mystic hermits in the Middle Ages continued to attract pilgrims until just a few decades ago.

The second reason is that witches and snake charmers descended upon the Abruzzo from the west in ancient times, when a people called the Marsi streamed over the mountains to settle around what is now Avezzano, leaving their name on many a village still there: *nei Marsi*. They brought their spells with them, and their ability with snakes, too. Every year at his festival at Cocullo, near Scanno, the image of San Domenico is carried forth covered with a writhing, hissing brood. Children here are taught to handle snakes without fear, and these reptiles even turn up on the coat of arms of the monastic order of San Celestino.

If you go to Pescara in July, you can combine the pleasures of listening to the jazz festival with those of people-watching on the city's long, hotel-lined stretch of sandy beach, which is chock-a-block with sunbathing families (because of the Adriatic's current pollution problem, swimming is not recommended). The seaside terrace of the **Guerino** restaurant, viale della Riviera 4, is a delightful spot to feast on tasty Adriatic dishes, especially the house fish soup (closed Thursdays except in July and August; Tel: 085-421-2065). Be sure to try the *parrozzo,* a rich chocolate cake that is a specialty of the area. The Guerino is expensive; particularly good value can be had at **La Cantina di Jazz**, via delle Caserme 61, which also serves regional specialties. (Closed Sunday evenings, Mondays, and June 24 to July 9; Tel: 085-69-03-83).

Right outside the city, up in the hills, is one of Pescara's finest restaurants. **La Terrazza Verde** (largo Madonna dei Sette Dolori 6, reached by via Rigopiano) enjoys a panoramic setting and specializes in rich duck and goose dishes, such as *pappardelle* in a goose sauce, which it serves in its attractive garden. Prices here are extremely reasonable. (Closed Wednesdays and Christmas; Tel: 085-41-32-39).

Roughly 8 km (5 miles) north of Avezzano, northwest of the Parco Nazionale, are the remains of the ancient town of **Alba Fucens**, near the village of Albe. A Roman settlement from the first century B.C., this site has been under excavation since the late 1940s and to date has revealed basilicas, a bath complex, a villa, and a huge amphitheater. Sprawled over three hills, these Roman ruins stand on top of an even older acropolis built by the ancient Equi.

Also near Avezzano, just off the A 25 autostrada about 13 km (8 miles) to the east, is the town of **Celano**. This small town, clinging to the side of a mountain, hosts a massive castle surrounded by quiet streets lined by medieval homes and churches. Each August the town holds a weeklong festival in honor of the local saints with a series of outdoor concerts and performances.

It was in the Abruzzo that the word *Italia* was born, after an ancient tribal people, the Itali, who inhabited the area. Whether Greek, Roman, or Italic, remains of Classical cultures litter the gentle slopes of Chieti and Molise as they descend toward the sea or toward Apulia to the south. **Chieti**, south of Pescara off the A 25, has its own sterling repository of pre-Roman and Roman artworks; visit the **Museo Nazionale Archeologico di Antichità** in the Villa Comunale, which itself is set amid spacious gardens. The museum's star attraction is the eight-foot statue known as the *Warrior of Capestrano,* which dates from the sixth century B.C. and may be the best portrait of the ancient Italic tribe, the Picenes. From the belvedere of the villa you'll also have a good view of the Maiella mountains. If you head toward the cathedral from the museum you pass the **Tempietti Romani** (the remains of three temples dating from the first century), a Roman theater, and at the edge of town, the ruins of baths.

Eating establishments in Chieti are of a more recent vintage, and **Venturini**, via de Lollis 10, offers tasty regional cuisine on a spacious terrace (Tel: 0871-33-06-63; closed Tuesdays).

For more liberal interpretations of Abruzzese fare, try **D'Angiò e Ristorante La Regine**, a hotel/restaurant enterprise with comfortable, moderately priced rooms and moderate-to-expensive meals (via Solferino 20; Tel: 0871-34-73-56). This glass house perched on a hill just a few miles outside of Chieti is the venture of Nicola Ranieri, a charming host who once owned the renowned Taverna Ranieri in Lanciano. His welcome couldn't be warmer, with wine, fruit, and autographed copies of his recipe collection awaiting you. Though the quarters are undistinguished, the food is top-flight, with dishes such as shrimp over saffron risotto and tender boar atop polenta. Wines are superior here, and there's a good "tasting menu" for 45,000 lire. Try the unusual Picolit dessert wine from Lipari (if you can afford 75,000 lire per bottle).

Chieti makes a good base from which to explore the

impressive abbey of **San Clemente a Casauria**. Take scenic route 5 southwest in the direction of Tocco da Casauria. Founded in the ninth century near the ancient settlement of Interpromium, the abbey was restored in the 12th century and is one of the most beautiful examples of the Romanesque-Gothic style in the Abruzzo, with distinct and individual interpretations of neighboring Apulian and Tuscan styles. The simple interior is a perfect backdrop for the ornate pulpit, a 13th-century Paschal candelabrum, and a stunning ciborium taken from an early Christian sarcophagus.

Molise

Molise, a province of the Abruzzo until it gained regional independence in 1963, is worth a detour to see some of Italy's most ancient towns, often Samnite in origin, with some ruins contemporary with the Golden Age of Greece. In the north of the province are the excavations at **Pietrabbondante**: a theater and scattered temples surrounded by the countryside and situated on a green tableland with views in every direction.

From here route 86, heading north, wraps around the Selvapiana forest and leads to the pristine town of **Agnone**, which sits high above the beautiful Trigno valley. The "Athens of the Samnites," as Agnone is known, shapes bells for worshipers around the world. Visit the Marinelli Pontifical Foundry, the oldest in Italy and supplier to the Vatican. Agnone itself makes for a refreshing stay. Streets are lined with shops redolent of marzipan and display a rainbow of *confetti,* and there are many fine copper stores where you can find every sort of pot and utensil. Although there are no grand hotels here, the **Hotel/Ristorante Sammartino**, situated right in the city, is pleasant and serves excellent food (largo Pietro Micca 44; Tel: 0865-782-39; inexpensive).

Larger in scale than the site at Pietrabbondante and not far south of Molise's capital, Campobasso (off route 87), is the ancient city of **Saepinum**, set in the lovely Matese valley. Mysterious and strongly evocative of Roman vigor, its forums, temples, and monuments are in a miraculous state of preservation, and still set amid bucolic surroundings that recall its role as the stopover for the massive movement of herds twice a year between the heights of the Abruzzo and the Apulian plain. Here, at this important crossroads, shepherds met with farmers to trade their wool. Saepinum began as a Samnite village, founded by the Petri, a Samnite tribe. During the frequent wars with Rome, the Samnites retreated to the surrounding hills to protect themselves. After they were defeated by Roman consul L. Cursor Papirius, they returned to Saepinum, which was later built up during the reign of Augustus (27 B.C. to A.D. 14). After Rome fell in the fifth century, the city was given by the Lombard duke of Benevento to the duke of Bulgari, but by this time its buildings had been abandoned and the surrounding farmland left fallow.

The outer wall of the theater has been converted into modest homes; otherwise, you can wander through the unspoiled ruins of the ancient town, similar to Ostio Antica. For the many travellers who will pass through here on their way south to the wonders of Magna Graecia, the museums of Bari and Taranto, and the temples of Calabria and Basilicata, it is a perfect preparation for things to come.

GETTING AROUND

Service between Rome and Pescara and L'Aquila is at present better by bus (ARPA line) than by train, which is direct but a longer ride by more than an hour. From Rome, buses leave from piazza della Repubblica about every two hours. L'Aquila and Pescara are linked by rail and bus to Sulmona. The Parco Nazionale can be visited by taking the bus (ARPA) from Sulmona to Pescasseroli, the park's administrative center, or the train to Avezzano, on the Rome–Pescara line. Other connections can be made by bus within the region.

ACCOMMODATIONS REFERENCE

The rates given below are projections for 1993; always check for up-to-date information before making reservations. Wide ranges may reflect the differences between low- and high-season rates. Unless otherwise indicated, the figures indicate the cost of a double room (per room, not per person). However, half-board (mezza pensione) rates, which include breakfast and one other meal per day, are per person. The service charge is included in the rate; inquire about tax and breakfast.

▶ **Abruzzo.** 67030 **Campo di Giove**. Tel: (0864) 401-05. Ł50,000; half board Ł50,000.

▶ **Le Cannelle.** Via Tancredi da Pentina 2, 67100 **L'Aquila**. Tel: (0862) 41-11-94; Fax: (0862) 41-24-53. Ł80,000–Ł120,000; half board Ł90,000–Ł115,000.

▶ **Castello.** Piazza Battaglione Alpini, 67100 **L'Aquila**. Tel: (0862) 41-91-47; Fax: (0862) 41-91-40. Ł88,000.

▶ **Castello di Balsorano.** 67025 **Balsorano.** Tel: (0863) 952-36. Closed in November. Ŀ82,500; suite Ŀ110,000.

▶ **Duca degli Abruzzi.** Viale Giovanni XXIII 10, 67100 L'Aquila. Tel: (0862) 283-41; Fax: (0862) 615-88. Ŀ74,000–Ŀ108,000; half board Ŀ84,000–Ŀ104,000.

▶ **Europa Park Hotel.** Strada Statale 17, km 93, 67039 **Sulmona.** Tel: (0864) 25-12-60. Ŀ95,000; half board Ŀ80,000.

▶ **Garden.** Via del Lago, 67083 **Scanno.** Tel: (0864) 743-83. Open Christmas–Easter and June–September. Ŀ80,000–Ŀ120,000.

▶ **Grand Hotel del Parco.** Corso Federico II 74, 67100 L'Aquila. Tel: (0862) 41-32-48; Fax: (0862) 659-38. Ŀ90,000–Ŀ140,000; half board Ŀ120,000.

▶ **Grand Hotel del Parco.** Via S. Lucia 3, 67032 **Pescas-seroli.** Tel: (0863) 91-27-45; Fax: (0863) 91-27-49. Open December–Easter and June 20–September 25. Ŀ180,000; half board Ŀ105,000–Ŀ165,000.

▶ **Hotel del Lago.** 67083 **Scanno.** Tel: (0864) 713-43. Open December 18–January 10 and Easter–October 15. Ŀ100,000; half board Ŀ85,000–Ŀ120,000.

▶ **Hotel/Ristorante Sammartino.** Largo Pietro Micca 44, 86061 **Agnone.** Tel: (0865) 782-39 or 775-77. Ŀ45,000–Ŀ60,000; half board Ŀ50,000.

▶ **Mille Pini.** 67038 **Scanno.** Tel: (0864) 743-87. Ŀ80,000–Ŀ110,000; half board Ŀ100,000.

▶ **Sporting.** Via de Gasperi 41, 64100 **Teramo.** Tel: (0861) 41-47-23. Ŀ75,000–L120,000; half board Ŀ85,000–Ŀ95,000.

NAPLES, CAMPANIA, AND THE AMALFI COAST

By Barbara Coeyman Hults

Campania, nature decreed, would be a balm to body and soul, a luxurious coastline of sheltered bays curving past Naples, down to the ancient Roman cities of Pompeii and Herculaneum, and beyond to the beautiful Amalfi coast and the ancient Greek city of Paestum. Running in back of the coastline are the Apennine mountains, and offshore lie Capri and the volcanic mysteries of Ischia. Even Vesuvius, the volcano that once covered Pompeii with ash, is lovely to look at, with its famous double curve completing the symmetry of the Bay of Naples. (Summer weekends here, however, are far from soothing, with Romans fleeing down the coast in their exhaust-spewing cars much as their ancestors did in their horse-drawn versions, dust billowing. Today's traffic jams, complete with noise and air pollution, make it imperative that you visit in the off-season. At the least, the month of August and summer weekends are to be avoided—or take the train from Rome to Salerno, and a taxi up the coast to the Amalfi Drive.)

Pompeii and Herculaneum are frozen moments, their life stopped suddenly in A.D. 79, when Vesuvius erupted. Paes-

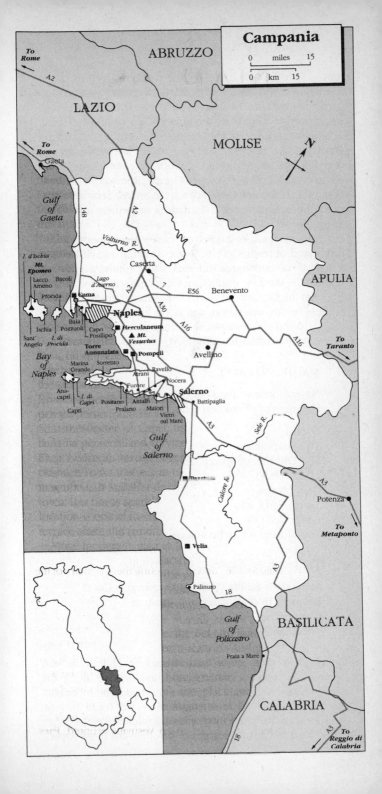

tum's Doric temples have kept their youth as a result of the site being abandoned when malaria swept the South; Tiberius's beautiful villa on Capri fared less well, but the site is so magnificent that ruins are secondary when visiting the island. At Amalfi the cathedral recalls an Arab-Norman past, and the churches and palaces of Baroque Naples are getting a long-overdue face-lift. Naples and Campania combine the influences of, in succession, ancient Greeks, Romans, Byzantines, Normans, Hohenstaufens, French Angevins, Spanish Bourbons, the Bonapartes, and Garibaldi's movement toward the *Risorgimento*.

While the past is preserved here, the present is also celebrated, at resorts as chic as the San Pietro in Positano or as happily untouristed as Palinuro farther south. As a place to relax in the shadow of antiquity, Campania still draws dreamers from throughout the world, rewarding them with days of endless beauty, relaxation, and good food—seafood, macaroni (in a thousand shapes, it seems), pizza, fine wines, and fruits and vegetables from the rich volcanic soil.

MAJOR INTEREST

Natural beauty along the coast
Unique mix of cultural influences

Naples
The Neapolitans
The Old City of Spaccanapoli (Gothic and Baroque
    churches)
Castel Nuovo
Teatro San Carlo
Castel dell'Ovo
The museums (Archeologico, Capodimonte, San Martino)
The bay, from Naples to Capo Posillipo

Antro della Sibilla (Cave of the Sibyl) at Cuma
Pompeii, Herculaneum, and Paestum
Capri, Ischia, and Procida
The Amalfi coast

Campania is one of the easiest regions of Italy to visit because the most sought-after destinations lie along the coast, accessible by car, train, bus, and boat. The mountainous interior is rich with towns and valleys that recall the past, but these are overshadowed by the formidable line of attractions along the seacoast extending southward from Naples.

NAPLES

Naples (Napoli) is not kind to the day visitor, who must combat traffic and noise in a city that offers no gracious piazzas in which to relax. The city bestows its favors only on those who take the time to know it; those who do often remain loyal friends of the city for life. The ancient city of hills follows the Bay of Naples, still a fine sight to behold. Unfortunately the port area itself is not a place to stroll in. From the Castel dell'Ovo west to Mergellina is the nicest bayside area, and by night Mergellina can be enchanting. The bay, with the famous curves of Vesuvius dramatically visible on clear days, is an integral part of the drama of Naples. At the top of the residential Vomero hill, or higher up at the royal palace museum of Capodimonte, the bay is still the star, with promenades and balconies theatrically arranged to view it in its best light.

The urban sprawl outside the city is perhaps the ugliest in Italy, but this is not necessarily the view of the inhabitants, who often left damp, dark, small apartments in the city for what is to them a far better place. Naples, like the rest of the South, suffers from high unemployment. This is caused partly by the long-held policy of the industrial North of keeping the South a source of cheap labor, and also by the Camorra, Naples' Mafia, whose history of extortion and forcing employers to hire their cronies has made moving to the South less than tempting for Italian businesses.

Naples began life as Parthenope, named for the nymph who, unable to lure Ulysses with her siren song, drowned herself in the bay. She was washed ashore at Santa Lucia near today's via Partenope. During the seventh century B.C. Greek settlers from nearby Cuma moved down to the Naples area, and the city grew despite raids by Etruscans. Called Neapolis, or new city, Naples supported Rome in most of its territorial ventures and was subjugated for its loyalty. Rome profited greatly from Naples, where Greek was the spoken language. Much of the Greek influence on Roman thought, art, and architecture was instilled through the Greeks of Naples.

The area was later given colony status as Rome found the hot springs, lovely harbor, and gentle climate enticing—and, of course, there was Capri across the bay. Who worried about the volcano Vesuvius?

Later invasions by the Goths created a somewhat unified society under a duke-bishop who combined church and state

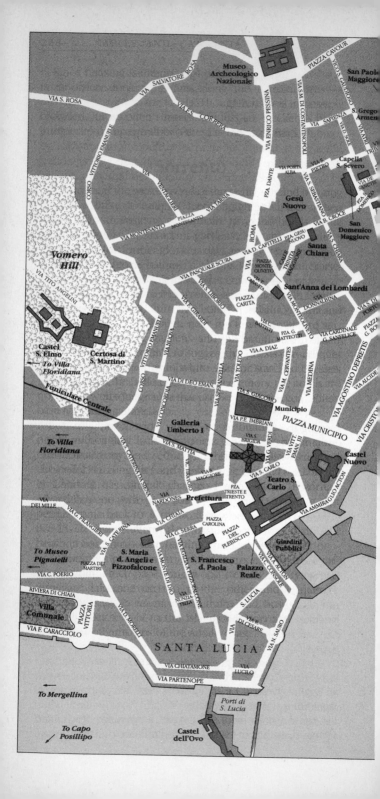

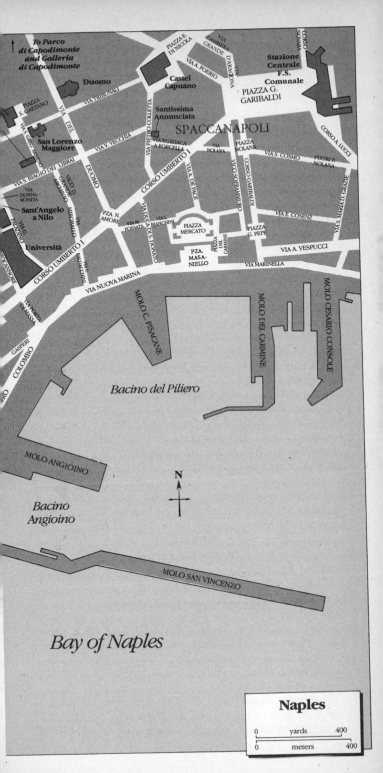

roles. The Normans came in 1140, and in 1224 Frederick II founded the university. Charles of Anjou took control in 1266. Unlike Sicily, Naples flourished under the Angevins—especially under Robert the Wise, who took the city to great heights of intellectual and artistic development during his rule (1309–1343).

When Aragon seized control, exploitive Spanish viceory rule was imposed, leading in turn to the abortive Masaniello revolt in 1647. The Spanish Bourbon Charles III led the excavations of Pompeii and Herculaneum, creating Naples' exceptional museum to receive their contents. The royal palaces at Capodimonte and Caserta were built during his reign, as was a duplicate of Caserta that served as a hospital for the indigent.

But revolution was in the air, spreading from America and France. In 1798 it came to Naples, but with little popular support. The Parthenopean Republic that resulted was short-lived. Napoléon threw out the Bourbons and placed his brother-in-law, Joachim Murat, on the throne. Murat became a popular hero but was executed in 1815 when Bourbon rule was restored. The Bourbons established the Kingdom of the Two Sicilies, but the forces of nationalism and liberty were ultimately stronger, and on September 7, 1860, Garibaldi and his forces entered the city. The following year it became a part of the united Italy. Naples suffered greatly during the two world wars, but practicing *l'arte de l'arrangiarsi,* a Neapolitan version of creative management, the city made do. Even today, its indomitable spirit is one of the world's wonders.

Watching a street scene in Naples is like watching a hundred television sets at once, each tuned to a different channel. The variety of expressions one eyebrow can engineer is amazing, not to mention the full repertoire of mime, both subtler and more obvious than most actors use in a lifetime.

Spaccanapoli District

Naples is known for having given Italy—and the world—some of its greatest thinkers: Saint Thomas Aquinas, Giovanni Batista Vico (who opposed Cartesian logic and saw history as the center of reality), and Benedetto Croce (1866–1952), among others.

Both Saint Thomas and Benedetto Croce lived in **Spaccanapoli**, an area that is the best introduction to a city that has no beginning and no end, only movement. Spaccanapoli was laid out along the precise grid plan favored by the ancient Romans, but don't let that fool you. Nothing else seems planned once you enter these streets.

To get there, take the number 140 bus from Mergellina or the Santa Lucia section, and get off at the end of the line, piazza del Gesù Nuovo, the heart of old Naples (the bus starts at Capo Posillipo). Remember to catch the bus here on its rebound, or you'll have neither sitting nor standing room; sit near the door. At piazza del Gesù Nuovo a tourist office offers color-coded maps of Spaccanapoli, one of the most colorful parts of town. The main tourist office in the Palazzo Reale can also provide these maps, which are worth looking for: Ask for *The Old City: A Stratified Multiple Itinerary Map*.

In the piazza del Gesù Nuovo stands the church of the **Gesù Nuovo**, and in front of it a *guglia*—a curious dethroned, steeplelike monument that seems to be waiting to be lifted back on top of the church. This one is especially Baroque in feeling—festooned with flowers, saints, and angels, with the Madonna on top, like a country processional captured in stone.

The rusticated façade of the Gesù itself is created of diamond-pointed *piperno,* a lava stone obviously easy to come by here in the shadow of the volcano. Inside is one of the typical surprises Naples has to offer: a joyous profusion of colored marble and frescoes. Neapolitans love to marry here in May (the month of the Madonna), with pomp and enthusiasm worthy of the setting. Despite earthquakes and bombs, the church has endured and kept its charm through restoration. The Jesuit architect Valeriani built this structure over an older palace between 1584 and 1601, when the Spanish viceroys ruled Naples. Above the door is *Heliodorus Driven from the Temple* by Solimena, which shows why he was unequaled as a fresco painter until Tiepolo appeared in the North.

After seeing the Gesù, enter the heart of the Spaccanapoli district, a sort of Baroque souk of flower stalls, street-corner transistor hawkers, dark cathedrals named after mysterious saints, and grand palace courtyards hung with flapping sheets and towels that signal the owners' presence.

Just left of the Gesù is via Benedetto Croce. Croce lived in the 14th-century palace at number 12, where he founded the Istituto Italiano per gli Studi Storici (Italian Institute for Historical Research) in 1947. This section of town has a certain cachet that is not always evident. Gray walls and unclean streets often hide some of the most interesting, artful apartments in the city. Croce was born in the Abruzzo in 1866, but he is considered Neapolitan because he was educated in Naples and lived here until his death in 1952. Although his life was spent in practical politics—as a member of the Liberal Party in Parliament and a strong anti-Fascist—in his philosophical system the spirit is the only reality, and history and philosophy cannot be separated.

But first there is the lovely church of **Santa Chiara**, now restored to its Gothic-Provençal charm, where Robert the Wise is buried. King Robert's court was as close as Naples ever came to Camelot—a time that Boccaccio described in the *Decameron,* though he changed the setting to Florence. Robert's wife, Sancia de Mallorca, had wanted to enter a convent, often a favored alternative to an arranged marriage, but fate or her father decided on Robert. As an act of secular devotion she had Santa Chiara and the cloisters built, giving Naples one of its most beloved churches.

Robert's regal tomb at the altar shows the king lying in the Franciscan robes he wore when he entered that order late in life. The section under the king's body, showing the Virtues, divided by six pilasters, is the only remaining part of the original monument. To Petrarch, of whom Robert was a patron, he was the "consummate king and philosopher, equally illustrious in letters and in dominion." His reign contrasted sharply with the Angevin rule in Sicily, which had ended in the bloody revolt of the Vespers in 1283.

The adjoining **cloisters** is a peaceable kingdom hidden from the noisy streets. The columns and garden walls, brightly decorated with majolica scenes of life beyond the convent walls, kept the nuns from being homesick. Italian convents often attracted the aristocracy, who added the good life to good works by enjoying the world's beauty and developing a high level of cuisine, still found in some convent bakeries that sell to the public. (Not here, unfortunately, though there is a wonderful baker up the street at piazza San Domenico.)

Past Croce's palazzo is another *guglia*—this one a votive offering against the plague. It marks the church of **San Domenico Maggiore** (1308), the church of the Aragonese nobility. During the late 1500s, when Naples was ruled by a Spanish viceroy, powerful religious landowners built hundreds of convents, monasteries, and churches here, creating a small ecclesiastical city for themselves, which is why churches seem to pop up on every block, though many are now closed or abandoned.

San Domenico is very much alive inside, with its elaborate Renaissance altars. In the candlelit Cappellone del Crocifisso, the painting of a crucifix is regarded as sacred because it spoke to Thomas Aquinas, one of the most prominent Neapolitan saints, who lived and taught in the adjoining monastery. Although Aquinas's rooms were destroyed by an earthquake and the bombs of World War II, a few relics remain: the bell he used, a portrait bust, the papal bull that proclaimed him Doctor of the Church. Stop in the sacristy to see the wonderful frescoes by Solimena and the unusual Aragonese tombs set into the walls. (Stop also at **Scaturchio**, across from the church, for coffee and *sfogliatelle,* light triangular layers of pastry with a soft ricotta center flavored with lemon or candied fruit bits.)

Off the right side of San Domenico is via De Sanctis, where the **Cappella San Severo** serves as a crypt/museum for the family of the alchemist prince Raimondo di Sangro (1711–1771). The bizarre statues *Modesty* (veiled) and *Disillusion* (netted) stand at the altar, flanking Sammartino's extraordinary *Veiled Christ,* a virtuoso work in marble that even shows Christ's wounds under a marble veil. Downstairs is something else again: two mummies, seemingly a mass of veins and arteries, preserved by an ancient Egyptian formula. Gossip says that the woman, obviously pregnant, was Sangro's mistress and was caught with her lover. A likeness of the prince appears on the medallion on his tomb upstairs.

On via Nilo the church of **Sant'Angelo a Nilo** contains the burial monument of Cardinal Brancaccio. Donatello carved the bas-relief of the Assumption of Mary, noted for its perspective, on the front of the sarcophagus, as well as the cardinal's head and the right-hand figure raising the curtain. (The church is open mornings.) The word *Nilo* here comes from the reclining figure lolling in the largo Corpo di Nilo, supposedly the river Nile, sculpted in Nero's time. For some reason the statue was beheaded, buried, and then resurrected, and a new head added. Perhaps it was his mischievous ways—he whispers to women who pass at night, say local residents. An espresso break at the **Bar Nilo** will let you observe wily Nilo and the passing throng.

A few blocks to the east is **via San Gregorio Armeno**, the street of Christmas past and present, where the makers of *presepi* fill their workshops with every object imaginable for their miniature Christmas villages. The village is Bethlehem, Neapolitan style of course: Tiny kitchens are filled with wee pizzas and the utensils used to make them, as well as all manner of fruit and vegetables (young family members roll out the pea-size tomatoes and apples); cows and camels; wise men and townspeople; and, of course, the Nativity scene and walls of angels, who also swing from the ceiling on wires. Although December is the street's prime time, you can shop for inexpensive *presepi* at **Esposito's** (number 46), and for fine reproductions of classical *presepi* at **Ferrigno** (number 10, at the top of the street), all year round.

The church of **San Gregorio Armeno** has charming cloisters and Luca Giordano's frescoes of the life of Saint Gregory the Armenian. Giordano painted so many murals in Italy and at the European courts that he was called Luca *fa presto* ("Luca works fast").

At the top of the hilly, arched street stands the church of **San Lorenzo Maggiore**, built over the ancient pagan basilica of Neapolis (currently being excavated). In about 555 a church was built here to honor Saint Lawrence, but Charles of Anjou replaced it with this grander Gothic church in the 13th century. In this mystical setting Boccaccio first saw his Fiammetta—supposedly Maria, natural child of Robert the Wise—during Mass one Easter Eve when the Pascal candle was lit from a brazier and incense permeated the very French setting of pointed arches and parapets. "As San Lorenzo was favored by the Angevin kings and therefore fashionable, there were present besides the devout folk many young men with curled and frizzed hair and many young women more luring than lenten in their dark dresses, who loitered beneath the Gothic arches and perhaps lipped a prayer or two between glances and signals and ogles; for even sinners do sometimes pray.... Among them was young Messer Giovanni Boccaccio," writes biographer Francis McManus.

Petrarch, too, came to mass at San Lorenzo, and in 1345 prayed with the monks throughout the night during an earthquake and tidal wave. Another drama is remembered in the left transept, where Joanna I, Queen of Naples and granddaughter of Robert the Wise, is buried. Her adopted son Charles poisoned her when she supported Louis of Anjou against him. Her body was first displayed in the cloisters of Santa Chiara, though she was not yet dead, according to some observers. Adjoining the church is a fine museum related to its history. The enormous refectory, which can be visited, was once used for the parliament of the Kingdom of Naples.

Across the street, the figure of San Gaetano gestures to the sky in front of the church of **San Paolo Maggiore**, built on the site of the pagan temple of the Dioscuri. The columns on the façade come from the early temple, as does the torso under the statues of Saints Peter and Paul. Nero also had his singing debut in this temple, despite an earthquake that shook the building.

Since body and soul are intimately related in Spaccanapoli, the *pizzaiolo,* or pizza maker, is also venerated. At the **Trattoria Lombardi**, via Benedetto Croce 59, *pizzaiolo* Mazza produces the adored Margherita pizza—made with fresh mozzarella, tomatoes, and fresh basil—kept simple so that the delicious crust can be fully appreciated. Drowning pizza or pasta with sauce is not a native tradition; Italians like the taste of the crust as much as the topping. The best pizza makers use a brick oven, sometimes throwing a sprinkle of wood chips in at the last minute to singe the cheese and crust perfectly. The simple Margherita was named for Queen Margherita of Savoy, who in 1889 first tasted this version as prepared by *pizzaiolo* Raffaele Esposito. Another pizzeria (also serving a full menu), the **Bellini**, also in Spaccanapoli (via Santa Maria di Costantinopoli 80), wins approval from finicky Neapolitans. Hearty, even rough, wines accompany pizza; subtler flavors would be lost. Near piazza Dante, the **Porta Alba** is another venerated pizza spot (via Porta Alba 18; Tel: 081-45-97-13; closed Sundays). It's always crowded, so go early. All three restaurants are inexpensive.

From San Lorenzo it's easy to find the **Duomo**, off via Tribunali on via del Duomo. There the patron saint of Naples, San Gennaro, performs a miracle twice yearly (September 19 and December 16) by liquefying his congealed blood, which is kept in vials in a dazzling chapel here that has paintings by Domenichino. Multitudes gather for the occasion, waiting to judge the rapidity of the transformation—the quicker the blood liquefies, the better the outlook for the city. Gennaro, called Januarius by the Romans, was beheaded in nearby Pozzuoli in 305, after which he walked to Naples carrying his head (or so the story goes). The chapel where all this occurs is much admired in its own right. In the cupola is the fresco of *Paradise* by Lanfranco (1643). The other frescoes are the work of Domenichino, recently restored thanks to the Napoli '99 Foundation, a group of private and business patrons who choose individual artworks as projects for restoration. The entrance gate of gilded bronze was designed by Fanzago, as was the intarsia of marble on the floor.

In the crypt, or Cappella Carafa, a brilliant altar in Renaissance style contains San Gennaro's tomb. Among the other occupants of the Duomo are Charles Martel and Charles I of Anjou, entombed at the entrance door and surrounded by an elaborate Luca Giordano fresco. Opposite San Gennaro's chapel is the much-restored basilica of **Santa Restituta**, the oldest part of the Duomo, built during the fourth century on the site of a temple to Apollo, and with 27 columns that are probably relics of that early temple.

If you retrace your steps to piazza del Gesù Nuovo, detour briefly from the piazza down the calle Trinità Maggiore to piazza Monte Oliveto, where the church of **Sant'Anna dei Lombardi** is full of wonders, including a life-size pietà of eight figures by Guido Mazzoni (1492). The chapel to the right of the entrance contains an *Annunciation* by Benedetto da Maiano (1498), who also finished the tomb of Mary of Aragon in the opposite chapel, where there is a fine *presepio* by Antonio Rosellino.

On nearby via Maddaloni (4/b), musicians will savor the instruments displayed at **Panharmonikon**, Dottore Mario Ascione's wonderful store. Tel: (081) 522-04-37.

The Museums of Naples

Antiquity was once considered the province of the king, but Garibaldi relieved the royals of that responsibility in 1860, and now museums are open to all. At the **Museo Archeologico Nazionale**, north of piazza del Gesù Nuovo at the far end of via Santa Maria di Costantinopoli, the collection is one of the best in the world, especially the paintings from Pompeii and the small bronzes. Some of antiquity's most beautiful paintings are found here, especially those of *Sappho* and *Paquius Procolus and His Wife;* the latter were bakers whose portrait was found in their home in Pompeii. The equestrian statue of Emperor Domitian and the Farnese Bull are among the other treasures. Visit this museum before travelling to Pompeii and Herculaneum to get a clearer idea of those cities' original grandeur.

North of the archaeological museum is the **Palazzo e Galleria Nazionale di Capodimonte** (bus number 324 from piazza Vittoria), which occupies a hillside palace that enjoys a panoramic view of the bay. Charles III used the palace as a hunting lodge instead of a castle because it had no water. The art gallery has an important collection of works by Caravaggio, Rubens, Bellini, Titian, and Filippo Lippi. Napoli '99 has restored the brilliant portrait of *Antea* by Parmigianino and the *Assunzione della Vergine* by Pinturicchio. Also represented here is the lesser-known Artemisia Gentileschi. Influenced by Caravaggio, she favored gruesome scenes painted in bright, translucent tones with a strict attention to detail. Her paintings of Judith here and in the Uffizi in

Florence are especially dramatic. Stop also at the Royal Apartments to see the Salottino di Porcellano, an all-porcelain room delicately decorated in Chinese motifs—peacocks and flowers and other objects. (A museum devoted to porcelain is located in the Villa Floridiana on Vomero hill; see below for Vomero.)

The De Ciccio collection in Capodimonte includes porcelain, tapestry, and small bronzes. Charles of Anjou was entranced by the *presepio* tradition and started making his own figures from clay while the queen and princesses sewed and embroidered the costumes. As the king did, so did society, and this once-simple tradition of keeping Christmas all year became a new way for the nobles to outdo one another in grandiosity. The museum is open from 9:00 A.M. to 2:00 P.M.; closed Mondays.

On top of Vomero hill, to the north of the Santa Lucia area, is the **Certosa di San Martino**, a 14th-century monastery that is now home to examples of Naples' *presepio* art, including entire *presepi* as well as individual figures—not well presented but interesting nonetheless. Topographical maps, ship models, and the like evoke the city's cultural past, from the Bourbons to Garibaldi. In addition, the sweeping view of the bay and Vesuvius from the belvedere is one of the city's most dramatic. (Take the funicular from Piazza Duca d'Aosta near via Toledo.)

Fanzago's lovely white cloisters here contrast with the elaborately beautiful marble intarsia of the church, also his creation. The monks' chancel is the most remarkable section, with a superb marble communion table, a *Nativity* by Guido Reni, and *Christ Washing the Disciples' Feet* by Caracciolo, founder of the Neapolitan school, which opposed Mannerism in favor of Caravaggio's more emotional path. His young rival, the Spaniard Giuseppe Ribera (1591–1652), known in Italy as Spagnoletto, became the court painter because of his sensuous approach. In the treasury is his *Deposition* and Giordano's last work, *The Triumph of Judith*. Caracciolo's frescoes of *The Life of Mary* (1631) decorate the third chapel on the left. On the entryway arches are Ribera's *Twelve Prophets;* the *Deposition* (1638) at the door is the work of Massimo Stanzioni, the leader of the Neapolitan school at mid-century, known for his subtle chromatic values, melodious lines, and lyrical expressions.

The **Vomero** is a pleasant respite from the benevolent madness below. A short walk from San Martino will take you to the **Villa Floridiana**, a lovely park, scented with camellias in season, that has the added charm of a splendid view of the bay as far as Capri.

Dining up here is a pleasure: **Daniele**, via Scarlatti 104 (Domenico Scarlatti was born in Naples), is excellent and not expensive. Homey **Dona Teresa**, at via Kerbaker 58, serves a full dinner for about 20,000 lire—very reasonable.

From Castel Nuovo to the Villa Comunale

The enormous **Castel Nuovo**, a brick castle on the harbor northeast of Santa Lucia, was built (1279–1282) by Charles of Anjou and presents such a tough-looking, macho aura that it's called the *Maschio Angioino*. Naples, however, is ever the great deceiver, and the castle housed more than just artillery. In fact, the court of Robert the Wise enjoyed a style of life behind its walls that inspired much of the *Decameron*. Boccaccio and Petrarch were here, and Giotto painted frescoes here, though they were subsequently destroyed when the Aragonese redecorated and did away with the Angevin decor. Two magnificent features remain: the Renaissance arch and the Cappella Palatina. The Arco di Trionfo that welcomed Alphonse of Aragón to Naples has been restored, thanks again to Napoli '99. In the Cappella Palatina (also known as the church of Santa Barbara) is a Madonna by Laurana—one of the most sensitive sculptors of Madonna and Child themes—and a fine rose window. The Sala dei Baroni, though damaged by fire, gives an idea of the castle's finest hours.

Farther east, near the bleak central railroad station, **Mimi alla Ferrovia** is a boisterous trattoria that has long been enjoyed by Neapolitans not seeking a quiet lunch. The food is very good, the prices are moderate, and the people-watching at its peak. It's not for the timid, however (via Alfonso d'Aragona 21; Tel: 081-553-85-25; closed Sundays).

To relive the postwar years that de Sica portrayed, go to the **Forcella** flea market, near the station and the church of the **Santissima Annunciata**. The market is a warren of dubious salespeople selling even more ersatz products. (If they're real, they're contraband. Try not to look too much like a tourist, and don't carry anything you don't want to lose.) The church is a gem architecturally, but that's difficult to see beneath the rubble within and without. The 14th-century original was destroyed by an earthquake, but the building was restructured from 1760 to 1782 by the illustrious Luigi Vanvitelli and his son Carlo.

To the west of the castle, in the piazza del Plebiscito, stands the **Teatro San Carlo**, where a 250-year anniversary gala in 1987 brought music celebrities from around the world. The frayed red velvet and gilt interior has seen many of opera's most tearful moments. Although the season begins in December, musical productions are staged during much of the year. Take the tour if you can't see a performance.

Across the street is the enclosed shopping precinct **Galleria Umberto I**, usually less than sparkling clean and too drab to evoke its glamorous sister in Milan, and more interesting for its basic glass-and-steel form than for the shops inside. Finding a table for a coffee in one of the cafés affords you the pleasure of watching Neapolitans discuss politics. Nearby is the **Ristorante Ciro**, where most of San Carlo's musical stars have gained sustenance from the grilled meat and fine vegetable dishes (via Santa Brigida 74; Tel: 081-552-40-72; closed Sundays).

Next to San Carlo is the enormous **Palazzo Reale**, facing a piazza that is probably beautiful at dawn but for the rest of the day is a traffic cop's nightmare. The only effective preparation for crossing the street would be running with the bulls at Pamplona. Inside the 17th-century palace are a museum of paintings and the Bourbons' court theater, both at the top of a wonderfully dramatic staircase.

The piazza to the northwest of the palace, piazza Trieste e Trento, leads to via Toledo/via Roma, the main shopping street and the boundary imposed by the Spanish viceroy Don Pedro of Toledo in 1537 to separate royal Naples from the overpopulated streets beyond. The **Caffè Gambrinus** on the piazza still gives a hint of the Belle Epoque. The via Chiaia also starts at the piazza and leads to the most fashionable shopping areas in Santa Lucia and Mergellina. The **via Chiaia** is one of the nicest parts of Naples, a pleasure to explore (and the place to at least window-shop at Fendi and Armani).

From the Palazzo Reale you can also walk down the via Cesare Console to via Santa Lucia and straight on to the **Castel dell'Ovo** and its harbor, where you can have dinner at one of the seafood restaurants. None is particularly good, but all are entertaining for the views of fishermen and contraband runners plying their catches.

The sandcastle form of the Castel dell'Ovo is said to have been built over an egg that the Roman poet-magician Virgil placed inside a glass container and secured in the foundation. If the egg breaks, the castle will fall and take all of Naples with it. A castle of Lucullus stood here, too, and then the castle-building Normans erected a structure, which was enlarged by the Hohenstaufen monarch Frederick II, who kept his treasury and held parliament here before embarking on his crusade. Thirty years later his grandchildren, the sons of Manfred, died while imprisoned at the castle. In 1379 Joanna I received the antipope Clement VII here, and later she was imprisoned in the castle until being poisoned. The situation now is happier: The castle has been restored, and you can wander through its dungeons and parapets. At night it's brilliantly floodlit, and the tourist office sponsors folk-dance performances here.

Turning away from the city and along the harbor to the west, you'll soon reach the **Villa Comunale**, an attractive area refreshed by a park full of tropical trees and plants. A flea market operates here the third week of each month. At its far side is Mergellina, one of the prettiest parts of Naples and the place for a seaside walk after dinner. (Remember the 140 bus that plies this route.) You might want to stay in Mergellina, a less frenetic environment than center city—but then what isn't?

Mergellina and Posillipo

The **Museo Pignatelli**, opposite the middle of the park, is lodged in a splendid 19th-century Neoclassical villa. The carriage museum in the garden is charming; inside the villa there is a major collection of European porcelain. Evening chamber music concerts are frequently scheduled at the museum, and good trattorias are plentiful in the adjoining Mergellina district. A favorite with Neapolitans is **Palummella**, where the antipasto table is worth the trip and the amusing owner adds to the fun. Another small and charming place, **Al Poeta**, on piazza Salvatore di Giacomo, serves a wonderful *rigatoni alla montanara* made with artichokes, chopped meat, prosciutto, and mozzarella (closed Mondays; Tel: 081-769-69-36). At **Lo Scoglio di Frisio**, a bit fancier but still moderately priced, a variety of sea creatures pass through the kitchen to be transformed into imaginative combinations—squid and artichokes, for instance—and even the fritters have a taste of the sea (via Mergellina 1, Tel: 081-66-83-85; closed Tuesdays and August).

One of Naples' most fashionable restaurants, **La Sacrestia**, is located in a charming villa at via Orazio 116 in the

Mergellina area, with a grand view of the bay. La Sacrestia features traditional Neapolitan recipes and interesting culinary experiments in a sophisticated (and expensive) atmosphere. Reservations suggested; Tel: (081) 761-10-51; closed Mondays and August.

Neapolitan cuisine has touches of the Greek, Arab, French, and Spanish, yet the result is pure Parthenopean. Along the bay, *maccaruni* (the word used for all kinds of pasta in Naples) is prepared in as many ways as fish, meat, vegetables, and cheese require. A classic Neapolitan dish is *spaghetti alle vongole veraci,* made with tiny clams from the Naples area, the tastiest in existence. The sauce is white with garlic and parsley or red with small tomatoes. Vermicelli is sometimes served with a sauce of *polpetielli affogati* (tiny octopus in tomato sauce). *Lasagna alla napoletana, penne all' arrabbiata* (with hot peppers), *linguine alla puttanesca* ("whore's style"—spicy with black olives and capers), and the hearty *pasta e fagioli* all make eating here a joy. Vegetables, too, are given special attention. Eggplant is always a star, especially in *parmigiana di melanzane,* baked with cheese, tomato, and basil. *Peperoni* (large peppers) with cheese and *friarielli* (a kind of broccoli) cooked with a sauce of sausage can be eaten unadorned or in a pasta sauce. Meals often begin with *caprese*—fresh buffalo mozzarella from nearby Caserta's buffalo farms—and tomatoes with fresh basil. (Buffalo in Italy are water buffalo, not bison.)

Campania's volcanic soil is kind to grapes. Good whites include Fiano di Avellino, Vesuvio, Ischia, Falerno (of which Pliny spoke), Ravello, and Greco di Tufo. Lacryma Christi, best known because of its name (Christ's Tear), can be quite good. Taurasi is a great red for hearty meals. Falerno's red is excellent, as is Gragnano, which can be *frizzante* (sparkling). Ravello also produces a very good red as well as a *rosato* (rosé) with which to finish the meal.

Continuing in Mergellina: Near the church of Santa Maria di Piedigrotta and the Galleria Quattro Gironate, steps lead to the Parco Virgiliano and the so-called tomb of Virgil—which it probably is not but was so recorded by Seneca and Petronius.

If you continue on to the western limit of the curve of the Bay of Naples you'll reach **Posillipo** (po-SILL-ipo), a fashionable residential area that extends out along a cape—known to us from Clams Posillipo, found on many a menu. From the park near the cape's end a belvedere offers views of Naples, Vesuvius, and out to Capri. Under a wisteria-shaded terrace four generations of the Concetta family have served seafood and home-grown vegetables at their trattoria **Rosiello**. It's one of the most charming of the bay-view trattorias in Naples, albeit an expensive choice (via Santo Strato 10, Posillipo; Tel: 081-769-12-88; closed Wednesdays). At the busy fishing harbor at Capo Posillipo, **Giuseppone a Mare** (Tel: 081-76-96-002; closed Sundays), more moderately priced, has long served fine seafood to Neapolitans. Though lately it hasn't lived up to its old standards, it's still amusing, informal, and a good place to enjoy the harbor sights. You may want to take a taxi to Capo Posillipo because the number 140 bus stops inland of the cape itself. The trip from Naples is expensive, however.

STAYING IN NAPLES

Naples' most famous hotels, such as the **Excelsior** and the **Vesuvio**, line the waterfront of the Santa Lucia area opposite the Castel dell'Ovo. The **Royal**, their less attractive sister, is alongside, with dramatic views of the Castel dell Ovo's majestic form against the bay. On a stormy night this is the place to be. (The Vesuvio and the Royal have bay-viewing restaurants.) The **Santa Lucia** has its devoted clientele because of its very individual, flamboyant style in private and public rooms. All these hotels are expensive. The **Belvedere** is a far more economical version, on the Vomero, with fine panoramas of city and bay.

An alternative is to stay in the section Mergellina, which has the advantage over all of them in being a place where it's possible and desirable to go walking at night. Mergellina evenings have a summer-resort atmosphere, with fish restaurants and amusements along the sea promenade. Or stay at the comfortable **Hotel Paradiso** at the top of the hill in Mergellina; a funicular descends from the hotel to the port, where the Capri hydrofoils dock. The hotel restaurant is excellent and is graced with a perfect view of Vesuvius across the bay. Don't let the Best Western signs fool you—it's not a chain hotel in style. The **Pinto-Storey**, in the lively, attractive neighborhood of Chaia adjoining Mergellina, is a comfortable and old-fashioned *pensione* on several floors of an elegant apartment house. (Be sure to secure your room in this popular hotel with payment in advance; otherwise, the management is likely to give your room away.)

To see Naples economically, you would do well to take the short hydrofoil or ferry ride from the Mergellina dock out to **Procida**, a charming and usually tranquil island that has maintained its fishing-village look. Boat service to Mergellina and Capri is frequent from Procida, and the **Arcate** and the l'Oasi, both pleasant hotels on Procida near beaches and greenery—are currently remarkably inexpensive.

WEST AND NORTH OF NAPLES

Campania's northern region still steams with volcanic activity; here and there fumaroles (jets of steam and mud) escape the earth. The steamy land seemed magical to the ancients, who were both repelled and fascinated by the dance of gases over the earth, which they called the Campi Flegrei (Burning Fields).

LAGO D'AVERNO

To continue the mood, go on to Lake Averno (take the SEPSA bus from Pozzuoli; see below). It was here that Virgil located the mouth of the underworld, the Gate of Hell: "And here the unnavigable lake extends, o'er whose unhappy waters, void of light, no bird presumes to steer his airy flight. Such deadly stenches from the depth arise, and steaming sulfur that infects the skies. From hence the Grecian bards their legends make, and give the name Avernus to the lake." That no bird could fly over it and survive, as the legend has it, is not hard to believe—they may not have wanted to, after seeing this eerie place. Actually their deaths were caused by gaseous vapors that rose from the lake, then blocked from the sun by tall trees. But it must have been merrier when the Romans came to the Temple of Apollo; the remains of this vast spa can be seen on the other side of the lake.

Lago d'Averno today is not exactly paradise, but the infernal fumes are gone and the birds have returned. If it's Saturday and you want to hear more of the legend and to experience the true Neapolitan underworld, follow the path on the lake's south side (sign: **Grotta della Sibilla**). At the entrance to a vast underground grotto you'll find Carlo Sintillo, who guides (in his own English) people through the gallery and pools where a very mystical Sibyl bathed. His phone (at home) is (081) 867-32-56. The better-known Sibyl's Cave at Cuma may be an anticlimax after this.

The Greeks created myths around their fumaroles, but the Romans created spas and used the volcanic activity to heat the water and their villas. All the accoutrements of the good life (or bad life) followed quickly, especially around **Baia**, which became famous for its uninhibited lifestyle.

At Baia the **Scavi di Baia** (excavations) are reached by a steep path that begins near the station. The excavations are extensive and hard to decipher without a guide. Baia was a thermal spa and summer resort with nightlife suited to every taste, catering to wealthy Romans, whose extensive villas were built along this peninsula. The terraces at the site are splendid, and if most of the grandeur has been lost to earthquakes, this spot can sometimes evoke a touch of it. (Baia is also on the railroad line.)

CUMA

Cuma's history began before the Greeks arrived, but it was they who made Cuma the most important city of its time along the coast, with an area that stretched as far as Pozzuoli. At Cuma there stands a marvelous acropolis where the temples of Apollo and Jupiter, and a Roman crypt, are interesting sites, but by far the most-visited attraction is that of the famous Sibyl of Cuma, l'**Antro della Sibilla Cumana**, dating from the sixth and fifth centuries B.C. This was one of the most sacred places of Classical Greece. Aeneas came to consult the Sibyl in these long arched corridors, and she scattered leaves and read his fate. Virgil speaks of the "frenzied prophetess, deep in the cave of rock she charts the fates, consigning to the leaves her words and symbols. . . . " When the wind rushes through, it's easy to imagine the leaves flying about while the questor awaited life-or-death answers.

Though sibyls can't be found, a local *mago* often has fliers distributed here, listing the hours he'll be available to tell your fortune, sometimes with a drop of oil in water. Near the entrance to the site, the **Taverna Giulia** conjures up exquisite dishes.

To get to Cuma from Naples, take the Ferrovia (railroad) Cumana from Stazione Montesanto. From the train station a bus leaves for the site. There is a long, pleasant walk from the bus stop to the entrance. Plan to be in this area, as in the others, only when other people are around. The lunch hours, when custodians are away, are prime time for thieves on Vespa motor scooters.

POZZUOLI

Pozzuoli is multileveled, not by design but by bradyseism, a condition in which the earth shakes, rises, and falls. This condition has given the coast here a bizarre appearance. An ancient dock can be seen below the waterline, and water covers the floor of the **Serapeum**, part of the archaeological zone near the harbor. Although the area is the site of one of the oldest Greek settlements in Italy (530 B.C.), most of the ruins on view are Roman or Samnite. The Romans came in 194 B.C. and established the now half-sunken port for trade with the East. The Serapeum, which was a market hall, is often called the Temple of Serapis, although it was never a temple. A statue of the god Serapis was found there, which gave the structure its name.

Inland and across the railroad tracks stands the **amphitheater,** in its time (A.D. 67–79) one of the largest in Italy, and used for gladiatorial combat. The underground area where the wild beasts were kept is well preserved. It was in these cells that San Gennaro, Naples' patron, was kept before he was martyred by beheading. The amphitheater was originally decorated with statues and marble pillars, appropriate for the wealthy Roman weekenders down here for the hot springs at nearby Solfatara (see below).

Pozzuoli, known more today as Sophia Loren's birthplace, has been the site of frequent natural disasters. Attempts to remove the citizens to more secure foundations have largely run aground; as soon as new housing is built, squatters move in, and evicting an Italian in Italy is rarer than sangfroid in Naples in August.

The port area here is about as salty as a port can get. But many of the dubious-looking trattorias attract a lunch and dinner crowd of bankers and lawyers—all lovers of good food—as well as the more colorful locals. Among the favorites are inexpensive **Da Giggetta** at the port (via Roma 4/4; Tel: 081-526-15-63) and **Don Antonio** (via Magazzino 20; Tel: 080-867-39-41). If the earth moves, just exchange "this may be it" glances with your fellow diners and then go back to the *frutti di mare.*

When visiting this area, and particularly the more remote sites, stay near other people. Vespa-riding thieves are plentiful. Leave any valuables in your hotel. If you can take a small camera, do so, but camcorders and expensive SLRs will attract attention.

To reach Pozzuoli, take the Ferrovia Cumana, which you can pick up in Naples at piazza Montesanto, near Piazza Dante, or at Mergellina. To reach **Solfatara,** walk (or bus) along via Solfatara near the amphitheater in Pozzuoli for about ten minutes to see the steaming mud on the still-active crater, which is about a mile and a half wide. At the Bocca Grande (Big Mouth), vapors shoot up violently, reaching a temperature of 320° F.

If you have lots of time and the boat schedules favor it, return by sea to Naples from Pozzuoli, changing ferries at Ischia or Procida.

Caserta

Inland from Naples to the north (45 minutes by train), the **Palazzo Reale** at Caserta is not maintained royally but is still worth seeing for its evocation of regal splendor similar to that of Versailles. Charles III had the palace built in 1752 from the plans of Vanvitelli. Inside, the grand staircase and apartments, the chapel and theater, are lavish in their use of marble; outside, the gardens are stunning—vast fountains, groves, statues, and cascades. The English gardens are the most beautiful of all. All of this leads inexorably to a desire for wild boar, which you can enjoy in an amazing number of ways—from fillet to sausage—at **Ritrovo dei Patriarchi**, where venison and rabbit also star on the moderately priced menu (località Sommana; Tel: 0823-37-15-10; closed Fridays).

ANCIENT SITES SOUTH OF NAPLES

Ideally, you should allow three days to see Pompeii, Herculaneum, Vesuvius, and Paestum—after spending some time at the Museo Archeologico in Naples seeing its collection from the Roman sites. (Paestum has a fine museum of its own.) As the site at Pompeii is extensive, it requires the better part of a day. You can easily see Herculaneum and Mount Vesuvius in a day, since a bus for Vesuvius leaves from the town of Herculaneum, which is only about 6 km (4 miles) from Naples (closer than Pompeii). Paestum, farther south, can be reached by train from Naples or Salerno. We discuss Pompeii first because, although Herculaneum is closer to Naples, Pompeii is the premier site in this area. Be aware that this very touristed area is popular with thieves.

If you are starting from the Amalfi coast with a car, take the inland road from Ravello. Without a car, take the bus to Meta, before Sorrento, and then the Circumvesuviana train to Pompeii or Herculaneum. Returning, get off at Sorrento to ensure a seat on the bus (the bus stop is at the train station).

Pompeii

Pliny the Younger tells us what happened on August 24, A.D. 79, from notes his uncle (the Elder) took while watching Vesuvius's eruption from the sea before the fumes (or a heart

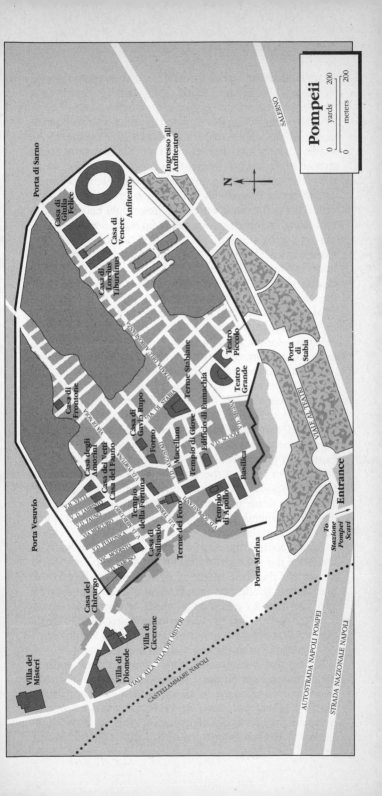

Pompeii

yards 0 200
meters 0 200

N

SALERNO

Porta di Sarno

Ingresso all'
Anfiteatro

Casa di
Giulia Felice

Casa di Venere

Anfiteatro

Casa di
Lorcius Tiburtinus

VICOLO DELL'ANFITEATRO

Casa di
Frontone

VIA DI NOLA

Teatro
Piccolo

Porta
di Stabia

VIALE AL TEATRI

Casa di
Gavio Rupo

Foro

Terme Stabiane

Teatro
Grande

VIA DELLA STABIA

Casa degli
Amorini

Casa del Vetti

Casa del Fauno

Tempio
della Fortuna

Macellum

Tempio di Giove

Edificio di Eumachia

VIA DI NOLA

VIA DELLE TERME

VIA VESUVIO

VIA DI MERCURIO

VIA FULLONICA

VIA VETTI

VIA DI LABIRINTO

VIA DEL FAUNO

VIA AUGUSTALI

VIA SOPPRAMURO

Basilica

VIA DEGLI AUGUSTALI

VD. CUOPI. VERGINI

Porta Vesuvio

Casa di
Sallustio

Terme del Foro

Tempio
di Apollo

VIA DELLE FORESE

VIC. MODESTO

VD. NARCISO

Casa del
Chirurgo

Casa di
Cicerone

Villa di
Diomede

Porta Marina

Entrance

To
Stazione
Pompei Scavi

Villa dei
Misteri

VIALE ALLA VILLA DEI MISTERI

CASTELLAMMARE-NAPOLI

AUTOSTRADA NAPOLI POMPEI

STRADA NAZIONALE NAPOLI

attack) killed him. Ashes were falling, hotter and thicker, as his ship drew nearer, followed by bits of pumice and blackened stone. It all seemed a great adventure to him at first. He went home and took a nap and awoke to find his house filling with pumice stone and ash. "Elsewhere," he wrote, "there was daylight by this time, but they were still in darkness, blacker, and denser than any ordinary night, which they relieved by lighting torches and various kinds of lamp."

The city of Pompeii itself tells the story clearly after that, especially in the tragic casts of figures caught under the ash, crouching under tables, struggling up stairs, a mother holding up her baby, a horribly contorted dog on a leash. The molten ash made sculptor's molds of them, which have been injected with a cement mixture to re-create the bodies displayed in the museum (Antiquarium) at the entrance to the excavations or returned to their original locations.

At both Pompeii and Herculaneum the fascination lies in the glimpses of everyday life frozen in time. Although Pompeii has a forum, major theaters, and all the trappings of a large Roman city, the private homes and small businesses are what intrigue archaeologists and social historians. The houses were often built in the classic Samnite style (the Samnites were settlers before the Romans arrived), with an atrium at the entrance; then a peristyle, or colonnaded courtyard, surrounded by the family bedrooms; then a dining area, or triclinium, where chaises longues were used for family and guests. The Samnites were the most influential architects in creating the city we see today, although the Romans, who had rebuilt it after an earthquake in A.D. 62, added grandiose touches and created a more luxurious lifestyle for themselves. (The famous Pompeiian red cinnabar dates from this period.)

Before starting the tour, which will take a few hours at least, buy the book (sold here) that has transparent sheets re-creating the look of the original buildings to aid the imagination. Guides and guards are also useful because they have the keys to everything—much of interest is locked away for security reasons. It's worth the tips. (For armchair explorations, read the new Time-Life *Pompeii: The Vanished City,* a treasure in its illustrations and text.)

A great deal of the artwork from Pompeii is in the archaeological museum in Naples, but the **Casa dei Vettii** here has been allowed to keep its treasures and has been partly restored. Researchers have studied friezes and dead roots to re-create the garden's original look. The brothers Vettii, Aulus and Restituti, bought this gracious villa during the first century A.D. Thanks to the beams and roofs that covered it when it fell, the floor remained in good condition through the centuries. The house, also Samnite style, faces inward and encloses both atrium and impluvium (rainwater opening) as it unfolds toward the colonnaded garden. In the vestibule a phallic symbol—a familiar charm that, along with coiled snakes, was thought to bring good luck—wards off the evil eye. The sight and sound of water were used to refresh the garden, as in the Arab houses that Romans had seen in Egypt and the East. The dining room is also exquisite, thanks to its black borders—bright with *putti* going about their daily chores—and the frescoes of gods and goddesses, which are almost Baroque in feeling.

A few other villas worth visiting are the Casa del Menandro, the Casa di Loreius Tiburtinus, the Casa del Fauno, and the Villa di Diomede. (Uniformed guides will encourage you toward the "pleasure houses," where for a contribution you can see paintings that require little imagination.) The Villa dei Misteri was the scene of Dionysian cult rituals, some of which are dramatically portrayed on the walls. Pompeii's extensive baths were spas to relax in, not for aerobics or pumping iron. They paid athletes to do those things.

There are four identifiable periods in Pompeii's painting: the first, Samnite, used stucco to imitate marble, as in the **Casa del Fauno**; the second introduced architecture with a skewed perspective, as in the **Casa di Sallustio**; in the third, imaginative architectural scenes abound—whole cities and harbors—as in the **Casa di Frontone**; and the last, as in the Casa dei Vettii, featured fuller perspective and dramatic scenes.

In addition to the artwork and villas at Pompeii, you can now enjoy 15 **gardens** that re-create their Roman originals, based on exhaustive research on burned pollen and seeds found during excavations (near the site on via Castriccio).

The excavation of Pompeii began during the mid-18th century, after a farmer discovered an enormous stone phallus while he was cultivating his garden. (At least that's the story told.) In any case, digging began, and continues. As Goethe summed it up, "Many disasters have happened in the world, but few have brought such joy to posterity."

Dining in the town of Pompeii can be an elegant (and pricey) affair at the much-praised **Il Principe** (piazza Bartolo Longo 8; Tel: 081-863-33-42; closed Mondays). At about half the price, **Zì Caterina**, at via Roma 16-22 (Tel: 081-863-12-63; closed Tuesdays), is a comfortable place to collapse after a day in the ruins. Scarcely less shocking than Vesuvius's eruptions is the news that a McDonald's will be opening near the excavations. The **Villa dei Misteri**, near the site, is an inexpensive hotel if you want to spend the night.

Pompeii is about 40 minutes from Naples on the Circumvesuviana railroad, a pleasant ride that begins in Naples' Stazione Centrale, which is less pleasant. A new major music festival, the Panatenee Pompeiane, presents concerts each August at Pompeii's theaters.

The site is open daily, from 9:00 A.M. until one hour before sunset.

Herculaneum

Herculaneum (Ercolano), named for its legendary founder, Hercules (Ercole), is much smaller and more intimate than Pompeii. Because the inhabited section of town above the site looks very similar to Pompeii, if you have seen Pompeii first it may seem as if Herculaneum were Pompeii come to life. When Pompeii, inland, was drowned in ashes, Herculaneum, on the coast, was flooded with mud churned up by the roiling sea. Consequently, even the wood survived in its mud and lava casing. Furnishings and foodstuffs, statues and mosaics, can be seen at the site.

Although Herculaneum's past is detailed in this manner, its full history—whether the lovely villas belonged to Pompeii's merchants or to Romans using it as another holiday resort—is not known. According to Seneca, Caligula was among the social set in Herculaneum.

The early history of eighth-century B.C. Oscan and later Samnite civilization is similar to Pompeii's; in fact, graffiti in Oscan can be seen on Herculaneum walls. Herculaneum remained packed in mud until 1709, when an Austrian prince who was having a well dug found a theater where the water table should have been. King Charles III got into the picture in 1738, and in 1755 he established the Royal Herculaneum Academy. *The Antiquities of Herculaneum,* a book of engravings published by the academy, influenced European taste for the next half century, from jewelry and clothes to interior design and painting.

As at Pompeii, guides or guards have keys, making them indispensable, and some of them are quite knowledgeable as well. Be sure to see the **Casa del Tramezzo di Legno** (House of the Wooden Screen), a patrician residence with a garden, and the new museum at the site, containing recently excavated material.

The **Terme**, for men and women, are also fascinating, with mosaics of Neptune and dolphins, seats for the bathers, and ledges for their clothing. In the **Casa del Mobilio Carbonizzato** (House of the Carbonized Furniture), the bedroom, painted in the warm red associated with Pompeii, has a bed and table from the original house. The **Casa di Nettuno** has a lovely nymphaeum in mosaic, and adjoining it is a shop with food staples still packed in storage jars. Be sure to visit the Palaestra and serpent fountain, the Casa dei Cervi (House of the Stags) and its fine sculpture, and the Terme Suburbane (Suburban Baths), with their marble rooms and windows opening onto the sea.

The site is open daily, from 9:00 A.M. until one hour before sunset.

For lunch in Ercolano, try **La Piadina**, via Cozzolino 10 (Tel: 081-771-71-41; closed Tuesdays).

The Circumvesuviana train goes to Herculaneum, as does a trolley (*filovia*) from the piazza Municipio (but never take the trolley on Sunday or during rush hour; at any other time, it provides a nice way to see the neighborhoods around Naples). From Herculaneum buses go to Mount Vesuvius.

If you have extra time, visit the **Villa di Oplontis** at Torre Annunziata, also on the Circumvesuviana route, between Herculaneum and Pompeii, where brilliant murals have been uncovered in a splendid villa currently being excavated.

Mount Vesuvius

Vesuvius has come through history with very good press, given the horror it inflicted on Pompeii. Nowadays Neapolitans look fondly at Il Cratere, as they call it, a dear sight on the horizon that means home, not to mention good wines like Lacryma Christi from its slopes and succulent fruits and vegetables. The plume of smoke is no more; only an occasional fumarole escapes to let us know it's down but not out. The famous truncated cone, Monte Somma, rises 3,714 feet above sea level. Probably the best way to see it is to take the blue SITA bus from Herculaneum. From the bus stop it's about an hour's climb to the top, and you'll need a guide. The views from the summit, however, are spectacular.

Paestum

At the ancient Greek city of Paestum, south of the Amalfi coast and Salerno, wonderfully preserved Doric temples are set in a grassy field surrounded by gardens and hills. Although the site is small, it's so charming that you may want to spend time just relaxing here. The museum is also exceptional.

Greek Poseidonia (called Paestum by the Romans) was founded around 600 B.C. and dedicated to Poseidon, or Neptune, in 400. The founding Greeks came from Sybaris (itself an Achaean colony in Magna Graecia near the modern city of Taranto), whose lifestyle made the word *sybarite* synonymous with luxurious comfort. Their influence on the region was considerable, and the city they built impressive. The magnificent **Tempio di Nettuno** (actually dedicated to Hera and misnamed), set in lovely countryside, re-creates the Hellenic spirit with its symmetry, serenity, and grandeur. The sacred interior area was originally covered with white stucco. The **basilica** is the oldest structure here (mid-sixth century B.C.). Its columns are curved (entasis), an unusual feature, but Greek Italy was more cavalier in its approach to temple art than was Athens, where the rules of symmetry, variety, number of columns, and such were strictly adhered to.

Paestum is rich in detail. Exceptionally graceful figures, carved on the metopes that stretched across the top of the columns of the **Tempio Italico**, are still on the site and can be admired at close range. In the museum itself, metopes from the Sanctuary of Hera, 13 km (8 miles) north of Paestum, are exhibited on an impressive model. Hercules' feats, centaur battles, and the *Oresteia* are the themes. The museum's star attraction, however, is the **Tomb of the Diver**, discovered in 1968 and considered the find of the century. Outwardly the tomb resembles others in this vicinity, but when opened it was found to be covered with intriguing frescoes, some subtly erotic. The diver is delightful, diving through frescoed space into eternity.

For lunch at Paestum go to **Nettuno**, near the site (Tel: 0828-81-10-28; closed Mondays). Paestum can be reached by train from Naples or Salerno; the excursion can also include a relaxing stop at a beach about a mile from the temples or at the little cove resort of **Palinuro** farther south along the coast, where simple accommodations are inexpensive and the coast is beautifully unspoiled. (Stay at the **Gabbiano**, with pool and beach.) Driving in this area is not the problem it is in Naples.

Palinuro was named for Ulysses' helmsman Palinurus, the inspiration for Cyril Connelly's *The Unquiet Grave*. Condemned "to lie naked on an unknown shore," he was finally buried at a place that "will always be called Palinurus," as Virgil tells the story in the *Aeneid.*

Just below Palinuro on the coast is the resort of Praia a Mare, where Calabria begins (see that chapter).

Velia, between Palinuro and Paestum, has a similar history, much that we know of it having been provided by Strabo. Founded as Elea in 535 B.C. by Greeks fleeing the Persians in Asia Minor, the town (whose ruins are not as well preserved as Paestum's, which were situated in the middle of a malarial swamp) is of great interest to archaeologists. However, as the remains are fragmentary, there is today little of interest to most visitors. Elea, which later became Velia, was the center of the Eleatic school of philosophy, which flourished during the fifth century B.C. and numbered Parmenides and Zeno among its leading lights. Parmenides, one of the most important of the pre-Socratics, represents the appearance of metaphysics in philosophical thought, and with him philosophy became a strict discipline. Parmenides applied his talents to daily life as well and drew up Elea's constitution.

The Phoenician Zeno, Parmenides' most important pupil and his successor in the Eleatic school, is considered the founder of stoic philosophy. Zeno developed the dialectic method of argument, in which the adversary's thesis is examined and the consequences of the thesis are shown to contradict each other or the thesis itself. Zeno and Empedocles in Sicily developed systems that led to the Sophists' art of rhetoric. Traditional customs and ethical principles were subjected to rational examination, raising the question— which would later cause the Cartesians sleepless nights—of how we know anything at all. (Zeno is well known even today for his various paradoxes.)

On a more worldly level, under later Roman domination Velia served as a base for Brutus when he was fighting Octavian. When Rome declined, trade routes moved to the Adriatic, depriving Velia of its prominent position and prosperity.

The very elegant **Palazzo Belmonte**, the property of Naples' noble Pignatelli Belmonte family, now rents spacious and tasteful apartments on a private beach at Santa Maria di Castellabate, near Paestum.

CAPRI

When Ulysses sailed past Sorrento, he looked westward and saw an island: "And lo, the Siren shores like mists arise. Sunk were at once the winds. . . . Some daemon calmed the air, and smoothed the deep. Hushed the loud winds, and charmed the waves to sleep."

Ulysses might find the Siren easier to resist these days if he dropped anchor alongside a ferryload of day-trippers. Capri in season is subject to package tours that visit the island to shop—good for the economy, bad for the Siren. The answer is to visit this still-enchanting island off-season. (The island of Capri is easily reached by ferry or hydrofoil from Naples's Mergellina dock, or from Sorrento or Amalfi.)

Go in the spring, when the island is pastel colored and fragrant with orange blossoms, jasmine, and roses, and the air seems to be filtered through a sparkling mist. In the fall the air becomes clearer, and the sea's emerald and sapphire tones are at their most intense. Some romantics even love the winter, when dark clouds shadow the steep cliffs and vineyards and the wind whips the waves about the harbor.

Capri is small, about two miles wide and four miles long. Almost entirely mountainous, the island rises from the port, Marina Grande, on the north side to the town of Capri at the next level, and high above, to Anacapri. At sea level the rocky shore, interspersed with small beaches, is deeply cut with grottoes, such as the famous Blue Grotto (Grotta Azzurra).

Marina Grande, where the ferry docks, is almost entirely given over to outdoor cafés during the warm months. On the quay, as you leave the boat, the tourist office dispenses maps showing the island's intricate paths, along with lists of hotels and apartments. The Caremar ferry ticket office, opposite the ferry landing, provides a baggage storage area and is open until 7:00 P.M. If you want to travel from Naples or Sorrento south to Amalfi and Salerno, you can take an early boat to Capri, leave your luggage while you visit the island, and then continue south by an afternoon boat. At Marina Grande you might hire a convertible-top taxi for a panoramic trip around the island.

From Marina Grande you can take the funicular to the *town* of Capri, in the center of the island. Buses leave both Marina Grande and Capri for Anacapri and for the Grotta Azzurra, or rather the cliff above it. Motorboats also leave Marina Grande for the Grotta, transferring their passengers to smaller boats that will clear the Grotta's low entrance. (This last method is not advisable in very hot weather, as the boats may sit in the sun for half an hour while awaiting entry.)

The town of **Capri** is charming—especially its tiny central *piazzetta*, occupied by outdoor cafés and smart shops. The small buildings, archways, narrow passages, wrought-iron decoration, and flowers recall Moorish Spain. The rest of the town is a flowery mall whose shops run from Armani to Yves, with many less-striking labels in between. On the piazzetta, **La Paresienne**'s windows show some of the year's most glamorous clothes. Custom-made pants can be picked up within two hours at **Caprese** on via Camerelle. **Chantecler** (on via Vittorio Emanuele) and **Campanile** have hand-crafted jewelry, and **Massimo Goderecci** on via Valentino offers interesting ceramics.

From Capri, a lovely walk of about two hours will take you to the **Villa Iovis** (pronounced YO-vis), Tiberius's villa. The path begins at the archway across the piazzetta and is fairly well marked. As you approach the villa's entrance you'll see the **Torre del Faro**, the ancient lighthouse used by Tiberius from A.D. 26 to 37 to relay messages to other lighthouses and on to Rome. (The Faro collapsed just a few days before he died; some historians believe that this event may have killed him, fearful as he was of portents.) Beyond the Faro, signs point to the Salto di Tiberio, the cliff from which he is said to have thrown his enemies (almost 1,000 feet down). Just how evil the old emperor was is debatable, but his exploits have made good copy since Suetonius described his "exquisite" tortures and his seductions of young boys and girls. The Villa Iovis itself was the grandest of the 12 villas supposedly constructed during the Roman "occupation" of Capri. Although there were probably not 12 (for the 12 deities), there were enough buildings to obliterate almost every trace of the earlier Greek and Phoenician cultures.

At the villa the baths, imperial lodgings, and kitchen, and the loggia with its spectacular views, can be seen, though all are mostly in ruins. This was a fortress as well as a home for Tiberius, built not just for the view but for the natural defense such a height provided.

Retrace your steps to the crossroads near the market, and follow the signs to the **Giardini di Augusto**, designed to provide even more flowers for the island, which boasts some 850 species. Along with the flora you'll see statues of gods, nymphs—and Lenin, who enjoyed Capri's charms after the 1905 uprising. From here the **Faraglioni**, two huge vertical stones offshore, are seen in their considerable splendor. (On clear days they are visible from Naples to Sorrento.)

Follow the signs down to the **Arco Naturale**, a fantastic upthrusted arch of limestone. On the way you might stop at the **Paradise Bar**, appropriately named given its location amid splendid scenery and the fragrant air and birdsong.

From the arch you can walk down to the **Grotta di**

Matromania, which may have been the site of ancient cult worship but was certainly used by the Romans as a nymphaeum, a place of art and beauty in which to relax. From here you can walk around the base of Mount Tuoro to the Porto di Tragara and then make the steep climb to the town of Capri.

From Capri you can reach the town of **Anacapri** by bus. Anacapri, at the western side of the island, is known for the brilliantly beautiful **Villa San Michele,** which was built on the ruins of a Roman villa (some of which is preserved inside) by the Swedish writer and physician Axel Munthe. Munthe lived on Capri for 40 years (arriving in 1910) and wrote *The Story of San Michele* here. The 17th-century furnishings, the Roman statues, and the garden are among the treasures to enjoy. The villa also is frequently the setting for concerts, so watch for notices. The church of **San Michele** nearby dazzles with its majolica floor depicting Adam and Eve in a medieval bestiary of an Eden.

While at Anacapri, take the chair lift to **Monte Solaro** if possible. The chair lift is just that—you alone on a chair attached to a cable that rises to the top of the world—or so Monte Solaro seems. (You are actually only about eight feet above the ground as you're lifted to the top.)

The **Grotta Azzura** (Blue Grotto) was, before the sea claimed it, a nymphaeum for Tiberius, filled with statues long lost or stolen. It gained international fame only in 1826, when a Slavic poet was enraptured by it and told his friends. It is the mysterious light, blue in one cavern, silver or pearl in another, that still draws tourists, and this light is best about midday. If there are many tourists about, you will probably have to wait in a long line: the larger boat you leave in will transfer you to a little rowboat so that you can enter the low opening into the Grotta. Take a book, a hat, and suntan oil, and then wait; it's worth it. Or, if you prefer, you can walk down to the grotto's entrance from above, near the ruins of the Roman villa at Damecuta, on the northwest part of the island. A taxi will take you there and wait as part of the trip.

The tour of the island by boat (from Marina Grande) is delightful, for Capri is as lovely and full of natural enchantments from without as within.

If you have a few days to enjoy Capri, there are other Roman ruins such as the Palazzo a Mare and the Baths of Tiberius, the monastery called La Certosa (if open), and many other grottoes and natural wonders you can visit.

From Capri you can also take day trips to Ischia, Procida, Naples, or Sorrento, or even farther south to Positano and Amalfi (in summer) if you decide to use the island as a base.

STAYING ON CAPRI

If a room with a view is of paramount importance to you, and you don't arrive in high season (when you'll usually need a reservation), you can leave your luggage at the Deposito Bagaglio at Marina Grande or at the top of the funicular in the town of Capri and set out to find the view that makes it all worthwhile.

The **Quisisana**, just off the piazzetta in Capri, is exquisite—and exquisitely expensive. In this private world of Oriental carpets, crystal chandeliers, and velvet cushions on gilt-frame chairs, the hotel guests discuss mergers and acquisitions and whither fashion around a dazzling oval pool, far from the cares of Naples. All bedrooms open onto the sea.

La Scalinatella is also luxurious and extremely charming, built on hillside terraces facing the sea. The **Villa Brunella**, nearby, is less expensive and also built on levels that reach the sea and its own little beach. The owners, Vincenzo and Brunella, pride themselves in keeping the hotel almost as a private home.

At the center of Capri, the newly renovated **Flora** maintains its personalized service in a fresh Pierre Deux setting. Each bedroom terrace overlooks the Faraglioni, the huge offshore rocks that act as marks for navigators. The **Luna** is magnificently situated on the cliffs just a short walk from the town. It is not as sparkling new in decor as the others, but its location is one of the loveliest. The pool and outdoor dining terrace share the superb views.

More moderate, also in Capri, are the **Villa Sarah** and the **Villa Krupp**. The Villa Sarah is situated on the road to the Villa Iovis but is close to the piazzetta. It has the homey air of a private residence. The Villa Krupp, nearby, has fine views, and each room has a balcony. Both Lenin and Gorky were guests here.

Near the Arco Naturale, the **Bel Sito** is a simple hotel with romantic views and its own trattoria and garden. **La Tosca**, via Birago 5, is inexpensive, and some of the rooms have views as dramatic as the hotel's name.

In general Anacapri is the place for more reasonable room rates. The **Caesar Augustus** is both glamorous and weathered, looking out to sea from high above the island.

They offer bus service from the port. The **Bellavista** is true to its name, with terraces opening to the sea; it's near the main piazza.

DINING ON CAPRI

In the town of Capri, **La Capannina**, located near the piazzetta, is one of the best restaurants. Their Capri wine is excellent, best enjoyed in the attractive inner courtyard. Very fresh *zuppa di pesce* (fish stew) and ravioli are specialties here. (Reserve; Tel: 081-837-07-32; open from March to October; closed Wednesdays except in August.) The inexpensive **Cantina del Marchese** (via Tiberio 7e; Tel: 081-837-08-57) is worth the uphill walk from piazza Umberto for its excellent fresh pasta dishes and homemade cheeses and cured ham. (Open daily in summer; closed Thursdays off-season.)

Down near Marina Piccola there are several interesting trattorias. You might seek out **Luigi's** (Tel: 081-837-05-91) near the Faraglione on strada dei Faraglioni, with a beach nearby, the latter a rare item on the island. Open from Easter to September (lunch only), it's a half-hour walk or a boat trip from Marina Piccola. Next to Luigi's, separated by a cliff, lies a languid trattoria, **La Fontelina**, a perfect retreat from the tourist hordes if you care to climb the cliff or have a boat. In Marina Piccola, the perennial sun-and-seafood luncheon spot is the **Canzone del Mare** (Tel: 081-837-01-04), where the food competes with the views and year-round tans for attention (open from Easter to October). The best beach is here, with lockers and showers.

In Anacapri, take a bus or taxi out near the lighthouse (the Faro) to **Nello al Faro**, carved out of the rocks. Nello serves good fresh fish and pasta—and provides changing rooms in case you want a swim. The surf out here is often rough, however, and thus is not for all swimmers. This is a great place for a late-night snack in summer.

ISCHIA

Beautifully green Ischia (ISS-kee-ah), a Greek trading station in the eighth century B.C., is the quiet sister island of chic Capri, with comfortable beaches, friendly people, and bizarre troglodytic dwellings high in its volcanic mountains.

Lacco Ameno is the smart resort town, where the luxury sister hotels **Regina Isabella e Royal Sporting** sheltered Liz and Dick from the paparazzi when love was new and *Cleopatra* was a wrap. Its spa is one of the best for mud (*fango*) baths; those of the **Jolly Hotel delle Terme** at Porto d'Ischia are also excellent, and one-day treatments are available. Whatever the volcanic mud from Monte Epomeo does for the body, it introduces an entirely new world of relaxation. The process begins in a darkened room, when a bell signals the approach of a scuttle of hot mud from somewhere below the floor, presumably Vulcan's forge. Then someone appears to spread *fango* on your sheeted bed; you sink in, are wrapped like a mummy, and are covered with the rest. Primeval ecstasy ensues, followed by a firehose-like shower, herbal wraps, almond rubs—whatever the new creature wishes. All cares are banished.

Elsewhere on the island, little towns like picturesque **Sant'Angelo** are interspersed with white beaches and gentle seascapes; less gentle but more mystical are the mountain roads that seem to go back in time as you climb. The restaurant **Girasole** can be reached by water taxi from Sant'Angelo, and you can precede your luncheon with a relaxing immersion in the hot volcanic sand followed by sauna and swimming (Tel: 081-99-92-97). At Sant'Angelo have seafood at salty but pricey **Dal Pescatore** (Tel: 081-99-92-06; closed January 15 to March 15). Near Lacco Ameno the **Negombo** has a great view of the bay. The Regina Isabella has an excellent dining room and a barman who remembers Liz's favorite drinks from the wild days. At **Forio**, on the western coast, stay at the **Residence Villa Tina** if you'd like an apartment sleeping four to six, with terrace and kitchen.

THE AMALFI COAST

Beyond Pompeii, where the Salentine peninsula curves seaward, the Amalfi coast begins. (The town of Amalfi itself is on the southern shore of the long peninsular coastline.) From the coast's northernmost town, Sorrento, to Positano, the road called the Nastro Azzuro (Blue Ribbon) rises over the magnificent crest of land at the top of the peninsula, with a long view north toward Naples and south toward Positano.

One of the most beautiful roads in the world, the **Amalfi Drive** begins at Postiano and continues to Amalfi. It curves along towering, massive, majestic cliffs terraced at intervals with vineyards and lemon groves, and is bordered by a rocky shore far below, dotted with fortress towers that once defended the towns from sea raiders. The sea views are as fresh as watercolors, splashed with pine and cactus and brightened by wild roses and bougainvillaea.

Since relaxing is the point of being here, a few days' stay is in order; don't try racing along the hairpin turns—a diversion best left to the locals. Though August is impossibly crowded, July is often surprisingly less so. Weekends bring bumper-to-bumper traffic to the narrow coast road.

Sorrento

Sorrento, near the western end of the peninsula and hugging the top of cliffs that reach 150 feet in height, is a big city when compared with Positano and Amalfi. Its grand hotels in the Belle Epoque style, luxuriant gardens, and splendid views recall Sorrento's former glorious days as a regal summer spot. The rocky shore has bathing pavilions built out like cruise-ship decks. Torquato Tasso, the 16th-century author of *Jerusalem Delivered,* was born in Sorrento, and is fêted with a statue and a piazza named for him. The hotels **Excelsior Vittoria** and **Parco dei Principi**, although near the town center, are surrounded by dazzling gardens and panoramic views, their grand appearance seeming to suggest that guests play croquet on the lawn all summer in white suits or starched dresses. However, with the Belle Epoque just a memory, the hotels are now filled with tour groups that use Sorrento as a convenient base for touring Campania.

Sorrento has a wide variety of accommodations at all prices. Although it lacks Positano's glamour, it has a faded charm that many find seductive. The **Hotel Elios** is a good choice for dazzling tiles and views of the bay, and the **Loreley et Londres** has similar charms. Dinner at **La Favorita– o'Parrucchiano** will give you a taste of the cooking that people come back to Sorrento for (corso Italia 71; Tel: 081-878-13-21; closed Wednesdays off-season). There is no real beach in Sorrento—only bathing pavilions at sea level.

Furniture is now a main industry here, particularly intarsia work, in which paper-thin wood stencils of varying patterns are laid one on top of the other and lacquered. Sorrento is also a terminal for trains and buses and has frequent boat service to the islands of Capri and Ischia as well as the other towns of the Amalfi coast.

Positano

Pastel sweet by day and as magic as a Christmas village by night, Positano is set into the cliffs. With Capri, it is the most fashionable place to be "seen." The town descends the hill from the main road (the Amalfi Drive) to the small harbor and the sea. The streets are steep or stepped, so espadrilles or rubber soles are necessary, especially after a rain. For a quick view of the town, take a ride on the orange bus marked "Interno Positano," which runs about every hour.

Some of Italy's best and most expensive hotels are located here, including the splendidly hidden San Pietro, dazzling with its azaleas and hand-painted tiles, thanks to the inventive whimsy of the late Carlino Cinque, who created this delightful place. However, its once international tone is now decidedly American. The San Pietro also has a lively restaurant. Reservations are suggested for non-guests; Tel: (089) 87-54-55. The hotel, just beyond town, has a private bus to provide transport.

In the town proper, the Sirenuse is a posh, sparkling hotel with antiques, huge terraces, and a pretty pool. Along the coast road near the San Pietro sits the Poseidon, a fine villa with a sweeping view of the coast as well as a pool and restaurant. In town, the charming hotel Palazzo Murat occupies an 18th-century palazzo where Murat, once king of Naples, spent some time.

Among the reasonably priced are the Hotel California, a comfortable spot with spacious rooms and terraces, tiles and greenery; and the Marincato, which also has comfortable rooms, many with terraces. Down on the beach the Buca di Bacco restaurant has created a hotel in a 19th-century villa; balconies face the sea. This tends to be a lively spot, and may be best in the off-season unless you like the late-night life. Both the Casa Albertina and the Casa Maresca are family-run and offer perfect views, and both are less expensive than most of the other hotels in Positano.

In addition to its flower-laden hotels and villas, Positano has a tiny harbor, a cathedral, and lots of boutiques—and not much else (aside, of course, from the marvelous scenery). The Cambusa (Tel: 089-87-54-32), Buca di Bacco, Covo dei Saraceni (Tel: 089-87-54-00; expensive), and O'Caporale are good places to eat fish while enjoying the harbor sights. Nightlife consists of a drink outdoors on a pretty terrace or checking out the discos that come and go.

Pretty Praiano, the next town east along the coast, is quieter than Positano, and has a lovely harbor and beach. The Tritone sits high on the cliffs and looks out at a dazzling panorama; each room has a terrace, and the swimming pool and restaurant are nestled on their own terrace levels. L'Africano, a late-night disco down at sea level, welcomes guests coming by boat or down the cliff steps.

Also at Praiano is the delightful Villaggio La Tranquillità, an

economical choice run by the handsome Maresca brothers:
private cottages with flowery sea-view terraces, outdoor dining, and a comfortable bar. The crowd here is usually young.

A fine small hotel, reopened by the original proprietors,
makes dramatic **Furore** a good place to stay. The **Hostaria di
Bacco**'s terrace extends along the sea, and meals and drinks
are served outdoors in season. Authentic local cuisine is its
specialty.

About 1,000 feet above the sea, Furore is famous for its
wines and its dramatic gorge, the Fiordo. At its base an old
fishing village is fast being replaced with tourist accommodations, alas.

Amalfi

The town of Amalfi, farther down the coast, has an imposing
history for a little place that's nestled beneath ponderous
cliffs and wanders up into the mountains. During Amalfi's
days in the sun, the city was an important maritime republic,
like Pisa and Venice, with trade routes extending as far as
Constantinople, where the bronze doors of its cathedral
were forged in 1066. The **Duomo** is among the most beautiful in southern Italy, intricate in its Arab-Norman design and
detail, with a cloister even more Eastern in its intertwining
arches and palm trees. The basic pattern, however, is Romanesque, greatly restored, its façade glistening with mosaic
saints on a gold background. Dedicated to Andrew, patron
saint of sailors, it was begun during the ninth century and
remodeled three centuries later.

The interior, jubilant even on the darkest day, has been
restored in Baroque style, with a ceiling of intaglio woodwork. Even the crypt is radiant, and the altar, the work of
Fontana, as well as the statues of Saints Peter and Paul by
Pietro Bernini, are magnificent. Under the altar lie Saint
Andrew's bones, but not quietly. The bones exude a fragrant
oil called the manna of Saint Andrew, and when it miraculously appears, it portends good fortune if it flows quickly,
like San Gennaro's blood. Slow manna is less auspicious.

The 11th-century art of papermaking is still practiced
here. At the top of the central street (number 92) is a mill
where fine paper with Amalfi watermarks is made. If you
ring and the time is right, you may get to see the production
process, from pulp to sheets. The watercolor paper sold
here is excellent, as is the stationery.

In the piazza near the harbor stands a statue of Flavio
Gioia, inventor, they say, of the compass he is consulting. In

back of him the Municipio (town hall) houses the Tabula Amalfitana—long accepted as the law of the sea—and the costumes for the Regatta of the Four Maritime Republics (Venice, Pisa, Genoa, and Amalfi), celebrated each year in alternating cities. Unfortunately, Amalfi's harbor area is largely used as a bus park, which takes away from its charm but is apparently necessary, given the rocky terrain the town has to cope with. The town extends from the large harbor up along a steep valley and into the high cliffs above.

Christmas and New Year's bring feasting and fireworks over the sea, making them a nice time to be here—it's never cold, just a little rain now and then. The **Santa Caterina**, Amalfi's luxury hotel, serves wild boar along with turkey, *baccalà,* and Champagne; at midnight the coast lights up with pyrotechnics from Positano to Amalfi and Atrani. The hotel curves along the coast, and many of its rooms open onto terraces above lush gardens and lemon groves, with only the sea beyond. The lemons are. used by the chef in a sauce for pasta that can be made successfully only with Amalfi's lemons. In summer, the hotel opens one long seaside terrace under a pergola of grapevines as an informal trattoria, complete with excellent pizza and a new favorite, pesto made with arugula.

High above Amalfi, the hotel **Cappuccini Convento**, reached by cliff elevator, evokes the medieval monastery it once was, set as it is amid a terraced garden with a grape arbor. Unfortunately it's owned by the town and badly maintained at present. The **Hotel Amalfi** is in town on the hill, amid terraces and lemon groves. It's one of the least expensive. Nearer to sea level, the **Luna Convento** hotel recalls its cloistered past, with vaulted rooms and antiques, and, of course, cloisters. Ibsen, a sign says, wrote *A Doll's House* here in 1879, and the hotel is still run by the same family as in the playwright's day. Near the harbor the **Residence** is inexpensive and pleasantly old-fashioned. The Santa Caterina and the Luna also have fine restaurants. The **Baracca** on piazza Ferrari (Tel: 089-87-12-85) is the town's oldest trattoria—friendly and family-run. Near the cathedral are the **Taverna degli Apostoli**, at via Sant' Anna 6 (Tel: 089-87-29-91), which has a traditional atmosphere and good pasta sauces such as *frutti di mare* (seafood), and the simple, family-run **Gemma** (Tel: 089-87-13-45; closed Thursdays). For an apartment by day or week, the **Bellevue Residence** offers new sea-facing spacious apartments, with terraces and kitchenettes, on the main road. The cost is about the same as for a hotel.

At night, a drink on the Caterina's outdoor terrace or in town, at the seaside promenade, is the activity of choice.

The white town of **Atrani**, east along the coast from Amalfi, is easily missed because the highway overpass obscures part of it. From Amalfi, walk down the hill to the right of the highway, just past the town, until you come to a small beach and arches (the highway's supports). Walk through the arches and you'll reach a delightful piazza, from which a maze of houses rises up the hill. These can be reached only by staircases, as private and elusive as in a North African village. A few alfresco restaurants on high are worth the climb; the cathedral bears a bronze door like Amalfi's, made in Constantinople during the 11th century.

Ravello

On the cliffs high above Amalfi, Ravello rises serene and aloof, embodying a rare combination of spaciousness, grace, and mood. Even the light at Ravello is rarefied, and is most beautiful during the afternoon when the air is clear. Buses provide frequent service to Ravello from Amalfi. Taxis cost about 25,000 lire to make the trip, and walking involves traversing a vertical cliff.

Just off Ravello's central piazza, the **Villa Rufolo** is so romantic and atmospheric that Wagner, on seeing it, exclaimed, "The magic garden of Klingsor has been found." He was then (1880) living in southern Italy and orchestrating *Parsifal.* Today, each July a Wagner festival is held on the grounds. During the 12th century the noble Rufolo family had the Villa Rufolo built in front of the boundless sea; Boccaccio was one of their guests, and he mentioned it in *The Decameron.* No ruins are more evocative of the period, and the effect is heightened by the gardens, with their palms, Judas trees, papyrus, and flowers—all serving as a counterpoint to the arabesques of the arches and the rugged old tower, now tastefully crumbling.

The **Villa Cimbrone**, near the Villa Maria (below), evokes another mood entirely, without the romanticism of the Rufolo but with its own humor and panoramas to satisfy even the wide-angle weary. Over the central arch of the entryway are two boars' heads representing the coat of arms of Lord Grimthorpe, the eccentric gentleman who was behind the villa's creation.

The first unusual sight is in the cloisters: the seven deadly sins, represented by seven little unrepentant heads. Then, across wide lawns, through rose gardens, past Greek statues, and into a nymph's grotto, a belvedere seems to unfold above the whole Mediterranean. Grimthorpe is buried nearby. His epitaph (1917) is as bizarre as his villa: "Glad I came, not sorry to depart."

Before leaving Ravello, stop at the **cathedral** (built in 1086) named for the doctor/saint Pantaleone. The cathedral façade is obviously restored, but the great door, made by Barisano of Trani in 1179, is the original, divided into 54 panels featuring beautifully executed lives of Christ and the saints. Inside is a superb pulpit by Niccolo di Foggia, commissioned by the Rufolo family in 1272. Topped with a majestic eagle, it glitters with mosaics, while its columns rest on sculpted lions. In front of it the smaller pulpit, a rare piece built in 1130, shows Jonah and the whale, a metaphor of Christ's resurrection, delightfully documented in mosaics.

The museum downstairs is singular. The bust of the Signora da Ravello is thought to be of a Rufolo family member, and the elegant silver head is that of Saint Barbara, perhaps with her real skull still inside. (During the Middle Ages trade in saints' relics was frantic. For all of them to have been authentic, saints would have had to have had myriad necks and thighbones and hundreds of extra fingers.)

The newly refurbished **Villa Maria** is perhaps Ravello's best hotel at present, especially for its restaurant. Take the half pension for evening meals, and enjoy a late drink on the grassy terrace in the cool air, with views of the hotel's garden and the hills beyond, framing the sea. Its companion hotel, the simpler **Villa Giordano**, in town, has a swimming pool that Maria guests can use. In 1992 a restaurant was opened here, too.

The **Palumbo** hotel is still very gracious and its view is superb, but Pasquale Vuillemier is no longer in charge and the hotel misses his touch. The **Caruso Belvedere** has exquisite grounds, but the hotel seems lackluster.

Ravello's wines are quite good—and even better on the Palumbo dining terrace, with the coast spread out below. The restaurant **Cumpa' Cosimo**, via Roma 48, is cozy, inexpensive, and serves exquisite pasta (Tel: 089-85-71-56; closed Mondays). The **Garden**, at about the same price, is beautifully situated at the cliff and serves crêpes and seafood (via Chiunzi; Tel: 089-85-72-26; closed Tuesdays). Staying in Ravello can be enchanting if getting away from it all is your desire. During the summer months a bus makes frequent connections between the piazza del Duomo and Amalfi's central piazza. Ravello is linked to Naples by a daily bus.

Vietri sul Mare and Salerno

If you are in the mood to shop for ceramics, head east from Ravello or Amalfi, along the coast, to Vietri, a town completely devoted, it seems, to ceramics, with its colorful wares displayed on every street. The **Solimena factory** is the one to see first; it's in an imaginative building designed by Solari on via Madonna degli Angeli. The little tourist office on the central piazza will guide you to the latest exhibits and other ceramicists.

Salerno, the next town east of Vietri sul Mare and famous in the Middle Ages for its medical school, has an excellent restaurant: **Maria Grazia** (località Nerano Marina del Cantone; Tel: 081-808-10-35; closed Wednesdays). After lunch, visit the **cathedral,** built by the Norman Robert Guiscard in 1086 and much restored. Many of its original details can be seen in the adjacent museum (open mornings and 4:00 to 6:00 P.M.)

GETTING AROUND

A sea express (hydrofoil, or *aliscalfo*) is available during the summer, connecting Rome's Fiumicino airport with Capri, Ischia, and Naples. For information contact Medmar, in Rome at via Ofanto 18; Tel: (06) 844-05-78. In Naples the address is via Caracciolo 11; Tel: (081) 66-73-27.

Campania is so well interconnected by boat, train, and bus that it is possible to stay almost anywhere and still be able to get to its main attractions. It's not necessary to stay in Naples, and in summer probably not desirable, given the heat and traffic. Stay on one of the nearby islands—Capri, Ischia, or Procida—and hydrofoil into Naples (less than an hour's trip) to take the train north to Cuma or south to Pompeii and Herculaneum. Then move south to Positano, Amalfi, or Ravello to enjoy the beauty of this popular resort area. Do not go in August, when all of Italy and Europe descends, and again, avoid weekend travel. (Get a copy of *Qui Napoli,* a bilingual booklet that features special events and tours, found at hotels with concierges and sometimes at the tourist offices.)

If you are travelling to Naples by train from Rome, get off at the first stop, Mergellina, a nicer introduction to the city and a better place than the central station to find taxis, especially at night. (Ask when reserving—not all trains stop there.) Alitalia's new service provides a free train ticket to

Naples for incoming Alitalia passengers in Rome (see "Useful Facts" in the Overview).

Money belts are advised in the Naples area, and if possible do not drive in or near the city. Park at your hotel unless you know the territory.

From Naples there are good train connections to western and northern Campania as well as to Pompeii, Herculaneum, and Paestum. For the Amalfi coast you can take the train to Sorrento and the bus (all year) or the ferry or hydrofoil (in summer) to Positano or Amalfi. For Amalfi it's sometimes easier to take the train to Salerno and the bus or a taxi back up the coast.

Ferries and hydrofoils leave Naples frequently for Capri and Ischia. In summer the Amalfi Drive can be reached from Naples by hydrofoil to Amalfi or Positano. For the hydrofoil from Naples to Capri, Ischia, or Procida, go to the pier at Mergellina (ten minutes from the Royal or Excelsior hotel by taxi; a half hour, at least, by the 130 bus); the buses are usually crowded to the point of immobility, so you might consider walking, allowing a half hour or more. For the ferries, which take longer but cost less, go to the port in back of the Castel Nuovo in central Naples.

Cars are not needed on Capri, but one might be handy on Ischia and Procida. All three islands have good bus service, or you can hire a taxi for a few hours, which comes to about $15 per person for a group of four.

In Naples a car is a hindrance; traffic and parking problems make walking or getting about by bus or taxi a much more practical means of transit. Buses can be entered only by pushing and being pushed, unless you enter at the beginning of the route and leave at its termination. The Amalfi Drive should be approached with caution—it is an extremely tortuous, narrow, cliff-hugging road. If you want to drive, rent a car before leaving Naples and take an inland route to Vietri, near Salerno; then double back up the drive to Amalfi and Positano—a much easier approach, at least until you know the territory.

Many hotels in Positano and Amalfi will send a car to the Rome or Naples airport for clients if requested—for a healthy fee. A taxi from Naples to Positano costs about $70. To reach Amalfi or Positano from Rome, take the train to Salerno or Sorrento, and then a taxi, hydrofoil, or local bus to your destination. Local buses do not regularly transport luggage, however, so a taxi makes better sense.

If you stay in Positano, Pompeii is conveniently reached

by car; there are also regular bus excursions. Bus and train connections are less convenient but possible. A bus from Amalfi's central piazza climbs the high, winding road to Ravello at frequent intervals.

The Naples daily paper, *Il Mattino,* lists train and boat departures. Vietri adjoins Salerno, and from there the train leaves for Naples or Rome—a last-minute swim or a plate of *spaghetti con vongole veraci,* and you're on your way.

ACCOMMODATIONS REFERENCE

The rates given below are projections for 1993; always check for up-to-date information before making reservations. Wide ranges may reflect the differences between low- and high-season rates. Unless otherwise indicated, the figures indicate the cost of a double room (per room, not per person). However, half-board (mezza pensione*) rates, which include breakfast and one other meal per day, are per person. The service charge is included in the rate; inquire about tax and breakfast.*

▶ **Hotel Amalfi.** Via dei Pastai 3, 84011 **Amalfi.** Tel: (089) 87-24-40; Fax: (089) 87-22-50. L60,000.

▶ **Arcate.** Via Marcello Scotti 10, 80079 **Procida.** Tel: (081) 986-71-20. L85,000.

▶ **Bellavista.** Via Orlandi 10, 80071 **Anacapri.** Tel: (081) 837-14-63. L130,000.

▶ **Bellevue Residence.** Via Nazionale 163, 84011 **Amalfi.** Tel: (089) 83-13-49; Fax: (089) 83-15-68.

▶ **Bel Sito.** Via Matromania 11, 80073 **Capri.** Tel: (081) 837-09-68; Fax: (081) 837-66-22. L120,000.

▶ **Belvedere.** Via Tito Angelini 51, 80129 **Naples.** Tel: (081) 578-81-69; Fax: (081) 578-54-17. L150,000.

▶ **Buca di Bacco.** Porto, 84017 **Positano.** Tel: (089) 87-56-99; Fax: (089) 87-57-31. Open April 6 to October 25. L170,000–L200,000.

▶ **Caesar Augustus.** 80071 **Anacapri.** Tel: (081) 837-14-21. L90,000.

▶ **California.** Via Cristoforo Colombo, 84017 **Positano.** Tel: (089) 87-53-82. L65,000–L75,000.

▶ **Cappuccini Convento.** Via Annunziatella 46, 84011 **Amalfi.** Tel: (089) 87-18-77; Fax: (089) 87-18-86. L170,000–L200,000.

▶ **Caruso Belvedere.** Via San Giovanni del Toro 52, 84010 **Ravello.** Tel: (089) 85-71-11; Fax: (089) 85-73-72. L140,000–L190,000.

► **Casa Albertina**. Via della Tavolozza 3, 84017 **Positano**. Tel: (089) 87-51-43; Fax: (089) 81-15-40. Ł100,000–Ł160,000.

► **Casa Maresca**. Viale Pasitea, 84017 **Positano**. Tel: (089) 87-51-40. Open Easter–October. Ł90,000.

► **Elios**. Via Capo 33, 80066 **Sorrento**. Tel: (081) 878-18-12. Ł55,000.

► **Excelsior**. Via Partenope 48, 80121 **Naples**. Tel: (081) 41-71-11; Fax: (081) 41-17-43. In U.S., Tel: (800) 221-2340 or (212) 935-9540; Fax: (212) 421-5929. In U.K., Tel: (071) 930-4147 or (0800) 28-92-34; Fax: (071) 839-1566. Ł286,000–Ł429,000.

► **Excelsior Vittoria**. Piazza Tasso 34, 80067 **Sorrento**. Tel: (081) 807-10-44; Fax: (081) 877-12-06. Ł280,000–Ł326,000.

► **Flora**. Via Federico Serena 26, 80073 **Capri**. Tel: (081) 837-02-11. Ł160,000.

► **Gabbiano**. 84064 **Palinuro**. Tel: (0974) 93-11-55; Fax: (0974) 93-19-48. Ł60,000–Ł120,000.

► **Hostaria di Bacco**. 84010 **Furore**. Tel: (089) 87-40-06; Fax: (089) 87-45-83. Ł85,000–Ł100,000.

► **Hotel Paradiso**. Via Catullo 11, 80122 **Naples**. Tel: (081) 761-41-61; Fax: (081) 761-34-49. Ł180,000–Ł250,000.

► **Jolly Hotel delle Terme**. Via de Luca 42, 80077 **Porto d'Ischia**. Tel: (081) 99-17-44; Fax: (081) 99-31-56. In U.S., Tel: (800) 221-2626 or 247-1277; Fax: (212) 213-2369. In U.K., Tel: (0800) 28-27-29; Fax: (923) 89-60-71. Open mid-March–mid-November. Ł175,000–Ł320,000.

► **Loreley ct Londres**. Via A. Califano 2, 80066 **Sorrento**. Tel: (081) 878-15-08. Ł65,000.

► **Luna**. Viale Matteotti 3, 80073 **Capri**. Tel: (081) 837-04-33. Ł280,000.

► **Luna Convento**. 84011 **Amalfi**. Tel: (089) 87-10-02; Fax: (089) 87-13-33. Ł140,000.

► **Marincato**. Via Cristoforo Colombo 36, 84017 **Positano**. Tel: (089) 87-51-30. Ł100,000.

► **L'Oasi**. 80079 **Procida**. Tel: (081) 896-74-99. Ł75,000.

► **Palazzo Belmonte**. 84072 **Santa Maria di Castellabate**. Tel: (0974) 96-02-11; Fax: (0974) 96-11-50. Ł180,000.

► **Palazzo Murat**. Via dei Mulini 23, 84017 **Positano**. Tel: (089) 87-51-77; Fax: (089) 81-14-19. Ł135,000–Ł160,000.

► **Palumbo**. Via San Giovanni del Toro 28, 84010 **Ravello**. Tel: (089) 85-72-44; Fax: (089) 85-73-47. In U.S., Tel: (212) 599-8280 or (800) 223-9832; Fax: (212) 599-1755. Ł200,000–Ł240,000.

► **Parco dei Principi**. Via Rota 1, 80067 **Sorrento**. Tel: (081) 878-46-44; Fax: (081) 878-37-86. Open April–October. Ł200,000–Ł300,000.

▶ **Pinto-Storey.** Via Martucci 72, 80121 **Naples.** Tel: (081) 68-12-60. Ł69,000–Ł90,000.

▶ **Poseidon.** Viale Pasitea, 84017 **Positano.** Tel: (089) 87-50-14; Fax: (089) 87-58-33. In U.S., Tel: (212) 599-8280 or (800) 223-9832; Fax: (212) 599-1755. Open April–mid-October. Ł138,000–Ł240,000.

▶ **Quisisana.** Via Camerelle 2, 80073 **Capri.** Tel: (081) 837-07-88. Open March–November. Ł315,000–Ł475,000.

▶ **Regina Isabella e Royal Sporting.** Piazza Santa Restituta, 80076 **Lacco Ameno.** Tel: (081) 99-43-22; Fax: (081) 98-60-43. In U.S., Tel: (212) 599-8280 or (800) 223-9832; Fax: (212) 599-1755. Open mid-April–mid-October. Ł267,000–Ł480,000.

▶ **Residence.** Via Repubbliche Marinare 9, 84011 **Amalfi.** Tel: (089) 87-11-83; Fax: (089) 83-03-03. Open April–October. Ł95,000.

▶ **Residence Villa Tina.** Via delle Vigne 6, 80077 **Porto d'Ischia.** Tel: (081) 99-77-82. Ł80,000.

▶ **Royal.** Via Partenope 38, 80121 **Naples.** Tel: (081) 764-48-00; Fax: (081) 764-57-07. Ł196,000–Ł293,000.

▶ **San Pietro.** Via Laurito 2, Località San Pietro, 84017 **Positano.** Tel: (089) 87-54-55; Fax: (809) 81-14-49. In U.S., Tel: (212) 599-8280 or (800) 223-9832; Fax: (212) 599-1755. Open April–November 1. Ł475,000–Ł580,000.

▶ **Santa Caterina.** 84011 **Amalfi.** Tel: (089) 87-10-12; Fax: (089) 87-13-51. In U.S., Tel:' (212) 599-8280 or (800) 223-9832; Fax: (212) 599-1755. Ł310,000–Ł380,000.

▶ **La Santa Lucia.** Via Partenope 46, 80121 **Naples.** Tel: (081) 41-65-66. Ł180,000–Ł240,000.

▶ **La Scalinatella.** Via Tragara 8, 80073 **Capri.** Tel: (081) 837-06-33; Fax: (081) 837-82-91. Open March 15–November 5. Ł220,000–Ł450,000.

▶ **Le Sirenuse.** Via Colombo 30, 84017 **Positano.** Tel: (089) 87-50-66; Fax: (089) 81-17-98. In U.S., Tel: (212) 838-3110 or (800) 223-6800; Fax: (212) 758-7367. In U.K., Tel: (0800) 18-11-23; Fax: (071) 353-1904. Ł490,000.

▶ **La Tosca.** Via Dalmazio Birago 5, 80073 **Capri.** Tel: (081) 837-09-89. Ł75,000.

▶ **Tritone.** 84010 **Praiano.** Tel: (089) 87-43-33; Fax: (089) 87-43-74. Ł134,000–Ł250,000.

▶ **Vesuvio.** Via Partenope 45, 80121 **Naples.** Tel: (081) 41-70-44; Fax: same. Ł200,000–Ł290,000.

▶ **Villa Brunella.** Via Tragara 24, 80073 **Capri.** Tel: (081) 837-01-22; Fax: (081) 837-04-30. Open mid-March–November. Ł260,000.

▶ **Villa Krupp.** Via Matteotti 12, 80073 **Capri.** Tel: (081) 837-03-62. No credit cards. Ł80,000.

▶ **Villa Maria.** 84010 **Ravello.** Tel: (089) 85-71-70. Ł130,000–Ł140,000.

▶ **Villa dei Misteri.** Via Villa dei Misteri, 80045 **Pompeii.** Tel: (081) 861-35-93. Ł60,000.

▶ **Villa Sarah.** Via Tiberio 3/a, 80073 **Capri.** Tel: (081) 837-06-87; Fax: (081) 831-72-15. Open Easter–October. Ł100,000–Ł180,000.

▶ **Villaggio La Tranquillità.** Via Roma 10, 84010 **Praiano.** Tel: (089) 87-40-84. Ł50,000.

APULIA

By Louis Inturrisi

Often described as "the heel of the Italian boot," Apulia (Puglia in Italian—pronounced POOL-ya) has from prehistoric times had the heels of various peoples planted onto its vulnerable topography. It has been occupied to a greater or lesser extent by the ancient Apuli tribes (from which it takes its name), Greeks, and Romans; it was at various times subjugated by Byzantines, Lombards, Franks, and Saracens; was heavily built up by Normans and Hohenstaufens; and was then ruled at a distance by Angevins, Aragonese, and Bourbons.

The region's most distinctive architectural style is a complex blend of French and northern Italian architectural forms with Byzantine ornamentation of Saracen inspiration, all of it brought together under the Normans. Whatever its confusing origins, the Apulian Romanesque resulted in some of Italy's most significant cathedrals, stretching heavenward above the Adriatic coastal plain. Yet the region draws visitors not just because of its peculiar artistic heritage but also for the natural wonders of its spectacular coastline, caves, and forests; for its own distinct cuisine; and for the chance to venture off the well-beaten tracks in Italy.

MAJOR INTEREST

Coastal drive along the Gargano massif
The Foresta Umbra Nature Reserve in the Gargano
Romanesque cathedrals in and near Bari
Frederick II's castle at Castel del Monte
Limestone alabaster caves of Castellana Grotte
The *trulli* structures in and around Alberobello
Baroque architecture of Lecce

Treasures of Magna Graecia in the Taranto National
    Museum
Folk pottery from Grottaglie

Most of Apulia's overlords were either passing through on
their way to more strategically protected destinations or
were occupying territory that formed part of a greater empire. The overwhelming exception—and the dominant figure of Apulia to this day—was Frederick II of Hohenstaufen,
stupor mundi et immutator mirabilis, a progressive 13th-
century leader and man of letters whom Dante called "the
father of Italian poetry." With his son Manfred, Frederick was
responsible for much of what Apulia still looks like. He not
only filled it with castles but stayed on to make use of them.
Later, the demise of the Hohenstaufen family dragged
Apulia's prosperity down with it.

Most modern invaders were as negligent toward Apulia as
the rulers who preceded and succeeded Frederick. Apulia
was seen as a place to pass through on the way to and from
the port cities of the Adriatic. Today, however, the region is
on the rebound. Witness Bari's thriving Fiera del Levante, a
trade fair, or the bounty of the region's extensive fields
(Apulia is the largest olive oil– and wine-producing region
of Italy). The tourist trade has also begun to flourish—
mostly on the coastline.

Apulia is Italy's most fairy-tale–like region. The whimsical
cone-shaped stone dwellings known as *trulli* in Alberobello
seem to be straight out of the *Wizard of Oz;* the shadowy
Foresta Umbra on the Gargano massif is the closest thing
Italy has to an enchanted forest; and the dolmen-like burial
markers of the Daunian people, who inhabited northern
Apulia in ancient times—thin, flat stones with helmet-
headed tops—are reminiscent of Alice's pack of cards. The
Rubian drinking vessels shaped like animal heads in the
Museo Jatta in Ruvo would put Walt Disney to shame, as
would the beast motifs on Apulian Romanesque cathedrals.
Animals figure prominently in folklore to this day in rural
Apulia, where farmers won't slice milk-soaked bread for fear
their cows will go dry and horses wear beads to ward off the
evil eye. In the caves of Castellana Grotte, unusual rock
formations have prompted imaginative names. And the already exuberant Baroque found especially fertile ground in
Lecce, far down the heel of Italy's boot, where the soft tufa
stone, as Osbert Sitwell wrote, "allows the rich imagination
of the south an unparalleled outlet."

Apulia has a lot of food prepared especially for religious

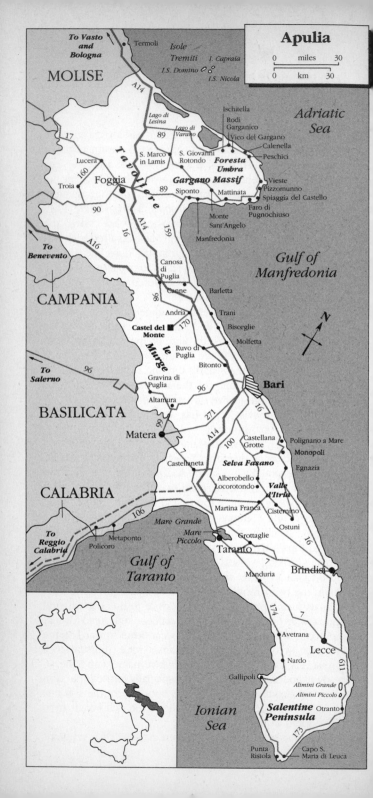

holidays, but dishes to be savored year-round include *ore-cchiette con cime di rapa,* the "little ears" pasta ubiquitous in Apulia, here cooked with garlic and turnip greens; *troccoli con sugo di seppie,* a kind of flat spaghetti in a sauce of squid's ink; *capriata,* puréed fava beans served with wild chicory or other vegetables; *tiella di funghi,* a mushroom casserole; lamb, kid, or game; and local versions of such cheeses as pecorino, ricotta, scamorza, and the local provolone. Usually it is all accompanied by the ring-shaped, fennel-flavored bread called *scaldatelli.* Much rosé wine is drunk in Apulia; among the best is the tasty pink Rosato del Salento. Puglia's robust cooking is best accompanied by an elegant red Castel Mitrano or a medium-bodied Copertino; the region's many seafood dishes go well with Puglia's best-known dry white wine, Castel del Monte, or its up-and-coming second, Locorotondo. Liqueur lovers might try the local Amarella, made from black-cherry tree leaves.

CAPITANATA

The northernmost section of Apulia (and therefore its most frequent point of entry from the rest of Italy), the Capitanata region is a union of topographical opposites. Jutting out into the Adriatic to form the spur of the Italian boot is the mountainous and forested Gargano massif; below it is the flat and treeless Tavoliere (Italian for chessboard, from the grid pattern of roads traced here by the ancient Romans), the largest plain in southern Italy, undulating with waves of wheat and barley.

Nature and sea lovers might want to stay (with large numbers of northern Europeans) on the Gargano at the quiet and modern **Hotel del Faro**, on its own rocky promontory in Faro di Pugnochiuso, near Vieste, or among century-old olive trees at the more moderately priced **Hotel Apeneste** in Mattinata on the south coast. However, the **Albergo Grand Hotel Cicolella** in Foggia, the bustling provincial capital, is a more convenient base than either for exploring the immediate area and, because it is primarily a businessperson's hotel, has the advantage of housing the town's best restaurant, also called **Cicolella** (Tel: 0881-38-90; closed Sundays and mid-August), which provides a superb introduction to most Apulian specialties.

Foggia, Lucera, and Troia

Despite Frederick II's frequent stays in Foggia, nothing remains of his palace there, as a result of an 18th-century earthquake and later heavy bombing during World War II. In fact, except for a moderately interesting Baroque cathedral and an archaeological museum, Foggia serves best as a place to gather your energies for exploring the rest of Capitanata (Foggia is just off Autostrada A 14 and a main train line, and has a small airport), perhaps invigorated by a walk on the extensive grounds of the **Villa Comunale** or through the six little outdoor chapels leading to the **Chiesa delle Croci**.

You can sample your first dish of *orecchiette con cime di rapa* at **Ristorante del Cacciatore** at via Pietro Mascagni 12, near corso Vittorio Emanuele (Tel: 0881-200-31; closed Sundays) or at the very elegant **La Pietra di Francia**, viale 1° (Primo) Maggio 2 (Tel: 0881-348-80; closed Sunday evening, Mondays, and August 10–31). For a less expensive meal, try **La Locanda di Hansel** at via Ricci 59 (Tel: 0881-67-38-71; closed Sundays).

LUCERA

From Foggia it is a short, straight hop by car or bus 21 km (13 miles) west across the Tavoliere plain to Lucera. Just outside the city is its magnificent castle, the **Fortezza Angioina**, begun by Frederick II. Norman Douglas begins his *Old Calabria* ("Calabria" once referred to more of southern Italy than it does at present) with a description of the castle's position, looking toward the Apennines and the Gargano, as the "key of Apulia." The castle itself is equally impressive, with dozens of towers and almost half a mile of encircling walls. Also on the outskirts of town is a Roman amphitheater, which is used for performances during the summer. In the Arabian-looking town proper (Frederick II stocked it with Saracens from Sicily) we get our first of many glimpses of Saint Michael, the patron saint of Puglia, on the **Duomo**, one of the few intact examples of Angevin architecture in Italy: The archangel is in the center portal, flanked by two lesser angels.

The **Albergo Al Passetto**, built into the ancient walls, is the best of the few hotels in Lucera, and **La Contessina** at via Mazzaccara 4 (Tel: 0881-94-10-18; closed Sundays) is an inexpensive restaurant-pizzeria.

TROIA

Troia, 18 km (11 miles) directly south of Lucera by car or bus, has another fine view of the surrounding countryside.

Though Frederick II destroyed much of the evidence of Troia's past, its 11th-century **Duomo** remains the happiest marriage of Romanesque architectural forms with Eastern sculptural ornamentation in Apulia. The intricate latticework of its splendid rose window shows Saracen sources, while beneath it the bronze doors teem with Byzantine dragons, animals, saints, and a portrait of the sculptor of the doors, Oderisio da Benevento, less than humbly placed next to Christ.

The Gargano Massif

The Gargano—the "spur" of the boot, northeast of Foggia—is served by a slow train and faster buses from Foggia and gets two types of tourists: nature lovers from Italy and northern Europe during the summer and tour buses full of religious pilgrims from all over the world year-round. From Foggia, pilgrims generally head north across the Tavoliere to the town of San Marco in Lamis to see the convent of San Matteo; then they go east to San Giovanni Rotondo to pay homage to a statue of the Madonna in the 16th-century convent of Santa Maria delle Grazie, to Padre Pio's tomb in the modern church of the same name, and to see the American-funded Fiorello La Guardia Hospital.

The final stop on the route is **Monte Sant'Angelo**, the windswept town perched on a rock high above the Gulf of Manfredonia, where the Archangel Michael is believed to have appeared to San Lorenzo, Bishop of Siponto, on May 8, 490, leaving behind his flaming red cloak. Subsequently, the **Santuario di San Michele** became one of the most important religious sanctuaries in the Christian world. Its miraculous grotto was consecrated in the fifth century, making it one of the oldest Christian shrines in Italy. The bronze door at the entrance to the inner vestibule comes from Constantinople and is the oldest in Apulia; also significant is the stone bishop's throne in the grotto, where a marble statue of the saint, attributed to Andrea Sansovino, presides. Devotees often make the steep descent to the grotto in their bare feet, and some continue their penance by licking the floor.

The Gargano coast road—route 89—east from Foggia begins with a stop at **Siponto** (about 36 km/22 miles east) to see the remarkable 11th-century church of **Santa Maria di Siponto**, which has recently been restored. It was the sole survivor of the earthquake that leveled the important Daunian town in the 12th century. Built in pristine Pugliese-Romanesque style, the noble edifice has a square design embellished by blind arches and an exquisite 13th-century portal, and stands in a pine grove surrounded by pre-Roman ruins.

From here it is a very short distance east to industrial **Manfredonia**, founded by Frederick II's bastard son Manfred, who later became the hero of Byron's famous poem. Its massive castle houses the **Museo Nazionale Archeologico del Gargano**, which contains the enchanting Daunian stelae, or grave slabs, covered with cartoonlike representations of nature. For lunch, **Ai Vecchi Mulini** (corso Roma 178; Tel: 0884-241-59) has excellent *antipasto di frutti di mare* (seafood salad), but you can eat more cheaply at one of the pizzerias on the beach, such as the air-conditioned **Capriccio** (viale Miramare 6; Tel: 0884-271-57).

It is 16 km (10 miles) from Manfredonia to **Monte Sant'Angelo**, where in addition to the sanctuary discussed above there is an interesting 12th-century structure called the **Tomba di Rotari**, which originally may have been a baptistery or a mausoleum, and the **Museo delle Arte e Tradizioni Popolari del Gargano**, a museum devoted to daily life in former times. (The folk tradition is still evident in the town's production of wood carving.) Before leaving, go to one of the bakery shops (*pasticceria*) near the sanctuary to try the delicious almond-and-honey cookies called *ostie* because they look like large communion wafers, or hosts.

Driving back down to the coast you pass through **Mattinata**, where a curious private collection of local art from Daunian stelae to alabaster statues of Saint Michael is on display in the **Farmacia Sansone**. Mattinata also boasts the **Trattoria dalla Nonna** (Mattinata Mare; Tel: 0884-492-05; closed Mondays and October–May), where *zuppa di pesce* (fish stew) and other delights from the sea may be enjoyed *in situ* overlooking the Adriatic.

The coast road around the promontory is spectacular. Odd rock formations and intriguing grottoes rise above a series of beautiful coves and clear-water beaches. Medieval **Vieste**, with its narrow winding alleyways and whitewashed houses, clings to the eastern tip of the Gargano promontory. The old town contains a **castle** from the time of Frederick II and an 11th-century Apulian-Romanesque **cathedral**. In summer Vieste's population increases fivefold, with masses of Italians and Germans crowding its beautiful sandy beaches at Castello, Pizzomunno (The Edge of the World), and Pugnochiuso (Closed Fist) bay. Boats depart several times daily in summer from Vieste's port for a tour of the grottoes carved out of the limestone cliffs. The elegant **Pizzomunno**

Vieste Palace Hotel also has a (pricey) restaurant, **Il Trabucco**, overlooking the sea. **Al Dragone**, a trattoria near the duomo (via Duomo 8; Tel: 0884-70-12-12), serves delicious pasta with cauliflower (*cavolfiore*), and **La Kambusa** (viale 24 Maggio 13; Tel: 0884-70-86-25) has flavorful mussels and clams in a garlic and parsley sauce.

PESCHICI
The next town as you move counterclockwise around the spur of Italy's boot is Peschici, perched high on a rocky promontory jutting out into the sea. Peschici was founded by the Slavonians in the tenth century; part of the original walls encircling the city are still standing. Like Vieste, Peschici, with its bay harbor, hotels, camping sites, and resort villages, is crowded in summer. Boat tours are available in summer to the nearby San Nicola and Manacore caves or to the Tremiti Islands (see below), and equipment for deep-sea fishing can be rented at the port.

Peschici has one of the best restaurants in the Gargano, which attracts clients from as far away as Foggia and Bari. Housed inside one of the natural limestone caves that are emblematic of this region, **La Grotta delle Rondini** (The Swallows' Cave; Tel: 0884-96-40-07) is more than a restaurant—it's an event. Diners feast on *zuppa di pesci* or *troccoli* (flat homemade spaghetti) with a seafood-tomato-and-mushroom sauce while watching the fishing boats glide in and out of the grotto in the illuminated clear green water below. (The restaurant is open from Easter to October.) Up in the town many restaurants have balconies overlooking the sea. One of the best is **Vecchia Peschici** (via Roma 31; Tel: 0884-96-20-53; closed Mondays), where the specialty is *strascinete,* ribbon pasta with an eggplant sauce.

If you want to use Peschici as a center for exploring the Gargano or the nearby Tremiti Islands, the modern **Hotel Residence Solemar**, about a kilometer (half a mile) past the town, has a private beach and swimming pool located in a quiet park. It also has a good restaurant, a sauna, and its own cinema. On Peschici beach, **Hotel D'Amato** is open from April until late September and has a swimming pool, a famous restaurant, and beautiful views of the sea. Alternatively, you might choose to stay at one of the many camping sites in this part of the Gargano. You do not have to have a camper to do so, as most of the camping sites offer everything from tents to mini-apartments to bungalows for rent. With a little advance notice, the AGRITUR agency (Tel: 0884-96-49-91; Fax 0884-96-22-08) will arrange for you to rent an apartment for a week or longer directly on the seashore surrounding Peschici.

The road winding 15 km (9 miles) west from Peschici to the next large town, Rodi Garganico, has two notable attractions: the pine forest at Calenella, which is also the terminus of the Garganica, the scenic Toonerville Trolley–like train that slowly puffs its way from Foggia through the whole of the Gargano (many insist this is the best way to see the region), and the many picturesque examples of rustic eating places run by fishermen. You can see these *trabucchi* along the coastal road. Never more than a wooden wharf on stilts with a few tables and benches and a rudimentary sign to show it is open, a *trabucco* is one place you can be sure of getting fresh fish.

RODI GARGANICO

Rodi Garganico is a sleepy little fishermen's village that fills to capacity during the summer months. Its whitewashed houses have ornamental chimneys (all different) and the tile roofs with three-layered eaves that are typical of this region of Puglia. The **Hotel Miramare** at via XX Settembre 2 has rooms with a view of the sea, and **Ristorante Da Franco** (via Pietro Nenni 22; Tel: 0884-96-50-03; closed Mondays except in summer) has a terrace and serves delicious spaghetti *alla pescatora,* in a tomato, garlic, and seafood sauce topped with fresh parsley.

From Rodi Garganico you can take boat trips to the Tremiti Islands (discussed below), visit the nearby coastal **Lesina and Varano lakes**, or take a ferryboat back around the whole of the Gargano to Manfredonia. The two saltwater lakes are worth visiting for their beauty and because they yield one of the largest productions of mussels and eels in Italy. The **Hotel La Bufalara** in Ischitella, southeast of Rodi Garganico, is in a pine grove on a tiny strip of land that separates Lake Varano from the sea. The hotel has a swimming pool and a restaurant (closed Tuesdays) and will arrange tours of the mussel beds in the lake with local fishermen. Naturally, all the restaurants in the area serve dishes featuring mussels. One of the simplest and best such dishes is *le cozze arracanate,* mussels on the half-shell covered with bread crumbs, olive oil, garlic, parsley, red pepper, and a little white wine, then baked in the oven. Try them at **Da Tonino** (via Umberto 177; Tel: 0884-996-66-65; closed Fridays).

Families travelling with children will appreciate the **Casino di Caccia** near Ischitella (7 km/4 miles off the superstrada in the direction of Carpino; Tel: 0884-99-68-91). It has the only outdoor pizzeria in the area, a roller-skating rink, beach volleyball and archery facilities, and a drive-in movie (in Italian).

Equally pleasant is the majestic **Foresta Umbra** (Shade Forest) near Vico del Gargano and about 100 km (62 miles) from Foggia. This extensive forest of tall, ancient beech, oak, pine, and chestnut trees is surprisingly clean, well-kept, and peaceful—except on weekends, when it fills up with picnickers. The State Forestry Bureau operates a deer reserve and Visitors Center (Centro Visitatori) inside the forest that includes a restaurant and has information on hiking and sports facilities.

Isole Tremiti

The Tremiti Islands, the only Italian islands in the Adriatic, require a full day's trip from the mainland no matter how you get to them—from May to September by ferry from Termoli, Manfredonia, Vieste, Peschici, Rodi Garganico, or Vasto; by hydrofoil from Peschici, Rodi Garganico, or Termoli; or even by helicopter from Foggia. The ferries land at San Nicola; water taxis and local ferries connect San Nicola and San Domino. The large number of hotels on **San Domino**, the largest of the islands, allows visitors to stay overnight as well, provided they have reservations. The *Insulae Diomediae* of Greek mythology, these were the isles inhabited by Diomedes' Illyrian companions, who were transformed by a vengeful Aphrodite into herons and are still said to be heard crying for their hero at night. The islands have been a place of exile, self-imposed or otherwise, from the days when Augustus's granddaughter Julia was banished to them for adultery through to the Fascist years, when they held political prisoners.

These days, the preference is to escape *to* them, and pine-covered San Domino becomes especially overrun each summer. Its **Kyrie** hotel, with beach, pool, tennis court, and private garden, gets the cream of the local agriculture-magnate crop; the less expensive **Gabbiano**, also in a garden but with lovely views of the sea, gets a more diverse crowd.

Of the other two main islands, **Capraia** (rarely visitable) is known for its rock formations, while **San Nicola** has the most cultural pursuits, with a medieval fortress offering lovely views of the archipelago, and the abbey church of **Santa**

Maria a Mare, which contains a well-preserved mosaic pavement, a Byzantine crucifix, and a Venetian polyptych.

THE ROAD TO BARI

Apulia's most famous Romanesque cathedrals and more may be taken in during a day's drive from Foggia southeast to Bari, weaving in and out to towns and other places along the Adriatic coast. It is an ambitious drive, but as there is little of interest here outside of the architecture, a practical one. If you're interested in a more leisurely approach, break it up with a night at **La Vecchia Masseria**, a tiny and inexpensive hotel housed in an ancient farmhouse in Andria, 22 km (14 miles) north of Castel del Monte (described below) along route 170. Most of the towns are also served by trains and buses, but you must allow ample time to make connections.

The first stop is **Canosa di Puglia**, which was founded by Diomedes, according to legend. Its cathedral contains the oldest bishop's throne in Apulia as well as the tomb of Bohemond, son of the crusader Robert Guiscard. Continuing toward the coast, you pass the site where Hannibal won the battle of Cannae (Canne in Italian) in 216 B.C., only to lose the war later.

It takes a lot of imagination to make this archaeological site come alive, however; it's best, instead, to move on to **Barletta** on the coast. Its Romanesque cathedral, now in rather sad repair, houses a sensuous Madonna commemorating the "Disfida di Barletta," a 16th-century battle reenacted in costumed pageantry each July. Outside the basilica of San Sepolcro stands Barletta's major monument, a 16½-foot-high **Colossus**. This fourth-century bronze statue from Constantinople was washed ashore after a shipwreck in the 14th century and was almost immediately dismembered by Dominican monks, the arms and legs melted down to make bells for their church in Manfredonia and new limbs added to the original head and torso. The best dining in town, and priced accordingly, is at **Ristorante Bacco** (via Sipontina 10; Tel: 0883-57-10-00; closed weekends and August).

CASTEL DEL MONTE

Heading inland again, drive due south to Apulia's most famous single piece of architecture, Castel del Monte, a masterpiece of civil architecture of the 13th century. Built by the Holy Roman emperor Frederick II, it was his favorite hunting lodge and retreat, as well as the place where he composed *De arte venendi cum avibus,* to this day the standard text on falconry. The golden octagonal stone castle, sitting like a crown on an isolated hill, still conveys a sense of majesty and peace. Castel del Monte is open Mondays through Saturdays, April to September from 8:30 A.M. to 7:00 P.M. and October to March from 9:00 A.M. to 2:00 P.M. On Sundays it is open from 9:00 A.M. to 1:00 P.M. The nearby restaurant **Ostello di Federico** (Tel: 0883-830-43; closed Sundays) is moderately priced and excellent. It serves carefully prepared regional specialties like *capriata* and *strascinete,* Puglia's version of tagliatelle, which here are made with whole wheat and served with ricotta cheese and arugula. With these you should try a Castel del Monte DOC rosé, which is considered one of the best rosé wines available. At night Ostello di Federico becomes a pizzeria as well—with the illuminated castle as a background.

Returning to the coast southeast of Barletta: In the white town of **Trani** is one of Apulia's most impressive Romanesque cathedrals, situated dramatically at the edge of the Adriatic. Farther along the coast past Bisceglie (its Romanesque cathedral was much altered during the Baroque period and can be skipped in good conscience) is **Molfetta,** a commercial town whose old cathedral is also on the sea (ask directions to the Duomo Vecchio, as there is also a less interesting Baroque Duomo Nuovo). The town also has one of the area's nicest restaurants, **Alga Marina** (strada Statale 16; Tel: 080-94-80-91; closed Mondays and November), which serves regional pasta and fish specialties. Inland, **Ruvo di Puglia** has another lovely Romanesque cathedral as well as the **Museo Jatta,** which contains an extensive private collection of terra-cotta vases and is especially noted for its rhytons (drinking vessels in the shape of animal heads) from the city's ancient incarnation as Rubi. From here it is a short drive to see the 13th-century cathedral at **Bitonto,** considered the culmination of the Apulian Romanesque, and then on to Bari.

BARI AND ENVIRONS

La gente di Bari o vende o muore (the people of Bari sell or die) is a saying that aptly describes the city, whose September Fiera del Levante is the most important trade fair in Italy after Milan's. Apulia's largest and busiest city, Bari is primarily a port and commercial and administrative center (it is the regional capital of Apulia), but it does have some sights worth seeing. These are found mainly in the **Città Vecchia** (Old City), which boasts the prototypical Apulian Roman-esque church of **San Nicola di Bari**, housing an important bishop's throne as well as Saint Nicholas's tomb in the crypt below. (He *is* the same as Santa Claus. Saint Nick is also the patron saint of sailors, and the anniversary of the arrival of his remains in Bari, brought from Asia Minor by local sailors, is celebrated each May 7–10 with an elaborate procession of floats from the cathedral to the sea.)

Another Frederick II castle stands in the Città Vecchia, and is most comfortably explored if you leave your valuables elsewhere. Points of interest outside the Old City are the **Museo Archeologico** in piazza Umberto and the **Pinacoteca Provinciale** in the Palazzo della Provincia on lungomare N. Sauro, the seafront. The latter has paintings by Veronese, Tintoretto, and Bellini as well as by Francesco Netti, Italy's most impressive Impressionist painter. The archaeological museum is open from 8:30 A.M. to 1:30 P.M., closed Sundays; the Pinacoteca is open from 8:30 A.M. to 1:00 P.M. and from 4:00 to 7:00 P.M., closed Sunday afternoon and Mondays.

Bari is also proud of its contemporary aspect, best exem-plified by its modern soccer stadium, which was designed by internationally renowned architect Renzo Piano for the 1990 World Cup soccer finals. On Bari's main shopping street, traffic-free **via Sparano**, most major Italian designers are represented at prices competitive with the rest of Italy. Halfway down the street is the Belle Epoque **Mincuzzi** emporium, an impressive reminder—with its wrought-iron marquee and glass-domed atrium—of the grandeur and elegance Bari could boast of at the turn of the century. A block away is the bookshop of the prestigious Italian pub-lisher Laterza. Handwoven baskets of a type used by fisher-men to display their catch and the distinctive Bari chocolate-brown ovenproof folk pottery are both available at a tiny shop without a name on via delle Crociate (number 14) in the Old City near the duomo. A lively flea market takes place Monday mornings on via Califati.

Virtually all the city's accommodations are geared to busi-nesspeople and thus are of the practical and pricey per-suasion. The most unusual hotel in the city is the **Villa Romanazzi-Carducci**, a modernized mansion set in its own private garden. Expect crowds during the mid-September Fiera del Levante, when reservations are a must. The most central hotel in Bari is the **Palace Hotel** on via Lombardi near the castle. Less expensive alternatives, like **Villa Meo-**

Evoli, are located a few miles outside the city in the Apulian countryside. A luxurious alternative to the Bari hotels is Il Melograno in nearby Monopoli (44 km/27 miles down the coast). The hotel itself is a converted *masseria,* or farmhouse, and boasts one of the area's best regional restaurants (closed Tuesdays).

Bari also has many excellent restaurants. Ai Due Ghiottoni (via Putignani 11; Tel: 080-523-22-40; closed Sundays and August), for example, makes an excellent light, non-greasy *fritto misto,* a fry-up of different kinds of lightly floured seafood, and a delicious risotto with baby shrimp and baby squid. The name of this moderately priced restaurant means The Two Gluttons in English, and it is easy to see why. La Pignata (via Melo 9; Tel: 080-523-24-81; closed Wednesdays and August) serves traditional Apulian dishes with a modern experimental touch. Try the *timbale di macaroni,* a baked macaroni and vegetable casserole, or the wood-pigeon soup. Ristorante alla Vecchia Bari (via Dante Alighieri 47; Tel: 080-521-64-96) and La Credenza (via Verrone 25; Tel: 080-523-87-18; closed Wednesdays) are good places to try the famous earlobe-shaped pasta, *orecchiette,* in a meat sauce (which in the not-too-distant past was made with horse meat). Recommended regional wines are Rosso di Barletta, a tart red, and dry whites from Castel del Monte and Locorotondo. The local liqueur, flavored with walnuts, is the potent Padre Peppe.

Bari is a haven for snack foods. For *focaccia* (pizza bread made with sun-dried tomatoes and black olives), try Arciuli (via Roberto da Bari 74); for *panzerotti* (fried puff pizza made with bran flour and mashed potatoes and filled with tomatoes, mozzarella, and oregano), try Pizzeria La Mezzaluna (corso Vittorio Emanuele 109); and for *calzone alla barese* (a pizza pocket filled with onions, olives, and raisins), try Pizzeria Piccadilly (via Crispi 86). The mecca for snackers in downtown Bari is the SAICAF café (corso Cavour 121), which has a wide selection of hot and cold snacks, delicious pastries, and take-out entrées. Finally, the ultimate snacks in Bari are the fresh oysters (*ostriche*) at the *bancarelle* (stands) along the Molo San Nicola (the San Nicola Wharf) in the old port, where a lively fish market is held every morning.

Inland from Bari

Some odd spots in the rocky, rolling inland plateaus known as Le Murge make a pleasant day trip from Bari by car; again, trains and buses service the area (including a special vintage train for tourists; see "Getting Around," below), but such a trip requires precise schedule-juggling. You begin innocently enough in the hilltop town of **Altamura**, southwest of Bari, admiring the delicate rose window and richly carved door of its cathedral, which was begun by Frederick II when he reestablished the Saracen-sacked city on its ancient, privileged site and stocked it with neighboring Latins, Greeks, and Jews, who were given further privileges.

In **Gravina di Puglia**, built into the side of a ravine to the west of Altamura, things get a bit bizarre. First, outside the train station there is the church with an enormous mean-looking spread-winged eagle, the coat of arms of its patron, covering the façade; then there is the Purgatorio church in piazza Domenico, with a gable over the door surmounted by two fey reclining skeletons; finally there are the dark, dank, and mysterious grotto churches of San Michele and San Vito Vecchio, with faded, peeling frescoes and a bone cemetery (in the former) that houses the remains of more than 400 victims of a Saracen massacre.

MATERA

The neighboring province of Matera (once part of Apulia but since redesignated to the otherwise largely undistinguished region of Basilicata) is the site of another ravine city, Matera, 26 km (16 miles) southeast of Gravina. Inhabited since Paleolithic times, it is famous for its **sassi**, the extensive area of dwellings carved into the side of the ravine, whose inhabitants' poverty was so poignantly described by Carlo Levi in *Christ Stopped at Eboli*. By now most of the residents have been relocated to proper housing projects in the modern upper town, but urchins still prowl the rocks and will divulge the secrets of the caves' chapels and cubbyholes for a fee, though they're not needed to explore the town's Apulian Romanesque cathedral and the macabre façade of its Purgatorio church.

For those who want to try Basilicata's cuisine, stop in at the **Nuovo Terrazzino** restaurant on vico San Giuseppe 7 (Tel: 0835-33-25-03; closed Tuesdays). It serves pasta, lamb, and kid dishes adorned with the region's spicy sausages, all to be respectfully downed with the extremely robust red wine Aglianico del Vulture and an appreciative toast to Horace (he was born in the Basilicatan city of Venosa). (*Aglianico* means Hellenic, another example of the mix of history here.)

On the way back to Bari, movie buffs may want to loop over to **Castellaneta**, perilously perched over yet another ravine. This town was the birthplace of Rudolph Valentino, and the ceramic monument erected here in his honor stands as silent as a silent-screen star, at once as odd and as devout as any piece of Apulian religious sculpture.

Southeast of Bari

Some of Apulia's most primitive and most sophisticated sights can be seen as a day trip by car in the area southeast of Bari; more time is necessary to see it using public transportation. This area makes for one of the region's most pleasant drives, filled as it is with gnarled gray-green olive trees, often planted side by side with almond trees, on red earth sectioned off with dry-laid walls made of weathered gray stone. This same stone is used for the area's most singular architectural feature, the conical dwellings known as **trulli**, most of which are less than 300 years old (although the construction method is prehistoric). In this part of Apulia you also begin to notice another type of structure characteristic of Apulian architecture: *masserie,* or fortified farmhouses, some of which date from Roman times.

Castellana Grotte, 40 km (25 miles) southeast of Bari on route 634, is the site of the largest and most spectacular caverns in Italy. Though people have left their imprint on nature through litter and the inevitable coins tossed into any body of water that can be loosely construed as a fountain, the names of the beautiful colored alabaster rock formations— such as the Madonna, the Altar, and the Leaning Tower of Pisa—attest to Italians' devotion to the caverns; the in-depth two-hour tour is recommended over the hour-long one.

ALBEROBELLO

Alberobello, about 20 km (12 miles) southeast of Castellana, is a town with more than a thousand shimmering gray and white *trulli* that must have looked like the Land of Oz before it gave in to some pretty heavy pandering to the tourist trade. Despite the town's status as a national monument, most of the *trulli* here have been transformed into snack bars, souvenir shops, and pizzerias, while very persistent hawkers line the two main streets offering tourists a chance to look inside "an authentic *trullo,*" which, it turns out, also happens to be a jeans shop.

You may stay in one of the *trullo* cottages at the **Hotel dei**

Trulli—which has clean and surprisingly spacious accommodations, complete with garden and pool—and have lunch in another *trullo* at the **Trullo d'Oro** at via Cavallotti 27 (Tel: 080-72-18-20; closed Mondays and January), which offers a number of lamb specialties along with local wines. Even more acclaimed is **Il Poeta Contadino**, at via Indipendenza 21 (Tel: 080-72-19-17; closed Sunday evening, Mondays, and the middle of January), serving many of the same local specialties with a much larger wine list.

Fortunately, the *trulli* are not confined to Alberobello; in fact, those in the nearby **Valley of Itria** or along the road to Martina Franca (see below) are often more interesting because you see them as they once were, dotting the countryside in small groups—some of them colored blue or yellow—or standing alone in a field of poppies, their white hex sign–like symbols standing out against the gray stone. Having a *trullo* in the countryside has recently become a status symbol for city dwellers in Bari or Taranto. Driving through the lush **Selva Fasano** (the Fasano Woodlands northeast of Alberobello, where there is also a safari park with wild animals), you can see several *trulli* joined together into villas that are now the homes of wealthy Italians.

Locorotondo, halfway between Alberobello and Martina Franca, overlooks the Valley of Itria and is known as the *balconata sulla valle* (the balcony over the valley). It is worth a stop not only for its panoramic views of the valley and the vineyards below, where its dry white wine—one of the best in Puglia—is produced, but also for its narrow concentric streets lined with white terraced houses and ancient portals with Latin inscriptions. For lunch here, try **Centro Storico**, in the center (via Eroi di Dogali 6; Tel: 080-931-54-73), where, if you haven't had them by now, you should try the shallot-like *lampascioni,* a kind of onion pickle that accompanies every Apulian meal. Here they are prepared *al forno*—baked in the oven *alla parmigiana*.

MARTINA FRANCA

Continuing southeast on route 172, you will soon come to elegant Martina Franca, a charming Baroque town whose grandiose **Palazzo Ducale** (1668), ornamented with wrought-iron balustrades and balconies, is the appropriate backdrop each summer for a festival of 17th- and 18th-century music (Festival della Valle d'Itria: July 15–August 15). The church of **San Martino**, in piazza Plebiscito, is one of the jewels of the Apulian Baroque. Note especially the fanciful high-relief sculpture on its façade. Martina Franca is famous for its sausages: *Cervellata* is made with veal and pork and flavored with fennel seeds, while *soppressata* is a salami made with pork and bits of lard. Many butcher shops in the old town have grills on which they will roast sausages and pieces of meat while you wait.

Hotel Villa Ducale in piazza Sant'Antonio reflects the charm of the old town while providing modern, comfortable (and expensive) facilities. The roof garden dining room (Tel: 080-70-50-55; reservations recommended) has views of the Itrian Valley and serves excellent lamb (*agnello*) dishes. **La Tavernetta** (via Vittorio Emanuele 30; Tel: 080-70-63-23) is an inexpensive, usually crowded trattoria off piazza Roma that serves homemade pasta. For a special pasta, try the air-conditioned **Creperie** on corso dei Mille (number 2; Tel: 080-880-69-83; closed Tuesdays), where they make a local pasta called *frusciti* (macaroni with arugula, shrimp, and artichokes). About 5 km (3 miles) east of town is Martina Franca's restaurant in a *trullo*, the **Trattoria delle Ruote**, at Contrada Primicerio, via Ceglie E (very reasonable prices; reservations needed; Tel: 080-70-54-29; closed Mondays). Closer to the Baroque churches and palazzi (the town hall is attributed to Gianlorenzo Bernini) is an excellent and inexpensive restaurant: **La Rotonda**, at the Villa Comunale (Tel: 080-70-58-45).

On the way to Ostuni near the coast you may pass through **Cisternino**, a whitewashed hill town 10 km (6 miles) east of Locorotondo that gives a tiny taste of the splendor to come in Ostuni. Built on three hills, with a Gothic cathedral and some Renaissance and Baroque buildings, **Ostuni** itself is most remarkable for the immaculate appearance of its white-washed houses, which give the city its nickname, *La Perla Bianca* (The White Pearl). Ostuni, another 14 km (9 miles) east, offers two relaxing accommodations (also white): the modest and modern **Incanto** in town (a restful spot with spectacular views of the city, plains, and Adriatic), and the huge **Grand Hotel Rosa Marina** resort on the coast, with private beach, tennis facilities, and restaurants much frequented by the more prosperous local gentry.

Alternatively, the coastal road (route 379) back to Bari makes for a lovely drive. Along the way is **Egnatia** (Egnazia in Italian, from the Greek Gnathia), a Messapian town written about by Horace and inhabited until early Christian times. Today it is a vast, flat archaeological site with a recently opened museum housing examples of Gnathian ware, the delicate yellow, purple, and white pottery on a black background that takes its name from the town. Closer to Bari, at **Polignano a Mare**, is the hotel/restaurant **Grotta Palazzese**, at via Narciso 59 (Tel: 080-74-06-77). Its seafood, regional cheeses, desserts, and wines are all quite good, but the location—in a cave overlooking the Adriatic—is what makes it so spectacular. (You'll pay fairly dearly for the view.)

THE SALENTINE PENINSULA

The southernmost part of Apulia is the true "heel" of Italy's boot. Called the Salentine peninsula (Salento in Italian), it is easily explored from Lecce, which has two comfortable hotels, the modern and efficient **President** and the more centrally located **Risorgimento**, which has seen better days and is all the more charming for it. Both have good regional restaurants.

Brindisi

From Bari southeast to Lecce by car or train, the routes hug the coast to Brindisi, a city worth a quick visit—if only as a passing nod to history, as its present aspect is rather horrendous—even if you are not passing through its port to Greece, the city's raison d'être since ancient times. Strabo praised its wines (*fare un brindisi* still means to make a toast), Horace mentions it in his first *Satire,* Virgil died here, and many other ancients saw Brindisi because it was the end of the Appian Way. One of the two columns that marked this terminus may be seen near the harbor (Lecce took the other one).

The **Museo Archeologico** (open weekday mornings only), the Cathedral of **San Benedetto** (where Frederick II married his second wife), and the churches of **San Giovanni al Sepolcro** and **Santa Maria del Casale** (just north of town) also merit seeing, but expect tumultuous traffic during the summer.

If you can brave the cars, have a meal at **La Lanterna** restaurant in the piazza della Vittoria near the Duomo (via Tarantini 14; Tel: 0831-22-40-26; closed Sundays and August). The setting—inside an antique palazzo—is rustic, with a coffered ceiling and a fireplace. In summer, tables are set outside in the garden. This is the most fashionable place to eat in Brindisi, and the menu sometimes gets a little overinventive—as in the pasta made with Cognac. But the grilled fish is simple, fresh, and delicious (along with a heady Malvasia di Brindisi wine), as are the homemade pastries for dessert. **Trattoria le Colonne**, above the port near the Roman columns, is a simple trattoria with a garden; it offers dishes that use the local artichoke, one of Puglia's main crops (via Colonne 57; Tel: 0831-280-59; closed Tuesdays).

Lecce

Lecce's 16th- and 17th-century literary academies gave it the nickname "The Athens of Apulia," and its architecture from the same period earned it the epithet "The Florence of the Baroque." Whichever you prefer, it is one of the most beautiful towns in southern Italy. The soft pink-tinged local sandstone is easily carved and was handled with such vigor that it gave rise to an indigenous style called *Barocco Leccese*, a religious and secular architecture known more for its lavish decorative elements than its formal innovation. (The decorative tradition continues today with a flourishing production of papier-mâché and terra-cotta figurines available in many shops. The most extensive display of these and other crafts is in front of the Municipio at **Mostra Permanente dell'Artigianato**, via F. Rubichi 21. **I Messapi**, in front of Santa Croce, also makes very elegant figures in papier-mâché, or *cartapesta*.)

Lecce, which had been an important center of Magna Graecia, was much sought after by the Romans, was made a capital by the Normans, and came into its glory in the 16th century, when the architects and artists of the Spanish court created churches and public buildings here in a style unrivaled for its originality and exuberance. The best example of this style is the church of **Santa Croce** and the adjoining **Palazzo del Governo**. Together they form a block-long sweep of sculptured garlands, saints, putti, and pillars that are best viewed not for individual details, but as a single shimmering whole.

Wandering about the clean, quiet, uncrowded streets of Lecce's old town, you will find other examples on almost every street corner of the same florid style in which the tenets of Renaissance architecture have been turned inside out. Note, for example, the phantasmagoric **Chiesa del Rosario** (Church of the Rosary) or the church of **San Matteo**, which recalls Borromini in its concave-convex façade, or the dignified church of **Santi Nicola e Cataldo**, with its Norman-Arab ornamentation. Continue wandering under billowing 17th-century wrought-iron balconies and amber street lamps noticing details, like the pair of strong-armed caryatids flanking the doorway of **Palazzo Marrese** on via Palmieri or the little angels carved out of tufa that decorate almost every building.

You should eventually wind up at the **piazza del Duomo** on via Vittorio Emanuele, a harmonious complex of graceful buildings that includes a five-story bell tower; the 17th-century cathedral designed by Giuseppe Zimbalo, the master of most of Lecce's Baroque buildings; the Bishop's Palace, to the right; and the Episcopal Seminary, which contains a beautiful wellhead watched over by a pair of garland-bearing putti.

You could easily spend a day in Lecce, an elegant, bustling provincial capital. The town's long history is further evidenced by a half-excavated Roman amphitheater and the **Museo Provinciale**, which is noted for its collection of Italian archaeological artifacts dating from Paleolithic times (open 9:00 A.M. to 1:30 P.M. and 4:00 to 7:30 P.M.; closed Saturdays).

In July and August Lecce sponsors a festival of music and dance, the **Estate Musicale Leccese**, in its Baroque churches and palaces and piazzas.

Some of the Salento's regional food specialties include *ciceri e tria,* tagliatelle pasta cooked in chick-pea broth; *cappello da gendarme,* a pastry shell stuffed with veal, eggplant, and zucchini; and *mercia,* a hard-to-find sheep's-milk mozzarella cheese. The Belle Epoque dining room of the **Hotel Patria**, near Santa Croce (piazzetta Riccardi 13; Tel: 0832-294-31; closed Sundays and August), is a good place to try the Pugliese specialty *tiella,* a dish made of layers of rice, vegetables (usually potatoes), and seafood baked in a clay pot (*tiella*). While you're waiting, munch on *tarallini,* hard, twisted bread rings flavored with fennel seeds or hot peppers, which are first boiled and then baked. At the elegant restaurant **Carlo V** (via Palmieri 45; Tel: 0832-460-42; closed Sunday evenings, Mondays, and August), you dine under vaulted ceilings with frescoes that glow in the evening candlelight. You may be ready by now to try the *involtini* (stuffed meat rolls made from horse meat). For snacks and sweets, the Belle Époque **Caffè Alvino** in piazza S. Oronzo near the Roman amphitheater makes the best *granita di caffè* (iced coffee) and *panzerotti* (fried stuffed pastries) in Lecce.

The full-bodied Salice Salentino, which is exported to North America, is the area's best-known red wine; the mellow Malvasia is the popular choice for white. Gran Liquore San Domenico, made in Lecce's convent of San Domenico, is the local liqueur.

The Salentine Coast

The Greek influence in Apulia becomes most apparent toward the end of the peninsula, where cultural ties with Greece are still evident in the local dialects. The coastal drive is the most pleasant way to see it, since train and bus routes generally take you inland.

OTRANTO

Otranto, the easternmost city in Italy, was founded by the Greeks and became an important center of the Byzantine Empire. Until recently, residents practiced the Greek Orthodox religious rite, and they still call themselves *Idruntini,* a reference to the town's ancient name of Hydruntum. In 1480 Otranto was the site of a vicious Turkish attack, and its castle, made famous by Horace Walpole's Gothic novel *The Castle of Otranto,* was built soon afterward for defensive purposes; these days it is more likely to serve as a backdrop to a lazy game of bocce played by the elderly men of the town. ("I did not even know there was a castle of Otranto," Walpole later wrote. "When the story was finished, I looked to the map of the kingdom of Naples for a well-sounding name, and that of Otranto was very sonorous.") The 12th-century mosaic of the Tree of Life on the floor of Otranto's medieval cathedral takes up the entire nave. Also worth a quick look is the chapel containing the bones of 800 martyrs slain by the Turks in 1480.

Below the old town, near the port, rises the 15th-century Aragonese **castle**. Halfway between the old town and the castle is the moderately priced **Duca d'Aragona** restaurant (via Scupoli 32; Tel: 0836-80-61-65; closed Wednesdays), where you can try an Otranto specialty—roast eel; otherwise, try the more expensive **Il Gambero** (lungomare dei Eroi 22, largo Porta Terra; Tel: 0836-80-11-07; closed Wednesdays), which makes perfect risotto with lobster (*aragosta*) or crabmeat (*polpa di granchio*).

Otranto is famous for its handmade baskets fashioned out of olive branches. Strolling through its narrow streets, you will find grandmothers sitting in front of their whitewashed houses weaving baskets, their hands sometimes as gnarled as the branches.

Eight kilometers (5 miles) north of Otranto are the two **Alimini lakes**, one of salt water (Alimini Grande) and the other (the smaller) fed by a freshwater spring. Cypress and pine trees grow along the edges of both, and the Sierras protect them from the hot winds off the Ionian Sea.

Apulia's natural drama has its denouement at **Capo Santa Maria di Leuca**, a lonely white limestone cliff at the very tip of the peninsula. (The southernmost point of Apulia, however, is actually at Punta Ristola, a nondescript beach a short distance farther on.)

From Otranto to the tip, the Ionian coast of Apulia is one long procession of yachting clubs and tourist resorts. The beaches have not only pebbly sand and clear water, but also waves big enough to have made this part of the Ionian coast Italy's Big Sur for water skiers, surfers, and Windsurfers.

GALLIPOLI

Up the western coast of the Salento is Gallipoli, a fishing town and agricultural center founded by the Greeks, who gave it the name Kallipolis (Beautiful City). The name is still an accurate description of the town, as evidenced by the lavish Baroque interiors of its **Duomo** and the church of **San Francesco**, which contrast with the simple whitewashed façades of the Old City. There is also the inevitable imposing castle and museum, but Gallipoli's setting will put you in the mood instead for lunch at its fine seafood restaurant, **Marechiaro**, which overlooks the Ionian Sea on lungomare Marconi (Tel: 0833-26-61-43; closed Sundays and October to May). An excellent, if expensive, place to linger in the area is the modern resort of **Costa Brada**, on its own private beach 6 kilometers (3½ miles) south of town. Inland to the north, the noble Baroque churches and palaces of **Nardo**, reminiscent of Lecce, are worth inspecting, as is the town's oddly Oriental-looking pavilion, the Osanna. In the surrounding area, you can see a number of typical *masserie,* the fortified farmhouses of the 16th and 17th centuries.

From Lecce to Taranto

The highway and railroad from Lecce west to Taranto pass through **Manduria**, a town once surrounded by three circles of cyclopean walls and now containing some interesting Renaissance and Baroque buildings—but known mostly for the nearby ruins of the Messapian civilization that ruled the Salentine peninsula before the Greeks arrived. The archaeological site (where the Messapians battled the Tarantines) contains a necropolis and the Fonte di Plinio (Pliny's Fountain), a natural grotto, so called because the phenomenon of its constant level is thought to be the one mentioned in Pliny's *Natural History*.

TARANTO

Most of the colonies of Magna Graecia were in what is now Calabria. But the port of Taranto (the ancient Spartan colony of Taras, or Tarentum), situated between two bays called Mare Piccolo and Mare Grande, was its greatest city, with a population exceeding the present one. Then, as now, it was famous for the oysters plumped in the Mare Piccolo, but the city's current role as Italy's second largest naval dockyard and headquarters of the country's largest steel corporation, Italsider, should make you wary of finding more than pearls when biting into them. Taranto's seafood is safely sampled at its best restaurant, **Al Gambero**, which overlooks the harbor at vico del Ponte 4 (Tel: 099-471-11-90; closed Mondays and November). Whatever is fresh goes well with Verdea Bianca, a local white wine; the local vanilla-and-chocolate–flavored liqueur is called Amaro San Marzano.

Taranto's Città Vecchia occupies an island. Like Bari's Old City, it has a magnificent if somewhat rundown castle and cathedral and is the scene of important religious processions during Holy Week. Also like Bari's Città Vecchia, it is poverty-stricken and reputedly dangerous. The remains of a Doric temple dedicated to Neptune, which is the only outdoor remnant of Taranto's Greek past, are also located here. The city's real Greek treasures are in the **Museo Nazionale**, just over the ponte Girevole, a swinging bridge connecting the old city with the newer part of town. The collections of sculpture, gold filigree jewelry, and pottery make this the world's most important museum devoted to Magna Graecia; at least half a day should be spent seeing it. (The museum is open from 9:00 A.M. to 1:30 P.M. and 3:00 to 7:00 P.M.; closed Sunday and Monday afternoons.)

Hotels in Taranto, again as in Bari, are generally pleasant but impersonal in appearance; try the expensive waterfront **Grand Hotel Delfino** (with swimming pool) or the more moderate **Plaza**. Both are modern and centrally located. Otherwise, a half hour's drive down the coast at Avetrana is the **Castello di Mudonato**, which offers excellent accommodations in the peaceful country setting of a refurbished *masseria*.

To further the study of Magna Graecia, each year in October Taranto hosts the *Convegno di Studi sulla Magna*

Grecia, an important meeting on various aspects of that ancient civilization.

Apulia is famous for its pottery and ceramics—both of which are still a good buy in Italy—so before leaving this part of the region, you may want to make a stop at the nearby pottery town of **Grottaglie**, about 25 km (16 miles) northeast of Taranto. The ceramics industry in Grottaglie goes back to Roman times and has been maintained until today. *Botteghe,* or artisan shops, line both sides of via Crispi, which is the center of the ceramics quarter. Here you will find everything from table services with the ubiquitous *pugliese puntini* pattern, consisting of a circle of cobalt-blue *puntini* (points) resembling flowers on a cream background, to various crocks and vases with delicate geometric designs. Also available are the famous *pugliese fischietti*—painted terra-cotta figures of everything from animals to *carabinieri,* which are really whistles. Two of the best *botteghe* in Grottaglie are **Domenico Caretta** (via Crispi 20), where you can find unusual polychrome doll bottles (*pupe*), and **Fasano** (via Caravaggio 39). The **Ristorante Arcobaleno** (via La Sorte 3; Tel: 099-86-71-49; closed Mondays) is a good place to have lunch until the shops open again about 4:30.

GETTING AROUND

Foggia, Bari, and Brindisi all have airports served by Aliblu Airways or Aerea Trasporti Italiani out of Rome and Milan. Trains connect the major cities with Rome, Naples, and Milan; the smaller towns can be reached by local trains (which are very slow) or by (faster) buses. As connections can require some time, a car (rented at the airports or in the larger cities) offers the most freedom, although it should be closely watched when parked, especially in Bari and Taranto.

A guided tour of Apulia is organized by Central Holiday Tours (Tel: 800-526-6045).

One unusual way of seeing part of Apulia is with the Murge Express train. The turn-of-the-century carriages leave Bari each morning for a day-long excursion (combined with coach connection) to the Murge sites. For information, contact Italsud Tours, 101 Ridge Avenue, Passaic, NJ 07055; Tel: (201) 779-2495; Fax: (201) 779-4538.

Monte Sant'Angelo celebrates Saint Michael on May 8 and September 29. Barletta's Disfida (a reenactment of the battle of 1503) takes place on the third Sunday in July. In Bari, Saint Nicholas's feast takes place from May 7 through May 10. In Martina Franca the music festival takes place in July and

August. In Taranto, the processions of Our Lady of the Sorrows (L'Addolorata) and the Mysteries (Misteri) take place on Maundy Thursday and Good Friday, respectively.

ACCOMMODATIONS REFERENCE

The rates given below are projections for 1993; always check for up-to-date information before making reservations. Wide ranges may reflect the differences between low- and high-season rates. Unless otherwise indicated, the figures indicate the cost of a double room (per room, not per person). However, half-board (mezza pensione) rates, which include breakfast and one other meal per day, are per person. The service charge is included in the rate; inquire about tax and breakfast.

Unusual accommodations in the beehive-shaped structures called trulli *may be rented by the week or month through Agenzia Fittatrulli, via Duchessa Acquaviva 5, 70011 Alberobello; Tel: (080) 72-27-17.*

▶ **Albergo Al Passetto.** Piazza del Popolo 28, 71036 **Lucera.** Tel: (0881) 92-11-24. £50,000.

▶ **Albergo Grand Hotel Cicolella.** Viale 24 Maggio 60, 71100 **Foggia.** Tel: (0881) 38-90; Fax: (0881) 789-84. £168,000–£288,000; half board £195,000.

▶ **Castello di Mudonato.** 74020 **Aventrana.** Tel: (099) 67-45-97. £95,000–£105,000.

▶ **Costa Brada.** Lungomare Costa Brada, 73014 **Gallipoli.** Tel: (0833) 225-51; Fax: (0833) 225-55. £160,000–£198,000; half board £121,000–£195,000.

▶ **Gabbiano.** San Domino, 71040 **San Nicola di Tremiti.** Tel: (0882) 66-30-44; Fax: (0882) 66-30-90. £55,000–£110,000; half board £79,000–£89,000.

▶ **Grand Hotel Delfino.** Viale Virgilio 66, 74100 **Taranto.** Tel: (099) 32-05; Fax: same. £110,000–£160,000; half board £130,000.

▶ **Grand Hotel Rosa Marina.** 72017 **Ostuni.** Tel: (0831) 97-04-11. £85,000–£99,000.

▶ **Hotel Apeneste.** Piazza Turati 3, 71030 **Mattinata.** Tel: (0884) 47-43; Fax: (0884) 43-41. £57,000–£98,000; half board £60,000–£85,000.

▶ **Hotel La Bufalara.** Via Uria, Isola Verano, 71010 **Ischitella.** Tel: (0884) 970-37; Fax: (0884) 973-74. £95,000; half board £70,000–£95,000.

▶ **Hotel D'Amato.** Località Spiaggia, 71010 **Peschici.** Tel: (0884) 96-44-11; Fax: (0884) 96-22-38. Open Easter–September. £100,000. Half board £70,000–£100,000.

► **Hotel del Faro**. 71019 **Faro di Pugnochiuso**. Tel: (0884) 70-90-11; Fax: (0884) 70-90-17. Open April 20–October 20. Ł129,000; full board Ł234,000.

► **Hotel Miramare**. Via XX Settembre 2, 71012 **Rodi Garganico**. Tel: (0884) 96-50-25. Ł70,000.

► **Hotel Residence Solemar**. Località San Nicola, 71010 **Peschici**. Tel: (0884) 96-41-86; Fax: (0884) 96-41-88. Open May 12–September 20. Ł115,000; half board Ł91,000–Ł115,000.

► **Hotel dei Trulli**. Via Cadore 32, 70011 **Alberobello**. Tel: (080) 932-35-55; Fax: (080) 932-35-60. Apartments Ł220,000–Ł240,000; half board Ł150,000–Ł180,000.

► **Hotel Villa Ducale**. Piazza Sant'Antonio, 74015 **Martina Franca**. Tel: (080) 70-50-55; Fax: (080) 70-58-85. Ł130,000.

► **Incanto**. Via dei Colli, 72017 **Ostuni**. Tel: (0831) 30-17-81; Fax: (0831) 33-83-02. Ł80,000–Ł120,000; half board Ł80,000–Ł100,000.

► **Kyrie**. San Domino, 71040 **San Nicola di Tremiti**. Tel: (0882) 66-32-32; Fax: (0882) 66-30-55. Open May 15–September. Ł130,000–Ł240,000; half board Ł95,000–Ł175,000.

► **Il Melograno**. Contrada Torricella 345, 70043 **Monopoli**. Tel: (080) 690-90-30; Fax: (080) 74-79-08. Ł484,000; half board Ł220,000–Ł286,000.

► **Palace Hotel**. Via Lombardi 13, 70122 **Bari**. Tel: (080) 521-65-51; Fax: (080) 521-14-99. Ł340,000; half board Ł216,000–Ł270,000.

► **Pizzomunno Vieste Palace Hotel**. Via Spiaggia di Pizzomunno, 71019 **Vieste**. Tel: (0884) 70-87-41; Fax: (0884) 70-73-25. Open April 15–October. Ł343,000–Ł424,000; half board Ł190,000–Ł360,000.

► **Plaza**. Via d'Aquino 46, 74100 **Taranto**. Tel: (099) 49-07-75; Fax: (099) 49-06-75. Ł83,000–Ł118,000.

► **President**. Via Salandra 6, 73100 **Lecce**. Tel: (0832) 31-18-81; Fax: (0832) 59-43-21. Ł100,000–Ł172,000; half board Ł130,000.

► **Risorgimento**. Via Augusto Imperatore 19, 73100 **Lecce**. Tel: (0832) 421-25; Fax; (0832) 455-71. Ł59,000–Ł103,000.

► **La Vecchia Masseria**. 70031 **Andria** (Castel del Monte). Tel: (0883) 815-29. Closed December–February. Ł46,000–Ł76,000.

► **Villa Meo-Evoli**. Via Provinciale per Conversano, Contrade Cozzana, 70100 **Bari**. Tel: (080) 80-30-52. Ł110,000.

► **Villa Romanazzi-Carducci**. Via Capruzzi 326, 70124 **Bari**. Tel: (080) 522-74-00; Fax: (080) 536-02-97. Ł222,000–Ł350,000.

CALABRIA

By Nuccio Ordine

Nuccio Ordine teaches at the University of Calabria. His book on the 16th-century philosopher Giordano Bruno, La cabala dell'asino, *has been published in Italian and French.*

Calabria's mountains, forests, and seacoast draw Italians from the steamy North in summer, and athletes and nature lovers throughout the year. They come for the Calabrian segments of the Appenine mountain ranges—especially the thickly forested Sila, which is generously endowed with lakes and wildflowers, and Calabria's 485 miles of wrap-around coastline. Hotels and tourist villages have developed at a fast pace here during the last 40 years, and the tourist lira is extremely important to the local economy. Because of the almost-encircling Tyrrhenian and Ionian seas, mild weather prevails in Calabria for much of the year. Summer, however, can be extremely hot and winter is often rainy, a condition the arid parts of the hills need desperately.

Calabria, the toe of the boot, is still one of Italy's poorest regions, where centuries of exploitation and neglect have combined with organized crime, in the form of the *n'drangheta,* to keep the economy marginal. The impact of tourist lire is not inclusive enough to reach those who attempt to farm with implements used by their grandfathers—the ones that interest anthropologists and collectors but mean backbreaking labor for those who use them.

The isolation that Calabria's geologically varied landscape—a full 90 percent hills and mountains—has brought the region has meant that ancient ways of life have continued in other ways as well. Customs that originated in Greece, Albania, and Provence centuries ago are still followed in mountain villages, and traditional dress is often

267

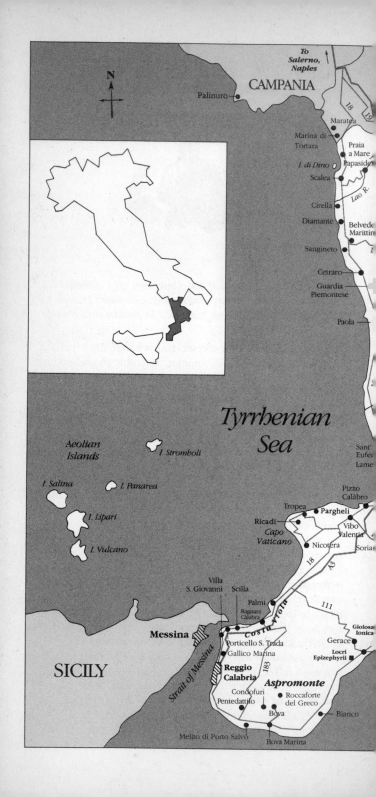

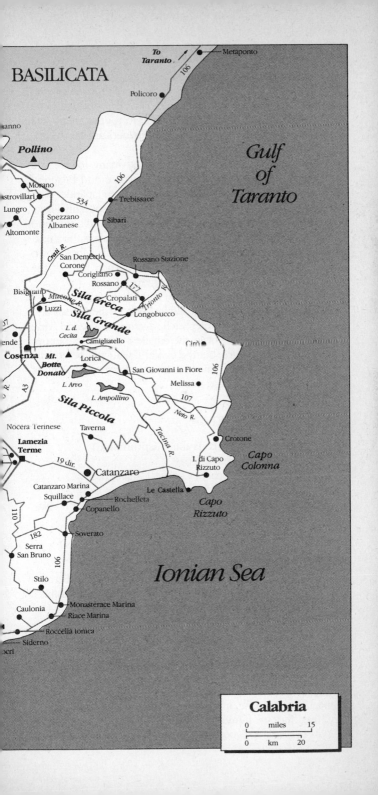

worn. Television antennas sprout from rooftops, but some of the beauty of ethnic traditions continues. The traveller who wants to explore the interior would do well to practice some Italian, for English is usually confined to tourist areas—ski resorts or coastal towns—although teenagers are apt to have learned a few words in school.

Earthquakes and war have destroyed many towns, and Calabria is not the place to expect pristine and beautiful villages. Although the towns do not often sparkle with Tuscan-style glamour, many are spectacular, especially Pizzo, Tropea, and Scilla on the western shore and Stilo and Rossano on the Ionian. The grandeur of nature is the thing: Dramatic mountain crags and clear, serene lakes look down on rocky shores and crashing waves. At each turn of the winding roads a startling new panorama unfolds.

The food is excellent, the fresh and wholesome fare now considered to make up the healthiest diet. Grilled meats and fish, pasta, beans, vegetables, rich olive oil, and good wine make up the menu in even the smallest town. Hot-pepper sauces are prized here, but the cooler palate will be equally pleased. Pastry shops entice with an amazing variety of cakes, rich with fruits and nuts.

MAJOR INTEREST

The mountains (Sila, Pollino, Aspromonte)
The rocky Tyrrhenian coast
The white sand beaches of the Ionian coast
The ancient relics of Magna Graecia (Crotone, Locri, and the Bronze Warriors at the Reggio Calabria National Museum)
Ethnic minorities (Albanesi, Valdesi, Grecanici)
Byzantine churches at Rossano and Stilo
The *Codex Purpureus,* Rossano
Gastronomy and local products, especially the permanent Sapore di Calabria (Taste of Calabria) exhibit at Diamante
Maratea (in adjacent Basilicata)

From prehistoric relics we know that Calabria has been inhabited for almost 120,000 years. When the Greeks arrived, they established thriving Greek cities such as Locri, Sibari, and Crotone, intermixing with an already developed culture, fed by numerous foreign influences because of Calabria's strategic position in the Mediterranean. Among the Greeks of note here was Pythagoras (570–500 B.C.), who established the first Pythagorean community in Crotone (Croton in English) in 532 B.C.

Rome expanded its consular roads into the southern peninsula, and later, the atrocities of Alaric (A.D. 410) included the destruction of Reggio Calabria. Alaric died at Cosenza and was buried beneath the Busento River there—along with the immense treasure he had accumulated, which has yet to be uncovered.

When Byzantine Greeks dominated the region, vast tracts of land (*latifundas*) were given to or taken over by monks who had emigrated because of persecution by the iconoclasts. Then Arabs and Normans, Lombards and Swabians arrived, those last encouraging commerce and bringing Jewish traders from Campania.

With the Renaissance came the New Man, exemplified in the humanist philosopher Bernardino Telesio (1509–1588), a native of Cosenza. Subsequent feudal struggles between Angevins and Aragonese led to the Kingdom of Naples taking over. Feudal lords exacted heavy taxes from the local people, and minorities, such as the Waldensians, were brutally persecuted. The philosopher Tommaso Campanella of Stilo led an uprising against the Spanish and was condemned to prison.

During the 18th century efforts were made at wresting the estates from the church, but the nobles, fearing a precedent would be set (redistributing land), opposed reform. The Bourbon ventures in the South, aimed at excavating the antiquities, led to the opening of Calabria to the European world.

In the light of the revolutionary late 18th century, Napoleon's brother-in-law Joachim Murat became king of Naples, but the Bourbons soon expelled him. When he attempted to land at the Calabrian town of Pizzo to regain the throne, he was imprisoned and executed. Soon afterward, Garibaldi marched through, relieving the Bourbons of command and helping create the Italian nation.

Writer-explorers such as the Frenchman Astolphe de Custine and later Norman Douglas (1868–1952) inspired wealthy travellers to include Calabria on the Grand Tour.

Although many travellers will simply follow the coastal route (Autostrada Salerno (SA)–Reggio Calabria (RC)) along the western shore just as far as Reggio Calabria and then go on to Sicily, those who extend their itinerary into the mountains will be rewarded with exquisite scenery, good food, and the opportunity to combine mountain and sea vacations, with side trips to the Byzantine splendors of Rossano and Stilo and the drama of the Greek statues at Reggio.

Our itinerary starts at the Pollino mountains at the northeast, takes serpentine paths through the mountains, and then follows each coastline, the Tyrrhenian (west) and the Ionian (south). (If you're travelling south down the coast from Campania, you may want to stop first in Maratea, as discussed in the Tyrrhenian Coast section below.) You'll probably want to choose some aspects of each as you travel. For those without a car, train and bus service does exist, but a good deal of patience, and a willingness to take early-morning buses if need be, will be required.

THE POLLINO

The highest peaks of the Pollino mountains, which separate Basilicata from Calabria, rise higher than any others of the region, to almost 7,500 feet. Difficulty of access has protected this range from the usual problems human contact creates for the natural environment, and the area has recently been declared a national park. Thick beech forests give way to the Calabrian fir, which looks like a tree from a Japanese water color. Its silvery bark has scales like chain mail that grow out as far as the needles, giving the tree a misty look. Meadows of cyclamen, crocus, bluebells, and daisies reward the early-spring visitor.

To explore the Pollino, leave the Autostrada del Sole (the A 3) at Mormanno, Morano, or Castrovillari, each of which is a convenient starting point for touring the most interesting parts of the mountains.

MORMANNO

Mormanno, whose roots go back to the Lombards, sits on a mountain spur about 2,640 feet above sea level. When summer's heat is scalding the coastal areas, Mormanno's cool breezes are inviting. The church of **Santa Maria del Colle** in Mormanno contains fine Baroque altars of the Neapolitan school. To stay here, your best (and almost only) choice is the **Sant' Elena**, which has its own garden and restaurant. From here the mountains can be climbed on foot or on the back of a mule.

From **De Gasperi**, at about 5,000 feet, you can climb to **Timpone di Mezzo** (5,500 feet), overlooking the river Frido as it rushes through the Vacquero plateau. Still higher, at about 6,600 feet, the Pollino plateau takes the form of a natural amphitheater, opening to the rocky cliffs of the Serra Crispo and the Serra delle Ciavole, and extending as far as the *grande porte del Pollino* (the entrance to the Pollino), where there is a huge pine tree, the symbol of the park.

Guided excursions can be arranged through the Prosertur organization, located in Mormanno on the corso Municipale (Tel: 0981-810-47 or 801-68). Take a dictionary if your Italian needs help, and a backpack equipped with a selection of regional salamis (perhaps spicy *capicollo*) and cheeses and the traditional pastry called *bocconotti,* filled with marmalade or almond paste.

Still using Mormanno as a base, travel toward the Tyrrhenian coast along route 504, a narrow, winding road through the valley of the river Lao. At the Avena crossroads, about 10 km (6 miles) before you come to Papasidero, a sign points to the entrance to a cave with **Neolithic drawings**. Umberto Cersosimo, the *simpatico* elderly proprietor of the cave, will be happy to act as guide. (It's his cave, after all.) Language may be a slight problem, but he will definitely know why you're there (to see *il graffito*). Three tombs here date from 9200 B.C. Inside, skeletons and funerary objects were found that reveal Italy's most ancient burial practices. You'll see the sketch of an ox, about 4 feet long, on a mass of rock. It's in perfect proportion, executed with a sure hand. You may want to toast this ancient ox with the local wine (called Rosso di Papasidero) at Papasidero.

MORANO CALABRO

Farther to the south along the autostrada, on the slopes of a hill graced with the ruins of a Norman castle, stands Morano Calabro, the ancient *Moranum* included in the itinerary of Sant' Antonino in the fourth century. The city forms a triangular shape on the hill, a shape repeated in the nearby mountain's silhouette, which is often splashed with snow. Morano's past is visible in many buildings and works of art, including the monastery of **San Bernardino**, one of the few examples of 14th-century architecture in Calabria, with a beautiful coffered wooden ceiling and a 17th-century wooden pulpit and baldachin. Its most important treasure, however, is a polyptych by Bartolomeo Vivarini (1477), intense in color, painted by the artist when he was at the peak of his artistic maturity. At present it can be seen in Cosenza at the Convento di San Francesco, as discussed below.

The **Collegiata della Maddelena** here is one of the most impressive Baroque churches of the area, although its foundations are pre-Christian. Its bell tower is covered with majolica. Inside, the choir loft, all in wood, is exquisite. Several paintings here are by Antonello Gagini, whose work can be seen in hundreds of southern Italian churches. A visit to the **Museo della Storia dell'Agricultura e della Pastorizia** adds insight into the pastoral nature of the area with nicely arranged displays of home and farm implements.

Those who want to plunge back into a mountainous landscape can continue from Morano into the **Vallone Guidolino**, the **Serra del Prete**, and the **Pollinello**. At Castrovillari, south of Morano, stop at the Comunità office on via del Lavoro for a map and a book (in Italian) by Giorgio Braschi, describing the area for hikers. Near Castrovillari you may want to enjoy rural Calabria at the Agriturist farm of **Pasquale Vacca**, where you can taste the apples and pears and his own wine.

CASTROVILLARI

Unfortunately the first glimpse the traveller from the north has of Castrovillari is the sight of the huge cement works outside town, a blight on the countryside. However, the town lies at the center of a fertile and well-cultivated crescent-shaped valley, irrigated with waters that descend from the Pollino. At its center and meriting a visit is the **Museo Civico Archeologico**, with both paleological relics and works by the painter Andrea Alfano (1879–1967). The many-turreted **castello** was built by the Aragonese in 1490. In its keep, the church of San Giuliano has a lovely (restored) Renaissance portal. You may not drop in, however, as it serves as a jail, like many other Spanish fortresses in Italy. Nearby, at the summit of a hill, stands **Santa Maria del Castello**, founded by the Normans (Robert and Roger Guiscard were both here) in 1090, and often restored since. Inside the church there is an icon of the Madonna that local people believe to have remarkable problem-solving qualities; you will see that countless women have dedicated their hair to her, surrounding the icon with it. Outside you can enjoy a panoramic view of the Pollino and its valleys.

While at Castrovillari, dine at the **Ristorante Alìa**, considered the best in all of Calabria. Pinuccio Alìa, the priest of this (expensive) temple of gastronomy, treats his guests to authentic traditional Calabrese cooking with his own creative interpretations (via Jetticelle 69; Tel: 0981-463-70). In his shop you can also find typical regional foods, including dried tomatoes, marinated mushrooms, and in winter a variety of figs, stuffed and sugared or plain with herbs. Lacrima di Castrovillari is a good full-bodied dry wine.

Two hotels at Castrovillari are comfortable: the **Motel A.S.T.J.** (no air conditioning) and the hotel **President Joli** (with air conditioning).

ALTOMONTE

Heading south on the autostrada, turn off for Altomonte, a peaceful, well-kept hamlet seemingly constructed by artists who got lost on their way to Siena, to see its church of **Santa Maria della Consolazione**, in Calabrese Gothic style. Inside are several works of art, including the 14th-century tomb of Filippo Sangineto, one of the noble rulers of the town, under whose patronage the church was built. Its marble bas-reliefs were sculpted in the tradition of Tino di Camaino.

In the **Museo Civico**, adjoining the church, is the *Madonna of the Pears*, painted, it's thought, by a student of the great master Antonello da Messina. There are also three sections of a polyptych, one done by Simone Martini and the others by Bernardo Daddi. (Open 9:00 A.M. to 1:30 P.M. and 3:30 to 6:30 P.M.)

The **Hotel Barbieri** overlooks Altomonte and has a good (moderately priced) restaurant. Try the homemade pasta with hot pepper sauce (*scoppiettanti*). Wild boar, kid, and grilled rabbit may make up a hearty second course. You can buy local products at their shop.

Eleven km (7 miles) northwest is the town of **Lungro**, the cathedral city of one of the two Greek dioceses in Italy. If you travel there near Easter time, you're likely to see some of the original Albanian costumes. The residents still speak their original dialect. Albanians make up Calabria's largest ethnic minority.

THE SILA

To climb the Sila the lazy way, take the autostrada to Cosenza (see below) and then the superstrada (route 107) from Cosenza to **Camigliatello**, at an altitude of over 4,000 feet, a modern tourist resort for winter and summer sports. Here every season offers choices: skiing, swimming, hiking, mushrooming, or just enjoying the landscape.

The Sila is rich with water, not an insignificant element in southern Italy. The rivers Neto, Crati, Trionto, Tacina, Corace, and Mucone feed beautiful large artificial **lakes** that bring electrical power to the area. All were created during the first decade of this century. Among the most beautiful are Lago

Cecita near Camigliatello; Lago Arvo, on whose shores Lorica is situated; and Lago Ampollino, near the hamlet of Palumbo in the Sila Piccola. Woodland, meadow, and granite cliffs are everywhere inset with lakes and rivers.

Thanks to these lakes the area is lush and green, varying from pinewoods to pastureland. Wolves, foxes, wild boar, and roe deer roam the slopes. The adventurous can search out the most remote, untouched areas of this vast landscape. The pinewoods of Fallistro, near Camigliatello, boast trees some 50 centuries old, called "the giants of the Sila" because of their dimensions. The Sila is locally called the "dark mountain" because of the tones of the wood.

Just below the ancient woods, 5 km (3 miles) east of Camigliatello, the very modern **Magara Hotel** comfortably jolts hikers into the world of hydromassage and sauna, swimming pool and disco. At Camigliatello the hotel **Sila** and the hotel **Camigliatello** provide less lavish but perfectly acceptable comfort.

In order to get to know this part of Calabria, you can follow two itineraries, each using Camigliatello as a base.

Rossano

From Camigliatello, follow Lago Cecita and route 177 until the crossroads, and route 283 for Fossiata and on to **Longobucco**, which is noted for its handmade woollen blankets and other handicrafts whose designs reveal Byzantine and Arab influences and whose colors come from local herbs. From here the highest peak of the Sila Greca, almost 5,000 feet, can be seen. Then follow the descent to Cropalati, and from there proceed west to Rossano. The total distance from Camigliatello to Rossano is 83 km (52 miles).

Rossano, dramatically set into a sandstone cliff, looks out to the Ionian coast through majestic olive groves. Roman in origin, it became an important center of the Byzantine Greeks, who established flourishing monasteries here, despite opposition from Rome. The church of **San Marco** was constructed during the 11th century on a cliff at the edge of the town; it's an interesting example of Byzantine style, with five small cupolas. If it's closed, try alerting the sacristan at via Marco 37.

The **Cattedrale** is a Baroque interpretation of an earlier structure. Inside you'll find a ninth-century Madonna supposedly painted by a supernatural hand. But the treasure of Rossano lies in the **Museo Diocesano**, next to the cathedral. The *Codex Purpureus* (Purple Codex) is one of the oldest and richest of evangelical manuscripts, composed of 188 leaves and dating from the sixth century. Seventeen brilliantly painted miniatures illustrate some of the best-known Gospel stories. One of its most famous illustrations is that of the Last Supper, showing Christ and his disciples reclining on the floor in a circle and eating out of a communal bowl, in Eastern (and Roman) fashion, thought by many scholars to be a realistic portrayal of the actual event. How the *Codex* came to Rossano is not known. Some say that it was written and illuminated in Syria and carried to Calabria by Greek monks fleeing during the Iconoclastic Controversy, which began during the eighth century.

With things ecclesiastical you may want to blend the delicious local licorice called Amarelli, produced here for more than a century. In spring the wild strawberries are woodland treats.

At Rossano Stazione (6 km/3½ miles north), the modest, modern hotel **Europa Lido Palace** is a good choice for an overnight base. The Lido Palace is on the sea, and its restaurant serves local specialties.

Ten minutes away on route 107 and the Vecchia Strada Ionica lies **Corigliano**. At its center stands a medieval castle, occupied by the Ruffo family during the 15th century. It has four merloned towers and a drawbridge. Inside you may visit the chapel and furnished rooms dating from the castle's 18th- and 19th-century residents.

About 5 km (3 miles) from Rossano is the **Convento del Patire**, which rivaled Mount Athos as a center of learning during the 12th century.

San Giovanni in Fiore

Starting again from Camigliatello, route 107 leads us 25 km (16 miles) east to San Giovanni in Fiore. A slow-moving narrow-gauge railroad also links the two towns along a lakeside route of stunning beauty (unlike the destination). There are two trains a day in summer, more in winter. This busy town's name is derived from Gioacchino di Fiore, the abbot who was mentioned in Dante's *Paradiso* as one gifted with a prophetic spirit, and founder (1189) of the **Florense Abbey**. Many of the original elements can be seen in the abbey today—the large Gothic doorway, the ancient walls, and the rose window. Women still wear the black and white costumes Fiore reputedly designed, or his temperament inspired.

The town has a flourishing Armenian-inspired textile trade, and shops are filled with bedspreads, rugs, and hangings in brilliant colors; ceramics are also created here. Stop at the **Centro Artigianato Tiano**, open all year, in via Vallone 225 (Tel: 0984-99-15-15) for an overview of the local crafts. If shopping makes you hungry, head for the bakery **Fratelli Mancini** at via Panoramico 83, where you'll find the local *pitta mpigliata.*

The goldsmith **Giovan** has an atelier in via Nazionale, where he sells original jewelry based on local traditions.

Traditional meals are served at the **Albergo Scuola Florens** (hotel school) in viale della Repubblica (Tel: 0984-99-28-51). Trout and wild boar are often menu choices, as is *butirro,* a dollop of creamery butter encased in *cacciacavallo* cheese. For an overnight, go to **Dino's Hotel**. It's not elegant, but friendly. Taste the local ricotta salata cheese. Italians are often sensitive to the subtle changes in the taste of foods, such as cheese, that occur from town to town, depending on climate and what the animals are fed. A few hours spent at one of its simple tables with a bottle of Savuto or Pollino is one way of paying homage to Pliny or another ancient who praised the site.

From San Giovanni in Fiore it's easy to get to Lago Ampollino (to the south) and the **Villaggio Palumbo**, a modern sports complex featuring year-round bobsledding on metal tracks, water skiing, helicopter tours, and festive dinners. Farther south, the town of **Tivolio** sits high on a rocky spur. Elegant striped silk and wool shawls are made here.

From Camigliatello, it's 31 km (19 miles) southwest to Cosenza on routes 107 and 19. There is also train service.

Cosenza

One of the most important economic and cultural centers in Calabria, and the site of the University of Calabria, Cosenza is located at the confluence of the Crati and Busento rivers; its picturesque historic quarter trails up the Pancrazio hills. According to legend, Alaric and his stolen treasures were buried in the river Busento (A.D. 410); the river was diverted from its course and then turned back after the burial. (The Busento is not wide.)

Like many "barbarians," Alaric was probably better educated and less barbarous than the Normans and the Saxons, who were adept at pillage but have had a better press. Alaric was a Romanized Goth, an Arian Christian with ambitions to command an army, who decided to take what had not been given. The sack of Rome lasted four days, and then the Goths moved south with their treasures, to set sail for Sicily and Africa. The palaces of the Aventine Hill in Rome may have been the source of the treasure that was buried, allegedly, with Alaric. Soon after Alaric's death, Galla Placidia, stepsister of the Western Roman emperor and cousin of the Eastern Roman emperor, married his brother Ataulphus, becoming queen of the Goths and scandalizing her family.

During the 16th century a flourishing humanistic culture developed here, inspiring the creation of the prestigious Accademia that is still important today, named after Cosenza's most illustrious citizen, Bernardino Telesio (1509–1588), an anti-Aristotelian who stressed empirical investigation, and regarded self-preservation as man's fundamental goal and the basis of his ethics.

Today's Cosenza is both ancient and modern. In the old town, built on a steep hillside, narrow, winding streets lead, under iron balconies and the morning's wash, to the **Castello** (closed between 1:00 and 4:00 P.M.). From its 14 bastions you'll have a fine view of Cosenza.

On a lower older level in the town stands the **Duomo**, built during the 12th century in Romanesque-Cistercian style and consecrated in 1222 with Frederick II in attendance. Its façade and rose window are especially graceful. Ask to see the Treasury and the small, magnificent cross that Frederick gave to the cathedral to honor the occasion. The fine tomb of Isabella of Aragon was erected here following her death from a fall from a horse in 1270. Avoid this area at night.

Near the Duomo the monastic complex of **San Francesco di Assisi**, founded in 1217, contains paintings by the 17th-century painter Mattia Preti, born in Taverna. The entrance to the Convento, where Preti's paintings are found, is on via San Francesco. The polyptych discussed earlier, by Vivarini, is also there. To see them, however, requires permission. Ask at the Cosenza tourist office and you may be lucky (via Rossi, near viale della Repubblica; Tel: 0984-39-05-95). The **Biblioteca Civica**, in piazza XV Marzo, houses a collection of precious antique manuscripts.

Cosenza's restaurants usually feature local specialties. The family-style **La Calavrisella** in via De Rada serves a superb *pasta e fagioli* (pasta with beans) as well as the local *cacciacavallo* cheese, similar to provolone (closed Sunday and Monday evenings; Tel: 0984-280-12). At **Da Armando**, in an old converted farmhouse on via Montegrappa 32, wood fires flavor the local delicacies (usually hearty), and the prices are moderate. In Rende, northwest of Cosenza, Il Setaccio is an ancient osteria where the proprietor, Domenico Ziccarelli, offers an inexpensive menu with porcini from the Sila, escarole, and *fagiole,* and above all, delicious desserts like *mpigliata,* which originated in ancient Greece. His backyard garden provides the salad and fruit. (Contrada Santa Rosa; Tel: 0984-40-17-86). It's a five-minute ride from the center of town.

The modern city, near Corso Mazzini, across the narrow river, is where the activity is. Have coffee and dessert at the Caffè Renzelli for a touch of old Cosenza. It's just to the right of the Bruzzi palace, in the southwest corner of the modern city, not far from the river.

For a good pizza go to the Luna Rossa (also a restaurant), on via Sicilia in front of the Tribunale (Courts). Try the *mazzacorde,* too, ground offals of pork and mutton in hot pepper sauce. (At least try it.)

Another good place to enjoy culinary Calabria is at the Ente Sviluppo Agricolo Calabrese (ESAC), at viale degli Alimena 71, a shop where you'll find and can taste wine, cheese, olive oil, and other local specialties.

The Hotel Executive, one of the most modern hotels in the South, is a good place to stay; it's located at the Cosenza-Nord exit of the autostrada about 5 km (3 miles) from the center of town in a residential area. The swimming pool is a plus.

THE TYRRHENIAN COAST

As you've meandered through the mountains, you've been conscious of the sea to the east and west of the peninsula. The fine western coast from Marina di Tortora (south of Maratea) to Paola is called the Citron Riviera because that ancient tree is cultivated here; citron is important in the production of candy, liquor, ice cream, and cosmetics, as well as for its beauty. Wide beaches, jagged cliffs, and stupendous grottoes characterize this coastline. Unfortunately an overdeveloped tourist industry obscures its natural beauty along parts of the coast, but you'll find many respites along this route.

PRAIA A MARE

Praia a Mare, on the sea as its name says, was perhaps the first tourist center constructed in Calabria. When summer crowds diminish you might want to stay here awhile in order to visit the interior and Maratea. The **Germania** is a good, moderately priced beachfront hotel. You may, however, prefer to stay in **Maratea**, a few miles to the north, across the border in Basilicata. (The region of Basilicata, usually thought of as inland between Calabria and Apulia, with a coast on the Gulf of Taranto, also has a small coastal strip separating Campania from Calabria.) It's at the foot of Monte San Biagio, a pretty fishing village and resort town. If you climb up Monte Biagio you'll find, at the statue of Christ with his arms outstretched, a magnificent view of the very beautiful gulf of Policastro. The hotel **Santavenere** is delightful and expensive. Each bedroom has its own balcony or terrace, with long sea views.

The sanctuary of the **Madonna della Grotta** in Praia a Mare is a vast cave that has been used in some way since the Paleolithic era, judging by the archaeological relics that have been found here. It's reached by a long staircase. The adjoining campanile contains a bell that came from an English ship torpedoed offshore in 1917, in an example of wartime recycling.

On the beach near the Fiuzzi Tower you can rent a boat to visit the **Isola di Dino**, a triangular island that forms a plateau about 200 feet above the sea. Take a counterclockwise route around the island to see the grottoes, one of which has a cascade inside. The waters beyond the Blue Grotto are similar to the waters around Capri, except that the colors vary from copper green to an opaque, intense blue. Dino offers a pleasant respite from the mainland coast lined with sunbathers. Beyond Praia, San Nicolo Arcella has a good, wide beach. Tourism has overwhelmed Scalea, a bit farther south along the coast, but you might enjoy the Norman castle here.

Down the coast about 15 km (9 miles) from Praia a Mare, **Cirella** lies opposite an island of the same name. The sea here is marvelous, and the rocky coast lends drama. Slightly inland but visible from the autostrada are the remains of Cirella Vecchia, also a Sybarite colony, which was destroyed by Hannibal, then again by the Saracens, and then by the French, who bombarded it by cannon from the sea in 1806. If you climb the winding old streets of the town you'll be rewarded with a splendid panorama of the sea and the island. Roofless houses, ruins of a castle, and a church with traces of a 15th-century fresco are still visible.

DIAMANTE

Five kilometers (3 miles) south is chic Diamante, much admired for its wide beach and clear water. The town's prosperity comes from the cultivation of citron trees, an enterprise linked to the earliest Jewish immigration, in the first centuries of the Christian era. The citron is important to the Jewish religion for the Feast of the Tabernacle and for Sukkoth, which may explain why the tree was first planted in this area.

Diamante has the added attraction of contemporary murals—about 100 frescoes painted on the walls and houses of the town by Italian and international artists under a government program begun in 1981. **Sapore Calabria** is one of the best places to taste and buy products from the entire region, thanks to the passionate devotion of journalist-*gastronomo* Enzo Monaco. A gourmet store where tasting is encouraged, it's located in via Amendola near the Madonnina Lungomare. Among the unusual tastes are the citron liqueur, salami made by Albanians, and a pecorino shot with chile pepper. As is common along the shore, a truncated 16th-century lookout tower is a landmark.

At Diamante, stay at the **Hotel Ferretti**, a mile away, at the center of the area called the Blue Riviera. It has a private beach and views of the rocky coast. Also on the sea, at Cirella, the **Hotel Guardacosta** provides attractive rooms. It's surrounded by olive trees on a rocky spur above the sea, and has a seawater pool. The **Corvino** is one of the best restaurants in the area for local cooking. Try *lagano e ceci* (pasta with chick peas), barbecued chicken, or rabbit. A citron liqueur is a good finish to the meal.

Ceramics fanciers will want to visit **Belvedere**, 10 km (6 miles) to the south, where a long tradition has led to interesting pottery and kitchenware, with Greek and Roman influences. They are often yellow and green, with stylized floral motifs. The sea and rock formations here are splendid, and the town boasts an Aragonese castle.

Sprinkled along the coast as far as Paola, 45 km (28 miles) south, you'll find pleasant beach towns, enjoying a climate tempered by the mountain chains at their backs. In Sangineto an important film festival takes place in August. At Guardia Piemontese, southeast of Cetraro, you can take the waters at the nearby Terme Luigiane and ponder the fate of the Waldensians. At Cetraro, the **Grand Hotel San Michele**, on statale (SS) 18, is a beautiful hotel, with a pool, set in the midst of greenery. Below it is a rocky coast cut by grottoes.

The Valdesi of Guardia

Arriving at Guardia Piemontese (about 24 km/15 miles south of Diamante) for the first time, you're apt to think that you've stumbled into a living crèche. This *presepio* village of low stone houses and narrow streets takes you with a sudden leap into the Middle Ages. And when you start to walk around, the impression will be reinforced: an ancient door inscribed *Porta del Sangue* (Bloody Door) and another labeled *Porta dei Valdesi*—referring to the group of refugees called Waldensians (Valdesi) who fled here from near Turin, escaping the fires of the Inquisition. Only after the Protestant Reformation were they able to practice their religion freely, but repression soon began again (1561), and many were forced to renounce their faith. During the following year their entire neighborhood was destroyed. The Waldensians were hanged and burned alive, women and children included, in a horrifying massacre. Two hundred quartered torsos were hung from poles along the streets. In 11 days 2,000 people were executed, 1,600 jailed. A few managed to flee to the mountains. Blood flowed in streams through the town, finding an outlet finally at the Porta del Sangue.

Today not even a trace remains here of that persecuted faith, although the Valdesi church has branches in other parts of Italy. The only remaining link is the *lingua d'oc* (*langue d'oc*), a Provençal language passed down through the generations and still spoken by some of the older residents of the town. The Waldensians originated in Lyons, France, during the 12th century, where they were called the Poor Men of Lyons.

On the piazza in front of the Porta del Sangue, the cultural center **Gian Luigi Pascale** has a permanent exhibit of Valdesi history; the English-speaking staff can answer your questions. In the *centro storico* there is also the **Museo delle Tradizioni Populari di Guardia**. To visit the museum ask at the Comune (town hall). (The Valdesi of Guardia make up one of three ethnic minorities in Calabria, the other two being the Albanians and the Greeks.)

Paola

Paola, with about 15,000 inhabitants, is the most important town along the Riviera dei Cedri (citron trees), partly because it's the rail and road junction for Cosenza, and an agricultural center. It's set at sea level and on a level above, a terrace carved out of the foothills. The sanctuary of **San**

Francesco di Paola here was built, it's said, over the home of the saint, and it contains relics of his life. On May 5th, his feast day, his statue is rowed out to sea to commemorate one of his saintly feats: It is said that he was once blown across the sea to Sicily. The church's sumptuous façade is built of tufa and decorated in Baroque style. Its interior has recently been restored to its original Late Renaissance splendor, with its flowering of polychrome marble and its impressive paintings. The monastery stands alongside, and its 12th-century cloister is open to the public. Adjoining it is the *biblioteca,* where illuminated manuscripts and rare books are kept. Among the monastery's treasures is an *Ecce Homo* by Caracciolo. (Open 9:00 A.M. to 1:00 P.M. and 3:00 to 6:30 P.M.)

Across from San Francesco on strada Statale 18, the hotel **Alhambra**, a modern building in Gothic style, is a good place to stay. Food lovers can abate their passions at **Le Bistrot**, on via Roma at the center of town (Tel: 0982-55-78), but it will be an expensive evening.

As you continue south along the coastal route on the Superstrada Tirrenica, you may want to make a detour inland to **Nocera Terinese**, especially if it's Good Friday, when *vattienti* flagellate themselves as they pass along the streets in penitence.

Farther along the plain of Sant' Eufemia, you cross the *Strada dei Due Mari* (the Street of the Two Seas), as this highway linking the Tyrrhenian and the Ionian seacoasts is known (between Lamezia Terme on the west and Catanzaro east). On a precipice another 18 km (11 miles) down the coast, **Pizzo** has an enchanting little port far below the town where excellent ice cream (*gelato*) and a *tartufo* (renowned in the area) may be just what the traveller yearns for before detouring inland to Serra San Bruno. Stop at the **Aragonese castle** where Murat was executed in 1815, after a failed attempt at recovering his kingdom. His jailor related the dramatic story of his last hours. Murat himself asked to give the order to fire. After saying "Prepare arms ... present ... " he took out a gold revolver with his wife's miniature portrait set into it, raised the gun to his lips, and called "Fire!" (The revolver was empty, the rifles weren't.)

Serra San Bruno

Heading south from Pizzo along strada Statale 18, you'll reach Vibo, where route 182 leads off to the heart of the Serre mountains. Stop at **Soriano** for the famous *mostaccioli,* a sweet made with flour and honey, or just to watch the artisans making wicker objects if you overindulged in *tartufo*. The **Certosa** (abbey) **di Santo Stefano del Bosco**, located at the center of luxuriant woods not far from Serra San Bruno, is the most exciting building in the area. It was established by San Brunone, founder of the Carthusian order, at the end of the 11th century and reconstructed at the end of the 16th century. Its tall campanile, coupled with the geometric grace of the building, has given rise to speculation that Palladio lent his ideas to its creation. Destroyed by the earthquake of 1783, it was rebuilt shortly afterward in Neo-Gothic style (open all year except Sundays, Mondays, and Lent). Women are not welcome, unfortunately, although some have passed through in disguise.

The town gossip (with no discernible foundation) about the monastery, which is denied by the monks, is that Lehmann Leroy, one of the airmen who flew the plane that dropped the bomb on Hiroshima, lives here. And Ettore Majorana, a prominent nuclear scientist, is supposed to have died here recently after disappearing in 1938 without a trace. But you won't get any help in solving the mystery here. To enter, ring the bell (11:00 A.M. to noon and 4:00 to 6:00 P.M.) and a monk will escort you.

Capo Vaticano

Back on the coastal route, **Tropea** sits like an acropolis on Capo Vaticano, still relatively unspoiled on sandstone cliffs. It was discovered, according to Pliny, by Hercules, who happened to glimpse its cliffs from the sea. You'll find the hotel **Villaggio Rocca Nettuno** comfortable; it's situated atop a 120-foot-high cliff, overlooking private gardens and the sea. The **Park Hotel Santa Maria** in Ricardi, close to Tropea, is another choice. The enchanting former Benedictine monastery of **Santa Maria dell' Isola** here is dramatically situated on top of a cliff that was once an island.

Past the cape, the coast southward is known as the Violet Coast because of the color it turns at sunset. The road hugs the sea and snakes through olive groves.

Near **Palmi**, about 40 km (25 miles) south of Tropea, you might want to head toward Monte Sant'Elia, covered with pine trees (and campgrounds), where you'll have a fantastic view of the coast as far as the Aeolian Islands. Palmi's **Museo Civico di Etnografia e Folclore** contains about 300 objects, including terra-cotta presipio figures, pastry molds, musical instruments, and traditional costumes. (Open 8:30 A.M. to

1:30 P.M.; also 3:00 to 6:00 P.M. Mondays and Wednesdays; closed weekends.)

The shoreline at Tonnara is quite beautiful, facing a little rocky island called L'Oliva because of the stouthearted olive tree at the summit.

At **Bagnara**, 17 km (11 miles) south of Palmi, you'll want to stop to buy a nougaty *torrone,* a local product, or to watch the swordfishermen ply their adventurous trade, which began with the Phoenicians. The catch of the day is grilled at trattorias in Bagnara (such as the **Taverna Kerkira**) and in **Scilla**, another 10 km (6 miles) south. A good trattoria here is **Al Timone**, opposite the cathedral. (Scilla today is a pretty popular bathing spot, giving no hint of the trouble it, with its companion monster Charybdis, caused Ulysses. It's thought that volcanic activity may have quieted the whirlpool's fury.) The only current gyrations come from the discotheque in the castle.

Farther along, at **Villa San Giovanni**, you can embark for Sicily; or you can continue on to Reggio, where ferries also leave for Sicily.

The Aspromonte

The Aspromonte—in the very toe of the Italian boot—offers some of the most spectacular mountain scenery, with terraces and plains at various levels on steep slopes where torrents plunge to deep riverbeds. The highest peak is Montalto, at more than 6,450 feet. It's famous as the place where kidnap victims are kept for years. But fortunately tourists are not the targets.

To reach the area, turn off the autostrada at the exit for Gallico, after Villa San Giovanni. Travelling northeast, head for Delianuova, Scido, and then the Zillastro plain (over 3,000 feet), the core of the Aspromonte, which, like the other mountains, make up part of the National Park of Calabria. If you hike up to the peak of Montalto, the world is your reward. Sicily stretches out in the distance, as if part of Calabria (the Strait of Messina being obscured by the mountains).

Reggio Calabria

Calabria's largest city and busiest commercial center facing Sicily, Reggio Calabria stretches along the shore of the Strait of Messina where it opens to the Ionian Sea, enjoying a mild climate year-round. Its wide seaside esplanade is almost always filled with strollers. Reggio Calabria's origins go back at least to the seventh century B.C., when the same Greeks who settled Messina came here. War and destruction was its lot until the Romans took over, and little remains of antiquity. Alaric had a hand at the devastation, and following him the city was dominated by the interests of the Byzantines, the Turks, and the Aragonese. Then the Spanish Bourbons moved in until Garibaldi moved them out. Not even nature has been kind to Reggio Calabria: Earthquakes, especially in 1783 and 1908, almost destroyed the city, and what we see today was almost entirely built in the 20th century.

Although Gabriele D'Annunzio might no longer call the *lungomare* (seaside esplanade) the "most beautiful kilometer in Italy," it does still have its charms, and some remnants of a Greek wall and a Roman bath can be found here.

The main attraction of Reggio is *I Bronzi,* exhibited at the **Museo Nazionale** on corso Garibaldi. If you've come by train just to see the museum, get off at Reggio Lido, a closer station. *I Bronzi* are mysterious Greek bronze figures recovered from the sea by a fisherman near the town of Riace in 1972. They are unforgettable, as much for their aura as for their artistic merit. Apart from these famous Greeks, the museum also contains impressive collections of ancient objects found at Greek and Roman sites. Near the bronze warriors, look for the Head of a Philosopher (fifth century B.C.), which is considered to be the only Greek portrait head in existence. The equestrian group from the Marafioti temple at Locri and a group featuring the Dioscuri (in another section of the museum) are prized. The painting collection includes works by the great masters Antonello da Messina and Mattia Preti.

The **Cattedrale** was reconstructed in 1920 in Neo-Romanesque style and contains an exquisite Baroque Chapel of the Sacrament salvaged from the earlier church. (Reggio, like all major cities in Italy, requires that you pay special attention to pocketbooks; a money belt makes travelling easier.)

If you're staying overnight, go to the **Grand Hotel Excelsior**, which is near the museum. *Buon gustai* (gourmets) will want to experience a meal at the **Taverna degli Ulivi**, an inexpensive place to taste *pesce spada,* fresh *maccaruni, pesce stocco,* and pork chops (*braciolette*) Calabrese-style (via Eremo Botte 32; closed Thursdays; Tel: 0965-914-61. **Da Peppino** is a simple trattoria with excellent grilled swordfish (corso Vittorio Emanuele 27–29; Tel: 0925-33-12-24).

Before leaving Reggio, look across the strait to Sicily; you may catch sight of the mirage, the Fata Morgana. Apparently the Normans brought this bit of Morgan le Fay lore with them. A magical city of towers and turrets sometimes seems to arise in the strait when the sea and air are miraculously calm.

THE IONIAN COAST

From Reggio Calabria, circling around the "toe" and north up along the eastern coast, the wide beaches of soft white sand begin—among the finest in the Mediterranean.

Melito di Porto Salvo, about 30 km (19 miles) from Reggio, is famous as the place where Garibaldi landed on his way from Sicily to Naples, to begin the war that would make Italy independent of foreign domination. Turn inland at Melito for 8 km (5 miles) to **Pentedattilo**, whose name comes from the Greek for "five fingers," referring to the shape of the rock on which it stands, huge, vertical "fingers" of stone, rising in front of a bare-rock mountain. Today the town is almost uninhabited, a ghost town interesting to behold in its starkness. Then back along the coast you'll encounter the towns of Bova (slightly inland), Bova Marina, Roghudi, Roccaforte del Greco, and Condofuri, towns with minorities that still speak a Greek dialect. Because the people have remained relatively isolated here, living on small farms, they have preserved some of their ancient language and customs. Traditional wood, copper, and fiber handicrafts are flourishing. Flowers are grown in this area that make up the essences of perfumes and teas—Bergamot and jasmine.

Heading north along the coast, you might want to stop at **Bianco** to sample the Greek wine Bovalino. Twenty kilometers (12 miles) beyond Bianco is **Locri**, an important center of Calabrian archaeology. The town, noted as a seaside resort, was built near the ruins of the Greek colony of **Locri Epizephyrii** (seventh century B.C.), one of the earliest Greek settlements in Italy, today known for its terra-cotta sculptures, including clay tablets with scenes from the cult of Aphrodite and Hades. It is thought to have been the first Greek city to possess a code of law. The excavations (Scavi di Locri Epizephyrii) are located about 3 km (2 miles) south of Locri. Along with the ruins of Greek temples and a theater, there is a sanctuary of Persephone where a collection of votive objects were found. The **museum** at the site contains many of the objects uncovered here.

A lovely stop along the way north is the ancient Roman **Cocynthum Promontorium** at Punta Stilo, 35 km (22 miles) up the coast. Turn inland here to see the cliffside town of **Stilo**, for the view overlooking mountains and sea and also to admire the **Cattolica**, a superb 11th-century Byzantine church with five domes. Stilo is the birthplace of the important Italian philosopher Tommaso Campanella (1568–1639), author of treatises on nature and poetic composition. An admirer of Telesio, he was accused of heresy and imprisoned for conspiring against Spain. Knowledge of God, to Campanella, came from self-knowledge; the love, wisdom, and power we feel must come from the whole that is God. This view won him no friends among the established priesthood and the nobles who championed them. Among other monuments are the **Duomo** (13th–14th century), in which a canvas depicting San Francesco d'Assisi is attributed to Mattia Preti. The hotel **San Giorgio** is the hotel of choice here, small and charming and occupying a 17th-century cardinal's palace. There is a swimming pool, and the views of a rocky cape are superb. It's one of Calabria's few hotels with a past.

Return to the coast road and continue north to see the wonderful rock formations at **Campanello** and **Squillace**, another town of Greek origin. At **La Cripta** in Squillace, the chef has done extensive research into the lively cooking of the area, delving into the ancient writings of Cassiodorus to find recipes.

About 1 km (½ mile) before you reach the overbuilt Catanzaro Lido, an immense edifice, the **Roccelletta del Vescovo di Squillace**, will catch your eye. Once the largest basilica in the region, now roofless, the structure has three circular apses and a long central nave. Perhaps Byzantine, it is dated at about 1000, although outside there is a fountain from about 800, with a seventh-century bas-relief; Roman relics have been uncovered nearby.

Catanzaro

The newest of the Calabrian cities, Catanzaro derived its name from the Greek Kata' Agkos ("above a mountain gorge"), reflecting the original site of the city atop a spur of rock more than 11,000 feet high, a few miles from the sea. The city is not known for its beauty.

In the old part of the city, particularly significant is the Norman church of **Sant'Omobono**, with its Byzantine decor. Along corso Mazzini, visit the church of the **Immacolata** and "the **Duomo** that refuses to die" (it having been rebuilt twice, after the earthquake of 1783 and again in 1960 after wartime bombardment). The Renaissance church of the **Rosario**, farther on, was also rebuilt after an earthquake (1832). Inside are exceptional wooden furnishings, the choir loft, and cermonial chair.

From the Villa Trieste, in the southeastern part of the city, a public garden with a fine view of the sea and the Sila Piccola, go to the nearby **Museo Provinciale**, which houses a collection that includes objects from prehistoric eras and 17th-century Italian paintings.

The traditional osterias in the city center often feature *morsello,* a specialty of Catanzaro that uses the tasty innards of the calf, excluding the liver. It's cooked for about five hours and flavored generously with hot pepper. Be daring!

The elegant hotel **Villagio Guglielmo** is a good place to stop here, as is the reliable **Motel Agip** near the viaduct, across the river.

Not far from Catanzaro, about 16 km (10 miles) inland, in the town of **Taverna**, the well-known Calabrian painter Mattia Preti was born (1613–1699). His works can be seen in the church of **San Domenico** here. Note especially the painting of John the Baptist in which the artist depicts himself as a Knight of Malta, an honor that had been given him by the pope. The church of **Santa Barbara** also contains some of his paintings.

Capo Colonna and Crotone

Forty kilometers (25 miles) along the coast is **Le Castella**, a marvelous little island, almost attached to the mainland, with an ancient Aragonese castle on it, like the creation of giant children on a summer day. It's open daily, and you can climb to its tower or swim from the rocks below. The coastline here is varied, interrupted with rocky masses that form a large bay ending at Capo Colonna, where you can see the sole remaining Doric column of the 48 that formed the temple of Hera Lacinia, sanctuary of the Italioti, the ancient Greek colonists. On the site there are also remnants of Roman life, including a furnace.

Still heading north, you reach **Crotone**, which unfortunately contains little of its glorious past, when it was one of the most important cities of Magna Graecia and Pythagoras and his school enjoyed its sea views—until the townspeople expelled them, finding their ways a bit too bizarre. As with many Greek sites, Crotone's columns and pediments were carried off to grace some new construction. You can see some of the relics in the **Museo Archeologico Statale** on via Risorgimento (open 9:00 A.M. to 1:00 P.M.; closed Mondays).

The **Crotone Castello** is imposing, with bastions and cylindrical towers, and in the **Duomo** there is a canvas of the *Madonna of Capo Colonna* in Byzantine style.

Among the Baroque churches in Crotone are the Immacolata and San Giuseppe. Ancient baronial residences—the Palazzo Barracco and two of the **Berlinguer** family—symbolize the period (which ended only in the 1950s) of the landed aristocracy, known in this area as the Marchesato. Today the city is industrial rather than aristocratic, a welcome development for many but regretted by many others.

Sibari

Thirty-five kilometers (22 miles) farther north, past crowded summer resorts, stop for some excellent wine at **Ciro**. It's the best wine in Calabria, and has a DOC label.

Ahead, north along the Gulf of Corigliano, is the extensive plain of Sibari (Sybaris), the site of an early Greek settlement, developed during the eighth century B.C. Unfortunately hardly a trace of its grandeur remains; apparently it was the victim of flooding. Those interested might go to the Parco dei Tori, at kilometer sign 25 on strada Statale 106, where part of the city can be seen.

In this area, beginning about 1448, Albanians fleeing religious persecution established numerous settlements. San Demetrio Corone, Lungro, and Spezzano Albanese are the three most important of these towns, where residents speak their ancestral language and enjoy an autonomous religion with their own bishop, in accordance with the Greek Orthodox rite. If you're fortunate enough to be here when a wedding is taking place, you'll be treated to a full day of singing and dancing in traditional costumes, and you'll be a very welcome guest.

GETTING AROUND

Trains and buses ply the coast and crisscross Calabria, and there are airports at Reggio Calabria, Lamezia, and Crotone. Take the airport bus to the city centers. However, unless you have a car you'll find travel very difficult in the mountains.

The autostrada Salerno–Reggio Calabria (SA–RC) is well marked and is intersected by superstradas in a network of highways.

Ferries and hydrofoils leave the ports of Villa San Giovanni and Reggio Calabria for Sicily.

ACCOMMODATIONS REFERENCE

The rates given below are projections for 1993; always check for up-to-date information before making reservations. Wide ranges may reflect the differences between low- and high-season rates. Unless otherwise indicated, the figures indicate the cost of a double room (per room, not per person). However, half-board (mezza pensione) *rates, which include breakfast and one other meal per day, are per person. The service charge is included in the rate; inquire about tax and breakfast.*

▶ **Alhambra.** Strada Statale 18, 87020 **Paola.** Tel: (0982) 27-90 or 22-40; Fax: (0982) 29-14. Ł48,000–Ł58,000.

▶ **Barbieri.** Via San Nicola 30, 87042 **Altomonte.** Tel: (0981) 94-80-72. Ł68,000–Ł80,000.

▶ **Camigliatello.** Localita Camigliatello, 87058 **Spezzano della Sila.** Tel: (0984) 57-84-96; Fax: (0984) 57-86-28. Ł125,000.

▶ **Dino's Hotel.** Viale della Repubblica 166–168. 87055 **San Giovanni in Fiore.** Tel: (0984) 99-29-90; Fax: (0984) 97-04-32. Ł44,000–Ł59,000.

▶ **Europa Lido Palace.** 87068 **Rossano.** Tel: (0983) 220-95; Fax: (0983) 220-96. Ł80,000–Ł89,000.

▶ **Executive.** Via Marconi 59, 87100 **Cosenza.** Tel: (0984) 40-10-10; Fax: (0984) 40-20-20. Ł210,000.

▶ **Ferretti.** Via Pastani 4, 87023 **Diamante.** Tel: (0985) 814-28; Fax: (0985) 811-14. Open April–September. Ł110,000–Ł132,000.

▶ **Germania.** Via Lungomare 3, **Praia a Mare.** Tel: (0985) 720-16. Ł90,000.

▶ **Grand Hotel Excelsior.** Via Vittorio Veneto 66, 89100 **Reggio Calabria.** Tel: (0965) 81-22-11; Fax: (0965) 930-84. Ł210,000–Ł250,000.

▶ **Grand Hotel San Michele.** Strada Statale 18, 87022 **Cetraro.** Tel: (0982) 910-12; Fax: (0982) 914-30. Ł190,000.

▶ **Guardacosta.** Localita Cirella, 87020 **Diamante.** Tel: (0985) 860-12; Fax: (0985) 862-27. Ł65,000–Ł100,000.

▶ **Villagio Guglielmo.** Localita Copanello, 88060 **Staletti.** Tel: (0961) 91-13-21; Fax: same. Ł99,000–Ł140,000.

▶ **Magara Hotel.** Localita Croce di Magara, 87050 **Spezzano Piccolo.** Tel: (0984) 57-87-12; Fax: (0984) 57-81-15. Ł78,000–Ł110,000.

▶ **Motel Agip.** Viadotto sulla Fiumarella, 88044 **Catanzaro.** Tel: (0961) 77-17-91; Fax: (0961) 77-33-66. Ł148,000.

▶ **Motel A.S.T.J.** Corso Calabria 103, 87012 **Castrovillari.** Tel: (0981) 48-92-38; Fax: (0981) 217-20. Ł70,000–Ł80,000.

▶ **Park Hotel Santa Maria.** Localita Santa Maria, Capo Vaticano, 88036 **Ricadi**. Tel: (0963) 66-31-21; Fax: (0963) 66-35-70. Ł96,000–Ł120,000.

▶ **President Joli**. Corso Luigi Saraceni 22, 87012 **Castro-villari**. Tel: (0981) 211-22; Fax: same. Ł95,000–Ł130,000.

▶ **San Giorgio**. Via 1 Maggio, 89046 **Gioiosa Ionica Marina**. Tel: (0964) 41-50-64. Ł80,000–Ł120,000.

▶ **Santavenere**. 85040 **Maratea**. Tel: (0973) 87-69-10; Fax: (0973) 87-69-85. Ł250,000–Ł350,000.

▶ **Sant' Elena**. Via Scesa Laino, 87026 **Mormanno**. Tel: (0981) 810-52. Ł68,000.

▶ **Sila**. Via Roma 7, Località Camigliatello, 87058 **Spezzano della Sila**. Tel: (0984) 57-84-84; Fax: (0984) 57-82-86. Ł95,000–Ł133,000.

▶ **Vacca, Pasquale**. Terrarossa, 87016 **Morano Calabro**. Tel: (0981) 303-66. Ł20,000.

▶ **Villaggio Rocca Nettuno**. Via Annunziata, 88038 **Tropea**. Tel: (0963) 616-12; Fax: (0963) 627-17. Ł130,000–Ł157,000.

SICILY

By Stephen Brewer and Barbara Coeyman Hults

Stephen Brewer travels in Italy frequently. He is an editor and writer for several other volumes in this series, as well as for other publications. Barbara Coeyman Hults is the editorial consultant for this guidebook.

Even though Sicily lies in full view of mainland Italy, across the Strait of Messina from Calabria, Italians from other regions still regard the island as a region apart, a seductive puzzle. Sicilians, for their part, still talk of "going to Italy" when they travel 20 minutes across the strait by hydrofoil.

In many ways, Sicily *is* a world apart. Colors are more brilliant: The sea is bluer on the southern coast, the contrasts of light and dark greater in the almost tropical sun; the pottery has taken on the hues of the natural world and explodes in reds, yellows, and greens. Jasmine and orange blossoms, mint and wild fennel, produce strong scents here, and the perfumed air of a cloister garden or private patio recalls *The Arabian Nights*. Food is tinged with sweet and sour blends from the East and North Africa, and desserts— sweet mulberry ices or super-rich *cassata*—could have been served by Scheherazade. The architecture, too, recalls other times and places: Greek temples overlook the sea, softened by pink and white almond blossoms each spring; massive Norman walls are lightened by interlacing arches that open onto cloisters of lemon and orange trees, bamboo and papyrus. The architecture of the Sicilian Baroque renders many of the island's cities and towns fascinating, otherworldly treasuries of bygone eras. The 5 million Sicilians themselves are intense. Glances become penetrating stares—not hostile, just fascinated. Life is lived more for its own sake here, even today, when the highway system has connected the island's cities and television has entered almost every home, for better or worse.

The Sicilian writer Tomasi di Lampedusa and the director Luchino Visconti captured some of this spirit in *The Leopard*—the colors of the plains, the love of show inherited from the Spanish Bourbons, the feasts, feuds, and passions. The recent murders of some of the island's most aggressive anti-mob crusaders attest to another force in Sicily, the strong presence of the Mafia.

Tourists are more likely likely to by menaced by motor-scooter-mounted street criminals looking for wallets and gold chains, like their counterparts throughout the world. Avoidance is the key: Don't take anything of value with you, and be aware of your surroundings in Palermo or Catania. Smaller towns have fewer problems of this nature.

Although it takes time to see beneath surface impressions in Sicily, spending a week or two here will open some doors to this fascinating conundrum that remains a mystery even to Sicilians. For a look at today's Sicily, read *On Persephone's Island,* a year's journal by Mary Taylor Simeti, an American expatriate who divides her time between the archaic rhythms of a Sicilian farm and the corroded and corrupt beauty of Palermo.

The Sicilian Heritage

Sicily (Sicilia) has been inhabited for more than 20,000 years. Cave drawings dating back to the Ice Age have been found on Monte Pellegrino near Palermo as well as on the island of Levanzo. In fact the early tribes, the Sicani and the Siculi, along with the Elymi, were already established residents when globe-sailing Phoenicians dropped anchor here during the eighth century B.C.

Greek settlement began along the east and north coasts and soon spread throughout most of the island. By the fifth century B.C. Sicily as a group of Greek colonies was more powerful than Greece itself. Its sophisticated cities attracted Plato and Pindar; Empedocles and Archimedes were native sons. Legend-loving Greeks found a natural home on an island that worshiped the Mediterranean fertility goddess Astarte in a mystical temple high on Erice's peak, and where Sicilian myth had Persephone kidnapped near Lago di Pergusa. Carthage had a foothold here, too, contesting con-

Sicily

miles 0 — 25
km 0 — 25

Tyrrhenian Sea

Egadi Islands

I. Marettimo

I. di Levanzo

S. Vito lo Capo

Gulf of Castellam-mare

Mondello

Mt. Pellegrino

Monreale

Soluto

Bagheria

Erice

Scopello

Contrada Lenzitti

Palermo

I. Favignana

Trapani

187

111

I. Mozia

A29

Segesta

● Calatafimi

115

● Salemi

Marsala

● Gibellina

188

● Sambuca di Sicilia

A29

188 bis

Castelvetrano

Marinella di Selinunte

● Menfi

● Caltabellotta

Selinunte

Mt. San Calogero

Porto Palo

Sciacca

Agrigento

Mediterranean Sea

Porto Empedocle

Caos

I. di Pantelleria

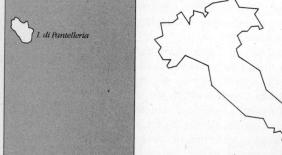
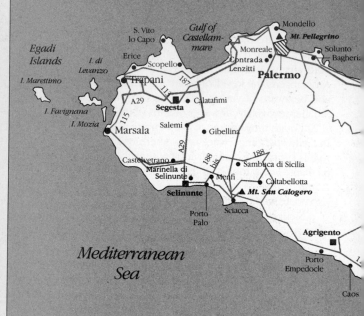

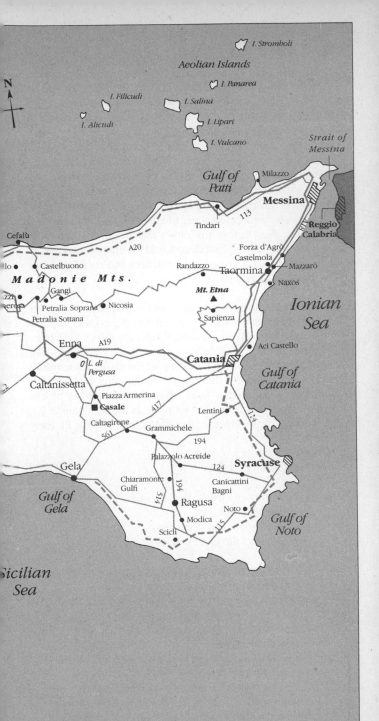

trol of the island first with the Greeks and then with the Romans. Not until Garibaldi and the Thousand landed at Marsala about 2,500 years later would Sicily be rid of foreign domination.

This intricate web of historical roots has created an emotional tug-of-war in the Sicilian of today. Contemporary novelist Leonardo Sciascia writes: "They love their island, but they constantly escape or dream of escaping from it. And when they are away from it, they love it even more and dream of returning." Young Sicilians, surrounded by TV, rock music, and videotapes, often think of themselves as Italians or even Europeans, rather than just Sicilians as their grandparents did. The modern world here, as everywhere, is a mixed blessing: greater conveniences but conflicting values and less direction.

To see Sicily in all its variety, start at Palermo and travel around the coast, with occasional forays into the interior. (We make this trip in a counterclockwise direction, beginning and ending in Palermo.) Avoid the summer months, especially August, when heat everywhere in Sicily is extreme and Taormina and other beach resorts are packed with vacationing Europeans. June, when the wildflowers bloom and temperatures aren't too extreme, is the best time to go. March can be lovely, too, but showers are likely in early spring.

MAJOR INTEREST

Unique mix of Greek, Roman, Arab, Norman, Spanish, and Italian cultures

Lush Mediterranean vegetation

Sophisticated Sicilian cuisine

Palermo for Norman and Baroque architecture, and for dining

Segesta, Agrigento, Syracuse, Selinunte, and Taormina for Greek temples and amphitheaters

Trapani, Marsala, and Sciacca on the west and south coasts

Erice and Taormina for medieval mountaintop villages with unparalleled views

Piazza Armerina for a Roman villa and mosaics

Caltagirone for ancient and contemporary ceramics

Syracuse, Catania, Noto, Ragusa, and other towns of the southeast for Baroque splendor

Cefalù for scenery and the duomo
The Aeolian and Egadi islands
Mountain villages of the Madonie near Cefalù

PALERMO

This chaotic capital of Norman kings and Spanish viceroys is likely to overwhelm travellers before it charms them. The street sounds, ridiculous traffic, poverty and decay (much of the old city still lies in ruins, from both sheer neglect and Allied bombing during World War II), and the surrounding hillsides laden with Mafia-built apartment blocks garner more attention at first impression than the city's richer charms. It takes only a short time, though, for Palermo to reveal itself as a city of great warmth and panache, an intriguing seaport and bustling capital that retains much of the élan of earlier eras.

Not the least of Palermo's attractions is its outstanding location on the Golfo de Palermo, flanked by Monte Pelligrino and the fertile hills of the surrounding Conca d'Oro, the lush agricultural lands that come up to the ever-expanding outskirts of this city of a million-plus residents.

Palermo's grand days, when the Arabs made it their capital from the ninth through eleventh centuries, rivaled the splendor depicted in *The Arabian Nights*—a world of jasmine and roses, mosques and fountains, harems and the good life as only Oriental potentates knew how to live it. The Normans and then the great Hohenstaufen Frederick II continued this tradition. This rich past is readily apparent in the city's Arab-Norman buildings, the Baroque oratories, and museums.

Palermo is an interesting and sometimes beautiful city, intriguing to explore on foot for its street sounds, for its savory street snacks (many found only in Sicily), and for conversations with Palermitani, who often speak some English and, like most Sicilians, usually have a relative in America, England, or Australia. The best place to experience city life at its fullest is the Vucceria, an outdoor market overflowing with olives of every tint, pyramids of blood oranges, mounds of purple cauliflower, and burgeoning banks of sea creatures that would astonish even Jacques Cousteau. When walking about, take big-city precautions (a money belt and an eye on the camera).

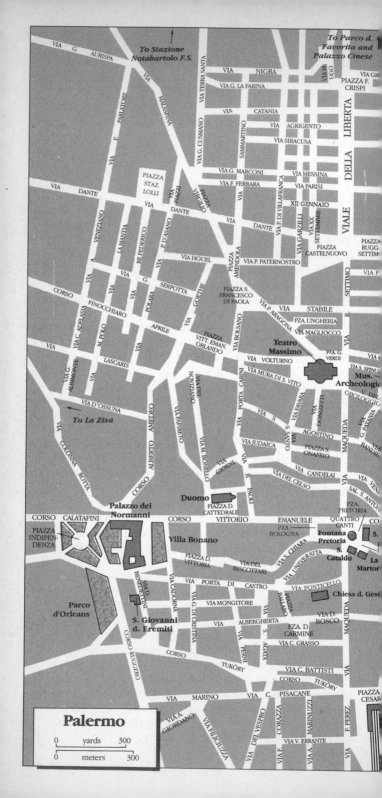

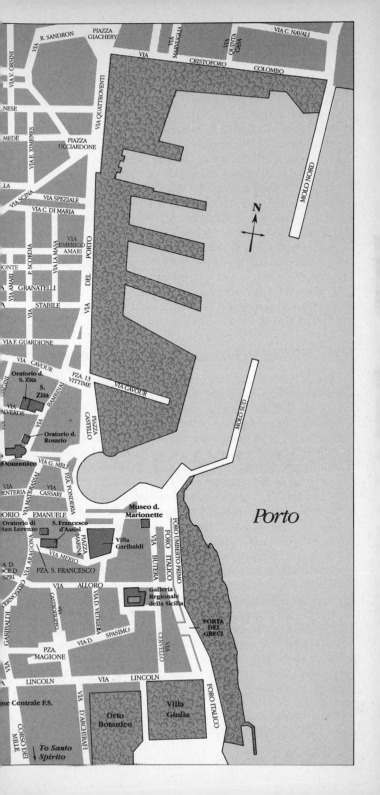

The Quattro Canti

You may well want to make the Quattro Canti (the Four Corners) your base for excursions into the intriguing quarters of the old city. At the intersection of via Maqueda and corso Vittorio Emanuele, the Quattro Canti produces a circular effect that recalls the Quattro Fontane in Rome. The concave, soot-blackened façades of three palaces and the church of **San Giuseppi dei Teatini** face one another from each corner, each building festooned with fountains and with figures and symbols that represent a season, a king of Sicily, and the saint who protects one of the traditional quarters of Palermo that stretch out in each direction from the intersection. If you are lucky enough to find the 17th-century church open, you will step out of the noise and traffic into a different sort of hubbub—a riot of swirling angels and flamboyant statuary, a good introduction to the Sicilian Baroque.

Piazza Pretoria and Piazza Bellini

Piazza Pretoria, just south of Quattro Canti on via Maqueda, is dominated by the vast **Fontana Pretoria**. Intended for a Tuscan villa, this Baroque creation is called the "Fountain of Shame," either because of the nudity on display or because of Venus's obvious enchantment with a virile-looking horse. When fighting was at a brutal pitch in adjoining streets during the 1870 Garibaldi campaign, the Great One showed his powers of leadership by calmly sitting on the fountain steps day after day while local residents brought him flowers and fruit. Though much of the square was destroyed, he was not touched, and his heroism gave the citizens fresh courage. The piazza's church of **Santa Caterina** is amazing, every inch of it busily Baroque. Yet even here Sicilian restraint in linear boundaries can be seen. At the right transept is a statue of Santa Caterina by Antonello Gagini (1534).

In the adjoining **piazza Bellini**, a few steps to the east, the red domes bulging beneath a graceful campanile announce the churches of the **Martorana** and **San Cataldo**. Together they make up a charming Arab-Norman complex, complete with palm trees and cloister. George of Antioch, Roger's admiral, founded the Martorana (also known as Santa Maria dell' Ammiraglio) in 1143, and its lovely campanile survived the church's Baroque renovation. Inside, as historian John Julius Norwich says, you must run the gauntlet of "simpering cupids and marzipan Madonnas" to get to the Norman original. But it's worth the run. The interior, created with marbles and mosaics, is charmingly intimate. Services in the Greek rite are still conducted here—most dramatically at Easter. At the west end are original mosaics of Christ crowning Roger (thought to be a true likeness of the Norman king) and of George of Antioch at the Madonna's feet. Across from the Martorana, the church of San Cataldo (1161) has been restored to its original Norman simplicity.

The Quartiere dell'Albergheria

This lively neighborhood, inhabited largely by Palermo's North African population, spreads westward from the piazza Bellini. Across the via Maqueda from the piazza, via Ponticello enters the maze-like district, every block of which still shows the scars of World War II bombs. After a few blocks you will come to the extravagant Baroque church of the **Gesù**, built by the Jesuits in the 16th and early 17th centuries. Just beyond the church lie the secular delights of the piazza Ballaro and the street of the same name, given over to a tumultuous outdoor vegetable and meat market. The golden dome of the church of the Carmine rises high above this souk-like scene, which is liveliest and most colorful in the early evening.

From Quattro Canti to Palazzo dei Normanni

A short walk up the corso Vittorio Emanuele brings you to the greatest treasures of Palermo's exuberant architectural mix. The first monumental building you'll come to on the corso—a fine old-fashioned street lined with Baroque palaces (many now being renovated) that house shops serving this old neighborhood—is the Duomo.

The Duomo
Though it suffers from too much redoing, the façade of this mighty structure, begun in 1185 and not completed until the 19th century, is a record of the city's history, bearing the marks of centuries worth of architectural styles. The best part of the exterior is the back, still Norman despite some embellishment. Roger II is buried in a simple tomb near the entrance, next to his daughter Constance and directly behind Frederick II. (Roger wanted to be interred in the cathedral of Cefalù, east of Palermo, but city politics kept the king here.) The Cappella Novella features the *Madonna*

della Scala (1503) by Antonello Gagini, a fine sculptor who, with his family, is responsible for hundreds of little-heralded works throughout Sicily. Francesco Laurana, the great master who was Gagini's teacher, is known for his exquisite Madonna and Child statuary. The *Madonna* in the chapel before the left transept is his work, with student participation.

The old neighborhood behind the Duomo is given over to antique shops and the Mercato delle Pulci (Flea Market), just south of the church off the via Papireto. Treat yourself here to a very figgy pastry, the *buccellato,* made superbly at the **Pasticceria Scimone** a couple of blocks north of the flea market at via Imera 8 (closed Tuesdays).

The Palazzo dei Normanni

The pleasant public gardens of the Villa Bonanno are a few steps farther west up the corso, and just beyond is the eclectic palace where Roger II and the Normans established their court. Today the palace is the seat of the Sicilian parliament.

The **Cappella Palatina** (Palatine Chapel), constructed for King Roger between 1132 and 1140, is a rhythmic fusion of the best of Latin, Byzantine, and Islamic architecture. Guy de Maupassant found it the "most amazing jewel ever imagined by human thought." Not only the fine mosaics but even the wooden stalactite-style ceiling is extraordinary, and the Persian-influenced Arab paintings rival anything in Cairo. These paintings are the earliest known of their kind: a magic world of camels and lions, dragons and monsters, scenes of hunting and picnicking with the harem, and Kufic inscriptions praising the Norman king Roger.

Upstairs in the **royal apartments** (which, for security reasons, are not always open, especially when Parliament is in session) court life was as exotic as any ever lived. Frederick II's court rivaled the Norman's as one of the most sophisticated in Europe, a center of arts and sciences where Arab mathematicians and astronomers had their theories translated and propagated, Greek philosophy and poetry influenced European literature, and Italian poetry and music flourished.

Church of San Giovanni degli Eremiti

This little church, built in 1132 and arguably the most beloved in Palermo, is just south of the palace on via dei Benedittini. Bursting with pink domes and set amid gardens and cloisters planted with lush palm trees and papyrus, the church is a blend of Norman and Arab architecture and looks more like an exotic pleasure palace than a place of worship. The shady precincts of the Parco d'Orleans, the grounds of the villa that houses the president of Sicily, is just west of the church across the corso Ruggero.

The Vucceria Market Area

This busy market, the throbbing heart of Palermo commerce, is just north and east of the Quattro Canti. Follow the corso Vittorio Emanuele east for a few blocks to the via Roma, and walk north for a few more blocks; steps descend into a warren of vendor-jammed streets. You could easily emerge from this enticing, raucous market with a new suit, an exotic bird or two, a Persian carpet, a statue of your patron saint, and just about anything else you've ever contemplated owning—plus things you've never thought of buying.

Most of all, though, the Vucceria is an introduction to the basics of Sicilian cooking. Traditional Mediterranean blends of eggplant, tomato, olives, onions, and garlic are combined with capers, wild fennel, and other bitters—cheese and pine nuts are added to soften the edge—to produce hundreds of sophisticated sweet-and-sour tastes. *Pasta con sarde,* a tradition in Palermo, is the perfect paradigm: a blend of sea and forest derived from fresh (no kin to canned) sardines, fresh wild fennel, sultanas, pine nuts, tomato paste, and saffron. The taste is exotic, and the following devoted. Like many such dishes, a bit more of this or that or a change in flavor because of regional soil differences will create a wholly new taste; as a result, each dish is orchestrated differently in each kitchen.

The seafood in the Vucceria will be difficult to resist or, on the other hand, may scare the wits out of you: sea urchins and lamprey, oysters and swordfish, crabs, and even that blob of gray called *neonata,* the newborn fish that are a delicacy in Palermo. These creatures are sold raw or frittered, though the cacophony of the hawkers is rarely directed at nonbuying tourists, except to amuse. Two simple Vucceria restaurants, the **Shanghai**, on a terrace above the clamorous market, and the nearly adjacent **Da Toto**, will sometimes cook what you point to. At the Shanghai, so called because the white canvas that covers the stalls reminds the owner of the sails that fill the Chinese port, the cook often lowers a basket off the terrace to haul in provisions. (The owners at both sing to the guests when the mood hits.) Here and throughout Sicily, fish is often stuffed (*a beccafico*) with bread crumbs, sultanas, pine nuts, and lemon juice, and then rolled. Swordfish and tuna are staples: broiled, stuffed, *alla marinara,* with lemon and olives, or some home-devised variant.

The Oratories of San Domenico and Santa Zita

From the market walk north a few blocks along via Roma to piazza San Domenico, named for the Baroque church that dominates it. The real treasure here is the **Oratorio del Rosario** in back of the church on via Bambinai. If the Oratorio is closed, the custodian will unlock the doors (and expect a tip in return). Palermo's oratories are amazing fantasies of Baroque cum Rococo. At the Rosario, in 1720, Giacomo Serpotta created a world of stucco that climbs the walls like ivy and is dotted with tiny figures. Serpotta was not only a master of the *putti,* those cherubs so characteristic of the Baroque, but also a fine sculptor of refined, almost Neoclassical figures such as *Courage,* on view here in the form of a woman with a plumed hat. At the altar is Van Dyck's *Virgin of the Rosary with St. Dominic and the Four Saints of Quattro Canti,* created by the artist after a visit to Palermo. Beyond the Oratorio at via Bambinai 16 is, appropriately, a bizarre shop selling tiny, delicate wax *bambini,* elegantly dressed and mounted on velvet cushions as ex-votos.

Santa Zita (next to the church of that name, a few blocks north of San Domenico on via Squarcialupo) is another exquisite oratory, where extraordinary reliefs of the New Testament and the battle of Lepanto reveal more of the Serpotta genius.

The Kalsa

This seaside district, the oldest in Palermo, is as intriguing (or despair-evoking, depending on your temperament) a collection of architecture and humanity as you are likely to find anywhere. Vegetation sprouts from crumbling palazzi and deconsecrated churches; laundry flaps above the rubbish-strewn streets; a glance through a doorway may reveal a courtyard that is being painstakingly restored or the remains of a Baroque staircase climbing from overgrown ruins toward the sky. Once an aristocratic quarter where Sicilian nobility outdid each other building lavish palazzi, the Kalsa was already moldering when it suffered heavy bomb damage in World

War II, and it has been slipping further into decay ever since. Even now, for instance, many of the neighborhood's residents (including some rough denizens who are best encountered only by the light of day) have no plumbing and draw their water from communal cisterns in bombed-out piazzas.

The remains of gentler centuries—churches, palazzi, and museum treasures—will amply reward you if you venture into this exotic, chaotic landscape. From the Quattro Canti, you can follow the corso Vittorio Emanuele east to via Paternostro and south to the church of San Francesco d'Assisi.

Around the Piazza San Francesco

The elegant church of **San Francesco** dates from the 13th century, a period when devotion to the saint was most fervent. Serpotta's statues and Laurana's Mastrantonio chapel (1468) grace the interior. Just to the north of the church a gate leads to another of Serpotta's joyful marvels, the **Oratorio di San Lorenzo**, diminished by the loss of a large Caravaggio painting, stolen from the altar in 1969 and never recovered. Ring the bell for entry.

Stop at the **Foccacceria San Francesco** on the piazza San Francesco for a Palermo favorite, *guasteddu,* a sesame roll with slices of tasty spleen and *caciocavallo* cheese. The Foccacceria is a wood-and-mirrors place where Garibaldi probably enjoyed his *meusa* (Sicilian for "spleen"). Delicious *arancini*—rice balls with a bit of prosciutto and cheese inside—and *panelle*—light chick-pea fritters found everywhere in Palermo—are better here than they are anywhere else in the city. *Sfincioni,* high, light pizzas with tomato and onion, are also common fare in the Kalsa.

From piazza San Francesco, the via Merio leads east a few blocks to **Villa Garibaldi**, a public garden dominated by an enormous banyan tree and the Palazzo Chiaramonte, a graceful 14th-century noble home that later witnessed the grim doings of the Spanish Inquisition.

Just next to the garden, the corso Vittorio Emanuele passes through the medieval city walls at Porto Felice and ends at the seafront, with stupendous views of the gulf stretching to Monte Pellegrino beyond. Inside the walls, via Buttera leads south past some of the city's best-preserved palaces, one of them housing the **Museo delle Marionette**. Puppet shows based on the Carolingian cycle of Roland (Orlando) battling the Saracens (instead of the Basques, in this version) are a charming form of entertainment in Palermo, and the art form is nicely celebrated in colorful exhibits here. These puppets, even originals, are sold in all tourist areas of Sicily, competing with that other superstar, Pinocchio. Originals are also sometimes sold at Palermo's flea market and in antiques shops (see the section on shopping, below).

The Galleria Regionale

The via Buttera soon comes to the via Alloro, another street of fine palaces. The Galleria Regionale della Sicilia is housed here in the Catalan-Gothic Palazzo Abatellis—an excellent collection that includes such masterpieces as Antonello da Messina's *Annunciata*. Portraying a transcendent moment, the artist catches the Virgin between two worlds, physically resisting with her hand while spiritually accepting what she is being told. The bust of Eleanora of Aragon by Laurana and the *Triumph of Death* by an unknown painter are among other great works of the gallery.

At the southeastern corner of the Kalsa, the leafy precincts of the **Orto Botanico** (Botanical Garden) and the adjoining gardens of the Villa Giulia provide a shady respite from the quarter's Baroque decay.

Around Piazza Verdi

The commercial heart of Palermo (a rather lackluster area of banks and offices) surrounds the piazza Verdi, several blocks north of the Quattro Canti along the via Maqueda. Traffic on the square swirls around the hulking **Teatro Massimo** at its center, a grand late-19th-century opera house, one of the largest and most ornate in Europe but closed indefinitely for renovation.

The **Museo Archeologico** is in piazza dell'Olivella, just down the via dell'Obologgio from the theater. The fine collection of antiquities here includes some lovely metopes from temple friezes at Selinunte, a Greek city on Sicily's south coast, and a model of the cave drawings at Addaura on nearby Monte Pellegrino. (To visit the cave site, apply at the museum.)

Staying in Palermo

The important decision is whether to stay in the city or at a nearby resort—Mondello or Cefalù (see below)—and take the train or bus back into Palermo to sightsee. (Don't drive in; chaos and auto theft in the city make that prospect unattractive.)

In the Center

The **Grand Hotel delle Palme**, the stately palace where Wagner wrote parts of *Parsifal,* has been renovated. The suites are particularly lovely, but the back rooms are dark and crowded—and service wavers between less than gracious and downright surly. The hotel cannot be beaten for its convenience to Palermo's sights, however, and the restaurant, La Palmetta, under separate management, is delightful (see below). Via Roma 396, 90139; Tel: (091) 58-39-33; Fax: (091) 33-15-45. In U.S., Tel: (212) 599-8280 or (800) 223-9832; Fax: (212) 599-1755. ₤120,000; half board ₤140,000.

The **Jolly Hotel**, near the port at the edge of the Kalsa quarter, is not grand but is well equipped to satisfy clients, with good service and simple, comfortable rooms. Garden dining here is romantic, thanks to a vine-covered crumbling palazzo adjoining the hotel. The quietest rooms face the swimming pool. In front of the hotel lies a stretch of beach that Fellini fans will love—a tired Ferris wheel and other dubious amusements line an enervated, unswimmable sea. Foro Italico 22, 90133; Tel: (091) 616-50-90; Fax: (091) 616-14-41. In U.S., Tel: (800) 221-2626 or 247-1277; Fax: (212) 213-2369. In U.K., Tel: (0800) 28-27-29; Fax: (0923) 89-60-71. ₤145,000–₤190,000.

The good news for travellers who want to stay in the heart of old Palermo is the recent renovation of the **Hotel Centrale**, on the corso Vittorio Emanuele just off the Quattro Canti. The rooms have been redone with attractive reproductions of Sicilian antiques and equipped with commodious baths; the rooftop breakfast room looks across a sea of church domes. This is an appealing, convenient, and reasonably priced place to stay. Corso Vittorio Emanuele 387. Tel: (091) 58-84-09; Fax: (091) 33-48-81. ₤90,000.

The **Albergo Sole**, just off the famous Quattro Canti corner, offers simple rooms and caters to businesspeople. Corso Vittorio Emanuele 291, 90139; Tel: (091) 58-18-11; Fax: (091) 611-01-82. ₤72,000–₤102,000.

The **Europa** is simple, convenient, and also favored by businesspeople. Via Agrigento 3, 90141; Tel: (091) 625-63-23; Fax: same. ₤75,000–₤110,000; half board ₤90,000–₤110,000.

The **Albergo Orientale**, located on one side of a Renaissance palazzo and run with care, is one of the best of the lower-priced *pensioni* near the train station. Via Maqueda 26, 90100; Tel: (091) 616-57-27, ₤40,000.

Outside the Center

The **Villa Igiea**, on the sea just outside the center, has its own tropical garden, swimming pool, and outdoor dining terrace and bar. The Art Nouveau (Liberty-style, in Italian) rooms are stunningly decorated by Basile. The best rooms face the pool (and the sea beyond); rooms in the main building near the bar and disco (favored by affluent young Palermo) can be noisy. The management has changed frequently and staff enthusiasm is not always high, but this is a very nice place to stay. Salita Belmonte 43, 90142; Tel: (091) 54-37-44; Fax: (091) 54-76-54. In U.S., Tel: (212) 599-8280 or (800) 223-9832; Fax: (212) 559-1755. £260,000–£450,000; half board £260,000.

The **Excelsior Palace** is also located just north of the city center in an attractive residential area, but just off a main artery, the via della Libertà. Via Marchese Ugo 3, 90141; Tel: (091) 625-61-76; Fax (091) 34-21-39. £120,000–£210,000; half board £180,000.

Outside the City

Mondello and Monreale provide pleasant retreats from the urban chaos of Palermo. The **Mondello Palace** is set in lush palm gardens and has its own swimming pool, tennis courts, and private beach. Ask for a sea-view room with terrace. Viale Principe di Scalea 2, 90151. Tel: (091) 45-00-01; Fax: (091) 45-06-57. £135,000–£210,000; half board £145,000–£165,000.

In Monreale, the **Carrubella Park** hugs the mountainside, with attractive rooms that have incredible views of Palermo. Via Umberto 1, 90046. Tel: (091) 640-21-87. £85,000.

Dining in Palermo

L'Approdo da Renato is a little outside the center of town to the northeast—and well worth the 15-minute taxi ride. Gian Rodolfo and Francesca Botto have created one of Palermo's best restaurants, where *zuppa di pesce,* crêpes stuffed with *frutti di mare,* wonderful raw fish marinated in oil and herbs, and swordfish in almond sauce are happily devoured before the cannoli, which are specially made at Piana degli Albanesi (a town to the south that, as you would expect, has an Albanian population). The attractive seaside setting is enhanced by antique furnishings and the relaxing though fashionable atmosphere. Let the owner choose the wine. Sicily takes olive oil seriously; an olive-oil list is often available. Via Messina Marine 224. Reserve; Tel: (091) 630-28-81. Closed Wednesdays; expensive.

For a good, comfortable, inexpensive trattoria with traditional and innovative Palermo fare, go to **Papoff**, where you can taste *u maccu,* a purée of fava beans with herbs (via La Lumia 28/b; Tel: 091-32-53-55; closed Sundays). Anyone visiting Palermo will want to have at least one meal at **Shanghai** in the Vucceria market (see above). Lunch is the better choice here, since the lively midday market on the streets below is the best show in town.

The **Charleston** is still very good and quite fashionable (and expensive), despite its ups and downs. It's decorated with Art Nouveau charm, and the chef has made eggplant a vegetable of Dionysian aspects. Piazzale Ungheria 30; Tel: (091) 32-13-66; closed Sundays and June 16–September 25, when the restaurant serves at its seaside quarters in Mondello (see "Around Palermo," below).

The **Hotel Patria**—not a hotel, but a restaurant—has a charming outdoor court where veal and lamb are braised over a grill on cool summer nights. At via Aragona 6, the Patria has caught on with Sicilians (Tel: 091-616-11-36).

La Scuderia, near the Parco della Favorita, is a favorite with well-to-do Palermo—a sizable population. Its stuffed perch served with charcoal-grilled vegetables and *cacciaca-vallo* cheese is pointless to resist, as is its roast lamb with fresh mint. The super-rich dessert *sole* (sun) *di Sicilia* is a *semifreddo* (half-frozen) luxury spiked with Moscato wine from Pantelleria (Sicily's island down near Africa; see "Trapani," below), and the outdoor terrace is a joy in summer. Viale del Fante 9; Tel: (091) 52-03-23; closed Sundays.

Another favorite in the center of town is the informal **Bellini's** on piazza Bellini, where a full Sicilian menu includes such innovations as the red-leaf lettuce *radicchio* stuffed with meats, cheeses, onions, and eggs. Wonderful pizza can also be enjoyed here, most of the year at tables set outside.

La Trattoria Primavera, where basics are inexpensive and nicely presented, is found at piazza Bologna 4 (closed Fridays). Try the *sarde a beccafico* (stuffed sardines).

Al Fico D'India is a popular trattoria, also inexpensive and bright with Sicilian decor. Tournedos are a specialty. Via Emerico Amari 64; Tel: (091) 32-42-14; closed Fridays.

La Palmetta is one of Palermo's finest restaurants, with a menu of Sicilian and Continental dishes and an attentive staff. Weather permitting, book a table on its airy roof terrace with mountain views. (It's not as pricey as you might expect.) Grande Hotel delle Palme, via Roma 398; Tel: (091) 58-39-33.

For picnics, **Mangia** will see that you *mangia* well. Via Principe Belmonte 17. Then for bread it's **Spinnato**'s bakery across the street.

Pastry and Ice Cream

Palermo's pastry shops are not hard to come by, and the quality is generally high, given the collective Sicilian sweet tooth. The **Convent of St. Benedict**, piazza Venezia 38A, is famous for its *minne di Vergini* (virgin's breasts), cannoli, and *trionfo della gola* (the triumph of greed)—the last word on the deadly sin: layers of sponge cake, marzipan, and pistachio with cream fillings. Their *grappola d'uva* is a bunch of grapes made with almond and pistachio paste. Orders are placed and received through a convent wheel by a lay worker or novitiate with the silent order. The more elaborate pastries can be bought only in about four-pound quantities.

For secular sweets, try **La Martorana**, corso Vittorio Emanuele 196; or **La Rosa Nero**, via Lincoln at via Cervello, near the Botanic Gardens. Sicilian ice cream is an art form in which all sorts of fruits, nuts, and creams are utilized. Even *tiramisù* and *zabaglione* are *semifreddo,* and the jasmine-petal ice is a delicate treat. The **Gelateria Ilardo**, Foro Umberto Primo 6, near the Porta dei Greci, is a popular summer place. (Also see "Mondello," below.)

Shopping in Palermo

Shops in Palermo don't begin to compare with those in Rome, Milan, Florence, and other Italian shopping meccas. However, antiques shops, elegant boutiques, and jumbled flea markets offer some interesting items, though bargains are rare. You'll find some interesting antiques at the **Mercato di Pulci** (flea market) behind the cathedral on corso Alberto Amedeo.

Art Nouveau (Liberty) collectibles can be found at **Cravosio** at via XII Gennaio 1 and at **Il Mercato**, via Garzilli 73, a couple of blocks west of viale della Libertà.

Sicilian ceramics vary with the region: strong patterns of vivid color in Palermo; blue and white in the south and Caltagirone, the ceramics center; and intricate earth-tone patterns at Erice. The **Artigianato Siciliano**, via Amari 13, is the largest center, with ceramics from all over Sicily. Contemporary artisans are naturally more experimental. **De Simone** has stores throughout Sicily featuring bright, bold patterns and interesting shapes, some for dinnerware, some for decoration. In Palermo, De Simone shops are located at piazza Leone 2 and via Stabile 133.

AROUND PALERMO

Palermo's excellent public transportation system makes it easy to reach any number of outlying sights. Most buses stop at the central train station. Cefalù, described toward the end of this chapter, is also an easy day trip from Palermo.

La Zisa and the Catacombs

La Zisa, surrounded by apartment blocks about a mile west of the old center (take bus number 27), was King William I's earthly paradise, once surrounded by luxuriant greenery. The palace's interior, with its arches, fountains, and mosaics, has now been restored to its original grandeur. In Norwich's words, "Nowhere else on the island is that specifically Islamic talent for creating quiet havens of shade and coolness in the summer heat so dazzlingly displayed."

The **Catacombe dei Cappuccini** (a few blocks south of La Zisa; folow the vicolo Zisa) is one of Sicily's weirdest sights: About 8,000 corpses, sitting on the floor or hanging fully clothed from the walls in oddly vivacious poses, provide *memento mori* for all viewers. Males and females, virgins and married women, professionals and peasants—all have separate rooms; Sicilians are very proper about death. (Open 9:00 A.M. to noon and 3:00 to 5:00 P.M.)

Parco della Favorita and Monte Pellegrino

Palermo's favorite park climbs the lower slopes of Monte Pellegrino a mere mile or so from the central city. It's not a bad trek from piazza Verdi to the park along via le della Libertà, a leafy and prosperous avenue lined with old villas and new bourgeois apartment houses; the number 12 bus plies the route.

One of Palermo's most enchanting museums, the **Museo Etnografico Siciliano Pitrè**, is in the park. This is an earnest collection of puppets, folk dress, brightly painted carts, peasant furniture, and other items that were part of everyday life in an age before highways crisscrossed the island.

The museum occupies the servant quarters of the curious **Palazzo Cinese**, built in 1799 for Ferdinand III, Bourbon king of the Two Sicilies—as the realm whose capital was Naples was called. This bit of chinoiserie entranced his queen, Maria Carolina, and their guests Lord Nelson and Lady (and Lord) Hamilton at a time when Nelson and Lady Hamilton were the talk of the royals. Harold Acton described a nocturnal *fête champêtre* thrown by Ferdinand at the Palazzo Cinese to thank his English guests for saving his life: Life-size wax figures of the three "were enshrined in a classical Temple of Fame, topped by a goddess blowing a trumpet. Fireworks represented the explosion of *L'Orient* at the Battle of the Nile. Paeans of praise were sung to the deliverer, and the nine-year-old Prince Leonard, his mother's darling, dressed as a midshipman, raised the laurel wreath from the waxen admiral's brow and planted it on that of the living one."

Much higher up Monte Pellegrino lies the dark, creepy **sanctuary of Santa Rosalia**, where the hermit saint lived for many years in the 12th century. Legend has it that Palermo was saved from the plague in 1624 after Rosalia's bones were paraded through the streets of the city, and the grateful citizenry adopted her as their patron saint. Rosalia is still celebrated with processions and feasting from July 12 to July 15 and on September 3 and 4.

Mondello

Just on the other side of Monte Pellegrino (a 20-minute ride away on bus number 14), Mondello is Palermo's most popular getaway. During the day the beaches here are noisy and crowded, but the town is pretty and animated. At night its streets are lined with fish vendors, and you can eat oysters as you stroll. More likely you'll go to the trattoria **Sympathy**—the origin of its name is a mystery—or to the **Gambero Rosso** for a sit-down meal of one of the sea fantasies you saw at the Vucceria. *Ricci,* or sea urchins, are a great delicacy here (via Piano de Gallo; closed Mondays; Tel: (091) 45-46-85). The **Charleston Le Terrazze** (the summer quarters of the elegant restaurant in downtown Palermo) shimmers white against the sea at viale Regina Elena. (Call for reservations; Tel: 091-45-01-71.) Mondello is a popular spot for ice cream on a summer night. **Antico Chiosco** and other shops along the sea will sell you fresh flavors of everything from fruit ice to *tartufo* cream.

Monreale

William II (a.k.a. the Good), Roger II's grandson, was the guiding light behind the Monreale cathedral, which he had built in 1174. According to legend, William was resting in his deer park when the Madonna appeared to him, promising to show him where his grandfather had hidden treasure if he would use it for a holy purpose, and so we have the cathedral of Monreale, high above Palermo, about 20 minutes away by the number 8 or 9 bus.

Though William was a man of spiritual depth, his detractors claimed the story was a ruse to justify the vast sums he spent on construction of the cathedral. As heir to the creator of the Cappella Palatina and the cathedral at Cefalù, he could hardly build a simple shrine. However, politics entered in as well. Walter of the Mill, the bishop of Palermo, was busy creating a political constituency of his own, attracting barons and prelates. By building a new bishopric near and equal to Palermo's, William would be ensured of a direct link to the pope, a pipeline the pontiff supported. When Walter heard this he decided to build a new cathedral in Palermo (the present structure), whose grandeur, it turned out, never threatened Monreale's.

"If the Palatine chapel is a Medieval carol, then Monreale is the *Canterbury Tales*," wrote Vincent Cronin in *The Golden Honeycomb*. Against a gold background, cycles of the Old and New Testaments unfold, played out in 130 large mosaics inscribed in Greek and Latin. The dominating mosaic is of the Christ Pantocrator, brilliantly executed for so vast a work (his hand alone is six feet long). William receives the crown from Christ, and offers it in turn to the Madonna. Thomas à Becket (middle lower right at the altar), is a curious presence here, as William's father-in-law, Henry II of England, had martyred Becket only a few years earlier. It's the earliest portrait of the saint yet identified.

William is buried alongside his father, William I, in a chapel south of the choir. An inscription marks the place where the body of Saint Louis, brother of the later Sicilian king Charles of Anjou, lay briefly on its way back to France from his fateful Tunisian crusade. Some say his heart is buried here, for the Sicilians couldn't bear to part with him entirely. Charles himself was parted with easily, however, during the Vespers revolt, when he and those Angevins who weren't slaughtered were expelled from the island. The Sicilian Vespers, so called because the revolt erupted in

Naples at the start of vespers on Easter Monday in 1282, was supported by the Kingdom of Aragon and won for Sicily its temporary independence—until 1442—from Naples.

In the cloisters, 104 arches are suspended by slender columns and enhanced with mosaics and carved inlays. The capitals are a tour de force of Romanesque stone carving, with themes varying from daily life to the Bible to pagan Mithraic sacrifice. A belvedere just outside the cloisters opens onto a panorama of the Conca d'Oro valley, Palermo sprawling below, and the sea beyond.

The **Taverna del Pavone**, just above the duomo on via Vicolo Pensata, is a pleasant place to linger over a plate of pasta and a bottle of Corvo while you wait for the church to open after its noontime closing. In the pretty town of Contrada Lenzitti, a few miles south on route 186, **La Botte** serves lunch on an open terrace (Tel: 091-41-40-51; closed Mondays; taxis are available).

Bagheria

Bagheria, some 15 km (9 miles) east of Palermo (frequent service on AST bus), is a reminder of the Sicily that has slipped away, with decaying Baroque villas the nobility built in the 18th century. The most famous is the **Villa Palagonia**, the creation of a deformed prince who decorated his garden wall with 62 grotesques. Goethe catalogues the eccentricities carefully in his *Italian Journey*. The interior, though in sad ruins, can be appreciated still; it is easy to imagine what the room of cracked mirrors (to make everyone appear to be deformed?) looked like in its original state. In the prince's day, entire rooms were decorated with fragments of picture frames and broken glass, pyramids of porcelain teacups, and marble reptiles, and in the chapel there was a huge crucifix from which Saint Francis hung by his neck. Enjoyable—and less bizarre—is the **Villa dei Principi di Cattolica**, a contemporary-art museum where the works of the late Sicilian painter Renato Guttuso are exhibited.

An entirely delightful setting in Bagheria is the little town-house restaurant **I Vespri**, especially pleasant when the roof terrace is open. The exceptional cuisine is a mix of Sicilian and French (as are the owners), with seafood crêpes and linguine Wellington. Since it has now been discovered by chic Palermo, reservations are advised (corso Buttera 423; closed Tuesdays; Tel: 091-93-40-40). A simple trattoria, **Don Ciccio**, at via Stazione 8, is known throughout the island as one of the fine family-run places that serves the traditional Sicilian menu without pretense or elevated prices (Tel: 091-93-43-66).

Though the days of the Leopard are but a memory, Sicily's noble traditions are lovingly maintained at nearby Regaleali, a family estate and vineyard (producing one of Sicily's finest wines). Countess Franca and Count Guiseppe Tasca d'Almeira have arranged several weeks a year for cooking enthusiasts to live within the castle keep and learn the artistry of their cook, Mario lo Menzo, considered the last Monzù. *Monzù* (from "Monsieur") was a term given to French master chefs who became fashionable with southern Italian noble families during a brief French reign in 19th-century Naples. A rare and expensive week. For information, write Ann Yonkers, 3802 Jocelyn Street NW, Washington DC, 20015; Tel: (202) 362-8228; or Anna Tasca Lanza, viale Principessa Giovanna 9, 90139 Palermo; Tel: (091) 45-07-27; Fax: (0921) 54-27-83.

Another side trip from Palermo—and a must—is to **Cefalù**, some 50 km (31 miles) east of Palermo on the north coast. We cover this spectacular seaside town, its world-famous Norman cathedral, and the mountain towns to the south, at the end of the chapter.

THE WEST COAST

The western portion of the island, rich in the remains of ancient Sicily, is within easy reach of Palermo by car (most places are only an hour or two away). Frequent train and bus service connects Palermo with Segesta, Trapani, and Marsala.

SEGESTA

Segesta's lonely ruins evoke the romantic spirit: A **Doric temple** sits on a flower-dotted hillside, the Classical ideal of order amid wild nature. Segesta is some 100 km (62 miles) southwest of Palermo on autostrada A 29 or slower route 113; there is frequent train service to and from Palermo.

Along with nearby Erice, Segesta was settled by the Elymi about the 12th century B.C. Although little is known of them, it seems they were of Greek and Trojan ancestry and certainly got along better with the new Greek colonizers than the native Sicani and Siculi did, sharing many aspects of the former's religious and cultural life. The temple's singular charm lies partly in its roughness. Never finished, the columns were left smooth in preparation for fluting; bosses that held the columns' hoist ropes can be seen along the steps. The foundation for the *cella,* the shrine inside, was laid but never built upon. Why it was never completed is the subject of speculation; some think the temple itself was begun only to attract Greek backing for the Elymi's interminable struggles with Selinunte to the south. Down the hill toward the amphitheater, the two defense towers and a fortified gate were used in frequent battles with Selinunte and Syracuse.

The well-preserved **amphitheater** is still used for performances; situated with the Greek genius for capturing the best possible view from the *cavea,* or seating area, it looks out on sea and mountains.

In Calatafimi, 5 km (3 miles) north on route N 113, the **Mille Pini Hotel and Restaurant**, piazza Fosco Vivona 2, is a good road stop for lunch (Tel: 0924-95-12-60). Garibaldi fought a famous battle here in 1870; red shirts and scarves are sold as souvenirs.

SAN VITO LO CAPO

This pretty cape, whose white beaches are relatively unspoiled by tourism, makes a fine base from which to explore Segesta and the west coast. The cape is about 60 km (37 miles) west of Palermo on the coast road, route 187, and due north of Erice. The **Hotel Capo San Vito** here is a comfortable retreat.

The lovely town of **Scopello** is a perfect spot to overnight while visiting the **Zingaro Nature Reserve**, a spectacular combination of mountain and sea views. The place to stay is the comfortable and friendly **Pensione Tranchina**, whose owners take pleasure in helping their guests enjoy the peninsula.

TRAPANI

From Segesta it is only 30 km (19 miles) west on A 29 or route 113 to Trapani. This port city of white buildings jutting into the sea looks so North African it almost seems like a set out of *Casablanca,* and the air of the theatrical is heightened by the windmills that tilt with the blue Mediterranean sky on the salt plains just outside this bustling city. Don't be swept away by these romantic notions, though: Trapani is a rough town, a major Mafia drug port, and with banks on every block, it is a money-laundering center as well.

The interesting part of Trapani is the old port city, crowded onto a long, narrow promontory. From the modern quarter around the train station, follow the corso Italia westward past the church of **Santa Maria del Gesù** (where a Della Robbia *Madonna* is topped by a *baldacchino* by Antonello Gagini) to the large piazza Sant'Agostino and the massive 14th-century church of the same name. Trapani's lively main shopping street, the corso Vittorio Emanuele, begins on the other side of the pretty piazzetta Saturna, with a fountain gurgling in the center. On the corso you can continue seaward, past the 17th-century Municipio, then the Baroque Cathedrale San Lorenzo. Glimpses down the narrow lanes that run off the busy corso reveal swaths of turquoise sea.

Two other major sights are inland, a mile or so east of the train station down the via Fardella and via Conte Pepoli. Coral work was a local art form during the 17th century, and some notable examples, even a *presepio* (Christmas village), are found in the **Museo Pepoli**, which also has a good collection of paintings. The adjoining **Santuario dell'Annunziata** dates from 1315, but after a clumsy 18th-century restoration all that remains are the Gothic façade, doorway, and rose window. The sanctuary houses the beautiful *Madonna of Trapani* by an anonymous 14th-century Pisan sculptor.

Dining in Trapani

Couscous, the North African grain, is the thing to eat now that you're in the west; also sample some new wines, Feudo di Fiori, Donnafugata, Steri, and Etna. Honey-sweet desserts as well as almond concoctions are found widely in this part of Sicily, where ties with North Africa are strongest. **P & G,** an excellent and popular restaurant at via Spalti 1, near the train station, is the most elegant place in town to sample this exotic local cuisine; you'll feast on shrimp in Cognac, grilled meats, *palombo* ("dogfish") *alla marinara,* and a sugary *cassata*—all at moderate prices. (Tel: 0923-54-77-01; closed Sundays). At **Da Peppe,** a wonderful fish trattoria, also near the railroad station at via Spalti 54, the catch of the day is the specialty. (Tel: 0923-282-46; closed Mondays.)

ERICE

Monte Erice (pronounced AY-ree-chay) rises abruptly from the plains of salt fields and windmills that surround Trapani. From Erice, the gray-stone medieval city at its peak, the coast of Africa can sometimes be seen to the southwest beyond puffs of clouds that drift past the nearly 2,300-foot summit. Once a beacon for Phoenician sailors, Erice has enchanted mythmakers and travellers throughout recorded history. (You can make the steep, hair-raising ascent up the 10-km/6-mile road northeast to Erice from Trapani by bus from the via Malta, just south of the train station.)

The Phoenicians built a temple atop what they called Monte Eryx to pay tribute to Astarte, a Mediterranean fertility goddess. "A different goddess, this Eryx Astarte," wrote D. H. Lawrence, "in her prehistoric dark smiling, watching the fearful sunsets beyond the Egades." The temple stood on the rim of land where Roman, Greek, and Norman ruins now lie. The Pozzo di Venere (Venus's Well) was the fate of maidens cast down as a sacrifice to the goddess after a ritual orgy. (That version is from guides who tell stories with drama; its real use is unknown.) The historian Jacob Burckhardt described the festivities as practiced in the eastern Mediterranean to honor this goddess-mother of all living things: "Joyous shouts and mourning wails, orgiastic dances and lugubrious flute music, prostitution of women and self-castration of men had always accompanied this cult of the sensual life of nature."

When spring came, a flock of doves would be released from Erice to fly to Africa. In nine days they would return, preceded by a red dove, who was Astarte, ensuring a bountiful harvest after the summer to come.

The medieval maze of steep streets and alleys (rubber soles are needed) that run up and down the town is lined with gateways that look in on courtyards flowering with tubs of plants, giving the town a domestic, contented air. The oldest parts of Erice are also the highest: the Norman **Torretta Pepoli** and **Castello**, built atop the remains of the temple of Venus Erycina, hang high above the sea and surrounding plains; the 14th-century church of **San Giovanni Battista** clings to the side of the mountain just north of the tower. Beyond the lush public gardens that enclose the castle, the medieval town rolls across the crest of the summit down to the wonderful 14th-century **Chiesa Madre** and the main gate, the Porta Trapani. On the piazza Umberto I, deep in the stone city, the **Museo Civico A. Cordini** houses an eclectic collection of art and prehistoric finds, including a marble *Annunciation* by Antonello Gagini and a head of Aphrodite from the fourth century B.C.

Pottery of dark earth tones and almond pastries are Erice's specialties. Cafés here serve madeleine-light sweets to enjoy with your coffee.

Erice's cool nights, medieval quietness, and hopelessly romantic vistas provide a welcome respite from the rest of the noisy island. The town is also an excellent base from which to explore the western and much of the southern regions of Sicily: Segesta, Marsala, Selunite, even Agrigento, are within easy driving distance.

Several hotels provide comfortable and charming accommodations. The **Ermione** is on a bleak bluff, literally at the edge of town. The modern building already looks like a ruin from the outside, but the rooms are pleasantly appointed and the views all the way to the Egadi Islands are a pleasure to wake up to; the swimming pool is a refreshing rarity in these parts. The elegant **Elimo**, in town near the Porte Trapani, occupies a 17th-century palazzo (Tel: 0923-86-93-77; moderate).

Among Erice's many attractive restaurants (popular with Palermitani on Sunday excursions), the favorite seems to be the **Taverna di Re Alceste** on viale Conte Pepoli (Tel: 0923-86-91-39; closed Wednesdays and November). **Il Cortile di Venere**, on via Sales, serves game birds roasted in the fireplace of its rustic wood-beamed dining room at via Sales 31 (Tel: 0923-86-93-62; closed Wednesdays; inexpensive).

ISLANDS OFF TRAPANI
The Egadi Islands

Ferries leave from Trapani for the Egadi Islands—Favignana (the closest: a 25-minute trip), Levanzo, and Marettimo. On **Levanzo**, which is sparsely populated, the **Grotta del Genovese** contains Paleolithic drawings of great beauty and a Neolithic group of paintings, both sets discovered in 1949. Getting to the cave is an adventure, however. You can rent a mule from Giuseppe Castiglione, the cave's owner (Tel: 0923-92-40-32; 10,000 lire; 6 miles round trip). Or you can take a boat from the port of Cala Dogana (arrange a price with the boatman), which is a good way to see the grottoes and white sand beaches that dot the shoreline. To stay the night, reserve at the **Paradiso**, where all eight rooms in the pensione have sea views and the little restaurant serves good home cooking.

Marettimo, the most distant of the islands, remains very much in its natural state, thanks to the lack of roads and cars. Good walking shoes will come in handy for its cliffs and valleys, fishing villages and caves. Small seafood restaurants are open on the island during the summer months, and rooms are also available in private homes. If seclusion is your goal, this would be the place. **Favignana**, the large island, is better equipped for tourism, though its undeveloped western side is the more attractive.

Isola di Pantelleria

From Trapani you can also take a ferry (five hours) or hydrofoil (two to three hours) to the volcanic island of Pantelleria, which can be reached by air from Trapani and Palermo as well.

Pantelleria is so close to the African continent it could easily belong to Tunisia. Stark and fascinating, it is famous for its raisin wine, Tanit. Made from the *zibibbo* grape, this sweet and sometimes sparkling wine is usually called Moscato di Pantelleria. The dark earth is dotted with vines of capers as well, which contribute sizably to the economy.

Dammuso houses are tomblike cells used by early inhabitants, somewhat similar to the *nuraghi* of Sardinia. Tourist villages are built in this style to try to keep the island from becoming just another hotel-strewn resort. The **Cossyra Club** is a full-service hotel with pool and a restaurant that conjures up delightful island combinations such as salads of capers, meat, and potato, or sea bass seasoned with parsley, oil, and capers. For dessert ask for sweet ravioli or *budino de zibibbo*—a pudding made with grape sugar. Accommodations in private homes are the least expensive option. The **Zzú Natale**, at via Padova 65, is a fine spot for an inexpensive seafood dinner (Tel: 0923-91-10-11). Stay at the pretty **Del Porto** if you're a scuba diver.

Mozia

The mysterious island of Mozia was an eighth-century B.C. Phoenician base; today you can visit the Whitaker villa **museum of ceramics** and other objects from that period as well as a house decorated with fourth-century B.C. **mosaics**. The English Marsala merchant Joseph Whitaker and his friend, archaeologist Heinrich Schliemann, did the excavations here. At Tophet, on the opposite side of the island, is a Punic (Phoenician) burial ground dedicated to their goddess Tanit, to whom children were sacrificed, a practice discontinued during the fifth century B.C.

To get to Mozia, turn off the highway south of the Trapani airport. Signs say Mozia, Stagnone, or Ragattis. The custodian will row you across the narrow waterway. Tel: (0923) 95-95-98.

MARSALA

Marsala, on the coast 31 km (20 miles) south of Trapani on route 115, was founded at the westernmost tip of Sicily by Phoenicians during the eighth century B.C. as a trading port and resettled 400 years later by those latter-day Phoenicians, the Carthaginians. Then called Lilibeum, Marsala continued to have strategic importance under the Arabs, who gave it its present name, a derivation of *Marsala Allah,* the harbor of Allah.

Marsala's big day in modern times was May 11, 1860, when Garibaldi and the Thousand landed, the first footfall of the revolution. The town is much more famous, though, for an Englishman, John Woodhouse, who in 1773 began a profitable business by shipping the local wine—with alcohol added as a preservative—to England. Marsala, so-called, soon became a popular drink, rivaling sherry. In 1806 Benjamin Ingham and his nephew Whitaker founded another prosperous Marsala-exporting company, which eventually was taken over by the Sicilian entrepreneur Vincenzo Florio. The house of Florio, with new owners, still flourishes, and you can visit the premises at via Florio 1, just south of the center of town on the lungomare Mediterraneo. The pleasant, pervasive scent of the local product adds to the sleepy quality of this sunny port city. (The house produces Donnafugata as well, a good wine that is now exported.)

Marsala was almost leveled by bombing during World War II, and the city has been substantially rebuilt. The modern city stretches somewhat monotonously up and down the coast, but the old center is a pleasant place to wander for a few hours. The sunny piazza della Repubblica is overwhelmed by the Baroque Palazzo Pretorio and the **Duomo**, built in the 17th and 18th centuries and dedicated to Thomas à Becket, allegedly because its columns were originally destined for the saint's city of Canterbury. A storm forced the ship carrying the columns from Corinth to Britain to seek safe harbor in Marsala, and the cargo went no further. A fine assemblage of Gagini statuary graces the interior. The new **Museo degli Arazzi**, just behind the Duomo, houses a renowned collection of 16th-century Flemish tapestries illustrating the life of the emperor Vaspasian, the gift of King Philip II of Spain.

The via XI Maggio continues seaward from the piazza della Repubblica and, passing through the city walls at the Baroque Porto Nuovo, comes to a gracious promenade and the archaeological zone. Among the Roman ruins and artifacts scattered along the shoreline are those of the **Insula Romana**, a third-century villa with marvelous mosaics and an elaborate bathing complex.

In 1969 a Punic warship, 114 feet long and designed to be powered by 48 rowers, was found offshore at Marsala. Probably sunk by the Romans in the Battle of Egadi in 241 B.C., the ship is now dramatically on view beneath a protective tent at the **Museo Nazionale Lilibeo**, facing the sea at the southern end of the archaeological zone.

A pleasant place for a seafood meal and a glass of the local wine is **'Gnaziu 'U Pazzu**, an airy, friendly seaside trattoria just up the via Boeo from the Museo Nazionale (Tel: 0923-95-92-84; closed Wednesdays). **Zio Ciccio**, at lungomare Mediterraneo 211, is practically next door to the Florio winery, making it a handy place to retire for an inexpensive plate of spaghetti with clams after a generous wine tasting.

THE SOUTHERN COAST

In the south Sicily takes on the air of Africa, with whitewashed towns, flat-roofed houses, and sparse vegetation dotted with palms and papyrus. Two of Sicily's greatest antique cities, Selinunte and Agrigento, overlook the sea from the southern coast.

The area is well served by Sicily's ever-expanding highway network. If you are travelling around the island by public transportation, however, you can take the train no farther than the town of Castelvetrano. From there, buses continue on to nearby Selinunte and to Agrigento, where train service resumes.

SELINUNTE

Moving southeast along the coast from Marsala, about 70 km (41 miles) on route 115, you'll come to the extensive remains of the seventh-century B.C. Greek city of Selinunte, spread over three hills alongside the sea.

Selinunte is approached through **Castelvetrano**, a busy wine town about 60 km (37 miles) east of Marsala. (Selinunte is only 10 km/6 miles due south of Castelvetrano; there's frequent bus service from Castelvetrano's train station.) Even if you are just rushing through Castelvetrano, stop for a look at the magnificent **Ephebe di Selinunte**, a Roman bronze of an athlete from about 460 B.C.; it has pride of place in the City Hall in piazza Garibaldi.

The Ruins

Much of the marble (travertine) would still adorn the temples of Selinunte if the Spanish hadn't carted it off to build their palaces and churches. Segesta and Selinunte were always at odds over territory, but Segesta had the edge because Carthage was an ally; Hannibal destroyed much of Selinunte in 409 B.C. An earthquake during the seventh century A.D. delivered the coup de grâce.

At the center of the area is the Acropolis, and to the west is the sanctuary of Demeter, where more than 12,000 votive objects have been found around the graves that stretch for miles along the coast. The three temples to the east are in the process of being restored; the one called Temple E is now recognizable, with its righted columns. (It is missing the lovely metopes from the frieze that ran across the top of the columns, however, because they are in the archaeological museum in Palermo). Temple G was one of the largest in Greek Sicily, left unfinished when the slaves saw Hannibal's ships heading toward them in 409 B.C. Some of the huge unworked column blocks lie on the ground; other half-cut ones can be seen at the nearby Cusa quarries, with the chisel marks of the laborers still visible. On the Acropolis itself the familiar grid plan is evident; to the north of it are remains of the residential section.

Staying Near Selinunte

Marinella di Selinunte, a pleasant little fishing port of flat-roofed African-style houses and vacation flats adjacent to the ruins, is a nice spot to spend an evening; you can awaken early to the sight of sunrise on the temples and wander through the ruin-strewn meadows of the archaeological zone. The **Hotel Ristorante Alceste** here accommodates guests in comfortable rooms and serves a hearty plate of *frittura mista* on the terrace of its dining room. Or you might choose to stay at the little resort of Porto Palo, about 10 km (6 miles) east of Selinunte. The **Miramare** is a simple, fresh hotel here, with fine views of the gentle surf a few yards from the windows.

The place to eat here is **Il Vigneto**, housed in a hacienda-like building with a wide verandah overlooking fields of grain and fruit trees, about a mile inland from Miramare. Il Vigneto is the realization of a dream long held by proprietor Marco Bursi, who left his legal practice to prepare dishes using the best of the local products. Couscous, with fish in summer and meat in winter, is a specialty, but you might want to try the *tre assagi*—three ample tastes of pasta sauces, perhaps with salmon *seppia,* or just tomatoes and herbs. The fish is apt to have been caught that morning at Porto Palo. Turn left at the hotel Miramare and continue until you see the sign for Il Vigneto; the address is officially Bivio (cross-roads) Porto Palo–Menfi (Tel: 0925-717-32); it's closed Sunday evenings, and Mondays except in summer.

SCIACCA AND AREA

If you could drive blindfolded from Selinunte to Agrigento, you would miss little, because much of this coast is built up with a long line of unattractive cement-block construction. Exceptions, besides the spa town of Sciacca (pronounced SHAK-ka), are the white village of Caltabellotta and the Baroque town of Sambuca in the interior.

Sciacca

Sciacca climbs a hillside above the sea some 45 km (27 miles) east of Selinunte on route 115. This pleasant town, not yet overrun with tourists, has been a thermal spa since the Greeks colonized Sicily. **Monte San Calogero**, about 8 km (5 miles) to the northeast, is the spa's origin, a thermal station hollowed out by Daedalus (legend has it). Before him the Copper Age residents of the area made human, animal, and grain sacrifices to placate the steaming gods below the ground.

The newly renovated **Grande Albergo delle Terme** is a sparkling white complex on a promenade above the sea, where a healthful regimen of treatments in the mineral-rich waters attracts clientele from all over Europe; you needn't be a spa client to stay in one of the Spartan but comfortable rooms. Beyond the tidy confines of the spa, the whitewashed, flat-roofed houses of Sciacca scale a steep hillside. Your climb uphill into the maze-like streets begins near the spa on piazza Don Minzoni, presided over by the 12th-century Norman **Duomo**, with some fine statuary inside and out by Americo Gagini, and the enormous 17th-century Palazzo Municipale. The corso Vittorio Emanuele and via Incisa continue past the 15th-century Casa Arone to the piazza della Carmine, where the Baroque church of the Carmine, the Gothic church of Santa Margherita, and the crenellated, castle-like Palazzo Steripinto are just inside the main gate to the city, the Porta di San Salvatore. The rest of Sciacca is best seen on a leisurely ramble up and down steep streets, past the quiet courtyards and outdoor markets that lend this exotic town the strong and heady air of North Africa.

Caltabellotta

High above Sciacca in the Sicani mountains (35 km/22 miles northeast) is Caltabellotta, a sun-bleached medieval town where hermits and monks once sought solitude in the rock caves that dot the surrounding woods. The **Chiesa Madre** here was created in 1090 by Count Roger, who must have enjoyed the view across the sea and eastward as far as Etna. But the city's most important date is 1299, when Charles of Valois, the Angevin, and King Frederick of Aragon signed the Treaty of Caltabellotta, ending the war of the Sicilian Vespers.

Sambuca di Sicilia

Some 30 km (19 miles) north of Sciacca on routes 188 B and 188, Sambuca di Sicilia is delightfully floodlit by night, turning its Baroque palaces gold. Until 1921 the little town was called Sambuca Zabut, for the Emir Zabut's castle, now in ruins. Adjoining it is the tiny Arab quarter of seven streets and a merlon tower with an ancient clock. Sambuca has its own wax museum, complete with Chopin, George Sand, Garibaldi, and other notables, in the **Palazzo Panitteri**. Have dinner at the **Barone di Salinas**, part of a baronial estate that is now the property of Tommaso di Prima, a local farmer who bought the estate—his lifelong fantasy—and who enjoys showing visitors about the premises.

AGRIGENTO

"Fairest of all mortal cities" was Pindar's tribute to Akragas, now Agrigento. Its location in a rolling valley and the grandeur of its long line of Doric temples drew high praise from visiting Greeks, who found life here much as it was in Athens, a worldly blend of philosophy, science, and art.

Most travellers to Sicily sooner or later make their way to this ancient place, in the center of the southern coast, some 65 km (41 miles) southeast of Sciacca on route 115. Seen in the pink light of dawn, the gold-red sunset, or floodlit at night, Agrigento's temples constitute one of the most captivating sights in the world.

ANCIENT AGRIGENTO

The city was established when residents of Gela moved west along the coast in 582 B.C. to take advantage of the area's fine harbor (now the overbuilt Porto Empedocle) and immensely rich grain fields (which would feed the Roman legions a few hundred years later). The first ruler was Phalaris, whose tyrannical acts included roasting his enemies in a huge bronze bull, perhaps harking back to a Rhodian bull cult. That he was assassinated is hardly a surprise, even if not all the tales of his treachery are true. Carthage, by then grown from Phoenician outpost to major power, was not happy to see another important city expanding across the sea and launched an invasion in 480 B.C. With the aid of Gelon, tyrant of Gela and Syracuse, Akragas triumphed, winning 70 years of peace for Sicily—her Grecian golden age—until the final defeat by the Carthaginians in 406 B.C.

In a time when Greek philosophers were examining the very basis of prescientific understanding, Empedocles of Akragas developed the theory of the four elements: that all things are compounded of earth, air, fire, and water, with love and strife acting as alternating currents. Unlike the Eleatics (at Velia, across the Strait of Messina), Empedocles insisted that the senses, not just the mind, if properly used, were routes to knowledge. His *On Nature* covers subjects from astronomy to zoology, and his work in physics is basic to the field today. In later years he apparently believed himself a god, having already been a bush, a bird, and a fish.

To die a death worthy of a god he is supposed to have leaped into the crater at Etna. (Some contend he died in Greece.) Of his native city he said, "The Agrigentines enjoy luxury as if they would die tomorrow, but they build palaces as if to live forever."

Agrigento's wealth was so enormous as to be eccentric: Young girls even had tombs built for their birds. Although a dictatorship, the city did not maintain an army of highly disciplined warriors (one military directive limited soldiers to using only two pillows per bed). During the Punic wars Rome attacked Carthage at Agrigento, which Carthage controlled by that time. Victorious in 241 B.C., Rome sold its people into slavery and used its grain to feed the Roman armies, while the corrupt Roman governor Verres collected a crippling corn tax. The city subsequently fell to the Saracens, who were routed by the Norman Count Roger in 1087.

The magnificent **Valley of the Temples** is spread over meadow-covered hills just to the south of the modern city. The warm-ocher temples were originally painted with white stucco and are Doric in construction, simple and sturdy, yet elegant in this setting. In February the fields here are covered with pink and white almond blossoms, heralding the International Folk Dance Festival, which brings folk dancers from around the world.

The Museo Archeologico and Hellenistic-Roman Quarter

A good place to begin a visit is the austere 15th-century **Chiesa San Nicola**, overlooking the temples at the entrance to the archaeological zone and built with stone plundered from the ruins. Just beyond the cloisters is the **Museo Nazionale Archeologico**, which is well organized, well lit, and a pleasure to visit. It houses an impressive collection of antiquities that includes a child's sarcophagus depicting his birth, death, and journey to the next world; and Phaedra's sarcophagus, Greek in design but probably Roman in workmanship, decorated with scenes of her tragic love affair.

In the Hellenistic-Roman quarter, across the via dei Templi from San Nicolà, many of the gridlike streets and buildings of the ancient settlement remain, columns and mosaics intact. The major temples are strung across the top of a ridge just to the south and are reached by the strada Panoramica, bordered with tropical plants and ancient tombs and especially dramatic at night, when the valley is floodlit.

Tempio di Giumone

The first temple you'll come to as you walk south is the Tempio di Giumone (Temple of Juno), built by the Greeks around 460 B.C. and restored by the Romans. Earthquakes have laid waste to much of the temple, although 25 of its original 34 columns still stand.

Tempio della Concordia

Walking south, you'll come next to the Tempio della Concordia (Temple of Concord), one of the best-preserved Doric temples in the world, exuding solidity and self-confidence. Up close the tawny tones of the temple vary from pale yellows to rich ochers. During the sixth century A.D. the Tempio della Concordia was converted into a church, thereby escaping the vengeance of Christian iconoclasts. When the church was created the columns were walled in and the walls of the central Greek shrine, the *cella,* were removed. Beyond the temple to the east is the sacrificial altar. A sacred enclosure containing shrines and niches for ex-votos originally surrounded each temple.

The Villa Aurea, south of the temple, often houses temporary exhibitions of the latest finds from the ongoing excavations in the valley. A Byzantine cemetery surrounding the villa includes underground burial chambers dating from the fourth century B.C.

Tempio di Ercole

The Tempio di Ercole (Temple of Hercules), reached through a lovely garden, is the oldest temple at Agrigento. Built about 520 B.C., it is still scarred by the fires set by Carthaginian invaders. Once richly decorated and considered the most beautiful of the temples, it housed a splendid statue of Heracles whose chin and lips, according to Cicero, were worn smooth by the adoration of the faithful.

Temples of Giove Olimpio and Castore e Polluce

The enormous Tempio di Giove Olimpico (Temple of Olympian Zeus), the largest Doric temple in the world, is just to the west of the Tempio di Ercole, in a valley below the other temples. The huge stone sunbather on the ground, called the Sleeping Giant, is a copy of one of 38 *telamones*—figures used as columns—that once decorated the temple. The original of this figure as well as a scale model of the temple are in the Museo Archeologico (see above).

Chthonic rituals took place on the round altars and

around the three-column remnant of the **Tempio di Castore e Polluce** (Temple of Castor and Pollux), a pastiche of several buildings just west of the Tempio di Giove Olimpico. The temple complex is actually a collection of artifacts found around the area—no historical accuracy here. The temple incorporates some earth-goddess shrines built during the seventh century B.C., when such cults were popular.

Modern Agrigento

Strung out on a ridge above the Valley of the Temples, modern Agrigento is almost entirely new, as devoid of character as any town in Sicily. Much of the town collapsed some 25 years ago when unregulated construction of the type of modern apartment blocks you see everywhere caused massive mud slides.

The most interesting part of town is the small medieval quarter that climbs uphill from the piazza Pirandello toward the **Duomo**, built in the 11th century and remodeled many times since then. Ancient Greek fortifications still flank the eastern end of the city. The Norman church of **San Biagio** is just inside the fortifications, at the top of a road worn with ancient cart tracks. Just below the church, down steps carved out of stone, is a shrine to Demeter and Persephone around which hundreds of votive objects have been excavated. Beneath the shrine is an elaborate system of terra-cotta pipes used during the underground rituals of a water cult. The Rupe Athena, a high rock face at the top of the fortifications, is where the first colonies here were established.

The **Casa di Pirandello**, a mile or so south of the Valley of the Temples in the seaside hamlet of Caos (bus number 11 from Agrigento and the valley snack bar), is the birthplace of the 20th-century playwright, Sicily's most famous man of letters. The house is filled with mementoes, and his ashes are buried beneath a lonely pine tree in the garden. Of Caos Pirandello said: "One night in June I dropped down like a firefly beneath a huge pine tree standing all on its own in an olive grove on the edge of a blue clay plateau overlooking the African sea." He would scarcely recognize his Caos today, full as it is of condominiums and second homes.

STAYING AND DINING IN AGRIGENTO

The **Villa Athena**, just across a tropical garden from the fifth-century B.C. Tempio della Concordia, affords incredible views of the temples. The rooms are a bit faded, but the gardens, with a swimming pool, are lovely and the views enchanting. If you are not in the market for luxury, as good a choice as any in Agrigento is the **Pirandello**, on a hill high above the Valley of the Temples. The rooms are basic but certainly adequate, and the views out to the temples are terrific. The **Hotel della Valle** is a modern, impersonal place in a wonderful location at the edge of the valley, with all the conveniences and a swimming pool. A beautiful new addition to the hamlet of Caos is the hotel **Kaos**, owned by Francesco d'Alessandro, proprietor of the Villa Athena. The villa in Caos has been remodeled with great attention to form and color, and the swimming pool is exceptionally lovely, a white oval of blue water surrounded by bougainvillaea, with olive trees and the deep blue sea beyond. From each room, Pirandello's tree on the adjoining property is poetically framed.

Apart from the Villa Athena, which has a good restaurant that serves pumpkin sauce with pasta in the fall, try the **Taverna Mosé** for dinner, where the beefsteak is seasoned with fresh herbs and the *falsomagro* are delicious (*falsomagro* is a roast stuffed with meats, cheese, vegetables, and bread crumbs, thus "falsely thin," as the name says). Closed Mondays; Tel: (0922) 267-78. **Del Vigneto**, at via Cavalieri Magazzini II (Tel: 0922-443-19; closed Sundays), and **Le Caprice**, at via Panoramica dei Templi 51 (Tel: 0922-264-69; closed Fridays), both of which are near the temples, serve good grilled meats in the inexpensive to moderate range. Try the wonderful red Regaleali wine called Rosso del Conto.

THE EASTERN COAST

In spirit (and often literally), the eastern coast huddles beneath the fiery peak of Mount Etna. Sicily's two other large cities, Syracuse and Catania, are here, as is the stage-set town of Taormina. Highways and train lines run up the coast to Messina, the gateway to the mainland, which connects the eastern coast with all of Sicily.

SYRACUSE

Syracuse is reached most quickly from Agrigento by taking route 122 north to the autostrada, then speeding east to Catania and dropping south along the industrialized coast on route 114—a trip of about 240 km (149 miles). However, you may want to travel at a more leisurely pace through the southeastern corner of the island, stopping at several of the exotically beautiful Baroque towns we cover below, under the heading "Inland Around Syracuse."

Once even greater than Athens, and briefly capital of Byzantium when Muslims threatened the Eastern Empire, Syracuse (Siracusa) now shows off its Classical past in an archaeological zone just outside the modern city. But its greatest beauty today is Ortygia, an island of Baroque fantasy connected to the modern city by a bridge.

ANCIENT SYRACUSE

Before the Corinthian Greeks arrived in 734 B.C. and moved them out, Siculi inhabited this part of the island. The Greeks valued Syracuse's natural harbors for their beauty and defensibility, and so the harbors often saw violent battles, as Thucydides chronicles faithfully in *The Peloponnesian War*. Though tyrants dominated Greek Sicily, the court of one Hieron, or Hiero I, attracted Pindar and Aeschylus, who probably wrote *Prometheus Bound* for its theater. The tyrant Dionysius, who defeated the Carthaginians in 397 B.C., was a military genius and poet manqué. After years of hissing at him whenever he read his poetry in competitions, the Athenians finally awarded him a medal, but the honor prompted Dionysius to treat himself to an orgy so intense that he died as a result. His son Dionysius II was once admired by Plato, who was always on the lookout for a philosopher king, but Plato left Syracuse and Magna Graecia in dismay at his tyranny. Timoleon (343–337 B.C.) gave Syracuse the closest thing to good government it would ever have, rebuilding and concluding a treaty with its perennial enemy, Carthage. He died quietly, a rarity for the time.

When the Romans invaded Syracuse, they "failed to reckon with the ability of Archimedes," as Polybius put it, for Archimedes' genius had helped create the brilliantly strategic fort of Euryalus as well as ingenious war machines. The Greek forces were finally beaten, however, and Rome sent Verres to govern Sicily. His habit of taking every Greek statue

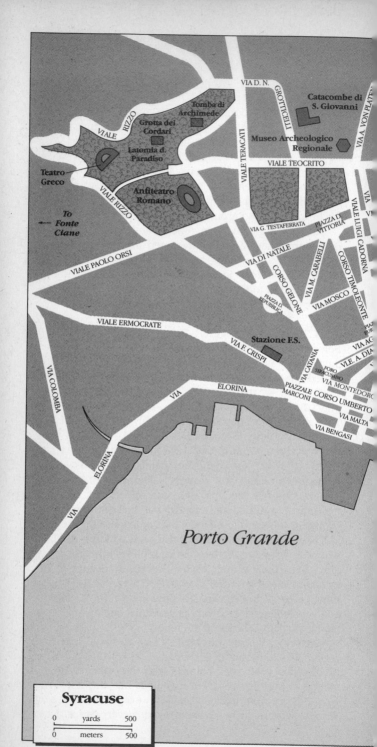

or frieze—no matter how large—was reported by Cicero in the *Verrine Orations*.

Syracuse would not flower again until the Spanish made it a Baroque fantasy, especially the city's island of Ortygia, where women still carry decorated lacy fans in summer and cover their shoulders with embroidered shawls.

Ortygia

Ortygia is a charming, seductive place, full of Baroque façades, balconies, and staircases, shadows and shady piazzas, and sun-drenched seaside promenades. Baroque here is more restrained than it is elsewhere in Sicily—more conscious of Classical order and simple elegance—perhaps because of the city's strong Hellenic past. Elegant as Ortygia is, many of the island's old palaces and churches have been left to ruin. Façades crumble and trees sprout from the roofs of churches, giving the island a melancholic yet evocative air.

Tempio di Apollo
Ponte Nuovo leads from the mainland to the piazza Pancali, where the Tempio di Apollo (temple of Apollo) was unearthed in 1943. Excavations continue here around the oldest Doric temple in Sicily, built about 565 B.C. It had six columns in front and seventeen along its sides, placed unusually close together. The name of Apollo derives from an inscription chiseled on the front of the temple, although Cicero attributed the temple to Artemis—an affirmation of the existence of the two cults here.

Piazza Duomo
From the temple, the shop-lined corso Matteotti is the most direct route to the commercial heart of the island, the piazza Archimede and its grandiose fountain. The via Roma continues south to **piazza Duomo**, the most beautiful piazza in Sicily, bounded by the splendid cathedral and grand palaces. The Duomo's site was sacred to the Siculi, who built a temple here, which was to have been followed by another one dedicated to Athena. Because the fleet-fingered Verres stripped the temple, we have a record of it only in Cicero's indictment: "More splendid doors, exquisitely wrought in ivory and gold, have never existed." On the roof stood a triumphant Athena whose gold shield flashed like a beacon for sailors at sea. (Some of the columns were used in the present-day church.)

The façade of the **Duomo** was designed by the Sicilian

Andrea Palma (1728–1751) to replace a Norman one that was the victim of an earthquake. The Duomo is praised for the brilliant execution of broken masses that create chiaroscuro. In front are statues of Saints Peter and Paul, the work of the Palermitan Marabitti. Inside, the centuries are harmoniously joined: Greek columns project from walls and chapels; fine wrought-iron work adds intricacy; a Norman font stands in the baptistery. At the end of the right-hand aisle is the chapel of the Crucified Christ, with a painting of *Saint Zosimus* attributed to Antonello da Messina. Antonello Gagini's *Madonna of the Snow* graces the north side.

At the far end of the piazza Duomo stands the church of **Santa Lucia alla Badia**, dedicated to the Sicilian-born patron saint fêted on December 13. In the other direction the splendid **Palazzo Beneventano del Bosco**, with its grand courtyard, retains its dignity despite the restaurant and disco on the ground floor. The palace is the work of Luciano Ali (1775) and is still inhabited by the descendants of the noble family that commissioned it.

Foro Italico and Fonte d'Aretusa

The western flank of Ortygia is given over to a tree-lined seaside promenade, the Foro Italico. Syracusans take the evening air here, looking out to the open sea, eating ices, and watching the night boat for Malta slip out of the harbor. This is the sort of evocative place that will make you feel you are in a rather exotic, far-flung corner of the earth—you are.

The freshwater Fonte d'Aretusa is next to the sea at the southern end of the promenade. Lord Nelson is the most famous admirer of the fountain, now overgrown with papyrus and home to a flock of swans. He took on freshwater provisions here on his way to the Battle of the Nile. The fountain, legend says, is actually the nymph Arethusa, who, fleeing the river god Alpheus, jumped into the sea in Greece. Artemis changed her into a fountain, and she travelled undersea across the Mediterranean and emerged here, with Alpheus in pursuit. The Delphic Oracle confirmed the story: "An isle, Ortygia, lies on the misty ocean, over against Trinacria [as Greece called three-cornered Sicily], where the mouth of Alpheus bubbles mingling with the bubbles of broad Arethusa." Strabo also reported that a cup thrown into the river at Olympia in Greece once reappeared here.

Galleria Regionale

From the fountain, the via Capodieci leads inland again to the delightful Galleria Regionale in the Palazzo Bellomo.

Among the masterpieces that grace this elegant palazzo are a damaged *Annunciata* by Antonello da Messina and Caravaggio's *Burial of St. Lucy,* moved for security reasons from the church of Santa Lucia around the corner. There's also a section devoted to folklore, with charming *presepi.*

Your explorations of the rest of the island will be more enjoyable if you abandon all hopes of following a logical route through the labyrinth of narrow streets and quiet piazzas; surrender yourself to the island's charms and wander randomly. If your rambles take you to the tip of the island, you will be allowed to venture no farther than the massive walls of the **Castello Maniace**, built by Frederick II in 1239 and now a military barracks.

Mainland Syracuse

Modern Syracuse hugs the mainland coast. It is a ramshackle though pleasing place, with broad, sunny avenues and lovely public gardens shaded by palms and oleanders, which also line the city streets with dark rose and white flowers. The corso Gelone, the main shopping street, runs from the port area north for about half a mile to the **Zona Archeologica**, the vast ruins of the ancient city.

The Roman amphitheater, off the corso Gelone's far (northwestern) end, is surpassed in size only by the arena in Verona, but much of its stone was carried away by the Spanish—a familiar story in Sicily. The *cavea* (audience section) built into the hillside is topped by a parapet engraved with the names of box holders. To the west is the largest sacrificial altar known to the Greek world, with ramps that could hold 450 oxen on their way to sacrifice. Once monumental in aspect, today it demands imagination. The structure called Archimedes' tomb is not, though Cicero did see the Greek mathematician's now-lost tomb somewhere in Syracuse.

The **Latomie** are deep limestone quarries where hapless slaves (often prisoners of war) cut stone for the city's buildings. The earlobe-shaped cave in the section of the quarries known as Latomia del Paradiso was dubbed by Caravaggio the Ear of Dionysius; legend has it that the acoustics are so good that the tyrannical one listened at the opening on top to hear what the slaves were saying. In the adjoining **Grotta dei Cordari** (Cave of the Rope Makers) the work is clearly evident, almost as if the site were recently abandoned. Despite the sinister history of the quarries, the Latomie are usually aflower with luxuriant vegetation: lemon and orange trees, capers, palm, prickly pear, and oleander flowers.

The **Greek theater**, among the most beautiful of its kind, originally enjoyed a view of the harbor and hills, but the Romans added a backdrop to facilitate their more elaborate productions—simplicity not being a Roman attribute. Syracuse was famous throughout the world for its dramatic productions, and Aeschylus and Euripides were performed regularly. When Hieron I founded a colony at nearby Mount Etna, Aeschylus wrote *Women of Etna* (lost) to be performed here; his Prometheus plays were also produced at Syracuse. All was not tragedy, however, for Epicharmus raised ancient comedy to artistic heights, and mime was popular as well. Above the theater are the remains of a nymphaeum to which Hieron's guests could run during a downpour.

Syracuse has inspired more than just great theater. Lentini, near Syracuse, was the birthplace of the philosopher Gorgias (483 B.C.), whose Sophist views led Cicero to say that doubt was born in Sicily. According to Gorgias nothing exists, for if it did it would have to come from something, and something can't come from nothing. And if something did exist, it could not be known, given the difference between thought and thing. Objective truth being thus impossible, there remained only the art of the Sophists: persuasion. Gorgias's challenge to speculative thought stimulated a more sophisticated approach to the problems of philosophy (see the eponymous dialogue by Plato), and he became known as the philosopher who introduced rhetoric, the art of persuasion that yields belief about things just and unjust, to Greece.

Many of the finds from the Zona Archeologica (including a remarkable stone diary tracing the history of Sicily from prehistory to the days of Greek and Roman occupation) are in the new **Museo Archeologico Regionale**, several blocks east on the viale Teocrito.

The **Catacombe di San Giovanni**, entered from the church of San Giovanni (St. John) just behind the museum, evoke the paleo-Christian past, a time when Saint Paul delivered a sermon at the altar of San Mariano in the catacombs on his way back from Malta. Frescoes, graffiti, and other remnants of the early Church lend the site a mystic aura (unless a school class arrives). The nearby **Galleria del Papiro** tells the story of papyrus—apparently introduced to Sicily by the Ptolemaic kings. The gallery owners demonstrate the Egyptian technique from stalk to finished painting.

Staying and Dining in Syracuse

Even Winston Churchill was entranced by the **Villa Politi**, where the rooms exude a faded charm and the gardens—part of the adjoining catacombs of the Cappuccini—are an organized jungle of palms and oaks, flowers and statues, and limestone quarries. (These catacombs are closed now, but they once held Athenian prisoners captive until they died—or could recite Euripides, a feat that would free them.) The views from the front rooms are enchanting at night, when garden lights turn the outdoors into a Gothic mystery. There's also a lovely pool.

The **MotelAgip**, in the center of the modern city near the Zona Archeologica, is well liked by Sicilian businesspeople for its comforts and very good food. This is not romantic Sicily, but it is a welcome retreat in a city so poorly endowed with hotels.

These days the only hotel on Ortygia is the **Gran Bretagna**, a simple though rather charming little place with bare-bones rooms (some with 18th-century frescoes to brighten things up) and communal bathrooms. Ortygia's Grand Hotel, with its soulful sea views, is closed up tight for renovations, and no one's saying when it might reopen.

Everyone who visits Syracuse has a favorite restaurant. A common (expensive) choice is **Jonico**, set on a beautiful quarry by the sea, just north of the center (near the Villa Politi) in a little garden filled with antiquity and kitsch. Fish is, of course, on center stage here—swordfish, bass, tuna, mackerel—seasoned with capers, fresh anchovies, wild fennel, black olives, and rich olive oil. Spaghetti may come topped with tuna eggs and herring. The menu is in Sicilian, but the staff speaks English (even Italians look at the menu in bemusement). When owner Pasqualino is there the food is exquisite, but alas, he too often travels, like many of the chefs of Italy. (Riviera Dionisio il Grande 194; Tel: 0931-655-40; closed Tuesdays.)

Arlecchino's proprietor, Baldassare Ponza, comes from Palermo and serves his native dishes, as well as local ones, in a pretty trattoria decorated with masks of the commedia dell'arte. Bass *in cartoccio* (baked in a paper case) tastes of the sea, fresh and moist, and the vegetable pastas are excellent (via dei Tolomei 5; Tel: 0931-663-86).

Acting students and actors who come to Syracuse to perform the classics at the Greek theater seem to have a preference for **Archimede**, at via Gemmellaro 8 in Ortygia (Tel: 0931-697-01; closed Sundays), filling the place almost every night and projecting over fresh fish, risotto with octopus in a sauce of its own ink, game, and seductive desserts. Nearby **Don Camillo** (via della Maestranza 100; Tel: 0931-671-33; closed Sunday evenings and Mondays) is an old Syracuse favorite. Also in Ortygia, the little **Minosse** (via Mirabella 6; Tel: 0931-663-66) is known for its wonderful fish stew (*zuppa di pesce*), breaded swordfish, and tender calamari steamed in white wine. (King Minos, the restaurant's namesake, came to Sicily to find Daedalus, the master sculptor, and take him back to Greece; but Minos was murdered in his bath by the daughters of Cocalus, the Siculi king.)

The pastries and ice cream in Syracuse are too good to ignore: almond pastry; super-rich *cassata* filled with pistachio cream and chocolate and candied fruit bits; the richest, lightest cannoli. Stop at **Marciante** in via Maestranza or at the **Bar Viola** in corso Matteotti (both in Ortygia) for ice cream.

INLAND AROUND SYRACUSE

In addition to the places described below, archaeological excursions, carefully outlined in a booklet available from the tourist office in Ortygia, will take you to the vast Siculi necropolis at Pantalica (thirteenth to eighth century B.C.) as well as to other ancient towns.

Castello Eurialo

This hilltop fortress 8 km (5 miles) northwest of Syracuse (you can take the number 8 bus from the corso Gelone; get off at the youth hostel) is a fascinating war machine engineered by Dionysius and Archimedes. Begun in the fourth century B.C., it is the best-preserved Greek fortress in the world. Underground trench networks allowed soldiers on the deck of a boat-shaped structure to drag bodies away, along with whatever objects of warfare the enemy propelled in.

Palazzolo Acreide

This dusty Baroque town, a colony of ancient Syracuse, is 45 km (28 miles) west of Syracuse on route 124. The **Zona Archeologica** contains the well-preserved remains of the early settlement: a Greek theater, a temple to Aphrodite, the agora, the council chamber, and the mysterious *santoni,* 12 figures carved into a rock face on an adjacent hillside, a place of worship for the cult of the goddess Cybele.

The town itself is sleepily beautiful but has done little to accommodate visitors. The **Museo Casa** (House Museum) on via Machiavelli has a pleasant little collection, showing how peasants lived until the early days of this century. Palazzolo Acreide is about an hour away from Syracuse by AST bus, which leaves from the gardens of the Foro Siracusano in the modern city. The Zona Archeologica is about a mile south of town; taxis are scarce, so be prepared to walk.

Noto

This small city 35 km (23 miles) southwest of Syracuse on route 115 is the masterpiece of Sicilian Baroque: Curving staircases sweep up to the ornate façades of churches; elaborate iron balconies overhang the narrow streets; the golden stone from which the entire city is built captures every ray of the Sicilian sun.

If Noto sounds theatrical, it was designed (by architects Rosario Gagliardi, Paolo Labisi, and Vincenzo Sinatra) to be just that. The stage-set city you see today was built in the 18th century, after an earthquake demolished the original Noto Antico in 1693.

In 1986 building authorities discovered that all of Noto was unsound and in danger of collapsing at the slightest tremor. The government rushed in to close many streets to the rumble of traffic, shore up buildings, and rebuild Noto's shaky foundations, so much of the city will be under renovation when you visit.

The central corso Vittorio Emanuele cuts through the center of the gridlike city, past three grand piazzas. Entering though the Porta Nazionale, you will soon come to the **piazza dell'Immacolata** and your first taste of Noto's flamboyant splendor at the sight of a grand staircase sweeping up to the church of San Francesco. A few more steps bring you to an even greater burst of extravagance, the **piazza del Municipio** and Noto's most important buildings. The **Duomo**, atop a long flight of steps, faces the **Municipio**, surrounded by an elegant portico. Farther along, the corso enters the **piazza Sedici Maggio**, with a garden at its center and the curved façade of the convent and church of San Domenico commanding its north side. If Noto's extravagance hasn't overwhelmed you by this time, leave the corso and walk up the **via Corrado Nicolaci**, which seems almost to be a trompe l'oeil (when cars aren't parked along it). Its balconies burst with griffins, mermaids, medusas, lions, and other oddities of decorative splendor.

The simple, inexpensive **Trattoria del Carmine** at via Ducezio 9 serves a pasta with vegetable sauce and grilled shrimp that causes even Nettini (as Noto residents are called) to flock to the popular spot (Tel: 0931-83-87-05; closed Mondays). In back of the Municipio is the **Gelateria Costanzo**, where wonderful ice cream, sometimes even *gelsomino*— made from jasmine petals—is prepared. Noto has a music festival and an ice cream festival during the summer, caring for both body and soul.

Ragusa

This ocher-colored city, 50 km (31 miles) west of Noto on route 114, is Sicily's exaggerated version of an Italian hill town (there is frequent AST bus service to and from Noto and Syracuse). Ragusa is actually two hill towns, the newer Ragusa Superiore and the old Baroque city, Ragusa Ibla. The two Ragusas face each other from their steep hillsides across a deep gorge. From Ragusa Superiore, where businesses and hotels are located and the AST bus stops, Ragusa Ibla is reached by a death-defying bus ride over precipitous, narrow streets or by a bracing climb down and up 242 steps (with a stop to catch your breath at the aptly named church of Santa Maria delle Scale (Saint Mary of the Steps).

Much of Ragusa Ibla was rendered unsound and uninhabitable by the 1693 earthquake; hence the prosperity of Ragusa Superiore. But Ragusa Ibla is the more appealing of the two, and a walk through its quiet piazzas and past its grand but often deserted palazzos can be a lonely and poetic experience. The place to set your sights is the **Basilico di San Giorgio**, in the highest, westernmost part of the town. The church is one of Sicily's most enchanting works of architecture, reached by a curving staircase from the palm-filled piazza Duomo. Just beyond lies the palm-shaded **Giardino Iblico**, with spectacular views across rolling countryside toward the sea.

The most comfortable accommodations in town are to be had at the simple, straightforward **Hotel Montreal**, near the cathedral in Ragusa Superiore. For a meal, you couldn't do much better than the simple fare (including Ragusa's gastronomic specialty, goat cheese with pepper, known as *pecorino piccante*) at **U Satacinu**, on via Convento.

It's worth the drive from Ragusa to have a meal at **Majore** (Tel: 0932-92-80-19; closed Mondays), an inexpensive family restaurant at Chiaramonte Gulfi (15 km/10 miles north) and the ultimate pork establishment (with wild rabbit and partridge, too). Pork—always with a special taste, for the Majore's pork is fed a special diet—is prepared in sausages, roasted, jellied, and thrown into pasta sauces. The province of Ragusa is the center for *caciocavallo* cheese, the taste of which changes noticeably from region to region.

CATANIA

Catania, 59 km (37 miles) up the coast from Syracuse, is Sicily's center of commerce and industry. This is a busy city of half a million people who, by the look of the modern office and apartment blocks, are more interested in the present and future than they are in the past. Founded by the Greeks in 792 B.C. and rebuilt by the Romans, Catania has withstood many subsequent sackings and occupations, but its worst foe has always been Mount Etna, looming barely 20 miles to the north and over the centuries shaking the city with catastrophic earthquakes. One recent eruption launched a swath of lava through the city's western suburbs.

The traveller willing to overlook Catania's noise, grime, and graceless modern precincts will find a rich and even elegant Baroque city. The place to begin your exploration is near the old port at the foot of via Etna, which stretches directly north toward the mountain's peak, snow-capped most of the year. The flamboyantly elegant Baroque **Porta Uzeda** opens into one of Italy's grandest squares, the piazza del Duomo.

Piazza del Duomo and Its Environs

The great Palermo-born architect Giovanni Battista Vaccarini settled in Catania in 1730, to rebuild the city after it was leveled in a 1693 earthquake that also killed most of the citizenry. Vaccarini brought about what the 20th-century art historian Rudolph Wittkower calls "a Sicilian Rococo, by blending Borrominesque with the local tradition." The stunning effect is readily apparent in this beautiful piazza. At the center is the **Fontana dell'Elefante** (Elephant Fountain), in which a black-lava pachyderm supports an obelisk, similar to the fountain that Bernini designed for the piazza della Minerva in Rome. Napoléon was so taken with Catania's most famous fountain, which has become the official symbol of the city, that he incorporated it in several of the monumental buildings he built in Paris.

The Baroque façade of the **Duomo** incorporates several

columns found amid Catania's Roman ruins. Only a small portion of the original 11th-century cathedral survived the 1693 earthquake; most of what you see is Vaccarini's deft rebuilding. Catania-born composer Vincenzo Bellini is buried inside the church, and Saint Agatha, the patron saint of Catania, who was thrown to the lions in A.D. 252, is buried in her own chapel to the right of the altar. Legend has it that Catanians narrowly avoided annihilation in 1669 when they stopped an approaching lava flow by waving the saint's veil in front of it. Agatha's breasts were cut off as part of her martyrdom, and they now reappear as pastries (*seni di vergine*) all over Sicily—an odd symbol of devotion. (Catania's pastries are perhaps the most elaborately designed in Sicily; Baroque didn't stop at stucco *putti*, after all. Pastry shops up and down the via Etnea display some amazing marzipan.)

Step west off the piazza onto via Vittorio Emanuele and you will shortly come to the pretty piazza Mazzini, with elegant arcades fashioned from Roman columns. From the piazza the via Castello Ursino leads a few blocks south to the grim **castle** that Frederick II built when he sacked Catania in the 13th century. Heavily restored several times over the centuries, the fortress now shelters the eclectic collections of the **Museo Communale**, ranging from Roman terra-cottas to *Saint Luke* by Mattia Preti to peasant embroidery.

The **Museo Belliniano** (Bellini Museum) is just north of the piazza Mazzini, in the adjoining piazza San Francesco. The composer's birthplace is filled with memorabilia, including many of his original scores. (Bellini is honored throughout Catania with *pasta alla Norma*—pasta with a sauce of tomatoes, basil, eggplant, and ricotta cheese—named for the composer's most famous heroine.) Venture around the corner to some remains of ancient Catania: the **Roman theater**, built over a Greek theater, and the **Odeon**, a small rehearsal stage.

Via Crociferi and San Nicolo

Running north from piazza San Francesco and lined with Baroque palaces and churches, the via Crociferi provides one of the most beautiful architectural vistas in Europe. Many of these fine structures have long been abandoned and look as though they are about to topple into ruin, but enough restoration is going on to suggest that Catania will preserve this street of treasures after all. Walking north you will pass a trio of especially elegant churches: **San Bene-**

detto, with the most elaborate façade; dei Gesuiti; and San Giuliano.

The **Chiesa di San Nicoló**, Sicily's largest and arguably its weirdest church, is just to the west of the via Crucifero, reached by the via Gesuiti. The church still functions, although its weed-covered façade (never completed and burdened with eight massive, ugly, truncated columns) suggests otherwise. The abandoned convent next door is (or was) Europe's second largest, topped only by Portugal's Mafra; it is now used as a storage barn for road-repair crews. The half-moon–shaped piazza Dante in front of the complex completes this desolate and eerily beautiful architectural mélange.

The Roman Amphitheater

The via Clementi will take you back east to the graceful via Etnea, which is crowded with shoppers and businesspeople by day and, come evening, with throngs of Catanese who take their *passeggiata* here. As you walk north on the street you will soon come to the busy piazza Stesicoro, with its monument to Bellini and the vast Roman amphitheater where Saint Agatha allegedly went to her martyrdom.

The leafy precincts of the **Giardino Bellini** are just a few blocks north. This is a beautiful spot, shaded by palms and laced with pretty walks that wind up a verdant hillside toward a viewpoint from which you can see the sprawling city, the port, and Etna looming above it all.

Staying and Dining in Catania

For tranquillity, the best place to stay is the **Catania Sheraton**, outside of town and connected by bus. It's ultramodern, and the saltwater pool and adjacent bar, restaurant, tennis court, and parking garage are up to Sheraton standards and are welcomed by business travellers. Ask for a sea-view room.

The **Villa Dina** is a strange and wonderful hotel that occupies an old palazzo near the center of things just off the via Etnea. The rooms could use some fresh paint, and everyone would sleep better if the gracious hosts battened down the creaky floor tiles, but this is a delightful place to stay. The **Albergo Moderno** (modern circa 1950, that is) is a simple but charming little hotel just off the magnificent via Crociferi and near the duomo. The **MotelAgip** is convenient and predictable (if anything is in Sicily).

A choice restaurant in Catania is **La Siciliana**, in a former villa at viale Marco Polo 52 (Tel: 095-37-64-00; closed Sunday evening and Mondays), where *rigatoni alla Norma,* made with eggplant sometimes seared for added flavor, is a delicious tribute to Bellini. Stuffed fresh sardines, roast lamb, *involtini,* and such can be accompanied by wines from Mount Etna or selections from the La Rosa family's extensive cellars. A specialty you might try is *ripiddu nivicatu* (lava of snowy Etna), a plate of rice blackened with cuttlefish ink, covered by snowy white cooked ricotta, and flaming with red pepper sauce. *Tiramisù* and *cassata* are sweet finishes.

The **Costa Azzurra**, a bit out of town at the port, Ognina, is worth the trip for the sea urchins (*ricci*) and similar treats. Località Ognina, via De Cristofaro 4, Tel: (095) 49-49-20; closed Mondays.

INLAND FROM CATANIA
Enna

Enna, practically in the middle of the island 85 km (54 miles) due west of Catania on austostrada A 19, is Sicily's highest city (almost 3,000 feet) and, blanketed in mist and dominated by the grim fortress that Frederick of Swabia built here in the 14th century, one of the gloomiest. (Enna also lies on the Catania–Palermo rail line, and is connected to both by frequent bus service as well.)

Enna is not without its pleasures. Most of its attractions are strung out along its one major street, the **via Roma**. From the west, you pass the church of **San Francesco**, then enter the **piazza Crispi**, where an airy belvedere affords views for miles over the surrounding wheat fields. (For the Greeks and Romans, the countryside around Enna was part of the breadbasket that fed their vast empires.) Beyond lies the 14th-century **Duomo**, and on a promontory high above the center of Sicily, the awesome **fortress**. If you climb the **Torre Pisana**, one of its six remaining towers, you can get an even better view of the countryside, including a look at the **Lago di Pergusa**, where mythology has it Pluto abducted Persephone, goddess of spring. You may well wish you'd left your images of the lake to the imagination, though, surrounded as it is by an auto-racing track.

Piazza Armerina

Most people pass though Enna en route to Piazza Armerina and the Roman villa at nearby Casale. Piazza Armerina is 35 km (23 miles) south of Enna on route 561; there is frequent bus service from Enna's bus station just off the via Roma, but if you are connecting with trains, beware: Enna's train station (where you can get trains to Catania, Agrigento, or Palermo) is 5 km (3 miles) outside the town. There's an hourly bus from the town to the station, but connections can be tricky.

Piazza Armerina is a dusty, mud-colored town dominated by its hilltop duomo. The luxurious **Roman villa at Casale** (3 km/2 miles south of town; taxis are available) was an imperial retreat during the third century A.D. Forty brilliantly preserved mosaics here, viewed from an ingenious network of catwalks, depict chariot races, hunts, picnics, and bikini-clad bathers, creating one of the world's most charming evocations of antiquity. The children's section shows imperial *bambini* at play.

Caltagirone

Caltagirone, 35 km (21 miles) southeast of Piazza Armerina on route 561, is a paradise for ceramics fanciers and worthy of a detour inland. Not only is there a museum devoted to pottery and tiles through the ages, but the town's walls, railings, even the 142-step staircase—each step differently tiled—glow with multicolored ceramic designs. Small arti-san shops continue the tradition, most of their tiles more modern than the age-old simple blue and white with an orange dab. This sophisticated town also has a charming Art Nouveau park designed by Basile. Stay at the modern **Villa San Mauro** here, with its lovely view and friendly bar for the travel weary.

Mount Etna

"Etna, that wicked witch, resting her thick white snow under heaven, and slowly, slowly, rolling her orange-colored smoke," was D. H. Lawrence's response to the still-active volcano. Pindar and Plato spoke of it, and Homer's Cyclops hurled rocks from its sides at Odysseus—rocks that now can be seen where they fell along the coast at Aci Castello (*I Ciclopi*).

Fierce and destructive as Etna has been and continues to

be, rare plants such as the Etna violet grow in the fertile soil on the broad slopes of the volcano, as do citrus, olives, and vineyards that produce very good wines. Chestnut trees from ancient forests turn golden in autumn, while in winter broom, lichen, and wildflowers are dazzling against the dark slopes higher up. Pistachio—probably planted by Arabs—is cultivated under the volcano, and the white birches are as noble as Robert Frost's.

Daily excursions to Mount Etna are arranged through CIT tours in Catania and Taormina. The Circumetnea railway leaves from Catania's Stazione Centrale, stopping at picturesque towns such as **Randazzo** that line the lower slopes. To reach the summit by car, follow the strada dell'Etnea out of Catania to the **Rifugio G. Sapienza**, operated by the Italian Touring Club. From here you can make the four-hour hike or take the cable car to the observatory (at almost 10,000 feet), and specially equipped buses continue on to the enormous and terrifying-looking crater. You'll get no farther than the refuge when the mountain is acting up, which it does often. Skiing on the slopes is also permitted when the volcano has been quiet.

TAORMINA

As you climb the steep, tortuous road toward Taormina, perched on a hillside just north of Mount Etna (38 km/24 miles up the coast from Catania on autostrada A 18 or route 114), the sea, the castle-topped cliff above the town, and Etna take their places in an incomparable panorama. Taxis and, irregularly, buses meet trains at Taormina's station, far below the town. If you're in the mood for an experience of centuries past, you can make the ascent on the rough-hewn steps carved out of the hillside.

The lure that has drawn the titled and the famous through the years is still strong, despite the hotels and shops that threaten to overwhelm the medieval charm of Taormina's steep streets, flower-bedecked balconies, Renaissance palaces, and tropical gardens. Avoid visiting in July and August, of course; but you couldn't find a more attractive setting in which to relax for a few days in spring or fall—or even to spend Christmas and New Year's, when the feasting boards groan and fireworks light up the sea.

Taormina was established by Dionysius I in 403 B.C. after he destroyed the nearby seaside settlement of Naxos (they were Chalcideans and Ionians; he was Corinthian). The

Arabs subsequently destroyed and rebuilt the city, and Count Roger rousted them in turn, as was his wont, in 1078. Its well-preserved medieval look is due in part to the care of the House of Aragon and in part to the Allied bombers' unwillingness to do much damage when they attacked Marshal Kesselring's fine quarters here.

Taormina climbs terraced levels above and below the corso Umberto. From the western edge of the city, the corso passes through the Porta Catania and soon comes to one of Taormina's picturesque squares, the **piazza del Duomo**, dominated by the crenellated, fortress-like 13th-century cathedral. The next square on the corso, the **piazza IX Aprile**, opens to stupendous views over Mount Etna and the sea. At its eastern end the corso comes to the piazza Vittorio Emanuele, where the **Palazzo Corvaia** (which houses the tourist office), like many of Taormina's many beautiful palaces, is rich with ornamentation of black lava and pumice inlaid in the limestone foundation.

Teatro Greco

From the piazza Vittorio Emanuele the via Teatro Greco leads to Taormina's main attraction, and one of the most beautiful sights in the world. The Teatro Greco is carved out of the rock and was so extensively made over by the Romans that most of the present structure dates from the Empire. But the site itself—affording views of Etna, the sea, the coast, and the sky framed by the theater's open walls—is a location only the Greeks could choose. The theater's acoustics are still excellent, and it is used frequently for a variety of artistic productions. Come here in early morning or late afternoon to see the light change over the sea and Etna's snowcap, and you'll experience a scene of sublime beauty that has awed Goethe, D. H. Lawrence, and generations of other travellers.

Taormina is perched high above the water; you can reach the beaches at **Mazzarò**, directly below, or at Naxos, visible from the heights, by car or funicular. **Naxos** was the first Greek colony in Sicily (735 B.C.), though its ruins are few compared with the treasures of Agrigento. Those that remain are found in the **Parco Archeologico**. Otherwise, Naxos is a long line of hotels.

Staying and Dining in Taormina

The best hotels in Taormina are the **San Domenico Palace**, a converted 16th-century convent that counts among its expensive charms spectacular panoramas from its many terraces, a pool, and a dining room; the less expensive **Jolly Hotel Diodoro**—where you should try to take an end suite with views of Etna, pool, and garden; the **Villa Belvedere**, still less expensive, and with the same panorama and its own flowery gardens and pool; and the small **Villa Fiorita**, with outdoor terraces, pool, and, of course, spectacular views. The most charming of the small hotels, however, is the **Villa Paradiso**, stylishly redesigned with Sicilian antiques and serving very good Sicilian food in its restaurant. Nearby, at via Bagnoli Croci 50, is one of the best trattorias in the area—the inexpensive **U Bossu**. Grilled fish is the specialty (Tel: 0942-233-11; closed Mondays).

Budget travellers will enjoy the **Villa Pompei**, across from the public gardens, and the **Pensione Svizzera**, with gorgeous coastal views.

At Mazzarò, on the beach just below Taormina, is the luxurious **Mazzarò Sea Palace** hotel and the charming **Villa Sant'Andrea**, which is merry with fabric prints and resembles an English seashore villa. The front rooms with terraces facing the sea are the best, but the back rooms face Taormina's semitropical lushness. And the price is right. One of its two restaurants is on the beach. Both hotels can be reached by cable car from Taormina.

If you've watched your calories, you may fit up the **Vicolo Stretto** (Narrow Alley) to the restaurant of that name at number 6—perhaps the best in Taormina and moderately priced (Tel: 0942-238-49).

For lunch go to the terrace of the sweet family-run **Il Faro**, high in the Taormina hills, which are terraced with vineyards above lush valleys and have views of the sea beyond (via Rotabile Castelmola; Tel: 0942-281-93; closed Wednesdays). After lunch, explore Castelmola's ancient streets and sample its almond cake drenched with almond wine.

FORZA D'AGRÒ

For a day's excursion from Taormina you can easily explore Mount Etna and the surrounding towns by train or tour. For a glimpse of medieval Sicily, go to Forza d'Agrò, a clifftop town reached by car only (bus service requires spending hours there between buses). In the town's piazza only the click of embroidery needles breaks the silence, except for an occasional blast of Michael Jackson from a passing tape deck.

MESSINA

About 40 km (25 miles) up the coast from Taormina, Messina is the busy ferry entrance to Sicily from Reggio di Calabria and Villa San Giovanni on the mainland. If you drive or take the train from the rest of Italy, you'll be ferried across the strait to Messina. It's well worth stopping for an hour or two, if only to see two Caravaggios and a magnificent fragment of a polyptych by the town's famous native son, Antonello da Messina, in the **Museo Nazionale**.

Messina has known destruction from its beginning—first by war, then by earthquake, tidal wave, cholera, and most recently by Allied bombs; but it is now cheerful-looking and energetic, a busy port and university town. In the central **piazza del Duomo** (north of the train and ferry stations on via IV Settembre), a noontime performance by the amazing clock tower features a crowing cock, a roaring lion, and Christ rising. The duomo is new, rebuilt on the model of the original 12th-century Norman cathedral after it was leveled by Allied bombs during World War II. The Museo Nazionale is a quarter of a mile farther north on the via Garibaldi and via della Libertà; if you make the trek on foot, stop in the piazza Unità d'Italia for a look at the extravagant Fontana del Nettuno, rebuilt after the war to its 16th-century grandeur.

If you spend the night in Messina, try the **Jolly Hotel**, which has a fine view of the harbor. The fashionable and expensive **Alberto** (via Ghibellina 95; Tel: 090-71-11; closed Mondays), considered one of Sicily's best restaurants, serves fish *carpaccio* with herb sauce, scampi in crab sauce, and superb lemon sorbets. Unfashionable, except in a radical chic way, is the **Trattoria del Porto**, a mariner hangout—and who knows fish better? (Via Vittorio Emanuele 71; Tel: 090-548-73.)

While in Messina you can cross the strait to see *I Bronzi,* the bronze warriors the sea gave up to a Calabrese fisherman, and now exhibited in Reggio di Calabria's Museo Nazionale (see the Calabria chapter). Hydrofoils from the via Vittorio Emanuele make the crossing in about 15 minutes; state-run ferries, carrying cars and trains, are slower and more likely to be running late.

THE AEOLIAN ISLANDS

The Aeolians (also known as the Lipari Islands), off Sicily's northeast coast, were once ruled by the god of the winds,

Aeolus, if we are to believe Homer—and we should, given the wildly sculpted shapes the wind has carved in the soft volcanic rock. The rich volcanic soil is excellent for growing grapes and vegetables, prickly pears, capers, carobs, and palms. During the Punic wars, Carthage used the islands as a base, until Rome conquered all in 252 B.C. The Aeolians were inhabited well before that, however—traces of Stentinello culture, especially pottery dating from the Neolithic period, have been found on Lipari. The Greeks were there later, but as early as 600 B.C. the Phoenicians and Greeks prized Lipari's obsidian, which proved ideal for making tools and weapons (because it is both strong and malleable), thereby putting the island on the map.

Daily sailings are available from Milazzo, about 50 km (31 miles) west of Messina (and in the summer from Messina and Palermo) for Lipari and Vulcano, less often (usually three times a week) to the others. During the summer there is daily hydrofoil service to all the islands, as well as among them. Palermo also is connected to the islands in summer by hydrofoil. An overnight ferry from Naples links them all, year-round (see "Getting Around," below). Leave your car at the car park at the piers; cars are permitted only on Lipari and Vulcano. Small motor vehicles take care of luggage and local transport.

Lipari

Lipari is the largest of the islands and the one best adapted to tourism. Its **Museo Eoliano**, in the little town of Lipari, is one of Europe's most important museums of prehistoric artifacts. Terra-cotta Greek theater masks and figures are attractively presented on an upper floor. The museum is enclosed within the walls of the **Castello**, where extensive excavations into Lipari's multilayered history can be observed.

The views from Lipari, and from all the islands, are striking in color and sculpturesque rock carvings. A friendly place to stay on the island is the **Villa Diana**, where terraces and private gardens overlook Lipari from on high; the local dishes and wines are wholesome. More hotel-like are the **Meligunis**, with beach and garden, and the **Carasco**, with fine sea views and a pool. The **Poseidon**, by the sea, is reasonably priced and well equipped.

It's worth the trip to Lipari if only to dine at **Filippino**. Signor Bernardi's restaurant on piazza Municipio is one of the finest in Italy, and surely the friendliest ever to have won the Michelin star—rarely awarded in Italy (Tel: 090-981-10-02). The house specialty is a pasta with a splendid eggplant sauce and flavored with local *pecorino* cheese. Seafood is king, of course, but all the grilled meat dishes are inviting. If you happen to be here when *cassata* is on the dessert menu, do indulge, for it's among the lightest and most subtly flavored in Sicily. (Moderate prices; closed November 10 to December 15 and Mondays in summer.)

Panarea

This is perhaps the most dramatically beautiful of the Aeolians, with its bizarre formations of volcanic rock and its clear water. Prehistoric villages dating from the 14th and 13th centuries B.C. can be seen on its volcanic slopes. Panarea is also a chic resort, attracting Italian celebrities who want to be alone—and who don't mind the island's limited electricity supply (stargazing here is an extraordinary experience). **Il Raya** is the place where they are found; no children, please. The **Residence** and **La Piazza**, with many amenities, are also charming. Scuba diving is the sport of choice.

Stromboli

The best way to approach this island is on the night boat from Naples; you can see its volcanic triangle rising out of the dawn mists. Nighttime trips are organized from Stromboli or Lipari to see the brilliant spectacle of fiery coals shooting into the air. On terra firma, if such can be said of Stromboli, the scene is surprisingly cheerful—white houses, bougainvillaea, almond blossoms, grape and caper vines, and even orange and lemon trees enliven the dark earth. Hotels are plentiful (usually open spring to fall); **La Sciara Residence** and **La Sirenetta–Park Hotel** even have swimming pools. The **Villaggio Stromboli** is somewhat less expensive, as is the **Pensione Scari**. If you arrive at night, be sure to have the hotel meet you: There are *no* streetlights. At La Sciara, look for **Teresa Trusnach's boutique**. If you're staying a while, she'll make you an exquisite outfit (she also carries ready-to-wear). This is the same Teresa who has a shop in Rome.

Climb the volcano only with a guide (avoiding the sort of problems Ingrid Bergman encountered when she made the ascent solo in the horrible film *Stromboli*). Smoke and rumbling will be apparent as you climb, as stones are constantly tossed about at the inside base of the cone. (Only those that shoot higher than 350 feet can be seen, however.) Allow about six hours to get to the top and back, assuming that you'll stop often to enjoy the view. Take a jacket, snack, and bottle of water, as there is no place to stop for a drink. Your hotel or the tourist office near the boat dock can arrange for a guide.

Vulcano

White steam and sulfur rise from the fumaroles here, and many of them have been designated for mud baths. You can walk along the rim of the dormant crater, which hasn't been heard from since 1890. Dine at **Al Cratere** (Porto Levante; Tel: 090-985-20-45) to know what "under the volcano" means. It's a good fish place with a cheerful terrace.

Filicudi and Alicudi

Prehistoric dwellings are to be found on these remote islands. Filicudi is extraordinary. The island swells upward from a small port toward a high tableland. Beyond the tableland, steep cliffs rush down to valleys of vineyards and caper plants and, in the spring, white almond blossoms. Nature lovers, artists, and lovers find the extravagant beauty and privacy of Filicudi ideal. The hotel at the port, the **Pensione Phenicusa**, has a restaurant and good views of the sea. Islanders also let rooms in their homes, and houses may be rented for longer periods. (The tourist office at the port has information.) While here, be sure to take an excursion by boat to Filicudi's **Bue Marino cave**, which is preferred by many to Capri's Grotta Azzurra, so dramatic are the displays of reflected light.

If you really want solitude, then **Alicudi**, farther west, is your island. Its *total* lack of electricity keeps away all but those most devoted to moonlight. The **Ericusa**, its tiny hotel, will supply you with lamps, but don't plan on nighttime reading.

TINDARI

En route back to Palermo along the scenic north coast from Messina, you may well want to stop at Tindari (about 90 km/ 56 miles west of Messina on A 20 or N 113) to see the fourth-century B.C. Greek **amphitheater**. Situated with the infallible

Greek eye for spectacular natural sites, the theater opens onto wondrous views of the Aeolian Islands ahead and Mount Etna in back.

CEFALÙ

Cefalù is unforgettable. An enormous cliff rises like a tidal wave above it; the town huddles below, dominated by the twin campanile of its cathedral. Cefalù is 200 km (124 miles) west of Messina on autostrada A 20 or route N 113, and 50 km (31 miles) east of Palermo.

Now a lively seaside summer resort, Cefalù has been inhabited probably as long as Sicily has, as witnessed by the prehistoric relics found in outlying grottoes. Carthage established a colony here, and Greeks, Byzantines, and Arabs followed. In 1063 Count Roger relieved the Arabs of command. It is to his son, King Roger, that we owe the extraordinary honey-colored **Duomo**. One night when he was caught in a storm at sea, Roger vowed to build a cathedral—a regal ex-voto—at whatever safe harbor he found.

The harmonious Romanesque façade of the duomo, in the center of the old town off corso Ruggero, the main shopping street, unfolds as you approach it from the piazza Duomo; the church is even more spectacular as you see it in the round. But it is the interior, being restored to its original simplicity after Baroque errors, that elicits the greatest admiration. The Christ who follows you with his mosaic eyes is unlike any other Pantocrator, and many observers consider it an unsurpassed representation, one where mercy is mingled with justice. The wisp of hair that has fallen over his forehead, the softened eyes, and the casual robes combine to create a portrait of power and majesty. The Bible he holds is open to "I am the light of the world," in Latin and Greek. The Madonna, too, is a rare creation and would be admired more if the Christ were not of such beauty. The strong-winged angels are transitional in Christian iconography— between the winged bull of Jewish art and the delicate winged messengers who would come later. In the left transept stands a *Madonna and Child* by Antonello Gagini, and in the narthex is a curious cat on the coat of arms of Monsignor Chat, who consecrated the cathedral.

Directly in front of the Duomo is the **Osteria del Duomo**, probably the best place to dine in Cefalù (Tel: 0921-218-38). Pastry and ice cream are the tours de force of the bakery across the piazza at the corso Ruggero.

Via Mandralisca leads west off the piazza Duomo to the **Museo Communale Mandralisca**. The treasure here is one of the world's greatest portraits, *Unknown Man* (1465–1470) by Antonello da Messina. His smile, sensuous and sly, has been called quintessentially Sicilian, as mysterious as that of the *Mona Lisa*. Among the archaeological relics here is a rare krater (Greek vase) from the Aeolian island of Lipari showing a tuna merchant arguing with a customer (fourth century B.C.). Just down the street, a flight of stone steps leads down to the dank **Lavatorio**, an Arab public washroom from the ninth century .

As you follow the corso Ruggero south through the old town, you'll come to the **Osterio Magno**, a fragment of Roger II's palace, with its graceful Norman touches still visible despite the weeds. In front is the **Osterio Piccolo**, the residence of the powerful Ventimiglia counts, who dominated the Madonie mountains to the south.

STAYING AND DINING IN CEFALÙ

If you decide to stay here—and it's an excellent choice, as the city is among Sicily's prettiest and cleanest (some people stay here and make the one-hour bus or train trip into the much less pretty or clean Palermo)—the best hotels are about a mile east of Cefalù. The **Kalura** and **Le Calette** are pretty little harbor-side resort hotels with swimming pools. Driving is easier, although you can go by bus or taxi. The **Carlton Riviera** is a modern, fully equipped hotel with a miraculous view of Cefalù and the surrounding sea; there are bus connections to town. The **Baia del Capitano**, located in an olive grove, has a private beach, pool, sauna, tennis court, and such. The price is right too.

In town, the **Riva del Sole** is nicely located across from the beach, with somber, reasonably priced rooms. There are two other nice hotels in the tree-covered hills just south of the center, but still within walking distance of the beach and town. The **Villa Belvedere**, south of the train station on via dei Mulini, is an old-fashioned pensione with big, comfortable rooms and a lush garden in which to relax. The young management is very friendly. The **Paradiso Club**, farther up the hill on the via dei Mulini, is a bit posher and more of a resort, with rooms in a pleasant modern building or in bungalows set amid a luxuriant tropical garden. The pool is lovely, and the hotel arranges cruises of the Aeolian Islands on its own yacht.

AROUND CEFALÙ

From Cefalù, trips to Solunto, Bagheria (see Around Palermo, following Palermo, above), and some of the small towns in the Madonie mountains are convenient by car. **Solunto**, a seaside town (about 40 km/25 miles toward Palermo) dating from the fourth century B.C.—with Phoenician, Greek, and Roman relics on a site above the sea and mountains—is one of the most evocative of these ancient settings. Much of the island, even Mount Etna, can be seen by taking bus excursions organized by Cefalù travel agencies.

The Madonie Towns

It takes a bit of driving along tortuous but scenic roads to reach the Madonie towns south of Cefalù. Castles and churches here are the legacy of Norman and feudal times, but the region owes its charm to its people and atmosphere, its food and way of life—in other words, the things that are the essence of a Sicily that is fast disappearing. If you go in the spring, the vast splashes of purple *sulla* and yellow mustard plants, along with frothy almond trees, will heighten the experience even further. The tours arranged by travel agencies in Cefalù are the best way to go for those who are uncomfortable driving the hairpin turns of mountain roads.

From **Castelbuono**, 14 km (9 miles) south of Cefalù on route 286, continue south another 30 km (19 miles) to **Petralia Soprana** (this mountaintop town is one of the most beautiful in Sicily, with its winding streets of sand-colored palazzi and churches), then west another 15 km (6 miles) to **Polizzi Generosa**, where you might want to stop at the tiny inexpensive restaurant **Itria** for fresh pasta with asparagus in spring, or hearty mixed grills or pizza (via Itria 3; Tel: 0921-885-43). Or head east to **Gangi** and **Nicosia**; stop and enjoy what you see at will.

Accommodations are few in the mountains, and fewer are very good. An exception is the **Milocca** in Castelbuono, which is beautifully situated and has a pool and riding horses. For a simple chalet with outstanding meals, go to Isnello's **Club Alpino Siciliano**, near Polizzi Generosa, an ideal mountain retreat (but with camplike rooms).

GETTING AROUND

You can reach Sicily by plane, arriving in Palermo or Catania, or by car or train across the Strait of Messina from Reggio di

Calabria or Villa San Giovanni. If you reserve this flight with Alitalia when making your reservations to Italy, the price will usually be considerably reduced. The most beautiful approach, however, is from Naples on the overnight car ferry (*traghetto*), which arrives in Palermo in time for the deep-pink African dawn over the city. First-class cabins (small, two beds, double-decker) and second-class (small, four beds, double-decker) can be reserved—and should be, for a soccer game will sell out second class easily. (A business-class ferry began service recently also.) The Naples–Aeolian Islands ferry lands at Stromboli, Salina, Lipari, Vulcano, and, on the Sicilian mainland, at Milazzo or Messina. Hydrofoil service from Naples also is available in summer.

In the U.S., bookings for the Tirrenia line can be made through Extra Value Travel, 683 S. Collier Boulevard, Marco Island, Fl. 33937; Tel: (813) 394-3384; Fax: (813) 394-4848. In Naples Tirrenia is located at the Stazione Marittima at the port (Tel: 081-551-21-81).

The Siremar line runs car ferries all year from Naples to Milazzo, and hydrofoils (in summer) that serve the Aeolian Islands as well. In Naples the address is via Depretis 78; Tel: (081) 551-21-12.

The Aeolians are also linked all year by SNAV (via Caracciolo 10, 80100 Naples; Tel: 081-66-04-44; Fax: 081-66-03-65. In Milazzo, Sicily, Tel: 090-928-45-09).

A car is the thing if you want to see the smaller towns, because bus service is infrequent. Train and bus connections to all major cities, however, are quite good. Taxi drivers frequently agree to reasonable rates for long trips. Cars are not recommended in Palermo and Catania, where traffic and auto theft make them a headache. (Nothing should ever be left in a car, even if it is locked.) Outside these two cities you'll encounter fewer problems, and the local people will be happy to tell you where to park.

Tour operators such as Italiatour and CIT offer independent packages, including hotel and car rental, or sometimes a rail pass, which can be booked ahead through a travel agent.

ACCOMMODATIONS REFERENCE

The rates given below are projections for 1993; always check for up-to-date information before making reservations. Wide ranges may reflect the differences between low- and high-season rates. Unless otherwise indicated, the figures indicate the cost of a double room (per room, not per person).

However, half-board (mezza pensione) rates, which include breakfast and one other meal per day, are per person. The service charge is included in the rate; inquire about tax and breakfast.

(See also the separate accommodations listings for Mondello and Palermo, above in the chapter.)

▶ **Albergo Moderno.** Via Alessi 9, 95129 **Catania.** Tel: (095) 32-53-09. ₤70,000.

▶ **Baia del Capitano.** Contrada Mazzaforno, 90015 **Cefalù.** Tel: (0921) 200-03; Fax: (0921) 201-63. ₤42,000–₤80,000; half board ₤84,000–₤126,000.

▶ **Le Calette.** Via Cavallaro 12, Località Caldura, 90015 **Cefalù.** Tel: (0921) 241-44. ₤80,000.

▶ **Carasco.** Porto delle Genti, 98055 **Lipari.** Tel: (090) 981-16-05; Fax: (090) 981-18-28. Open April–late September. ₤150,000; half board, ₤110,000–₤170,000.

▶ **Carlton Riviera.** Località Capo Plaia, 90015 **Cefalù.** Tel: (0921) 203-04; Fax: (0921) 202-64. Open March–October. ₤78,000–₤158,000; half board ₤83,000–₤145,000.

▶ **Catania Sheraton.** Via Antonello da Messina 45, 95020 **Cannizzaro.** Tel: (095) 27-15-57; Fax: (095) 27-13-80. In U.S., Tel: (800) 325-3535. ₤155,000–₤200,000; half board ₤149,000–₤189,000.

▶ **Club Alpino Siciliano.** Isnello, 90010 **Palermo.** Tel: (0921) 499-95. ₤40,000.

▶ **Cossyra Club.** Località Mursia, 91017 **Pantelleria.** Tel: (0923) 91-11-54; Fax: (0923) 91-25-46. ₤85,000.

▶ **Elimo.** Via Vittorio Emanuele 75, 91016 **Erice.** Tel: (0923) 86-93-77; Fax: (0923) 86-92-52. ₤110,000; half board ₤90,000–₤120,000.

▶ **Ericusa.** Via Regina Elena, 98055 **Alicudi.** Tex: (090) 988-99-02. ₤80,000.

▶ **Ermione.** Via Pineta Communale 43, 91016 **Erice.** Tel: (0923) 86-91-38; Fax: (0923) 86-95-87. ₤120,000.

▶ **Gran Bretagna.** Via Savoia 21, 96100 **Siracusa.** Tel: (0931) 687-65. ₤75,000.

▶ **Grande Albergo delle Terme.** Lungomare Nuove Terme, 92019 **Sciacca.** Tel: (0925) 231-33; Fax: (0925) 217-46. Closed December–January. ₤56,000–₤95,000; half board ₤79,000.

▶ **Hotel Capo San Vito.** 91010 **San Vito lo Capo.** Tel: (0923) 97-21-22; Fax: (0923) 97-22-59. ₤110,000.

▶ **Hotel Montreal.** Corso Italia 70. 97010 **Ragusa.** Tel: (0932) 62-11-33; Fax: same. ₤60,000.

▶ **Hotel Ristorante Alceste.** Via Alceste 23, 91020 **Ma-**

rinella di Selinunte. Tel: (0924) 461-84; Fax: (0924) 461-43. Ł65,000.

▶ **Hotel della Valle.** Via Ugo La Malfa 3, 92100 **Agrigento.** Tel: (0922) 269-66; Fax: (0922) 264-12. Ł190,000.

▶ **Jolly Hotel** Via Garibaldi 126, 98100 **Messina.** Tel: (090) 36-38-60; Fax: (090) 590-25-26. In U.S., Tel: (800) 221-2626 or 247-1277; Fax: (212) 213-2369. In U.K., Tel: (0800) 28-27-29; Fax: (0923) 89-60-71. Ł150,000–Ł190,000; half board Ł140,00– Ł195,000.

▶ **Jolly Hotel Diodoro.** Via Bagnoli Croce 75, 98039 **Taormina.** Tel: (0942) 223-12; Fax: (0942) 233-91. In U.S., Tel: (800) 221-2626 or 247-1277; Fax: (212) 213-2369. In U.K., Tel: (0800) 28-27-29; Fax: (0923) 89-60-71. Ł150,000–Ł210,000.

▶ **Kalura.** Via Vincenzo Cavallaro, Località Caldura, 90015 **Cefalù.** Tel: (0921) 213-54; Fax: (0921) 205-48. Ł94,000.

▶ **Kaos.** Frazione Caos, 92100 **Agrigento.** Tel: (0922) 59-86-22; Fax: (0922) 59-87-70. Ł170,000; half board Ł150,000.

▶ **Mazzarò Sea Palace.** Via Nazionale 147, 98030 **Taormina.** Tel: (0942) 240-04; Fax: same. In U.S., Tel: (212) 838-3110 or (800) 223-6800; Fax: (212) 758-7367. In U.K., Tel: (0800) 18-11-23; Fax: (071) 353-1904. Open April–October. Ł280,000–Ł400,000; half board Ł235,000–Ł295,000.

▶ **Meligunis.** Via Marte, 98055 **Lipari.** Tel: (090) 981-24-26; Fax: (090) 988-0149. Ł127,000–Ł215,000.

▶ **Milocca.** 90013 **Castelbuono.** Tel: (0921) 719-44. Ł80,000.

▶ **Miramare.** Via Piemonte 34, 92013 **Porto Palo di Menfi.** Tel: (0925) 712–78. Ł85,000.

▶ **MotelAgip.** Via Messina 626, 95126 **Catania.** Tel: (095) 71-22-300; Fax: (095) 71-21-856. Ł80,000–Ł130,000.

▶ **MotelAgip.** Via Teracati 30, 96100 **Siracusa.** Tel: (0931) 669-44 or 46-41-44; Fax: (0931) 671-15. Ł110,000–Ł140,000; half board Ł128,000–Ł157,000.

▶ **Paradiso.** Via Calvario 133, 91023 **Levanzo.** Tel: (0923) 92-40-80. Ł40,000.

▶ **Paradiso Club.** Via dei Mulini 18–20, 90015 **Cefalù.** Tel: (0921) 239-00; Fax: (0921) 239-90. Ł90,000.

▶ **Pensione Phenicusa.** Filicudi Porto, 98050 **Filicudi.** Tel: (090) 988-99-55. Ł60,000–Ł70,000.

▶ **Pensione Scari.** Contrada Scari, 98050 **Stromboli.** Tel: (090) 98-60-06. Ł75,000.

▶ **Pensione Svizzera.** Via Pirandello 26, 98039 **Taormina.** Tel: (0942) 237-90; Fax: (0942) 62-59-06. Ł60,000.

▶ **Pensione Tranchina.** Via A. Diaz 7, Scopello, 91010 **Trapani.** Tel: (0924) 59-60-63. Ł55,000–Ł65,000.

▶ **La Piazza.** Contrada San Pietro, 98050 **Panarea.** Tel:

(090) 98-30-03; Fax: (090) 98-31-76. Open April–September. £135,000; half board £110,000–£150,000.

▶ **Pirandello**. Via Giovanni XXIII, 92010 **Agrigento**. Tel: (0922) 556-66. £80,000.

▶ **Del Porto**. Via Borgo Italia, 91017 **Pantelleria**. Tel: (0923) 91-12-57 or 91-12-99; Fax: (0923) 91-22-03. £87,000.

▶ **Poseidon**. Via Ausonia 7, 98055 **Lipari**. Tel: (090) 981-28-76. £60,000.

▶ **Il Raya**. Costa Galletta, 98050 **Panarea**. Tel: (090) 98-30-13. Open June–September. £60,000.

▶ **Residence**. Contrada San Pietro, 98050 **Panarea**. Tel: (090) 98-30-29. £75,000–£187,000.

▶ **Riva del Sole**. Lungomare Colombo 25, 90015 **Cefalù**. Tel: (0921) 212-30; Fax: (0921) 219-84. £60,000; half board £85,000.

▶ **San Domenico Palace**. Piazza San Domenico 5, 98039 **Taormina**. Tel: (0942) 237-01; Fax: (0942) 62-55-06. In U.S., Tel: (212) 599-8280 or (800) 223-9832; Fax: (212) 599-1755. £360,000–£610,000; half board £330,000–£435,000.

▶ **La Sciara Residence**. Via Cincotta, Piscitá, 98050 **Stromboli**. Tel: (090) 98-60-05; Fax: (090) 98-62-84. Open May–October. £133,000–£186,000; half board £110,000–£190,000.

▶ **La Sirenetta–Park Hotel**. Via Marina 33, 98050 **Stromboli**. Tel: (090) 98-60-25; Fax: (090) 98-61-24. Open March–October. £80,000–£150,000; half board £88,000–£150,000.

▶ **Villa Athena**. Via dei Templi 33, 92100 **Agrigento**. Tel: (0922) 59-62-88; Fax: (0922) 40-21-80. £125,000–£190,000.

▶ **Villa Belvedere**. Via Bagnoli Croci 79, 98039 **Taormina**. Tel: (0942) 237-91; Fax: (0942) 62-58-30. Open March 16–October. £120,000–£155,000.

▶ **Villa Belvedere**. Via dei Mulini, 90015 **Cefalù**. Tel: (0921) 215-93; Fax: (0921) 218-45. £70,000.

▶ **Villa Diana**. Località Diana-Tufo, 98055 **Lipari**. Tel: (090) 981-14-03. Open March–October. £50,000–£80,000.

▶ **Villa Dina**. Via Caronda 129, 95100 **Catania**. Tel: (095) 44-71-03; Fax: (095) 43-69-35. £69,000–£180,000.

▶ **Villa Fiorita**. Via Pirandello 39, 98039 **Taormina**. Tel: (0942) 241-22; Fax: (0942) 62-59-67. £110,000.

▶ **Villa Paradiso**. Via Roma 2, 98039 **Taormina**. Tel: (0942) 239-22; Fax: (0942) 62-58-00. Closed November–mid-December. £120,000–£210,000.

▶ **Villa Politi**. Via Politi 2, 96100 **Siracusa**. Tel: (0931) 321-00; Fax: (0931) 360-61. £128,000.

▶ **Villa Pompei**. Via Bagnoli Croci 88, 98039 **Taormina**. Tel: (0942) 238-12. £40,000.

▶ **Villa San Mauro.** Via Portosalvo 18, 95041 **Caltagirone.**
Tel: (0933) 265-00; Fax: (0933) 316-61. Ł120,000–Ł160,000.

▶ **Villa Sant'Andrea.** Via Nazionale 137, 98030 **Mazzarò.**
Tel: (0942) 231-25; Fax: (0942) 248-38. Ł254,000–Ł274,000;
half board Ł243,000–Ł297,000.

▶ **Villaggio Stromboli.** Via Regina Elena, 98050 **Stromboli.**
Tel: (090) 98-60-18; FAx: (090) 988-01-70. Open April–
October. Ł90,000–Ł100,000.

SARDINIA

By Barbara Coeyman Hults

Sardinia (Sardegna), a name that conjures up images of the Emerald Coast, pleasure dome of the Aga Khan, is often ignored by those in search of less extravagant pleasures. Relatively few travellers, Italians included, take the island seriously on a cultural level. Perhaps because mainland Italy is so famous for the glories of Rome and the Renaissance, the natural beauty of the island seems less impressive. However, as congested cities and polluted water awaken both Italians and visitors to more basic treasures, the island is coming into its own. The rough energy of the thousands of stone structures that were built in ancient Sardinia is similar to that of much modern sculpture, an ironic twist of artistic fate. And although Sardinia has no cities of great beauty, Cagliari has its charms, and some of the towns, such as Castelsardo, are enchanting.

While it's true that the Aga Khan's lovely and expensive resort has brought fame and considerable fortune to that part of the northeast called the Costa Smeralda (Emerald Coast), Sardinia is much more than just another pretty beach.

Not that the coastline is to be ignored, for spectacular it is, and not only in the north. Long white beaches stretch out near Cagliari, the capital and commercial port on the island's southern coast, and brighten the coastline at frequent intervals around the rest of the island. Clear water of emerald and cerulean hues surrounds headlands of oak and pine, and rocks thick with macchia, a heatherlike shrub that provides ground cover, and splashes of color, from green to bright orange, are scattered everywhere. (Plan to go in June or September, definitely not in August, when Europe heads seaward en masse.)

Sardinia's interior is mountainous, but cut through with

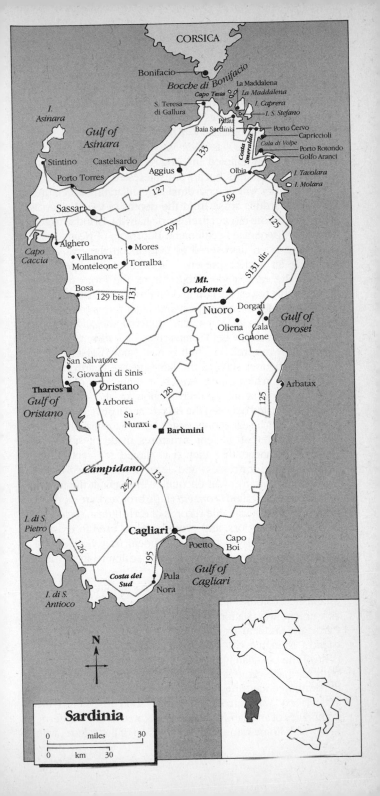

dramatic gorges and rivers. From Cagliari northwest to Oristano on the west coast extends the Campidano, a fertile plain that ends on the Sinis peninsula, where lagoons shelter flamingoes and salt mines have created mountain deserts.

On the north coast the wet mistral, blowing down from Provence in France—as if envious of the Emerald Coast's reputation—has sculpted amazing rock formations.

Not only naturalists, but anyone interested in art or in early human history will find Sardinia an exhilarating adventure. Although Sardinia arose from the depths of the Mediterranean long before most of prehistoric Italy, the island's rugged coastline discouraged settlement. But traces of Neanderthal man have been discovered at Dorgali on the east coast, revealing an ancient presence as early as the Paleolithic period. The earliest identified culture, the Protosards, left considerable traces: intriguing dolmens—huts made of massive stone slabs in square post and lintel forms (one of the best preserved is at Mores near Alghero); megalithic stone circles that generally held tombs (like the *tomba di gigante,* wonderfully restored on a hilltop near Nuoro); and a variety of fertility figures, such as the large-breasted earth mother and the ram, which can be seen in the museums of Cagliari and Sassari. The greatest civilization of the island, the Nuraghic, existed between the Bronze and Iron Ages (1600 to 111 B.C.), which seems only yesterday in Sardinia, given the 8,000 examples of ancient structures made of stones so perfectly balanced that they have lasted for centuries— houses, altars, fortresses, and even towns (especially at Barùmini)—that you will encounter throughout the island. Their sculpture, called *bronzetti* (little bronzes), are works of art that provide invaluable records of early human society, its gods and its warriors, and even the boats used to cross to Etruscan Italy. Early contact with Phoenicians, Greeks, and Etruscans is evident in ceramics and sculpture from these areas.

The Phoenicians, the Mediterranean's ubiquitous traders, established colonies here about 800 B.C.; Sardinia offered a convenient way station on their commercial routes. The Carthaginians (actually latter-day Phoenicians) overcame the island's Nuraghic colonies in about 600 B.C. in order to control the obsidian and other minerals to be found there. With Carthage came a social split in Sardinian culture, between the conquering Carthaginians and the earlier tribes, and slavery was introduced. Rome soon discovered the advantages of an island strategically located in the Mediterranean. With Rome came a further division of the culture, with the earlier societies retreating inland, creating a mountain people who today still prefer the interior to modern coastal settlements. At Nora, south of Cagliari on the southern coast, a fine Roman town is preserved, with its decorative mosaic-tiled baths—an essential to Roman well-being—and amphitheater nearly intact.

During this Roman period Sardinia became an island of deportation, a handy Siberia for discordant elements. Tiberius sent 4,000 Jews into exile here (A.D. 19), and Nero sent a few of his many enemies; Marcus Aurelius deported Christians to Sardinia, among whom was Callistus, who would become pope. Some of the early Christian churches in Sardinia, such as San Giovanni on the Sinis peninsula, are splendidly evocative of the simple faith of early Christianity.

The Roman legions left a lasting record here in the form of Vulgate Latin, which has been closely preserved in the Sardinian language.

The Vandals, after laying siege to Rome, did not neglect Sardinia, and remained here until the Byzantines arrived in 534. With Byzantium came the Greek language and churches in the Greek cross and round cupola form, such as Santa Sabina near Nuoro and the enchanting San Giovannini at Sinis, near Oristano. After Arab invasions from 711 to 1015, during the spread of Islam in the Mediterranean, Sardinia became tied to the Italian mainland more closely; expelling the Saracen had brought Pisa and Genoa, nearby seaports, into the fray, and they stayed on to enjoy the view. (The Doria family of Genoa made its mark on the island in many a castle and palace, notably at Castelsardo on the north coast.)

Now began a period that saw a flourishing of fine Romanesque architecture in Sardinia. This northern Italian style of the 12th and 13th centuries can still be enjoyed in cathedrals such as San Michele di Salvenero near Sassari and a wealth of other churches. At this time, Sardinia was partitioned into four political entities, as it is today: Cagliari, Nuoro, Sassari, and Oristano. Castles and towers arose on the hilltops as a new propertied class emerged and sought protection for their land; the others, the *servi*, did as their name implied.

The House of Aragon (1323–1478) kept its strong hold on Sardinia for centuries; in 1479 Ferdinand of Aragon married Isabella of Castile, and the Spanish language was heard until at least 1714, when the Peace of Utrecht gave Sardinia to Austria. In Alghero today you'd think the Spanish had never left, for Catalan is strong in the dialect, and street names appear in Catalan as well as Italian.

Apart from beautiful churches and a lilting language,

Spain left Sardinia bankrupt, as it was when the House of Savoy gained control in 1720; but the Savoy nobility were the ancestors of the kings of the united Italy that was to come. Although many Sardinians participated in the battle for Italian independence in 1870, Sardinia remained somewhat aloof from the struggle, its own advantages and disadvantages in the conflict never clearly understood. However, Garibaldi chose Sardinia for his own self-imposed exile later in life, and died here on the island of Caprera, off the northeast coast, where his house and grave can be visited.

Before World War II, the Fascist government initiated large-scale land reclamation programs, such as the agricultural development at Arborea, on the west coast, then called Mussolinia. But interest in the island was short-lived as new foreign wars created economic and manpower needs. In 1948 the Italian government conferred upon Sardinia a special status, giving it a degree of regional autonomy, which it holds today.

Today the island is divided between the political agendas of the Green parties and the developers, a struggle similar to those taking part in most developed countries.

Because Sardinia's culture has been so well insulated in the interior regions, we know a good deal about ancient daily life. The simple, nutritious diet of the past also survives— meat roasted with herbs on an open fire or in a pit; breads festively sculpted and touched with olive oil (called *carta da musica,* or sheets of music); goat and sheep cheese, creamy or sharp; and sweets made with honey, nuts, and cheese. *Cucina povera* (poor-person's cooking) is prized for its fresh and subtly delicious taste.

In many ways Sardinia is an island for the 1990s, a natural preserve for marine and wildlife, trees and flowers, as well as for natural foods, healthy lifestyles, and a connection with the ancient past. Unfortunately, ecological concerns have not yet been extended to transportation. Without a car, transit is difficult, for the most interesting parts of the island generally are not in the cities.

MAJOR INTEREST

The *nuraghi*
Nuraghic statues (*bronzetti*) in the museums of
    Cagliari and Sassari
Beaches and grottoes such as the Grotte di Nettuno
The cities: Alghero, Sassari, Cagliari
Romanesque architecture

The folk museum at Nuoro
Festivals, especially the Cavalcata at Sassari in May
Elegantly simple food
Handicrafts, especially gold rings

Oliena

A visit to Sardinia might well begin where Sardinia began, in a cultural sense: in the interior. Take the overnight ferry from Genoa or Civitavecchia near Rome to Arbatax or Olbia (or fly to Olbia) on the eastern coast. From there it is a short drive to Oliena, a town of about 8,000, just southeast of Nuoro. Here, in the wild, forested heart of Sardinia, you'll find **Su Gologone**, which has grown from a local café to a splendid white hacienda with red tile roofs, set amid glorious mountain scenery. The name is derived from a spring that gushes from between nearby boulders.

The restaurant is not for dieters—vast sides of meat and dozens of lake fish are roasted on the open hearth. The *carta da musica,* waferlike unleavened bread filled with herbs and dripping with olive oil, and the dessert menu destroy any plans for moderation. Swimming, horseback riding, and trips through the interior by Land Rover are arranged by the management. The only drawback is that its popularity brings small conventions and weekend luncheon groups out in force. Luckily the restaurant is laid out in separate sections, and proprietor Signora Palomera makes sure that no one is left out.

Oliena itself is famous for its wines, sweets, lovely jewelry, and the wonderful costumes its women still wear occasionally (and always on the feast day of San Lussorio, August 21). Although it is not a charming town, its site is superb and its friendliness is legendary. The winding streets, painted courtyards, and external staircases are set off by the sharp incline of the Sopramonte. In driving around Oliena you may find yourself on corso Martin Luther King: King's significance is keenly understood in Sardinia and the south of Italy, where economic and social discrimination are still common.

Using Su Gologone as your base, head northwest to Nuoro. About 10 km (6 miles) from the hotel you can detour to **Monte Ortobene** (some of the roads are tortuous). From the statue of the Madonna at the top, the view of Nuoro and the surrounding countryside is spectacular. The hills are covered with oak trees, cork (a major export), and a medley of flowers.

Nuoro

At Nuoro, a rather bedraggled-looking but ingratiating town of about 40,000, stop at the house of the 1926 Nobel Prize–winning writer Grazia Deledda on the street bearing her name. The house is charming, with mementos of her career in an unassuming upper room. The folk museum, **Museo della Vita e delle Tradizioni Popolari Sarde**, houses a marvelous collection of lavish costumes worn by Sardinian women through the ages, and in which the glamour of Spanish lace, the opulence of Greek and Arab jewelry, and the talent of local artisans have been combined with stunning results. In the room devoted to the pre-Lenten Carnevale costumes, frightening masks and costumes that were once thought to placate the gods vividly represent the primeval fear of the unknown. (Open 9:00 A.M. to 1:00 P.M. and 3:00 to 7:00 P.M.; closed Sunday afternoons and Mondays.) If you can be here for Carnevale, on Shrove Tuesday, you'll see one of the most memorable festivals anywhere. (Nuoro's other important folk festival takes place on the last two Sundays of August.) Also in Nuoro is the **Civico Museo Speleo-Archeologico**, where ceramics and bronzes retrieved from nearby caves are exhibited.

From Nuoro, you can either drive southeast to the Nuraghic city of Barùmini and then return to Oliena at night, or you can continue south and stay in Cagliari (see below) for a night or two, visiting Barùmini, about 48 km (30 miles) north of Cagliari, from there.

For splendid beaches, travel eastward to **Cala Gonone**. From here boat trips can be arranged to **Cala Luna** and **Cala Sistine**, small white-sand islands with clear pools and grottoes. Boat trips also leave for the **Grotta del Bue Marino**, a spectacular site but best undertaken when the tourists are not boat-to-boat. (If they are, take a sunshade and a book, and relax on the beach.)

Barùmini

Barùmini, or Su Nuraxi, as the village itself is called, is a rare treasure, a well-preserved Nuraghic city dramatically located on a hillside south of Nuoro. The town dates from about 1700 B.C.; its walls and towers and houses were built with basalt rock—so perfectly balanced without the benefit of mortar that the stones continue to withstand the ravages of time. In the "Parlamento" hut, the round seat and wall niches, as well as a number of objects found there, have led anthropologists to theorize that religious rituals were part of the governing process.

Cagliari

As buoyant and blowsy as most port cities, Cagliari (CA-lya-ree), on the south coast, has sights enough to detain anyone with an interest in art. Its **Museo Nazionale Archeologico**, inside a castle on piazza Indipendenza above the city, houses an exceptional collection of *bronzetti*. Gold jewelry from the Punic days and Roman glass are also well represented. (Open 9:00 A.M. to 2:00 P.M.; on Wednesdays, Fridays, and Saturdays also 3:30 to 6:30 P.M.) Stop at this museum early, since it is quite extensive. In back of the museum, the amphitheater, though not always open, is one of Sardinia's best-preserved Roman monuments. Dating from the second century B.C., it's almost entirely carved out of rock. Beneath the seating areas are three levels where "participants," men and beasts, were kept. Behind the arena, the **Orto Botanico** is the third largest in Italy, with local and exotic plants (open 8:30 A.M. to 1:00 P.M., and also 3:30 to 7:00 P.M. in season; closed Sundays).

Outside the museum, the **Torre Pancrazio** is part of a Pisan fortification. Pisa had moved into Sardinia ostensibly to defend it against the Arabs, but Sardinia soon needed defense against Pisa. Besides crops, salt, and animals, Pisa demanded gold tribute. When the pope gave Sardinia to the Aragonese, fortifications went up quickly, but Sardinia had become part of Spain.

Take a stroll through the public gardens to the **Citadella Museum**, where there are frequent exhibitions. From there you can head to the Roman amphitheater to the west or start down to the Duomo at the center of the Castello section, the old city. The **Duomo** (Cattedrale di Santa Maria) is a mix of styles, but the Pisan predominates. Inside, Maestro Guglielmo of Pisa sculpted two fine pulpits. The cathedral has a museum of some note, and members of the House of Savoy are buried in its sanctuary. The neighborhood around the church is fascinating; elaborate wrought iron and street life abound. At a lower level, off piazza Costituzione, the **Bastione di San Rémy** contains the Terrazza Umberto I, with a salty view from along the Spanish bastions. On Sundays this area turns into a flea market.

Have lunch at the elegant (and expensive) **Dal Corsaro**, considered Cagliari's best by many restaurant critics. If you want to try its Sardinian specialties, ask for *cucina tipica,* specifying *carne* (meat) or *pesce* (fish). (Viale Regina Margherita 28; Tel: 070-66-43-18. Closed Sundays and August.) Or try the charming St. Rémy, at via Torino 16 in the herbalist's shop of a former monastery (Tel: 070-65-73-77; closed Saturday lunch, Sundays, and August). You can watch the busy Sardinian business folk enjoying the fare at Italia, via Sardegna 30 (Tel: 070-65-79-87; closed Sundays), in the busy shopping area near the port (watch your wallet). Down the street at via Sardegna 60, the Trattoria Gennargentu is a good choice for palate and purse (Tel: 070-65-82-47; closed Sundays). And for a sweet finish, have coffee and ice cream at the traditional Caffè Genovese, piazza Costituzione 10-11 (closed Thursdays).

When you are in the port area, do stop at Giesse, a tiny shop at via Sardegna 32, where handcrafted delicate gold filigree wedding rings cost about $120. They seem to be made of gold petit point. If a wedding is not imminent, you can do as the doge of Venice did and marry the sea. The rings are worth a bit of artifice.

I.S.O.L.A., via Baccaredda 184, is a government-sponsored handicrafts shop, with very fine (and expensive) work on display (Tel: 070-48-67-07).

Since the sea is part of the reason for coming here, stay on the coast, 3 km (2 miles) outside of Cagliari, at the Hotel Calamosca, where you should ask for a room with a view of the *pineta,* or little pine grove. The view of the cove, its beach, and the working lighthouse makes this hotel well worth the few minutes' drive from Cagliari. A less expensive alternative is the Pensione Vittoria, in town, with interesting rooms, some of which have sea views.

For a seaside lunch go to Ottagono on the gulf strip called La Poetto, on viale Poetto (Tel: 070-37-28-79; closed Tuesdays, January, and February), not far from Calamosca. Have *aragosta* (lobster), the local specialty. Lo Scoglio, nearby, also has a sea-view terrace (Tel: 070-37-19-27).

If, instead, you'd like to experience Sardinian country life, you can stay with a family in a bed-and-breakfast–like arrangement that includes supper as well. The ecology-minded Terranostra organization (via Sassari 3, Cagliari; Tel: 070-668-83-67) arranges such stays. This is a new, exciting, and very inexpensive way to experience Sardinian life as it is lived by real families (about 26,000 lire per person, including dinner). You stay at the family's *azienda,* a small farm where they raise animals, fruits, and vegetables, probably have a small vineyard, and make their own sheep's-milk cheeses. From this bounty you'll be fed, and not sparingly, using traditional family recipes. (*Note:* These are working farms and not on the main highways, so be sure you can drive on unpaved roads. Take a dictionary, for English won't be spoken; communication should be easy, however, because the families are well briefed about tourists and their needs. Such farms are located throughout the island.)

Cagliari hosts a summer art festival, and its university presents concerts all year.

Travel down the coast about 45 km (28 miles) in the opposite direction from Poetto (southwest) and you'll reach the Punic-Roman city of **Nora**, with its columns brilliantly outlined against the sea (stop in **Pula** to shop for ceramics en route). A Roman amphitheater and baths (nicely mosaicked, as usual) are spread out amid earlier Punic remains, such as the temple to Tanit, a Mediterranean fertility goddess. You'll find a pleasant windswept beach near the site.

Su Gunventeddu is a tranquil restaurant, whether you can pronounce its name or not. Here fresh fish and seafood are the specialty. (On the road between Nora and Pula; Tel: 070-920-90-92; closed Tuesdays and from mid-December to mid-January.)

Tharros

Heading north along the western coast past marshland quivering with eel, you might fantasize flamingos in flight and find that they're real. Stop at Tharros on the flat Sinis peninsula, which has been inhabited since the Iron Age (ninth to eighth century B.C.), when it served as a port. Its calm harbor soon attracted the Phoenicians—the world's greatest traders. Rome moved in, and then bradysism (in which the earth rises and falls in a volcanic swoon) induced the population to flee. Much of the city is submerged. At the Tophet, the most important Phoenician shrine, found throughout the Mediterranean, infants were sacrificed to the deity.

Roman ruins are much in evidence here. The temple of Demeter was built over Punic construction. The familiar grid pattern of Roman streets, baths of course, and the Greek-Egyptian–style Roman temple made up a comfortable Mediterranean city.

On the way to Tharros you'll see another fantasy, the set for a Western movie at San Salvatore, a ghost town until the movie crew appeared, now returned to the tumbleweed. Some nice beaches line the coast, and so you might opt for a picnic, perhaps at **San Giovanni di Sinis**. The hotel **Da Cesare**, on a white sand beach, is an inexpensive place to linger. One of the oldest Christian churches in Sardinia, also called San Giovanni di Sinis (fifth century), is found in this village, close to Tharros.

Oristano, about 10 km (6 miles) east of Thanos, is a largish city, and you may want to have lunch there at **Il Faro**, where good soup and grills are rather expensive (via Bellini 25; Tel: 0783-700-02; closed Sunday nights and Mondays). The **Forchetta d'Oro** will give you a good pasta with squid ink, now becoming the rage in the United States, from its more moderately priced menu (via Giovanni XXIII 8; Tel: 0783-30-27-31; closed Sundays).

Alghero

Leaving Oristano, head north toward Alghero, stopping first at **Bosa** on the coast to see the **Castello di Malaspina**, whose dramatic walls and tower dominate a hilltop. Inside the walls is the church of **Nostra Signora di Regnos Altos**, in which a cycle of frescoes depicts scenes from the life of Christ. Bosa produces a good Malvasia wine, and you might want to stop to see some of the lacemakers at work, often outdoors. Continue along the sea until, past the town of Villanova Monteleone, the rugged outline of the coast at Capo Caccia appears, signaling that you are nearing Alghero (al-GAYR-oh).

Although Alghero was apparently founded in the 11th century by the Genoese, today the city is Catalan in look and spirit. Street signs are written in both Catalan and Italian, and the panache of Moorish Spain—vividly evoked by the inter-laced arches and arabesques that decorate windows and courtyards—is happily fused with the solemnity of tall Gothic windows and reliefs of leaves and lilies. The Old City is still bound with massive towers and walls, which protect it from the busy harbor and esplanade below. A walk around the town's sturdy sand-colored walls is an exhilarating way to begin the morning. Some cafés set up their tables on the walls near the port side for cappuccino and *cornetti* while the fishing fleet sets sail.

In 1353 the Catalan Aragonese—with the help of Genoa's rival, Venice—defeated the Genoese. Expelling Sard and Ligurian, Peter IV of Aragón repopulated the city with Catalans. Alghero remained a possession of the Aragón crown until 1714, when it was transferred to the House of Savoy. Since then the city has expanded well beyond its walls, and this part of Sardinia has become one of the most popular with tourists for its picturesqueness, its location near beaches and dramatic cliffs and grottoes, and its proximity to important Nuraghic sites and the museum at Sassari, with its fine collection of Nuraghic art (see below).

A walk through Alghero might start at the piazza Porta a Terra, at the eastern edge of the Old City. (Just outside the walls are the extensive public gardens.) In the piazza is the 14th-century Jewish Tower, or **Torre degli Ebrei**, so called because it was built by the Jews of Alghero before they were expelled by the Inquisition.

From here follow via Roma a short way, turning left at the via Barcellonetta, to via Machin, where a right turn leads to the beautiful 14th-century church of **San Francesco**. Here the marriage of two cultures is evident in soaring Gothic arches and dramatic Catalan sculpture. The statue by an unknown 17th-century Spaniard of Christ tied to the pillar, at the left of the central nave, is exceptionally fine. Along with the star vaulting at the altar, notice the fine cabinet (*paratore*) of intarsia in the sacristy, as well as the cloisters, where concerts are often held. From here, the view of the bell tower contributes a vertical accent to the horizontal harmony below. The Franciscans, who live in the adjacent monastery, provide simple rooms if you'd like to stay here overnight.

Turning right at the exit you'll reach via Roma, close to the **Cattedrale** (which closes at noon). Its late Renaissance portico of Doric columns lends it the solemnity appropriate to the burial place of members of the House of Savoy.

Close by is the piazza Civica, where you can stop for a coffee and sandwich at the delightful café on the ground floor of the palace. You might mistake it for an antiques shop, but inside there are tables and a handsome bar.

This is one of the busiest and prettiest sections of town. As in an Arab town, tiny streets head off in all directions. To buy some of the finest coral and gold (including the gold wedding rings), go to **Orafart**, nearby at via G. Ferret 53, where a model of the sea bottom illustrates how coral is formed. Today it is difficult to obtain coral because fishing boats scraping the bottom unintentionally have destroyed much of it. The largest pieces are found at such depths that divers can remain there only a short time. Since harmony of color is part of its beauty, a necklace must come from one piece of coral to be considered fine jewelry. There is much imitation and much Asian coral masquerading as Sardinian.

Right off the piazza Civica is the Bastione della

Maddalena, and beneath it is the port from which boats leave for a three-hour excursion to **Neptune's Grotto**, considered Sardinia's most beautiful. The cliffs at **Capo Caccia** (24 km/15 miles from Alghero) above the grotto possess great dramatic beauty (also enjoyed by tour buses, especially in summer, so go early in the morning or off-season). You can rent a bungalow near this glorious sight at **Campeggio Porticciolo**, with facilities that include a restaurant and tennis courts.

Between Capo Caccia and Alghero, be sure to visit the Nuraghic village of **Palmavera**, where 50 Nuraghic huts and a fine tower can be explored. The tower's intricate vaulting—called a "false dome" because from the outside only the usual truncated cone is visible—is well developed, and you can climb the prehistoric stairs to enjoy the view.

Ask at the Alghero Tourist Office (piazza Porta Terra 9) whether a trip to **Arca di Noë** (Noah's Ark) can be arranged. A guide is required to see this wild stretch of land where the rare white donkey (*asino bianco*), wild quarter horses, and the almost-extinct griffin vulture live in an Eden all their own.

In Alghero you may want to stay at the modern **Carlos V**, just outside the city walls, with a pool and terraces on the sea, or at the refurbished home of Spanish royalty located on a little rocky peninsula across from the Carlos V, the **Villa Las Tronas**, which has restored some of its grandeur of days gone by. The most beautiful hotel in the area is **El Faro**, on a private promontory 13 km (8 miles) from the city. The spacious white building is warmed with antiques, and each room has a sea-facing terrace. Pool and courts, sauna, and private beach plus water sports such as underwater photography, windsurfing, and sailing are all at hand. Full summer is the best time here, unless you like a little Gatsby-type off-season melancholy.

Less expensive and far less glamorous is the **Bellavista**, near the lovely beach at Fertilia, just outside Alghero.

Have a lavish dinner at **La Lepanto** at via Carlo Alberto 135 (Tel: 079-97-91-16; closed Mondays), where lobster is served Alghero-style—the meat is marinated in a sauce of lemon and orange peel, with tomatoes and herbs. A glass of Vernaccia, a fine Sardinian dessert wine, writes a happy ending to a moderately expensive meal here. At **Tuguri**, in a 15th-century palazzo at via Maiorca 57 (Tel: 079-97-67-72), try the risotto *con verdure* (with vegetables), or ask Carbonella to choose your meal for you. A fine wine with seafood is Tere Bianche (Torbato di Alghero). **Da Pietro**, near San Francesco, is charming, and lively at night (via Ambrogio Machin 20; Tel: 079-97-96-45). Less expensive is the Spanish-style **El Pultal**, at via Colombano 40 (Tel: 079-97-80-51).

When you leave Alghero, take the road toward Porto Torres, turning west a few miles before town when you see the sign for **Stintino**, which is located on a stretch of land that shoots up from Sardinia's extreme northwest coast. Stintino was strictly a fishing village until recently, but has made itself more attractive to tourists. Stay at the hotel **Roccaruja**, with a view of the island of Asinara, which has the dual distinction of being the only place where the white ass, *l'asino bianco,* is bred and also the home of a penal colony specializing in Mafiosi. No visitors.

To the southeast, 19 km (12 miles) from Porto Torres, lies Sassari.

Sassari

Sassari is an attractive, vivacious city, thanks to its nicely preserved medieval Old City (**Centro Storico**) and the presence of a major university; you would do well to include it in your itinerary. A visit to its Sanna Museum (see below) is a wonderful way to learn about Nuraghic society, for the exhibits are carefully arranged with both enjoyment and education in mind.

As capital of the province of the same name, Sassari is a major commercial center, yet it retains the quaint charm characteristic of smaller towns. If you stay at the modern, comfortable hotel **Grazia Deledda**, you can walk to most sights of interest.

The **Duomo,** at the center of the Centro Storico, was begun during the 12th century and rebuilt during the 15th. In its museum, reached from inside the church, is the *Madonna and Child with Saint Veronica,* considered one of the most beautiful paintings in all of Sassari. A few blocks away and just outside the city walls is the church of **Santa Maria di Betlem**, in which enormous painted candlesticks are kept until August 14 of each year, when (on the eve of the Feast of the Assumption of the Virgin Mary) they are carried in a procession through the city.

If possible come to Sassari on the next to last Sunday in May, when the Cavalcata Sarde with its galloping horses begins; look for the riders straddling two horses. The brilliant parade of Sardinians in lavish traditional dress lasts for hours.

Stroll from the cathedral along the viale Coppino past the **Giardino Pubblico** (city park), where the **Padiglione dell'Artigianato** (Folk Arts Pavilion) has exhibits of rugs, jewelry, and other folk crafts, as well as copies of *bronzetti* all made in the traditional way and thus somewhat expensive.

Nearby on via Roma is the **Museo Sanna**, the modern archaeological museum mentioned above. The museum is laid out spaciously, with minute attention paid to exhibits that range from prehistoric finds and Nuraghic-era relics to Punic and Roman collections and a sampling of folk art.

Sassari has several good restaurants. Among the best is the **Trattoria del Giamaranto** at via Alghero 69 (reserve; Tel: 079-27-45-98; closed July 22 to August 22, Saturday evenings, and Sundays in summer). Although the atmosphere is stylishly minimalist, the cooking is decidedly natural, offering such pleasures as homemade ravioli filled with porcini mush-rooms or artichokes. If you haven't yet tasted Sardinia's caviar, called *bottarga* (mullet eggs), now is the time. The grilled fish is always the freshest possible and may be a welcome option if you've indulged in the meat dishes typical of Sardinia. Meals here lean toward the expensive side. **L'Assassino** is simple in style but interestingly complex in its offerings, which include game dishes such as wild boar and rabbit, and pizzas for the lighter appetite (via Ospizio Cappuccini 1/b; Tel: 079-23-50-41; closed Sundays and Au-gust). Good and less expensive is **Florian** (via Bellini 27; Tel: 079-23-62-51-27).

About 32 km (20 miles) south of Sassari, some of the most interesting **nuraghi** await. The Nuraghi Santu Antine at **Torralba**, an enormous complex dominated by a building with a massive tower, dates from the ninth century B.C. Relics from as far back as the 15th century B.C. have been excavated here (open daily). In the town of Torralba, the **Museo delle Valle dei Nuraghi** (Museum of the Valley of the Nuraghi) provides interesting information about the site (via Carlo Felice 97; closed Mondays.)

The Fabled North Coast

From Sassari, head 32 km (20 miles) north to **Castelsardo**, one of Sardinia's most dramatic coastal towns, founded, it's thought, in 1102 by the Doria family of Genoa, in part because of its strategic importance. In 1448 the Aragonese conquered the city, but with less lasting impact than at Alghero. Today this fishing town is known for its *aragosta,* and you really should indulge in one or two. Local women can also be seen weaving baskets, which they sell (you'd better buy if you want to take their picture).

Continue along the beautiful coastal drive north another 71 km (44 miles) to **Santa Teresa di Gallura**. The coast from here to the Emerald Coast (the color is emerald here, too, and cerulean blue in broad expanses) on the eastern coast is composed of new settlements; the towers and churches of Aragonese days are rarely seen. Stay just outside town at **Shardana**, a pretty resort with private bungalows, swimming pool, private beach, and tennis courts.

The best place to try the local dishes is at **Canne al Vento** (named for a novel by Grazia Deledda). You need only ask for *cucina tipica* and a wealth of good food (and a pretty steep bill) will appear (via Nazionale 23; Tel: 0789-75-42-19; closed October, November, and Saturdays in off-season).

From town (or the Shardana, which is closer), you *must* take an excursion to **Capo Testa**, a promontory about 3 km (2 miles) to the west and one of Sardinia's most scenic places. Some of the mistral-sculpted rocks at Capo Testa are astonishingly beautiful; the odd animal shapes of others are amusing. At Tibula on Capo Testa you can walk along the cove of Santa Reparata to see the granite columns carved by the Romans for the Pantheon but left behind after their unexpected departure. If you'd like to stay in the area, try the **Bocche di Bonifacio**, where the owners do the fishing and the catch of the day is always fresh. **Da Colomba**, on a rocky shore with a nearby marina, is another simply furnished and reasonably priced hotel. The hotel **Li Capanni** at Cannigione, near Porto Cervo, is away from it all on a tranquil macchia-covered bit of land near the sea. Meals are quite good.

Sardinia also has many comfortable campgrounds, an excellent choice for families. For detailed information on sites and facilities, ask the tourist office in any major Sardinian city for *Campeggi 1993*.

Another excursion from Santa Teresa is to **Bonifacio** in Corsica, named for Napoléon. Or sail to the lovely islands of **La Maddalena** archipelago and the island of **Caprera**, just to the east across a causeway, to see Garibaldi's last home and final resting place. On La Maddalena, dine at **La Grotta** (via Principe di Napoli 3; Tel: 0789-73-72-28; closed Sundays and October), a traditional place for good Sardinian-style seafood, including of course the classic *spaghetti alla bottarga* (spaghetti with Sardinian caviar) and *aragosta* (lobster) with onions and tomatoes, a combination that works well with this variety of crustacean, unlike its American cousin. Vernaccia is the wine of choice.

Continuing on to the **Costa Smeralda**, you may find Porto Cervo a bit disappointing, given its advance publicity. The town is a pretty, suburban-type shopping mall with Rodeo Drive labels—a Disneyland for the inveterate shopper where Mickey and Minnie are stylishly played by Armani and Krizia. Watch the helicopters land on the power yachts in the harbor; Aga Khan's yacht has space for two.

The hotels of the Costa Smeralda complex, of which the Aga Khan is principal stockholder, are indeed luxurious. The **Pitrizza** is the most exclusive, with private villas scattered picturesquely about, spacious terraces, and lots of space to moor your yacht. The **Balocco** is a good choice at about a quarter the price, with scenic terraces and a swimming pool.

Apart from sailing, tanning, hiking, enjoying nature, grotto exploring, scuba diving, swimming, water skiing, eating, and shopping, there simply isn't a thing to do here; and when you're ready to return to the mainland, the air- and seaports of Olbia are only a short drive to the south.

GETTING AROUND

Sardinia can be reached from all Italian airports via Alisarda Airlines (sometimes you must change planes in Rome). Incoming flights land at Alghero, Cagliari, and Olbia. Many European airports—Paris, Geneva, Nice, Frankfurt, and Düsseldorf, among them—have direct flights to the island. By sea there are frequent overnight ferries from Toulon, Genoa, and Civitavecchia (near Rome). State railway-ferryboats take you to Sardinia directly from Rome and other cities; ask for information at the Italian Railways Information Service or from CIT, the Italian tour company. The Tirrenia Line in Italy services the island; tickets can be bought from travel agents in Italy. In Great Britain, booking can be made through Normandy Ferries, Arundel Towers, Portland Terrace, Southampton; Tel: (703) 321-31 and 441-41.

In Sardinia, Roberto Salmon, a well-informed guide who also teaches English, arranges tours for individuals and small groups. He can be reached at via Perpignan 27, Alghero; Tel: (079) 97-69-98.

Driving is the best way to see the island, since many sights are far from the main roads and public transportation is a sometime thing.

ACCOMMODATIONS REFERENCE
The rates given below are projections for 1993; always check for up-to-date information before making reservations. Wide ranges may reflect the differences between low- and

*high-season rates. Unless otherwise indicated, the figures
indicate the cost of a double room (per room, not per
person). However, half-board (mezza pensione) rates, which
include breakfast and one other meal per day, are per
person. The service charge is included in the rate; inquire
about tax and breakfast.*

For country living, call **Terranostra**. Via Sassari 3, 09100
Cagliari. Tel: (070) 66-83-67.

▶ **Balocco.** Liscia di Vacca, 07020 **Porto Cervo**. Tel: (0789)
915-55. Open April–October 15. £160,000–£370,000.

▶ **Bellavista.** Via Rovigno 13, 07041 **Fertilia** (Alghero). Tel:
(079) 93-01-24; Fax: same. £45,000–£74,000; half board
£65,000–£80,000.

▶ **Bocche di Bonifacio.** Capo Testa, 07028 **Santa Teresa di
Gallura**. Tel: (0789) 75-42-02. Closed November 10–March
10. £50,000

▶ **Hotel Calamosca.** Viale Calamosca 50, 09126 **Cagliari**.
Tel: (070) 37-16-28 or 37-02-52. £90,000.

▶ **Campeggio Porticciolo.** Capo Caccia, 07041 **Alghero**.
Tel: (079) 91-90-07. £60,000.

▶ **Li Capanni**. Golfo Saline, 07020 **Cannigione**. Tel: (0789)
860-41. £85,000–£120,000.

▶ **Carlos V.** Lungomare Valencia 24, 07041 **Alghero**. Tel:
(079) 97-95-01; Fax: (079) 98-02-98. £190,000; half board
£133,000–£173,000.

▶ **Da Cesare. San Giovanni di Sinis.** Tel: (0783) 520-15 or
533-02. £50,000.

▶ **Da Colomba.** Capo Testa, 07028 **Santa Teresa di Gallura**.
Tel: (0789) 75-42-72. £45,000.

▶ **El Faro.** Porto Conte, 07041 **Alghero**. Tel: (079) 94-20-
10; Fax: (079) 94-20-30. Open April–October. £160,000–
£240,000; half board £150,000–£220,000.

▶ **Grazia Deledda.** Viale Dante 47, 07100 **Sassari**. Tel: (079)
27-12-35; Fax: (079) 28-08-84. £91,000–£137,000; half board
£99,000–£121,000

▶ **Pensione Vittoria.** Via Roma 75, 09100 **Cagliari**. Tel:
(070) 65-79-70. £65,000.

▶ **Pitrizza.** Pitrizza, 07020 **Porto Cervo**. Tel: (0789) 915-00;
Fax: (0789) 916-29. In U.S., Tel: (800) 221-2340 or (212) 935-
9540; Fax: (212) 421-5929. In U.K., Tel: (0800) 28-92-34 or
(071) 930-4147; Fax: (071) 839-1566. Open May 15–
September. Half board £641,000.

▶ **Roccaruja.** Località Capo Falcone, 07040 **Stintino**. Tel:

(079) 52-70-38. Open May–October. Full board (3 meals)
Ł130,000–Ł190,000.

▶ **Shardana.** Santa Reparata, 07028 **Santa Teresa di Gallura.**
Tel: (0789) 75-43-91; Fax: (0789) 75-41-29. Ł88,000–
Ł110,000.

▶ **Su Gologone.** Oliena, 08025 **Nuoro.** Tel: (0784) 28-75-
12; Fax: (0784) 28-76-68. Closed November. Ł95,000.

▶ **Villa Las Tronas.** Lungomare Valencia 1, 07041 **Alghero.**
Tel: (079) 98-18-18; Fax: (079) 98-10-44. Ł160,000–Ł200,000;
half board Ł180,000–Ł200,000.

CHRONOLOGY OF THE HISTORY OF ITALY

Prehistory

Italian prehistory extends at least as far back as 700,000 B.C., when the earliest known relics of humanoids were left in Molise in central Italy. On the rugged hillsides of Sardinia, Stone Age inhabitants built towers called *nuraghi,* and archaeologists in Apulia and Sicily have uncovered Paleolithic cave drawings. After 3000 B.C. the peninsula was settled by migrating Indo-Europeans.

From their base in Carthage, the sea-travelling Phoenicians established settlements in western Sicily and Sardinia during the eighth century B.C. Their influence eventually spread across the sea to the shores of Latium.

Between the eighth and fifth centuries B.C., Italy was colonized in the North and South by Etruscans and Greeks, respectively. The Etruscans, an advanced people probably from Asia Minor, are believed to have absorbed the culture of Greece without relinquishing their own cultural identity. Little is known about their architecture, but wall paintings and decorated sarcophagi found at their burial grounds attest to a pronounced realism, a love for drama, and an attraction to the grotesque.

The Greeks

In the early eighth century B.C. Greeks from various centers founded more than 40 colonies on the coasts of Sicily and southern Italy, which in the aggregate were called Magna Graecia. A number of pre-Socratic philosophers, including Pythagoras and Parmenides, made important contributions here, and Plato himself lived in Magna Graecia for a time. The Greek Doric temples in Sicily are more numerous and better preserved than those in Greece.

The Foundations of the
Roman Empire

Some of the most lasting expressions of Roman artistic creativity are in the areas of architecture, engineering, and urban planning. Highly successful open spaces, such as the forum, continue to ensure the vitality of civic and commercial life today. As Jacob Burckhardt observed, the Romans set the seal of immortality on everything they did.

The major architectural contribution of Roman art was the refinement of vaulted construction (for the vast spatial advantages it allowed) and its use in the building of baths, amphitheaters, palaces, aqueducts, and triumphal arches. During the republican period (510–30 B.C.) portrait sculpture became more realistic, departing from the ideal.

- **753 B.C.**: According to legend, Rome is founded by Romulus on April 21.
- **800–500 B.C.**: Sardinia is occupied by Phoenicians from Carthage, who war with the Greeks and eventually take over large sections of Sicily.
- **600–501 B.C.**: Greeks bring olive trees to Italy.
- **700–500 B.C.**: Etruscan political and cultural power at its highest in Italy.
- **510 B.C.**: Rome is transformed from a kingdom into a republic.
- **500 B.C.**: The Greeks begin their intermittent war with the Carthaginians.
- **500–451 B.C.**: Viticulture begins.
- **494 B.C.**: Led by Rome, 30 Latium cities form the Latin League.
- **396 B.C.**: Rome captures the Etruscan city of Veii, which marks the decline of Etruscan rule.
- **390 B.C.**: Gauls invade Italy and occupy Rome.
- **348 B.C.**: League of Latin Cities dissolved.
- **312 B.C.**: Construction of Appian aqueduct and Appian Way begins.
- **264–241 B.C.**: First Punic War. Rome wars with Carthage and drives it out of Sicily.
- **220 B.C.**: Flaminian Way finished.
- **219–201 B.C.**: Second Punic War. Hannibal crosses Alps, invades Italy, and captures Turin; defeats Romans at Lake Trasimeno (217 B.C.). Romans, led by Scipio, carry war back to Spain and Carthage; Hannibal is defeated by Scipio at Zama (203–202 B.C.).

- **209 B.C.**: Taranto, the last Greek city-state in Italy, is subjugated by Rome.
- **149–146 B.C.**: Third Punic War—Carthage destroyed.
- **133–17 B.C.**: Sicily becomes the "granary of Rome." Numerous slave revolts, including one led by Spartacus, result in protracted, bitter wars; reform movement of the Gracchi.
- **60 B.C.**: The first Triumvirate is created by Pompey, Crassus, and Julius Caesar.
- **58–51 B.C.**: Julius Caesar conquers Gaul.
- **49–45 B.C.**: Caesar defeats Pompey; in 45 B.C. he is elected dictator for life.
- **44 B.C.**: At the height of the internal wars in Rome, Julius Caesar is assassinated. His great-nephew and ward Octavius ushers in a new form of government, the *principate*.
- **43 B.C.**: The second Triumvirate is formed by Mark Antony, Lepidus, and Octavius, Caesar's great-nephew.

The Early Empire

In the early Roman Empire the equestrian statue is perfected, as evidenced by the bronze statue of Marcus Aurelius (A.D. 165) on the Capitoline Hill in Rome. Painting reaches its highest achievement in the Roman cities of Pompeii and Herculaneum.

- **31 B.C.**: Battle of Actium; Mark Antony and Cleopatra defeated by Octavius, and commit suicide; Egypt becomes a Roman province.
- **30 B.C.–A.D. 14**: Octavius, given the name Augustus by the Senate in A.D. 27, establishes the Roman Empire and presides over a cultural awakening (Virgil, Horace, Livy, Seneca, and Ovid are among the writers and thinkers of the time); Pantheon in Rome is begun.
- **A.D.14**: Tiberius assumes *principate,* followed by Caligula in A.D. 37.
- **54–68**: Reign of Nero; has his mother, Agrippina, and wife, Octavia, killed; commits suicide.
- **79**: Pompeii and Herculaneum are demolished by the eruption of Mount Vesuvius.
- **98–117**: Under the emperor Trajan, the Roman Empire reaches its pinnacle.
- **161–180**: Reign of philosophical emperor Marcus Aurelius; writes his *Meditations;* beginning of barbarian attacks.

- **200**: Bishops of Rome gain predominant position.
- **212**: "Civis Romanus Sum"—every freeborn subject in the Empire is granted Roman citizenship.
- **220**: Arabs, Germans, and Persians, among others, begin attacking the frontiers of the Roman Empire.
- **249–269**: Persecution of Christians increases.
- **284–305**: The Illyrian emperor Diocletian reforms government.

Constantine and the Later Empire

- **313**: Emperor Constantine (306–337) formally recognizes Christianity with the Edict of Milan. In 330 he moves the capital to Byzantium and renames the city Constantinople. Rome is in decline.
- **349–397**: Saint Ambrose becomes bishop of Milan (374); refuses surrender of church to Arians; converts and baptizes Saint Augustine of Hippo.
- **391**: Theodosius declares Christianity to be the state religion; becomes last ruler of a united Empire.
- **395**: The Roman Empire is divided into a western empire, with its capital at Ravenna, and an eastern empire (Constantinople).
- **410**: Alaric, king of the Visigoths, invades Rome; Saint Augustine writes *The City of God* (411).
- **425**: Valentinian III is western Roman emperor under guardianship of his mother, Galla Placidia. During fourth and fifth centuries, Latin begins to replace Greek as the formal language of the Church.
- **455**: The Vandals, led by Gaiseric, sack Rome.
- **476**: The German general Odoacer brings an end to the western Roman Empire, although a strip of coast around Ravenna remains under eastern Roman rule until 751.

The Founding of the Holy Roman Empire

From the fourth century, when Constantine moved the capital from Rome to Byzantium, until the 13th century, Byzantine art, mainly Christian in its themes, dominates the Italian peninsula. The most significant monuments of early Byzantine art are its catacombs and basilicas (Ravenna, Venice, and Rome).

- **480–543**: Saint Benedict of Nursia, patriarch of Western monasticism, devises his "rule."
- **493**: Odoacer is succeeded by Theodoric the Great.
- **500**: First plans for Vatican palace drawn up.
- **524**: Boethius, Roman scholar and adviser to Emperor Theodoric, is accused of treason; while imprisoned, he writes his *De consolatione philosophiae*.
- **532–552**: Ostrogoth kingdom of Italy occupied by Byzantine general Belisarius; Totila ends Byzantine rule in Italy and becomes king; begins ravaging Italy.
- **553**: The Byzantine emperor Justinian succeeds in reimposing the rule of Constantinople on Italy.
- **568–572**: The Lombard king Alboin drives the Byzantines out of northern Italy, Tuscany, and Umbria. Lombards establish strong principalities in these areas. The rule of the eastern empire extends to Ravenna, Rome, parts of the Adriatic coast, and sections of southern Italy.
- **590–604**: Papacy of Gregory the Great, architect of medieval papacy.
- **751**: Ravenna falls to the Lombards.
- **754–756**: The Carolingian king Pepin defeats the Lombards and forces them to recognize Frankish sovereignty.
- **773–774**: Charlemagne unites the Lombard kingdom with the Frankish kingdom.
- **800**: Charlemagne is crowned emperor in Rome by Pope Leo III. In southern Italy, the sea republics of Amalfi and Naples and the duchy of Gaeta seek protection from Byzantium. Sicily and Sardinia are conquered by the Arabs as Islam expands in the Mediterranean.
- **Ninth century**: Rival states are established and anarchy reigns with the demise of the Carolingian Empire.
- **828**: Founding of St. Mark's, Venice.
- **846**: Arabs sack Rome and damage Vatican; destroy Venetian fleets.
- **879**: The pope and patriarch of Constantinople excommunicate each other.
- **962**: The German king Otto I is crowned emperor and founds the Holy Roman Empire of the German Nation. His attempts to conquer southern Italy fail.

The Papacy and the Empire

The Romanesque style developed from Early Christian architecture in the 11th century and embraced numerous regional variations. In architecture, the Romanesque style is characterized by round arches and by large, simple geometric masses. The Duomo at Pisa is one of the finest examples. The figurative sculpture and the painting that began to appear in the Romanesque churches of the 11th century showed considerable Byzantine influence.

- **1000–1200:** The Normans combine southern Italy and Sicily into a new kingdom. Byzantine and Arab cultural influences continue. Independent city-states emerge. The sea republics of Genoa, Pisa, and Venice emerge.
- **1053:** Under the leadership of Robert Guiscard, the Normans conquer Pope Leo IX's forces in Apulia. In 1059 the pope invests him with southern Italy and Sicily.
- **1076–1122:** In the confrontation between the empire and the papacy, known as the Investiture Conflict, the pope distances himself from the emperor and focuses on the emerging states.
- **1077:** The excommunicated emperor Henry IV humbles himself before Pope Gregory VII.
- **1095:** Pope Urban II declares the First Crusade.
- **1119:** Establishment of the first university in Europe at Bologna.
- **1130:** Roger II founds the Norman kingdom in Italy and is crowned king of Naples and Sicily.
- **1152–1190:** Frederick Barbarossa of Hohenstaufen wars with Lombard cities and destroys Milan; Saint Francis of Assisi is born (1182); communes arise and northern and central cities in Italy experiment with self-government.
- **1194–1268:** Southern Italy and Sicily come under Hohenstaufen rule. Emperor Frederick II moves the palace from Palermo to Naples.
- **1198–1216:** Papacy of Innocent III, great church reformer; Fourth Crusade; Venice leads in fighting Constantinople; introduction of Arabic numerals in Europe.
- **1224–1250:** Inquisition under Dominicans commences; Pope Gregory IX excommunicates Frederick II; Frederick II's court establishes first school of Italian poetry; crusades and commerce enlarge intellectual boundaries of Italy, and Arab scholars translate the Greek classics; commercial and industrial boom in northern and central Italy.
- **1256:** Hundred Years War between Venice and Genoa begins.
- **1265:** Pope Clement IV gives Sicily and southern Italy to Count Charles I of Anjou as a fief. The French put an end to the rule of the Hohenstaufen. In 1268 the last of the Hohenstaufen, Conradin, is beheaded in Naples.

The Renaissance and the Emergence of the City-States

From 1250 to 1600 a politically fragmented Italy saw its city-states grow in both cultural and economic importance. During this same period humanists (Dante, Petrarch, Boccaccio) rediscovered ancient (so-called Classical) literature.

The Gothic style, represented most notably in church architecture by pointed arches, was introduced into Italy by the mendicant orders. The earliest Gothic church in Italy was completed in Assisi in 1253. The Duomo in Milan maintains true northern Gothic style; large public buildings and palaces, among them the Palazzo Vecchio in Florence and the Doges' Palace in Venice, also exemplify its lofty principles. Gothic painting was advanced by Giotto (1266–1337), who, breaking away from Byzantine iconography, imbued biblical scenes with naturalism and humanism.

With the patronage of wealthy ruling princes, and a theologically less restrictive approach to architecture, painting, and sculpture, the Renaissance evolved. In 15th-century Florence it reached its zenith. The architects of the Quattrocento (1400s), as the early Renaissance is known, adopted a new style modeled on Classical architectural forms. The subject matter of sculpture, heavily influenced by Classical art, now included secular, mythological, and historical themes. Portrait sculpture emphasized greater realism.

- **Late 13th–early 14th century**: Thomas Aquinas (1225–12/4) writes *Summa contra Gentiles* and *Summa theologica;* teaches at Orvieto; Cimabue begins to soften the Byzantine look in art; Marco Polo (1254–1324) journeys to China, and returns to Italy in 1295. Giotto (1266–1337) revolutionizes painting by cracking the Byzantine mold; frescoes painted in Assisi and Padua. Dante Alighieri (1265–1321) writes *La vita nuova* (1290) and the *Divina commedia* (1307). Pisano family of sculptors works in major cities. Boccaccio (1230–1313) writes the *Decameron*. Petrarch crowned poet laureate on the Capitol (1341); Pisa University founded; plague devastates Italy and the rest of Europe.
- **1282**: The rule of the House of Anjou over Sicily comes to an end with the massacre in Palermo of the French, an event known as the "Sicilian Vespers." Charles of Anjou retains only the kingdom of Naples.
- **14th century**: Italian cities divide their allegiance be-

tween pope (Guelphs) and emperor (Ghibellines). The sea republic of Venice is at the height of its power. Florence establishes its reign over a large section of northern and central Italy. In Milan the House of Visconti emerges as sole ruler (later replaced by the Sforzas).

- **Late 14th–early 15th century**: Flourishing artistic period—works of Botticelli, Titian, Bramante, Piero della Francesca, Perugino. Ascent of Medici in Italy; become bankers to papacy. Great Schism (1378–1417) begins after Pope Gregory XI dies; two popes elected. Papal exile in Avignon (1309–1377); Saint Catherine of Siena (1347–1380) helps bring back popes from Avignon. Brunelleschi (1377–1446) discovers perspective.
- **1442**: Alfonso IV, king of Aragon, conquers Naples and becomes "King of the Two Sicilies."
- **1451**: Christopher Columbus (Cristoforo Colombo) is born.
- **1453**: Fall of Constantinople.
- **1466**: Probable year of birth of Andrea Doria, admiral and statesman, who governed the republic of Genoa and was instrumental in defeating Barbarossa.
- **1493**: Lodovico "Il Moro" Sforza is invested with the duchy of Milan.
- **1463–1498**: Giovanni Pico della Mirandola (1463–1494), humanist and wandering scholar, writes *Oration on the Dignity of Man*. Aldine Press in Venice publishes comedies of Aristophanes.

The High Renaissance

From the first half of the 16th century onward the High Renaissance spread to the great cities and courts of Europe. It was during this period that Donato Bramante (1444–1514) designed the new St. Peter's in Rome, and Michelangelo Buonarotti (1475–1564) executed the plan. Michelangelo's works in Florence included the famous statue of *David* and the mausoleum of the Medici in San Lorenzo. In Rome he painted the magnificent ceiling frescoes in the Sistine Chapel. Leonardo da Vinci (1452–1519), sculptor, architect, painter, scientist, and builder, worked in Florence, Rome, France, and at the Sforza court in Milan. Major scientific discoveries, particularly the Copernican revolution, shook the foundations of the religious community. The Neoclassical architecture of Andrea Palladio (1508–1580) evoked the splendor of ancient Rome in San Giorgio in Venice and the Venetian villas, and provided a model for all of Europe. Titian's (1477–1576) paintings presaged the development of the Baroque style.

- **1492**: Columbus sails from Spain on the flagship *Santa Maria* with a crew of 70; discovers Watlings Island (San Salvador), Cuba, and Haiti.
- **1493**: Columbus returns to Spain and then leaves for a second voyage, during which he discovers Dominica, Jamaica, and Puerto Rico. Travels for three years.
- **1494**: Italy is invaded by Charles VIII of France, who deposes Piero de Medici and then captures Rome.
- **1494–1498**: Leonardo da Vinci paints *The Last Supper* and develops his scientific studies.
- **1496**: Michelangelo's first stay in Rome; begins to paint Sistine Chapel (1508).
- **1502**: Columbus sails to Honduras and Panama, marking his fourth and last voyage. Returns in 1504 and dies in 1506.
- **1512**: Copernicus produces his *Commentariolus,* in which he asserts that the Earth and other planets revolve around the Sun.
- **16th century**: The Austrian House of Hapsburg and the French kings begin their struggle for northern Italy, which is divided into numerous small states as a result. Subsequently, almost all ruling houses of Italy are subjugated by either the Austrian or the Spanish line of the House of Habsburg. Palladio works on villas, theaters, and churches in the Veneto.
- **1521**: Machiavelli writes *Dell'arte della guerra,* and *Il Principe* in 1532.
- **1527**: Castiglione writes *Il libro del cortegiano;* Rome sacked by Charles V's troops.
- **1545**: Council of Trent meets to discuss Reformation and establish principles of Counter-Reformation.

The 16th Century to the Napoleonic Era

The art of the Counter-Reformation (mid-16th century to mid-17th century) became known as Mannerism because it emphasized the study of attitudes and expression. The Baroque style developed out of Mannerism in the 17th century and the early part of the 18th century. Painters of the Baroque style included Caravaggio (1573–1610), who delighted in the theatrical and emphasized the effects of lighting, movement, perspective, and trompe l'oeil.

No form of music is more Italian by nature than opera, and no country is more passionate about opera than Italy. Claudio Monteverdi (1567–1643) was the first composer to make opera available to a wider audience. The operatic music of Alessandro Scarlatti (1660–1725) and Giovanni Battista Pergolesi (1710–1736) set the stage for the flowering of Italian opera in the next century.

- **1570**: The Turks declare war on Venice.
- **1573**: Peace of Constantinople establishes peace between the Turks and Venice.
- **1578**: The catacombs of Rome are discovered.
- **1598–1680**: Life and works of Bernini, master spirit of the Baroque, in architecture and sculpture; splendid colonnade of St. Peter's.
- **1600**: First opera, Florence.
- **1601**: The University of Parma is founded.
- **1608**: Galileo constructs an astronomical telescope, which he uses in 1610 to observe the planets and discovers Jupiter's satellites.
- **1615**: Galileo faces the Inquisition for the first time. The following year he is prohibited from further scientific study.
- **1626**: The pope inherits the duchy of Urbino from the last of the Della Rovere family.
- **1633**: Galileo is forced by the Roman Inquisition to recant his acceptance of the Copernican view of the universe. Dies in 1642.
- **1648**: Aria and recitative become two distinct expressions in opera.
- **17th century**: The popes join the French in the battle against the Spanish-Austrian rulers. Savoy becomes the strongest state in northern Italy.
- **1706**: As a result of the victory of Prince Eugene near Turin, Austria controls all of Lombardy.
- **1713**: Following the Spanish War of Succession, Austria receives the kingdom of Naples and the island of Sardinia, making Austria the major power in Italy.
- **1713–1714**: With the Treaty of Utrecht, Austria receives large sections of central Italy, but in return must yield Naples and Sicily to the Spanish Bourbons. With the demise of the Medici in Florence, the Grand Duchy of Tuscany also becomes part of Austria.

- **1725**: Casanova, author and adventurer, is born. Dies in 1798.
- **1796**: Napoléon Bonaparte begins his Italian campaign.
- **1797**: The French defeat the Austrians at Marengo. With the Peace of Campoformio, Italy is ruled by France. Austria retains Venice and land south of the Adige. Eventually, Napoléon dissolves the papal states and incorporates them into Italy.
- **1805**: Napoléon crowns himself king of Italy.
- **1806**: Joseph Bonaparte, Napoléon's brother, becomes king of Naples.
- **1809**: The papal states are annexed to the French empire. Pope Pius VII is imprisoned in France in 1812.
- **1814**: The demise of the Napoleonic regime. Pope Pius VII returns to Rome.

The 19th-Century
Unification Movement

The ornate Baroque style of the 18th century gave way to the simpler lines of Classicism (or Neoclassicism), which was modeled after Greek and Roman art forms. The foremost Italian painter of the style was Antonio Canova (1757–1822). Verdi (1813–1901), whose works include *Rigoletto, Il Trovatore, Aida,* and *Otello,* escalated opera to an extraordinarily popular music form. Puccini (1858–1924) continued the development of the operatic form with *La Bohème, Tosca, Madama Butterfly, Gianni Schicchi,* and *Turandot.*

- **1814–1815**: The Congress of Vienna reestablishes the former state structure. The supremacy of Austria in Italy is reaffirmed. Lombardy and the Veneto become Austrian provinces. Tuscany is placed under Austrian rule, and Naples and Sicily are invaded. The papal states are reinstated.
- **1831**: Bellini's operas *La Sonnambula* and *Norma* are performed in Milan.
- **1831**: Following several popular revolts against the Austrians, Giuseppe Mazzini founds the secret movement for independence, "Young Italy." The national resentment of the Italians against the Austrians (the *Risorgimento*) grows.
- **1848**: A general insurrection against Austria under the leadership of the king of Sardinia is crushed by the Austrians.

- **1849–1850**: Victor Emmanuel II of the House of Savoy becomes king of Sardinia. Cavour's government organizes the state of Piedmont.
- **1858**: Cavour and Napoléon III create an alliance at Plombières.
- **1859**: War is declared by Austria against France and Piedmont. Victor Emmanuel II places his army under the command of Garibaldi. Franco-Piedmont victories result in Piedmont obtaining Lombardy, and France obtaining Savoy and the county of Nice.
- **1860–1861**: Garibaldi frees the South from the Bourbons. The kingdom of Italy is proclaimed, with Turin as its capital. Victor Emmanuel II is crowned.
- **1866**: Italy declares war on Austria but is defeated. The Austrian admiral Tefgthoff sinks the entire Italian fleet. The Prussians join Italy and defeat the Austrians near Königgrätz, forcing them to retreat from Italy.
- **1870**: France withdraws its troops from the papal states and Rome becomes the capital of Italy. The Italian unification is complete. The pope retains sovereignty over Vatican City.
- **1882**: Italy makes peace with Austria. Under Umberto I, Italy forms the Triple Alliance with Germany and Austria-Hungary.

Italy in the 20th Century

- **1900**: King Umberto I is assassinated, and Victor Emmanuel III ascends to the throne.
- **1909**: Marconi receives the Nobel prize in physics.
- **1913–1934**: Works of Luigi Pirandello; receives the Nobel prize for literature (1934).
- **1915**: Although initially neutral, with territorial guarantees from Britain and France, Italy declares war on Germany and Austria, annexes Istria, Venezia-Giulia, and Trentino–Alto Adige.
- **1919**: With the peace treaty of St.-Germain-en-Laye, Italy receives South Tirol up to the Brenner Pass, Istria, and a number of Dalmatian Islands.
- **1922–1926**: After his march on Rome, Benito Mussolini is granted dictatorial powers by parliament and his Fascists take over the government.
- **1929**: The conflict between church and state is settled with the Lateran Pact. The Vatican is established.
- **1935–1936**: Italy invades and annexes Abyssinia in North Africa.

- **1936**: Germany and Italy enter into the "Rome-Berlin Axis." Italian troops fight for Franco in Spain.
- **1940**: Although at first remaining neutral, Italy eventually sides with Nazi Germany and declares war on France and Britain.
- **1941**: Italy loses Abyssinia.
- **1942**: Enrico Fermi splits the atom.
- **1943**: Allied troops land in southern Italy and conquer Sicily. Italian forces surrender; Mussolini is arrested and the Fascist government falls.
- **1945**: The German army surrenders. While fleeing, Mussolini is executed by partisans. The Christian Democratic Party forms a government led by de Gasperi.
- **1946**: King Victor Emmanuel III abdicates.
- **1947**: In the Treaty of Paris, Italy cedes Istria to Yugoslavia, and the Dodecanese to Greece. Italy renounces its colonies.
- **1953**: The Christian Democratic Party loses control; the frequent rise and fall of governments becomes the norm.
- **1954**: Trieste is divided between Yugoslavia and Italy.
- **1957**: The European Economic Community (EEC) is founded in Rome. The reconstruction of the country moves quickly.
- **1966**: Northern and central Italy are flooded; irreplaceable works of art in Florence and other cities are destroyed.
- **1970**: Following widespread strikes and unrest, the Statuto del Lavoratore (the Statute of the Worker) provides job security.
- **1976**: Earthquakes in Friuli and in the province of Udine cause severe damage.
- **1978**: Aldo Moro, chairman of the Christian Democratic Party, is kidnapped by the Red Brigade and found murdered 54 days later.
- **1980**: Severe earthquakes rock southern Italy.
- **1981**: Pope John Paul II is gravely injured in an attack.
- **1983**: Bettino Craxi is the first Social Democrat to become head of the Italian government.
- **1987**: Italy ranks fifth among Common Market countries as an economic power, nosing out Great Britain.
- **1987**: Craxi's socialist government ends. A Mafia trial in Palermo results in the conviction of 338 people.
- **1988**: Bernardo Bertolucci wins nine Oscars for his film *The Last Emperor*.
- **1989**: Conductor Claudio Abbado assumes the director-

ship of the Berlin Philharmonic Orchestra following the resignation of Herbert Von Karajan.

- **1990:** Former porn star and stripper Ciccioloni is elected to Parliament.
- **1991:** The Italian Communist Party dissolves and is renamed the Democratic Party of the Left. Prime Minister Guilio Andreotti resigns, ending the 49th postwar government.
- **1992:** Festivities on both sides of the Atlantic commemorate Cristoforo Colombo's historic voyage to the New World 500 years ago.

Italy's worst political crisis since World War II leaves the scandal-ridden government in shambles, the lira devalued, and EC membership in question.

—Joanne Hahn

INDEX